STUDIES ON ETHNIC GROUPS IN CHINA

Stevan Harrell, Editor

D1566827

HENRY M. JACKSON SCHOOL
OF INTERNATIONAL STUDIES

STUDIES ON ETHNIC GROUPS IN CHINA

*Cultural Encounters
on China's Ethnic Frontiers*
Edited by Stevan Harrell

*Guest People:
Hakka Identity in China and Abroad*
Edited by Nicole Constable

*Familiar Strangers: A History of
Muslims in Northwest China*
Jonathan N. Lipman

*Lessons in Being Chinese: Minority Education
and Ethnic Identity in Southwest China*
Mette Halskov Hansen

*Manchus and Han: Ethnic Relations and
Political Power in Late Qing and Early
Republican China, 1861–1928*
Edward J. M. Rhoads

Ways of Being Ethnic in Southwest China
Stevan Harrell

Familiar Strangers

A History of Muslims
in Northwest China

JONATHAN N. LIPMAN

University of Washington Press

SEATTLE AND LONDON

STUDIES ON ETHNIC GROUPS IN CHINA
is supported in part by a grant
from the Henry Luce Foundation to the
Henry M. Jackson School of International Studies
of the University of Washington.

The Publication of *Familiar Strangers:*
A History of Muslims in Northwest China
is supported in part by a grant
from the Henry M. Jackson Foundation.

University of Washington Press
PO Box 50096, Seattle, WA 98145, U.S.A.
www.washington.edu/uwpress

Library of Congress Cataloging-in-Publication Data
Lipman, Jonathan Neaman.
Familiar strangers: a history of Muslims in Northwest China /
Jonathan N. Lipman.
p. cm.—(Studies on ethnic groups in China)
Includes bibliographical references and index.
ISBN 0-295-97644-6 (alk. paper)
1. Muslims—China. 2. Islam—China—History. I. Title. II. Series.
DS731.M87L56   1997   97–10814
951'.00882971—dc21   CIP

The paper used in this publication meets the minimum requirements of
American National Standard for Information Sciences—Permanence of
Paper for Printed Library Materials, ANSI Z39.48-1984. ⊗

For
Esther and Eugene Lipman,
Avi and Mia Lipman,
and Catherine Allgor

The stranger is thus being discussed here not in the sense often touched upon in the past, as the wanderer who comes today and goes tomorrow, but rather as the person who comes today and stays tomorrow—that is, he remains the *potential* wanderer. Although he has not moved on, he has not quite given up the freedom of coming and going.

Georg Simmel
"Exkurs über den Fremden," 1908

General Knowledge is Remote Knowledge; it is in Particulars that Wisdom consists & Happiness too. Both in Art & in Life, General Masses are as Much Art as a Pasteboard Man is Human.

William Blake
"A Vision of the Last Judgment," 1810

Contents

CONTENTS

Maps

Illustrations

Except when noted otherwise, these photographs were taken by the Rev. Claude Pickens, Jr., during two trips to northwest China in the 1930s. He traveled on horseback all over the Hezhou, Xunhua, Xining, and Ningxia regions and took thousands of photographs. The entire collection is deposited with the Harvard-Yenching Library, Harvard University.

following page 92

Acknowledgments

For financial support: The Danforth Foundation, Mount Holyoke College, the National Endowment for the Humanities, the Boston-Hangzhou Summer Study-Travel Program, Dr. Isadore Rodis, the Jackson School for International Studies of the University of Washington, the Associated Kyoto Program.

For scholarly resources: The directors and staffs of the East Asian Collection of the Hoover Institution (Stanford University), the Library of Congress, the Toyo Bunko (Tokyo), the National Diet Library (Tokyo), the Kyoto University Library, the Hangzhou University Library, the Harvard-Yenching Library, the John K. Fairbank Center for Research in East Asian Studies, the Yale University Library, the University of Washington East Asia Collection. Phil Mobley produced the maps from my inchoate lists of place names. Raymond Lum of the Harvard-Yenching Library helped me search for and produced the photographs from old positives and negatives, which were painstakingly collected and organized by Mary Ellen Alonso.

For instruction and guidance: Hajjī Yusuf Chang, Albert Dien, the late Joseph Fletcher, Nancy Gallagher, the late Iwamura Shinobu, Hal Kahn, Ma Qicheng, Ma Shouqian, Ma Tong, Nakada Yoshinobu, the late Rev. Claude Pickens, Morris Rossabi, Saguchi Toru, Sung Li-hsing, Lyman van Slyke, Ezra Vogel, James Wrenn, and Yang Huaizhong.

For critical readings: Françoise Aubin, Peter Bryder, Leila Chebbi Cherif, Daniel Gardner, Dru Gladney, Sohail Hashmi, Kavita Khory, Donald Leslie, Jim Millward, and Wang Jianping read parts of the manuscript and saved me from many errors. Pamela Crossley generously opened her reader's comments to discussion and helped me to refine my sense of our field and its issues. Stevan Harrell listened to the book as it developed and shared his knowledge of Chinese society and gift for prose style. Gao Zhanfu patiently guided a non-Chinese non-Muslim through the world of Hui scholarship.

For collegiality and discussion: Jere Bacharach, Linda Benson, Ming Chan, Helen Chauncey, Chen Yung-fa, Dr. and Mrs. Huan-ming Chu, Jim Cole, Juan and Liz Davila, Jerry Dennerline, the late Jack Dull, Jamal Elias, Joseph Esherick, Jay Fiegenbaum, Maris Gillette, Kent Guy, Kate Hartford, Raphael Israeli, Mohammed Jiyad, Kay Ann Johnson, Kim Ho-dong, Terry Lautz, Janis Levy, Beatrice Manz, Kathy Masalski, Bob Merkin, Dick Minear, Emiko Moffitt, Barbara Pillsbury, Mary Rankin, Justin Rudelson, Vera Schwarcz, Marilyn Sides, Miriam Silverberg, John Voll, Dennis Yasutomo, Elsie Young, and Aaron Zysow. Laurie Pollack ensured that my superannuated computer would not eat the manuscript, and Tom and the Computing Group in the basement performed some amazing transformations. Arienne Dwyer, Ali Igmen, Bill Clark, and the other graduate students at the University of Washington enlivened my days with talk and kept me working late nights.

Colleagues at Mount Holyoke College: All the members of the History Department past and present, Dan Brown, Lee Bowie and Meredith Michaels, Joan Ericson, Vinnie Ferraro, Samba and Fatoumata Gadjigo, John Garofano, Penny Gill, Stephen Jones, Girma Kebbede, Indira Peterson, Tadanori Yamashita, Katy and Ted Yao. At the Academic Computing Center, Vijay Kumar, Paul Dobosh, Teena Johnson-Smith, Cindy Legare, Sue Rusiecki, Ivy Tillman, and Jürgen Botz have kept me (barely) afloat on the cybersea. Holly Sharac was always there with an encouraging word, a tactful remonstration, and omnicompetence.

For publication of the book: The sure editorial hand of Lorri Hagman and the supervisorial presence of Naomi Pascal, both of the University of Washington Press,

And closest to home, the family that has put up with this project longer than anyone should ever have to live with a doctoral dissertation. Esther and Eugene Lipman helped me through every year of the lengthy preparation and research, never wavering in their support or love. Avi and Mia Lipman have spent their entire lives with the Sino-Muslims; I thank them and love them for their patience and, as my father wrote of my brothers and me so long ago, for their blessed distractions. Catherine Allgor has been an intellectual companion, an unrelenting critic, and a loving friend on the ten-page days and the ten-word days. To all of them I dedicate the work to which they have contributed so much.

It is said that a Muslim rug-maker always includes at least one error in every carpet, for only God can achieve perfection. Would that I had both the competence and the *chutzpah* to think that I could *choose* what would be wrong in this book. Its value surely comes from those who have written before and who have helped me write, and all of its errors must as surely be my own.

Preface

Since this book covers such a long period, in which the internal and external frontiers of what we now call China were in more-or-less constant motion, I have not attempted historical reconstruction of the frontiers or boundaries of states or substate administrative entities. Rather, for convenience in reference and to prevent cartographers' nightmares, the maps in this book are based on 1995 provincial and national borders as fixed or claimed by the People's Republic of China. Since in the narrative I refer to place names appropriate to the period under discussion, noting modern names and positions as appropriate, those anachronistic place names (e.g., Hezhou, now Linxia) have been included in the maps.

My subject requires that many names and terms be either translated or transliterated from Chinese, Arabic, Persian, and Turkish. I have used the *pinyin* system of romanization for standard Chinese pronunciation (*putonghua*) throughout, with occasional notes on local variation. The languages spoken in northwest China differ radically from standard Chinese in many ways, and it would be both difficult and feckless to try to reproduce local pronunciations. For Arabic, Persian, and Turkish, I have used the romanization system of the *Encyclopedia of Islam*, modified by use of *q* rather than *k* and *j* rather than *dj*, and by elimination of consonant underlining. Non-English terms, except those with common transliterations, are given in italics throughout. Islamic terms with common English transliterations are given in that form (e.g., Koran not *Qur'ān*, muezzin not *mu'adhdhin*).

The Chinese Character Glossary contains personal names and terms that are rendered in Chinese in the text (excepting the footnotes), but I have not included characters for place names, which may be found by consulting an English-Chinese gazetteer or geographical dictionary. Familiar terms such as dynastic names (e.g., Ming, Qing) and names of ancient historical figures (e.g., Laozi, Confucius), as well as those of contemporary scholars, have not been included in the character glossary.

All footnote citations are in shortened form; full citations are given in the Bibliography.

All dating of dynasties uses conventional Sinocentric dates.

Introduction

Purposes and Form of a
Muslim History in China

THE NEED FOR HISTORIES

Muslims have lived in China since the eighth century, but no comprehensive account of their 1,300-year history has ever been written in a European or Middle Eastern language. From the vantage of either Chinese or Islamic studies, Euro-Americans lack even an intellectual context for a focused treatment of this important cultural encounter and the millions of individuals who have participated in it. With a few notable exceptions, modern Chinese scholars have restricted themselves to narrow monographs or overblown theoretical models, and the most thorough Japanese book on the subject ends its narrative in the early nineteenth century.

Given the copious primary sources that deal with the Muslims of China, we would expect a larger body of scholarship from foreign academics. The presence of so many Muslims in China has stimulated occasional panic and consistent concern among China watchers, especially missionaries and players of the Great Game of Russian-British imperial rivalry in Central and East Asia. But most contemporary Euro-American scholars of Chinese history, not to mention their students, would be hard-pressed to say much of anything about the history of China's Muslim residents, except perhaps that they have been there a long time and are counted among the "minority nationalities" (*shaoshu minzu*) by the government of the People's Republic of China. But the stories of how they came to be there, how their lives and those of their ancestors might have differed from those of their non-Muslim neighbors, how they differ from one another and from other Muslims, and how their presence might have affected Chinese history do not appear in conventional histories of China, except when Muslims become violent. Islamicists know even less about Sino-Muslims, for mention of this far-flung margin of the Muslim world is generally confined to a few pages of exotica drawn from the thin secondary sources.

This lack of concern has not been exhibited toward the entrance, acculturation, and continued presence of the other three "world religions" in the Chinese cultural area. Despite the difficulty of the sources, the strategies, successes, and failures of Buddhism, Christianity, and Judaism in China have been extensively analyzed, including their sometimes degraded, sometimes exotic status as foreign religions and their adherents' identification as barbarians, or at least outsiders, who gradually became ordinary and normal—that is, Chinese. The linguistic and intellectual obstacles standing in the way of the study of Islam in China are similar to those facing scholars of other "foreign" religions there, but an additional difficulty lies in the entrenched notion that Muslims are everywhere the same—that Islam, more than the other world religions, demands a strict uniformity of its believers. We can comfortably describe Chinese Buddhists, cope with the cultural complexity of Chinese Christians, and even consider Chinese Jews as both religiously Jewish and culturally Chinese. But not Muslims—they must either be fanatical followers of the Prophet, and thus not Chinese at all, or entirely acculturated, and therefore not Muslim enough to be of significance. This complex of attitudes does not conform to the history of religions in general, certainly not of Islam in particular. For religion alone cannot ever determine how people behave in specific times and places; many other valences of identity constantly play in individual and collective decisions.

In addition to its relevance to the history of both Islam and China, the study of Muslims in China should be included as an element in the much larger study of frontiers both cultural and physical, of cultural contact and syncretism, and of multicultural societies. All over the world a vast variety of hyphenated or multiple cultural identities has been established over the course of millennia.[1] For many reasons—trade and long-term sojourning, migration away from military threats or toward natural resources, the expansion and contraction of kingdoms and empires, among others—people moved, acculturated to new human and physical ecologies, and became normal in new places. Some claim indigenous status after only a few generations (e.g., Afrikaaners, Anglo-Americans), while others keep (and/or are kept) separate and remain self-consciously Other after centuries (e.g., the Jews of Europe, the Hoa of Vietnam). The immigrants, the target culture, and the particular temporal moment all figure in the complex processes of mutual adaptation and coexistence.

---

1. For the creation of such combined identities among the Sino-Muslims, see Lipman, "Hyphenated Chinese."

In the past two centuries the nation-state as humankind's primary form of large-scale social, cultural, and political integration has become a crucial actor in the dramas of acculturation—those already in progress and the new ones created by colonialism, imperialism, and the break-up or consolidation of empires into "countries." Modern nation-states fix their borders, including under their sovereign power whoever happens to live in the territory thus enclosed. In most cases, that includes large numbers of people culturally different from those in control. Nation-states also possess the almost unconstrained power to grant citizenship, and thus full humanity, to their residents[2] and to count, classify, divide, and otherwise control crucial elements of personal identity.[3]

Though not utterly new in quality, these capacities of the modern nation-state do differ significantly from those of premodern states. The Qing (1644–1912) empire before the nineteenth century, for example, possessed an ethnological capacity, counting and ordering its subjects on the basis of language and other cultural variables, but it rarely went so far as to tell them who they were.[4] When the Qing emperors established and tried to enforce boundaries between their subject peoples, they did so to prevent combinations against themselves and to maintain the normative model of a Manchu center ruling over many distinct subordinate lords.[5] Following China's enforced inclusion in the world system of nation-states, the nation-state centered on cultural China—first in its embryonic Qing and Republican forms and now as the People's Republic—has created categories of humanity and superimposed them over existing social reality, to which they conform in wildly

2. Rubenstein, *Cunning of History.*

3. Anderson, *Imagined Communities,* esp. chap. 9, "Census, Map, Museum."

4. James Millward has found exceptions to this generalization at the northwestern edge of the Qing empire, law cases in which officials indicted Chinese-speaking Muslims (whom Millward calls Tungans) from Gansu who moved to Xinjiang as merchants. After acculturating in language and marrying local Turkic-speaking women, they cut off their queues. Were they Chinese, and therefore to be punished for defying the empire's tonsorial strictures on Chinese people, or non-Chinese, and therefore free to wear their hair as they chose? Both men protested that they had been forced to cut off their queues by invaders from Kokand, but Nayancheng, the pacification commissioner, believed that they would not have hesitated to do so themselves, so he punished them with exile. In addition, he requested a judgment from the Board of Punishments regarding their marriages to Turkestani women and was permitted to beat them with the heavy bamboo, separate them from their wives, and reinforce their sentence of exile under an antimiscegenation statute added to the Altishahr regulations only after these cases were decided (*Beyond the Pass,* chap. 6).

5. Hevia, *Cherishing Men,* chap. 2.

varying degrees. The People's Republic of China now employs the awesome apparatus of modern political and social technology to penetrate into local society far more effectively than its imperial predecessors could. In this (to date) century-long process, the Chinese nation-state has inherited, reimagined, and acted upon a modern, hegemonic paradigm of "Chinese" society, one based on the powerful concept of *minzu*.

THE *MINZU* PARADIGM

The People's Republic of China divides its citizens into fifty-six *minzu*, a word of late nineteenth-century Japanese origin with no obvious English equivalent. It probably originated as a translation of the German *das Volk* and is now variously rendered as "ethnic group," "nationality," "(a) people," and "nation." Qian Mu, in Dennerline's English, thought of it as the "whole people's descent group," and believed that its existence and power grew out of the Chinese lineage and the universality of the rituals and norms of propriety.[6] The *minzu* was conceptualized in late nineteenth- and early twentieth-century China as a powerful, invisible cement binding together the descendants of the Yellow Emperor, a definition that clearly illustrates its genealogical connection to late Edo and Meiji period (eighteenth–nineteenth century) Japanese nativism and more distantly to German Aryanism and other European racialist theories, as well as to indigenous Chinese discourses of race.[7] In the twentieth century, *minzu*, and various other compound words using the *zu* component to claim familial (i.e., genetic) descent, have been critical elements of the re-creation of Chineseness, deeply affected by evolutionism (especially Neo-Lamarckism) and the racial-eugenic theories expounded by Euro-American scientists.

The People's Republic of China, borrowing from the Stalinist "nationality" policies of the Soviet Union, has transformed the term into a bureaucratic classificatory tool. Since the 1950s it has been part of the governing project of the People's Republic to "identify" China's *minzu*, to classify and count the people within its borders as members of these *minzu*, and to educate and provide services and policies for them appropriate to their *minzu*. The state also undertakes verification and reification of the primordial quality of *minzu* membership and identity through institutions and policies ranging from ethnological and linguis-

6. Dennerline, *Qian Mu,* 8–10.
7. Dikötter, *Discourse of Race,* esp. chaps. 3 and 4.

tic research institutes to collections of *minzu* folktales to special schools for *minzu* children.

Justifying this immense enterprise, now involving over a billion souls, required the creation of a hegemonic narrative, a unified story that could demonstrate the bedrock truth of *minzu* continuity and consanguinity in the past, for the present. That narrative rests primarily on the teleological imperatives of Lewis Morgan's five-step journey from primitive matriarchy to socialist civilization, but, like all such national stories, it also embodies an ideology of domination, the superiority of Us over Them. In this account, each *minzu*, at its own pace and according to its own environmental and historical conditions, has followed the most advanced *minzu*, the majority Han people, toward higher steps on the ladder of history. The Han *minzu*, which is supposed to include the vast majority of China's citizens—most (but not all) of the people we would call "culturally Chinese"—has also been subjected to this most Procrustean of narratives, but not in the same way as the "less advanced" peoples. For Han—that is, *Chinese*—history, unlike other *minzu* histories, constitutes the story of Civilization or Culture itself and thus represents the Chinese version of History, the linear and rigidly structured narrative of progress that philosophers of the European Enlightenment imagined would happen to everyone, sooner or later.[8]

The "minority nationalities," formally the *shaoshu minzu* but often called simply *minzu* to distinguish them from the Han, have been placed in their "proper" historical positions by the construction of their individual narratives, published as *jianshi*, "simple histories." These books all tell more or less the same story, embellished with local detail and ethnological descriptions. From the Mosuo "living fossils" of Yunnan (who cling to archaic practices such as sex outside marriage) to the pastoral Mongols (many of whose families have been farmers for centuries) to the remnants of the Manchus (some of whom have had to be *convinced* to be Manchus), the various *minzu* move from primitive to slave to feudal to capitalist to socialist modes of production, progressing most effectively when they acculturate to Chinese ways and learn from the progressive classes of Han society.[9] The universal promulgation of these narratives, and the huge master narrative of the Han on which

8. On the Enlightenment narrative of History, see Duara, *Rescuing History*, chap. 1. To contrast Han History with those of the various *minzu*, see Harrell, "Civilizing Projects," esp. pp. 25–27. I have borrowed the notion of a "civilizing project" from Harrell's article.

9. For a detailed essay on the *jianshi* of the "Miao *minzu*" of southwest China, see Litzinger, "Making Histories."

they are modeled, has generated contemporary Chinese History, a story that can be amended or decorated but never questioned. These histories constitute a crucial part of the "civilizing project" of the People's Republic, which builds upon, expands, and transforms the efforts of earlier political centers—Mongol Yuan, Chinese Ming, Manchu Qing, Chinese Republican—to express their dominance over peripheral peoples. Now a centralized nation-state, twentieth-century China has reified the shape and size of the Qing empire at its greatest extent, minus much of Mongolia and some of Vietnam, as *what China has always been*. Historical figures as varied as Chinggis Khan, the Dalai Lamas, and the Kangxi emperor and the vast territories of Tibet, Turkestan, and Mongolia may thus be unambiguously identified as *Chinese*.

The problem of hegemonic narratives and the category systems on which they are based—that is, the objectification of the Other—lies close to the heart of this book. Euro-American scholars generally have accepted description of the "non-Chinese" people of China—as is done unproblematically in the People's Republic—as members of fifty-five clearly distinguishable *minzu*. But upon even cursory examination, the supposedly exclusive *minzu* categories break down, become muddled, invite deconstruction.[10] Consider some questions germane to this book: How is "Muslim" defined in the People's Republic? What is the relevance of this religious category to the *minzu* paradigm, which eschews religion as a determinant of *minzu* status? Are people Muslims by heredity, even if they do not practice Islam or believe in its tenets? How much intermarriage outside one's own *minzu* is required before ethnic identity shifts? These questions reiterate the difficulties Euro-American states have had with the categories "Jew," "Black," "Indian," and many other putatively genetic boxes, underlining the rigidity and inflexibility of state-established categories as hegemonic devices, not simple descriptors of ethnological reality.

The People's Republic of China, claiming to divorce its *minzu* paradigm from religion, divides its "Muslim" citizens into ten *minzu*, each supposedly distinguished by common territory, language, economy, and psychological nature.[11] Of these ten, nine are held to occupy their own

10. Many of the papers in Harrell (ed.), *Cultural Encounters,* undertake this work, especially those by Harrell, Diamond, Litzinger, Khan, Borchigud, and Hsieh.

11. Muslims may be divided by language group: the Uygur, Qazak, Tatar, Uzbek, Salar, and Kirgiz are Turkic-speakers; the Dongxiang and Bonan speak Mongolic languages; the Tajiks speak a Persian-based language; and the Hui, the default Muslims of China, are primarily Sinophone but include small populations that use Tai, Tibetan, and other "minority" languages.

ancestral land and speak their own languages, though several are now predominantly Sinophone. The tenth, the Hui, whose members make up almost half of China's Muslims (and ex-Muslims), constitutes the default category. Under the Ming, Qing, and Republican regimes, the word Hui meant "Muslim," and Islam was called the "teaching of the Hui" (Ch. *Hui jiao*). Muslims were distinguished from one another by additional ethnonyms: the Turkic-speakers of the Xunhua region were called Sala Hui, the turban-wearing residents of the eastern Turkestan oasis cities were called Chantou Hui, and Chinese-speaking Muslims were called Han Hui, among other names. Since the 1950s, however, only a Muslim or descendant of Muslims who lives in China but does not belong to one of the nine linguistically or territorially defined Muslim *minzu* is a Hui.[12] Most of the Muslim actors in this book would now be considered to belong to the Hui *minzu*—that is, they were Chinese-speaking Muslims—but they would not have used that name themselves.

The most common ethnogenetic account of the Hui *minzu*, found in the *Huizu jianshi* among many other sources, claims that during the Ming period (1368–1644) the Muslims of China became a *minzu*, despite their lacking at least three of the four defining characteristics of such an entity.[13] This Hui *minzu* is characterized by common descent from the foreign Muslims of the Tang (618–907) to the Yuan (1279–1368) period, a wide geographical distribution in China, and exclusive use of the local vernacular, usually but not always a form of Chinese, outside of ritual life. No such ethnonym exists in the Ming sources—there *all* Muslims are called Huihui, an erroneous generalization of the earlier Huihe, meaning Uygur.[14] Hui, a shortened version of that same

---

12. In pre-PRC China a Chinese who converted to Islam would become a Hui, that is, a Muslim. Now that is no longer the case, for *minzu* is not a category based on religion. Such a person would be a "Han who believes in Islam." Similarly, a Tibetan Muslim's *minzu* status would depend on when the conversion took place. If it were back in the 1780s, the male descendants of that Tibetan would now be members of the Hui *minzu*. (The *minzu* status of females often depends on that of their fathers, so only some female descendants—those whose fathers were also Muslims—would now be Hui.) If the conversion took place now, however, that Tibetan would remain a member of the Zang *minzu*, but one who believes in Islam. Dru Gladney has written an ethnography of the Hui, focusing on the diversity and local character of their cultures and Islamic practice (see *Muslim Chinese,* esp. chap. 7).

13. A concise version of this argument may be found in Lin and He, *Huihui lishi*, 1–12.

14. Nakada, *Kaikai minzoku,* chap. 1. The Uygurs called by this name in pre-Ming times were not of the same culture as twentieth-century Uygurs, though they came from the same part of the world. Members of the contemporary Uygur *minzu* must by definition be Muslims, and the Tang to Yuan period Uygurs were not.

word, was used to mean "Muslim" in Ming and Qing texts, a meaning changed decisively by twentieth-century governments intent on establishing *minzu* (contrasted to religion) as the crucial valence of ethnic identity in modern China.[15]

The People's Republic of China has been remarkably successful in imposing the language of the *minzu* paradigm on its entire population, including scholars and intellectuals of the "minority nationalities" themselves, so as a foreign historian I find myself in the position of disagreeing at the fundamental level of vocabulary—the meaning of words—with teachers, colleagues, and most of the Chinese secondary literature on this subject.[16] The reader should certainly be aware of these differences and judge the arguments in this book not on their conformity to a familiar vocabulary but on their historical merits. My subjects are predominantly Chinese-speaking Muslims, but I shall not call them Hui unless I am referring to the period of the People's Republic. Because the word Hui is now entirely subsumed in the Hui *minzu,* for historical narrative I prefer the categorical term Sino-Muslim, which combines Chinese linguistic and material culture and Islamic religion without relying on an anachronistic category scheme that would lump them together genetically with Tibetan-, Tai-, and Bai-speakers, among others. To go further, I find the entire *minzu* paradigm, with its putative antiquity of ethnic consciousness and common descent, to be highly

---

15. Some scholars, including Gladney (*Muslim Chinese,* chap. 7) and Harrell ("Civilizing Projects"), argue that the whole notion of "ethnic group" or "minority nationality" can be created only in the context of the modern nation-state, a position with which the evidence presented here leads me to concur (see chap. 6, this volume). Duara (*Rescuing History,* 52–56) disagrees, arguing against Anderson that the gap between modern and premodern self-consciousness is neither so wide nor so radical as he claims. Duara does, however, recognize the nation-state as a new kind of community, despite its potential ties to "archaic totalizations." There is an enormous literature based on the assumption that the Hui *minzu* was formed in Ming China and that it was firmly established by the Qing conquest. The simplest, most essentialized description may be found in *Huizu jianshi,* 13–21. An earlier, somewhat more academic treatment, with substantially the same conclusions, may be found in Xue Wenbo, "Mingdai yu Huimin." Many of the texts that will enable an accurate assessment of Islam under Ming rule have been collected and analyzed by Tazaka Kōdō in his magisterial *Chūgoku ni okeru Kaikyō* (esp. vol. 2, sec. 4–5).

16. I have had stimulating, frustrating discussions on this subject with colleagues in Beijing, Gansu, and Ningxia. They generally concluded that I, being a foreigner and a non-Muslim, did not understand correctly, while I found that they could not tolerate my argument, which challenged one of the crucial underpinnings of their view of the world, the *minzu* paradigm.

suspect in regard to the Sino-Muslims. One of this book's purposes lies in examining what actually happened in some parts of China in order to test the now politically enshrined *minzu* version of Chinese and Sino-Muslim history.

For the same reasons, I shall attempt to use ethnonyms contemporary to the sources of my narrative for non-Chinese-speaking Muslims, so Salar will appear in the Qing, and Dongxiang only in the twentieth century. Perhaps most annoying to contemporary readers, I shall try to avoid the word Han as well, preferring "Chinese," or, in some cases, "non-Muslim Chinese," as a more neutral marker. Though it certainly appears in pre-twentieth-century sources, "Han" did not mean what it does now, and historical accuracy demands that we understand what it meant then. As Almaz Khan has persuasively argued for the Mongols, Pamela Crossley more cautiously for the Manchus, and Frank Dikötter for the Han Chinese, I shall demonstrate with regard to the Sino-Muslims that ethnic consciousness of the *genealogical* kind inherent in the *minzu* paradigm is largely a modern phenomenon, based in a hegemonic ideology that belongs to the nation-state, not to premodern empires.[17]

CATEGORY SYSTEMS

Clearly one of the difficulties of a Muslim history in China lies precisely in determining what the categories—the limits that states, cultures, and other hegemonic systems place on what meanings are possible by control over the lexicon and syntax of primary and secondary historical expression—were at a particular time. Since I am writing for an English-reading audience, I confine myself largely to the category systems available in this language, some of which do not exist in Chinese or the other languages in which my sources are written. Like *minzu*, words such as "religion" (Ch. *zongjiao*), "Muslim" (Ch. Musilin, or earlier Huihui and Huijiaotu), "ethnicity," "China," and "nation-state" (Ch. *guojia*) have no neutral or precise referents but rather represent pieces of historically constructed category systems within discourses of power.[18] From the outset, then, I shall be clear about their meanings.

---

17. Almaz Khan, "Chinggis Khan"; Crossley, *Orphan Warriors;* and Dikötter, *Discourse of Race.*

18. It is both significant and fascinating that many of these Chinese words—*minzu, zongjiao, guojia*—were first created in Japan as translations of Euro-American terms.

Religion

The differentness of various Muslims from normative Chinese definitions of themselves, from the idealized descriptions of "Han" culture
and society, does not always lie in the four Stalinist criteria that qualify
Muslims for *minzu* status. Indeed, the *minzu* paradigm, as applied in
the People's Republic of China, embodies only some of the category
problems of a Muslim history in China. In this book, I have categorized
and separated the various actors from one another primarily by creed,
religious association, and the panoply of practices associated with Islam.
"Muslim" represents a powerful valence of identity, engaging us with
religious criteria invariably mediated by words and practices originating
far from China.

Though scholars of religion can supply strict and objective criteria for
membership in the *umma,* the universal Muslim community, like *minzu*
definitions they begin to bend and become more malleable under the
pressure of historical circumstance. In public behavior, not only in
China but also in Muslim heartlands as well, many adult Muslim males,
not to mention women, do not pray five times a day, some stint on their
charitable obligations, and many do not fast during Ramadan, but they
are nonetheless unambiguously Muslims (some would call them "bad
Muslims"). We have even less information to test Muslim identity with
regard to matters of the heart such as faith in God. From studying
Muslims in China, I would argue that "being a Muslim" strongly resembles "being a Jew" or "being a Christian" in the vast variety of religious,
psychological, social, political, and intellectual states it might describe.[19]
The sources for this book define "Muslim" in many ways, ranging from
silent participation to religious conviction to genealogical descent, and
readers should be aware that no single definition beyond self-ascription
or community membership informs the text. Euro-Americans must be
particularly cautious in ascribing specific collective consciousness or
behavior to Muslims, for we are bound with special tightness by our
own discourses of superiority and hegemony with regard to the Islamic
world.

19. Arguments among Muslims on "what it means to be a Muslim" are as common as
the remarkably similar debates over the meaning of Jewishness in Jewish communities all
over the world. Muslims have rhetorically, ritually, or even politically placed other Muslims outside the *umma* over many issues, a fact we often forget in our desire to formulate a
unified Muslim Other. I would not argue that anything is possible within Islam—or
Judaism, for that matter—but rather that the range is wider than we usually imagine, and
that this variation is germane to the study of Muslims anywhere.

Sects, Orders, Teachings, and Solidarities

The Muslims of northwest China have divided themselves into a bewildering number of groups by affiliation with leaders, ideologies, and religious communities.[20] The terminology describing these structures will be crucial to this historical narrative, for religious solidarity functioned as a central valence of identity in northwest China. Muslims also identified themselves with particular places, genders, age-cohorts, professions, and more, but the sources for northwestern Chinese history focus to a great extent on expression of loyalty to specific Muslim leaders, taken to embody the principles and character of their solidarities. I shall use the generic term "solidarity" to refer to all such groups, for they are, to a greater extent than many other components of identity, voluntary and self-consciously solidary.

The English word "sect" has in Islamic studies come to refer exclusively to groups that can consider other Muslims to be nonbelievers (Ar. *kafir*). In modern times the Sunni/Shi'i division is referred to as sectarian, while most others are not, and since that distinction is not relevant to this history of Islam in China, "sect" does not appear in this book with reference to Muslims. Islamicists use the word "order" to refer to Sufi brotherhoods, whose rise in China will be described in considerable detail. Chinese, of course, possesses its own terminologies and categories for such groups, and controversies have arisen over whether a particular group is a *jiaopai* (teaching), *menhuan* (Sufi group with hereditary leadership), or some other sort of *pai* (faction). Qing texts often refer to Laojiao (Old Teaching) and Xinjiao (New Teaching), while contemporary studies combine specifically Muslim terms with *minzu* categories, for example, Salazu *de* Zhehelinye (Jahrīya adherents among the Salar *minzu*). Because so many of the actors in this narrative are Muslim solidarities, usually personified in their leaders, I shall define them with care when they appear.

Ethnicity

The complex definitions surrounding the English term "ethnicity" continue to provide scholars with fertile ground for contumely. Rather than engage in the theoretical debate, I shall follow the definition proposed by a recent book: Members of an ethnic group share consciousness of

20. Gladney, *Muslim Chinese,* appendix A, includes a list of the names of many of these organizations or solidarities.

solidarity by virtue of sharing (putative) common descent and common customs or habits, and they similarly share consciousness of opposition to other such groups of "different" ancestry and customs. However ethnic groups might arise (and there is considerable controversy on the issue), they do seem to develop (are invented or transformed) "in situations where a group is confronted in some way by an outside power with whom it is in competition for resources of some kind, whether they be material . . . or symbolic."[21] This definition allows for ethnicity to be processual, rather than fixed by a list of characteristics in anthropological time, and it denies the primordial, eternal qualities often ascribed to ethnic groups by their members and their enemies. This definition also does not conform to that of a *minzu,* for the latter is rendered ahistorical by construction of objectified markers—in official doctrine, these are common territory, language, economy, and psychological nature—rather than processes of consciousness or opposition, so I shall not use the two words interchangeably.

Empire and Nation

The state must be an important actor in any history of Muslims in China, and here, too, problems of definition arise, especially as we observe the transformation of the Qing empire into the Chinese nation-state in the nineteenth and twentieth centuries. In a recent book James Hevia notes some crucial differences between Manchu imperial hegemony and earlier (specifically Ming) indigenously ruled Chinese states, such as the "multinational, multilinguistic, and multiethnic" nature of the Qing polity and the consequent necessity for the Qing rulers to create a powerful center and an effective balance among their subordinate lords.[22] We cannot place "the Muslims" in a single position in this state-centered model (nor did the Qing), for they lived in so wide a variety of cultural and political circumstances and in so many different relationships to the state. Some (e.g., the Turkic-speakers of Altishahr) were perceived as vassals, others (e.g., the Chinese-speaking Muslims of Gansu) as domestic subjects like the Chinese; some individuals received hostile attention from officials, while others achieved high rank. Transforming itself in historical time, and affected by internal and external forces beyond its control, the empire, like the personal or collective

21. Harrell, "Civilizing Projects, 28.

22. Hevia, *Cherishing Men,* chap. 2. As Pamela Crossley recently noted in a personal communication, "Empires pinpoint centers, nation-states construct boundaries."

identities of its subjects, should be viewed as processual rather than fixed, and this requires special care in the construction of an apparently straightforward narrative.

Even Qing authority over the Muslims of northwest China, the central subjects of this book, cannot be described as monolithic or consistent. Some of the non-Chinese-speaking peoples, the Salar for example, had been governed by *tusi*, local families that received hereditary patents of office and a degree of autonomy in local affairs from the Qing state.[23] After completing the conquest of eastern Turkestan in the 1750s, the Qing appointed local notables as hereditary lords (Tur. *beg*) over the urban Turkic-speakers of Xinjiang, but the Chinese-speaking Muslims of Shaanxi and Gansu remained entirely under the jurisdiction of the centrally appointed regular civil officials, though the military played a major role in local politics. The Qing perceived differences among the peripheral groups—in their ability or inability to use the Chinese language and in their historically demonstrated "governability"—and established local authority accordingly, altering its structure as local and regional conditions changed.

In local or regional history, we cannot simply examine central policy or imperial pronouncements and assume their implementation by "the state." Rather, we ask, within local structures of dominance, "*Who* is the state?"[24] The state's formal and informal apparatus in northwest China over the past three centuries has included a fair number of Muslims, some of them conventional graduates of the military and civil examination system, others holders of less obvious (but no less real) state-sanctioned authority. The empire governed many of its peripheral subjects from a considerable political—as well as physical—distance, and this, too, distinguishes it from the more intrusive modern nation-state, with integration and participation on its mind.

SOURCES AND PERCEPTIONS

Our interpretive problems do not end with the meanings of words. To repeat a common truism, historical writing depends to a great extent on what people choose to remember, usually by writing it down but by

23. The *tusi* had originally been established by the Mongols, and the Ming continued some of their appointments in the limited peripheral areas under their control. The Qing, of course, ruled an empire twice the size of the Ming state.

24. I am grateful to Stevan Harrell for this insight, based on his fieldwork in southwest China.

other means as well, and this is determined by what they think is important. For a history of Muslims in northwest China, most of our primary sources come from officials, literati, gentry, and other people associated with the state. The northwest has had the lowest literacy rate of any part of the Chinese culture area, so few Muslims wrote Chinese well enough to compose their own histories. Those who did tended to work, like their literate non-Muslim contemporaries, in the vocabulary and from the point of view of the imperial center. They did not necessarily agree with one another, for Chinese historiography and intellectual history are rife with conflict over interpretations of the past, but all of them, more or less unconsciously, utilized culturewide notions of human nature, of historical causation, of the working of human society to inform not only their analyses but also their decisions on what to include when they wrote.

In Chinese writing about Muslims over the past three hundred years, one theme overrides all others—that of violence. During the Ming and Qing periods, it became axiomatic that Huihui, or (if the writer was careful) *some* Huihui (meaning Muslims) were by nature fierce, predatory, and hard to control.[25] Like similar dominant stereotypes elsewhere in the world, and others rife in China itself, this image has a history; we can follow its formation in real time, as specific incidents combined with more diffuse perceptions of peripheral or "different" people to arouse fear and loathing.[26]

Particularly after the Qing conquest of eastern Turkestan—that is, by the mid-eighteenth century—the peculiar conditions of northwest China, pressuring the Sino-Muslims from both sides of their frontier homeland and on both aspects of their hyphenated identities, brought catastrophic change, which can be narrated in increasingly detailed and textured form. I am especially concerned with the weight of the stereotype of Muslims as violent people, which figured in state and local

25. Needless to say, this characterization is applied almost exclusively to *male* Muslims. I have found almost no premodern Chinese sources that even mention the existence of Muslim women except as victims of massacre, objects of pacificatory action by the state, or statistics in census or taxation records. A conversation in May 1996 with Ms. Ma Yaping, a graduate student at the Gansu Nationalities Institute in Lanzhou, confirmed that Chinese scholars have not found any sources, either. Ms. Ma must restrict her research on Sino-Muslim women in Gansu to the People's Republic (post-1949) for lack of information on any earlier period. For more detailed analysis of this theme, see Lipman, "Ethnic Conflict."

26. I have dealt with this problem of perception in detail in Lipman, "Statute and Stereotype."

sociopolitical and military practice from the mid-Qing into the twentieth century. To narrate a history of violence does not mean to accept the image as true. Rather, as a historian, I weave the stories the sources tell into a history of perception that lay beyond the consciousness of their authors. Hindsight, after all, has to be good for something.

EXPLANATIONS OF SOCIAL DISORDER

From 1949 into the 1980s Chinese historiography has been dominated by the supposedly materialist analytical construct of class struggle, the sole motive force of change in the Maoist vision of the past. In contemporary Chinese History, the hegemonic narrative centering on the Han *minzu,* class struggle remains a primary explanation for social disorder (including violence): the masses who are the subjects of history and objects of state control rise up against feudal oppression at moments of sharpening social contradiction, with varying degrees of success. Within that rigidly enforced conception of human motivation, however, Chinese historians have creatively integrated older causal conceptions from imperial China's Confucian discourse.

As the historian's focus narrows to specific events and individuals, the hoary ethic of "praise and blame historiography," canonized by the Han dynasty historian Sima Qian (145–87 B.C.E.?), appears alongside dialectical materialism, attaching judgments of "good" and "evil" to the crucial actors—emperors, rebels, officials, warlords, intellectuals, and more. Since Chinese nationalism (often permeated with Han *minzu* chauvinism) has come to dominate explanatory modes, the decision as to what is good and what is evil depends largely on whether the event or actor contributed to the good of the *nation,* its most progressive classes (the workers and peasants), and, in some cases, the *minzu,* as it is currently perceived. Historians therefore set out to judge whether Ma Hualong was a righteous rebel or a wicked bandit, whether Ma Hongbin was a virtuous warlord or a feudal warlord, whether Chiang Kai-shek was a reactionary villain or a national unifier. The objects of historical judgment include not only individuals but also collectives of various kinds, including Muslim solidarities, entire peoples or nation-states, residents of a particular place, foreigners (in general or divided into subgroups), and *minzu.* Such judgments have powerful impact on the construction of hegemonic narratives, while their praise-and-blame purpose ineluctably influences the ways Chinese historians read their sources.

The definition of "good," and for whom the person or event in question might be good, lies at the core of all such judgments. Prior to the rise of the modern nation-state, the conventional nostrums of Confucianism set the standard—goodness lies in acting out benevolence, righteousness, justice, filial piety, female chastity, and so forth. For officials and other public figures, loyalty to the throne—to the person of the emperor or his family—stood as an important definer of the good, as long as the dynasty's virtue could be seen to remain intact. The Mencian justification of rebellion against an unjust authority that had lost Heaven's mandate might also condition the evaluation, with appropriate hindsight, of a historical actor. Like many historians of China, I shall have occasion to mention the proverb "A winner a king, a loser a bandit." In the nineteenth and twentieth centuries the good of the nation-state, its leader, and the *minzu* has become the standard for historical judgment, joined since the rise of the Communist Party by that of the "progressive" or "virtuous" social classes and of the Party itself.

Under these judgmental, moralistic historiographical regimes—Confucian, nationalist, and communist—the behavior of Muslims in China has been evaluated. Not only did Muslims have to conform to the current standard of goodness, but they also suffered opprobrium from an intellectual elite that held its own texts and values to be exclusively true, thus condemning the Muslims' texts (and the Muslims themselves) to permanent or temporary barbarism. Confucian scholars usually argued that the barbarian was civilizable, and we will note many cases of Muslims who achieved high rank or reputation by their (Chinese) classical learning or (Chinese) moral action. Foreigners or barbarians were simply those who had not yet been adequately exposed to Civilization, to Culture.

Dikötter, however, notes that another, more defensive set of categorical differences between Chinese and non-Chinese was available in premodern China, in contrast to this Confucian cultural universalism. The alternative view defined non-Chinese as utterly and irremediably Other, different, savage, bestial. Though literati commonly invoked those categories only under pressure from external elites (e.g., conquest dynasties), when the standards themselves were threatened by unCivilized power, they nonetheless provided a potential counterbalance to the ideology of acculturation and absorption of foreigners.[27] They also enabled both officials and local gentry, in times of social strife, to call on wide-ranging stereotypes of Others (including Muslims) as evil and disorderly by nature, controllable only through *force majeure* applied by the state rather than by peaceful exposure to the civilizing influences of literary Culture (or its lower-class correlate, agriculture). In the People's

27. Dikötter, *Discourse of Race,* chap. 1, sec. 2.

Republic, with its statutory equality among *minzu,* "barbarian" has been replaced by "primitive" or "backward" as a characterization of those *minzu* who must be persuaded or educated into conformity with the dominant cultural norms of the Han *minzu,* while irreversible savagery is reserved for imperialists, feudal regimes, some foreigners (especially Africans), and, occasionally, the Japanese.

SPECIFICITY AND MULTIPLE CAUSATION

Facing a comprehensive, hegemonic narrative of Chinese history based on inflexible imperial or Sinocentric standards of judgment, we should aim not only to deconstruct but also to provide alternatives that comprehend the ambiguity and multiple causations inherent in any human history. In the construction of parallel or alternative narratives, we can avoid the errors of universalism and overgeneralization that plague the dominant paradigms; we can read the sources in pursuit of local stories revealing the same humane richness of motivation we would seek in order to explain or understand events in our own times and places.

So I present this book not as *the* history of *the* Muslims *of* northwest China but as *a* history of Muslims *in* northwest China—one of many, as firmly grounded in specificity as the sources allow. My own proclivities and opportunities led me to the region called Gansu Province by the Qing but which now includes Gansu and Qinghai Provinces and the Ningxia Hui Autonomous Region. There the Sino-Muslims' bicultural quality is sharply pronounced, for they occupy what Richard White, a historian of European relations with Native Americans, has called the "middle ground," a place of intimate contact and fear and adaptation, a place in which peoples adjust to their differences while positioned between cultures.[28] Though it may be dominated by one side or the other, the middle ground is always ambiguous ground, always capable of multiple interpretations. The middle ground of Gansu, like that of the Great Lakes, enabled a long process of sometimes expedient, sometimes deadly, mutual misunderstanding. Though I believe that Sino-Muslims inhabited similar middle grounds in Yunnan, Sichuan, and Turkestan, and elsewhere in China on a more local scale, those stories will have to await other investigations.

As I explain below, Gansu was the meeting ground of four cultural zones. In the past millennium the dominant cultural and political cores of Chinese, Tibetan, Mongolian-Manchu, and Central Asian civiliza-

28. White, *The Middle Ground.*

tions all have lain far from northwest China, making it a frontier of four cultures. Under imperial rule from a capital in eastern China, the region could usually function through negotiation of the terms of relationship and a careful eye to independent powers that might occupy the "other" side of the frontier in Tibet, eastern Turkestan, or Mongolia.[29]

PROGRESS BY NARROWING

We cannot begin such a history in medias res, however. Even the hegemonic narrative of Sino-Muslim history is not generally known by Euro-American scholars, so the very presence of Muslims anywhere in China must be narrated and explained. This story includes the evolution of social attitudes and socially constructed descriptions of Muslims in China as a group (stereotypes), providing a general context for more local history. Therefore I progress by *narrowing* in both space and time, beginning with a brief and rather general history of the arrival and diffusion of Islam in what we now call China and moving toward regional, local, and finally individual stories. Driven by the historian's inexorable logic of chronological time, my narrative cannot sustain the vast scope necessary to be *the* history of Muslims in China, nor can it amalgamate into accurate generalizations all the personal, local, and specific stories that represent the Sino-Muslims as human beings, as historical actors.

Following chapter 1's geographic and ethnographic introduction to northwest China, the narrative begins in chapter 2 with an overview that covers almost a thousand years and encompasses the entire Chinese culture area, setting the stage by placing Muslims as unfamiliar elements in the well-known context of Tang through Ming China. As sources become richer and more complex after the Qing conquest of the 1640s, chapters 3 and 4 examine specific Sino-Muslim solidarities and their leaders, covering only a century each, and only in northwest China. When the Chinese nation-state replaced the Qing empire in the late nineteenth and early twentieth centuries, complex processes of change, caused by both endogenous forces and others from Euro-America and from the Muslim world, enveloped the peripheries of China and forced people to make choices under unfamiliar pressures. Chapter 5 therefore narrows further to individuals, presenting four portraits of Sino-

29. In this millennium, only the Xixia kingdom of the Tanguts, a Tibetan-speaking people, created an independent polity in this region, but many local power-holders (including twentieth-century warlords) were able to establish semi-independent satrapies under distant regimes.

Muslim leaders who took very different but equally winding paths toward accommodation with modern China.

In the Qing and Republican periods Muslims played an important role in constructing Chinese identity—as Gu Jiegang claimed they would for a *modern* China—in part by resisting homogenization, by subverting the dominant definitions of Chineseness, by remaining different but present, the "familiar strangers" of my title. The results of this history of tension were often brutal and violent, well reported in the self-consciously moralizing histories of the keepers of public order, who were also the defenders of the monolithic hierarchy of virtue with themselves at the top and distant, uncivilizable foreigners at the bottom. But some of the Sino-Muslims' history took place within domestic settings that historians cannot reach, as Muslims and non-Muslims intermarried, or in marketplace encounters that ended in deals, not brawls, or in mutual and satisfactory adaptations resulting from centuries of ordered contact.

Over the past thousand and more years Muslims have come to belong in China, to think of it as their only home, to use its cultures and languages as their own. And Chinese culture, in many of its regional manifestations (especially, but not exclusively, in Gansu and Yunnan), has developed a "sense of itself" in part through constant interaction with and gradual inclusion of the Muslim strangers who lived there. Their myriad of stories cannot be told only in the aggregate, in terms of ethnic groups or regions. Rather, we meet individual human beings, follow their decisions and indecisions, try to understand their position as participants in what appear to be two cultures, as demanding and as exclusive and intolerant of domestic difference as cultures are prone to be. Complex choices about adaptation had always been available to Sino-Muslims, but the richness of our twentieth-century sources allows us to examine individuals as they faced the wrenching changes wrought by modernity.

THE VIEW FROM THE EDGE: FAMILIAR STRANGERS

The large processes examined here—acculturation, resistance, incorporation, integration—should not be allowed to obscure differences among places, times, and persons. In a book covering 1,300 years I have sacrificed a measure of specificity, especially in the early chapters, but I have tried to suggest in anecdotes the richness of sources that awaits us. Only a novelist's or poet's hand could describe adequately the extraordinary physical and human terrain of northwest China, but I hope to do it pale justice with maps, photographs, and narratives. This book is intended to create interest not only in further study of Sino-Muslims, but also in the broad issues of difference and conflict their stories embody. Most, if not all, of the contemporary world's nation-states are coming to terms with domestic minorities—people who belong to more than one culture simultaneously, people who live in the "middle ground" and who have created new and syncretic cultures there. (Another recent book called *Familiar Strangers* deals with the Gypsies in the United States.)

It would be feckless to claim that Gansu somehow represents China as a "typical" region. Gansu lies at the frontier, at the margin, of Chinese culture (though not of the contemporary Chinese nation-state), and thus, despite its apparently outlandish mix of cultures, it can provide us with what has now become a clichéd advantage—the liminal view. The Sino-Muslims of northwest China indeed live in a dual liminality, at the outer edges of the two worlds with which they identify as Chinese and as Muslims. I have written *Familiar Strangers* as a history of becoming and then being Chinese while remaining Muslim, of the evolution of a sense of home. If our understandings of Chineseness cannot encompass the history of Gansu, then we should revise them. If our generalizations about Islam, about cultural contact, about acculturation and sociocultural distinction cannot help us explain the society of northwest China and its processes, we should change them.

Familiar Strangers

A History of Muslims
in Northwest China

1 / The Frontier Ground and Peoples
of Northwest China

Well, I at least find myself reflecting on this point. A geographical
area keeps a certain *flavour,* which manifests in all its happenings, its
events. . . . I sometimes wonder if this thought may not be usefully
taught to children at the start of their "geography lessons." Or
would one call it *history?*

Doris Lessing, *Shikasta*

Muslims live almost everywhere in China. A few small clusters are located in the south, more in the northeast, and hundreds of thousands on
the north China plain, with the densest concentrations at Beijing and
Tianjin, though they constitute only a tiny minority among the non-
Muslim Chinese.[1] Tens of thousands of Muslims live in Yunnan's cities
and market towns, and smaller numbers may be found along the trade
routes leading to Burma and Tibet from the southwest. But Muslims in
contemporary China still live most densely along the ancient Silk Road,
which connected Central Asia with north China. Eastern Turkestan
(now the Xinjiang Uygur Autonomous Region) has had an indigenous
population that is almost entirely Muslim and non-Chinese-speaking for
centuries, joined only during the past forty years by millions of non-
Muslim Chinese.

Between north China and Turkestan are two zones of dense Muslim
habitation: the Ningxia region of the middle Yellow River valley (now
the Ningxia Hui Autonomous Region) and a crescent of territory in
southwestern Gansu and northeastern Qinghai Provinces. These zones,
one on either side of the regional core at Lanzhou, are the ground of most

---

1. A map including only the Muslims classified as Hui by the People's Republic of
China may be found on the flyleaf of Gladney, *Muslim Chinese* (table of distribution, p.
28). The Hui Muslims are largely Chinese-speaking, which sets them off from Muslims
who speak Turkic, Mongolic, or Persian languages, though the government has included
some non-Chinese-speaking Muslims among the Hui.

3

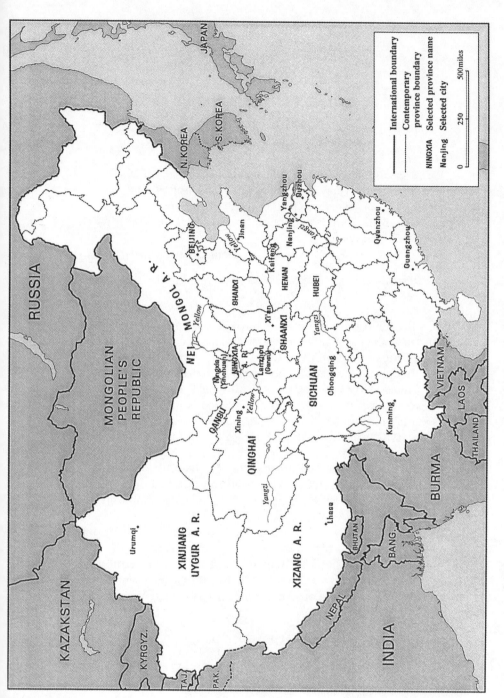

MAP I. Contemporary provinces, autonomous regions, and municipalities of the People's Republic of China. (Map by Philip M. Mobley)

of this book—a frontier of four cultures, a region known in China for little except poverty, marginality, archeological riches, and bellicose inhabitants. Though I must begin with a general history of Islam's arrival and development in China, since no such narrative exists in English, the lion's share of this work focuses on the northwest.

Therefore this book is not about China, but about a particular part of China, a frontier very distant from the core areas of Chinese culture and very strange to most Chinese. That does not, of course, reduce its importance in Chinese history. The distance of the northwestern frontier from "China proper" (which northwesterners call *neidi,* the interior) enhances its value as a lens on the range and diversity of Chinese life. Local history, not in the mode of case studies in search of the typical but as an understanding of the particular for its own sake, deepens and subtly diffuses our comprehension of what it is to be Chinese. The generalization and homogenization of Chinese society by scholars, both Chinese and foreign, distorts the real and compelling variety created by distinct environments and their particular histories.

The acts recorded by chroniclers of northwest China have tended to be violent and antisocial, construed as immoral by the Confucian judges of history. In a narration of this rowdy past, we must ask why people, often neighbors for years or for generations, take up weapons to kill one another at particular historical moments. What begins what Barbara Tuchman has called "the march of folly," leading to bloodshed on a small or large scale? It will not do to say, as many have, that Muslims are naturally violent and fanatical people because of their doctrine. Nor can we aver that Chinese people do not care about human life because there are so many of them. Or that frontiers are just violent places. Historians of the particular cannot ignore or devalue the often peaceful Muslims, the often life-affirming Chinese, the often calm fronters. In order to discover patterns and clues in the specific time and place, we must patiently explore what people actually did.

In the civil, avowedly antimilitary and culturally homogeneous China of the dominant mythology, violence may properly serve only the holder of the mandate of Heaven.[2] Yet in folk tradition, from the early legends to the battles of Cao Cao to the heroes of the *Shuihu zhuan* and the Luding Bridge, warfare and martial heroism have vaulted men and women into exalted memory, and many parts of China have dramatic, explosive local traditions of violence going back to the Han dynasty (206 B.C.E – C.E.

---

2. For a more comprehensive treatment of the problem of violence in the study of China, see Harrell, "Introduction."

220) or even before. A local historian of Jiangsu tells me that there are areas of central China where collective or large-scale violence plays almost no part in history. But to call such places "typically Chinese" ignores not only stereotypically violent frontiers such as the northwest but also counties in Zhejiang, Anhui, and even Jiangsu itself that have rich and troubled traditions of violence. To understand China in its particulars, we must assimilate that violence into our imagery.

Thus we can build on Hsiao Kung-ch'uan's famous metaphor—China as a vast mosaic of environments and histories. In this book I focus on a small part to discover the colors and textures of its many fragments, their brightness and sharp corners, their diverse shapes. As local history becomes more popular and more viable, a clear vision of the parts must, in our history of scholarship, clarify the complex human effort that created the whole.

FRONTIER GROUND

October 1938. Gu Jiegang was tired and worried. His father was dying back home in Suzhou, but the forty-five year old professor of ancient history knew he could not travel east to do his filial duty. He had been on the road for over a year, having left Beiping just ahead of the invading Japanese, and had arrived in Sichuan only in September, after an exhausting fact-finding tour of the northwest. Not yet ready to report to the Sino-British Cultural and Educational Endowment Fund, which had sponsored his excursion in the hope of learning more about education among the northwestern Muslims, he nonetheless agreed when an old friend asked him to give a lecture. He had to speak to his audience—the faculty and students of the Mongolian-Tibetan School of the Central Political College—in a makeshift hall, for Chongqing's universities, like its sewers and housing market, had been flooded by refugees fleeing the Japanese:

> When Demchukdonggrub [Ch. De Wang] started the autonomy movement in Mongolia in 1933, I met with him and his associates at Bailingmiao. Only after that did I realize the gravity of frontier issues, so I changed my direction and began to study frontier problems. . . .
> [On my recent trip] most of the places I visited were inhabited by Hui and Fan [Tibetans]. . . . Banditry is a really serious problem there. . . .
> Though we met with some local desperadoes, fortunately they didn't rob us.
> The most severe and most pressing problem in the northwest is

transportation. . . . If you haven't been there, you couldn't imagine it, but between neighboring counties, even townships, people rarely communicate. . . . If the northwest's transportation problem is not solved, there's no sense even talking about the others.

Of the places I visited, many were districts with complex racial [Ch. *zhongzu*] and religious intermingling. . . . The Muslims have Old Teaching, New Teaching, and New–New Teaching, while the lamaists have Red, Black, Yellow, and Flowery sects. Among the races there are Han [Chinese], Manchus, Mongols, Hui Muslims, Qiang and Fan, Salar Muslims, and Turen [Monguors, a Mongolic-speaking people]. . . . Because northwesterners have all these factions, all these mental barriers, they know only that there are sectarian divisions, and they don't know that they all are citizens of the Republic of China!

. . . people from the rest of China rarely go to the northwest, and those who do are all merchants, low-class salesmen, with small minds and love for high profits, who often jack up prices and cheat ignorant Tibetans and Mongols.

The places we went on this trip are actually in the middle of our country's territory; when people say we got to the frontier, it makes us feel really ashamed. . . . So our responsibility in "frontier work" must be gradually to shrink the frontier, while enlarging the center, so that sooner or later the "frontier" will just be the border.[3]

We have no record of the audience's reaction to Gu's lecture, but he remained convinced that the northwest held one of the keys to China's future, so he spent much of his career investigating its history. His father died that winter without ever seeing his son again.[4]

The Frontier Ground of Gansu

Gu Jiegang was right about the northwest's physical position inside China's border—the provinces he visited are only slightly north and west of the country's geographical center, if the vast areas conquered by the Qing are included in "China." But he was certainly ingenuous about culture. Despite its proximity to the "center" of China, what he called the northwest constitutes the meeting ground of four topographical

3. Gu Jiegang, "Kaocha xibei," 12–16.
4. For Gu Jiegang's interest in China's Muslims, especially their internecine conflicts, see Nakada, *Kaikai minzoku,* 75–77.

and cultural worlds: the Tibetan highlands, the Mongolian steppe, the Central Asian desert, and the loess of agricultural north China.[5] This frontier zone encompasses the perimeters of cultures that have been in evolving contact on this same ground for centuries. We might have a comparable area in the United States if large numbers of Navajo farmers, Sioux hunters, Anglophone ranchers, and Spanish-speaking herders all had been packed for a long period of time into a three-hundred-mile-square, ecologically diverse region of New Mexico. The comparison between northwest China and the American west did not escape a contemporary Chinese urbanite sent to work in Qinghai during the Cultural Revolution:

> The road passed through hills and valleys that were at times bleak and empty, reminding me of what I had imagined the American wild west would look like, based on a movie I had once seen in Shanghai. "Where were the cowboys and the Indians?" I asked myself, and later of course it turned out that I would be one of the cowboys and the Tibetans would be the Indians.[6]

In physical space eastern Gansu forms the transitional zone between steppe/highlands and arable lowlands, its climate dry and severe, its topographical contrasts sharp and sudden.[7] Both of the historically crucial roads in the region—between Central Asia and the cultural cores of China (west-east), and between Tibet (Xizang) and Mongolia (south-north)—pass through the Gansu corridor, the narrow gap between the northern Tibetan mountains and the Mongolian desert.

The complex topography has contributed to equally complex human geography. In historical time, most of Gansu has been numerically and politically dominated by Chinese people and the states ruling them, both the conquest dynasties and the domestic. As Gu noted, sharing or competing with them for the productive and strategic resources of Gansu have been diverse non-Chinese peoples, among them Tibetans sedentary and nomadic (including a few Muslims), Turkic-speakers (Muslim and

---

5. Fletcher, "A Brief History."

6. Frolic, *Mao's People*, 146.

7. "Northwest China" usually refers to the contemporary provinces of Shaanxi, Gansu, and Qinghai, plus the "autonomous regions" of Ningxia and Xinjiang. Before the late 1920s, however, northeastern Qinghai and the Muslim areas of Ningxia were included in Gansu Province. Since most of the region of concern here lies within pre-1928 Gansu, I shall use that province's name except when referring specifically to places that lay in Shaanxi or Xinjiang under the Qing.

non-Muslim), Mongolic-speakers (Muslim and non-Muslim), and mixtures among the four. New ethnic identities have evolved as peoples and states advanced, contracted, and mingled along this multicultural margin, strategically crucial to many states but central only to those who live there. Personal and collective identities, elusive and processual in all human societies, have proved particularly troublesome in frontier areas when modern states attempt to rigidify boundaries and classify people; Gansu is no exception.

In central Gansu, at Jiayuguan, lies the symbolic end of the Chinese agriculturalist's domain, the terminus of the Great Wall. Even inside the wall, however, the Gansu topography dictates a diverse economy, with livestock breeding and trade in animal products playing crucial roles beside cultivation of food grains and artisanal production. The eastern half of the province, with its New England–like climate, produces good tobacco, fruit, millet, and medicinal herbs. Both eastern Gansu and the Gansu corridor have soils and conditions well suited to the opium poppy, planted in great abundance in the nineteenth and early twentieth centuries.

Much of Gansu, however, does not look as agrarian China should (see plate 1). The hillsides and grasslands, especially in the high country of the Tibetan mountains and Alashan, provide pasture for sheep, goats, local breeds of hardy cattle, horses, deer, and yaks. Between the river valleys, away from water sources, much of Gansu lies barren, the loess deeply eroded into steep hills without sufficient topsoil or water for agriculture. There the population spreads more thinly across the landscape, and even the best roads wash out in the rainy season or collapse when earthquakes strike. Gu Jiegang knew from firsthand experience how many parts of Gansu, remote from regional or even local centers, remain difficult to reach because of the infrastructural obstacles posed by topography and climate.

Gansu Geographical Regions

The Yellow River, its tributaries, and the deforestation of its watershed have carved out much of this harsh terrain. The rivers—very rapid as they flow down from the high mountains—obstruct transport, irrigate narrow flatlands along their banks, and erode the slopes from which the trees have been removed. They also define the regions into which the province has traditionally been divided. Lanzhou, the provincial capital and commercial and transportation center of the whole region, lies on the Yellow River's south bank, directly between the two zones of dense

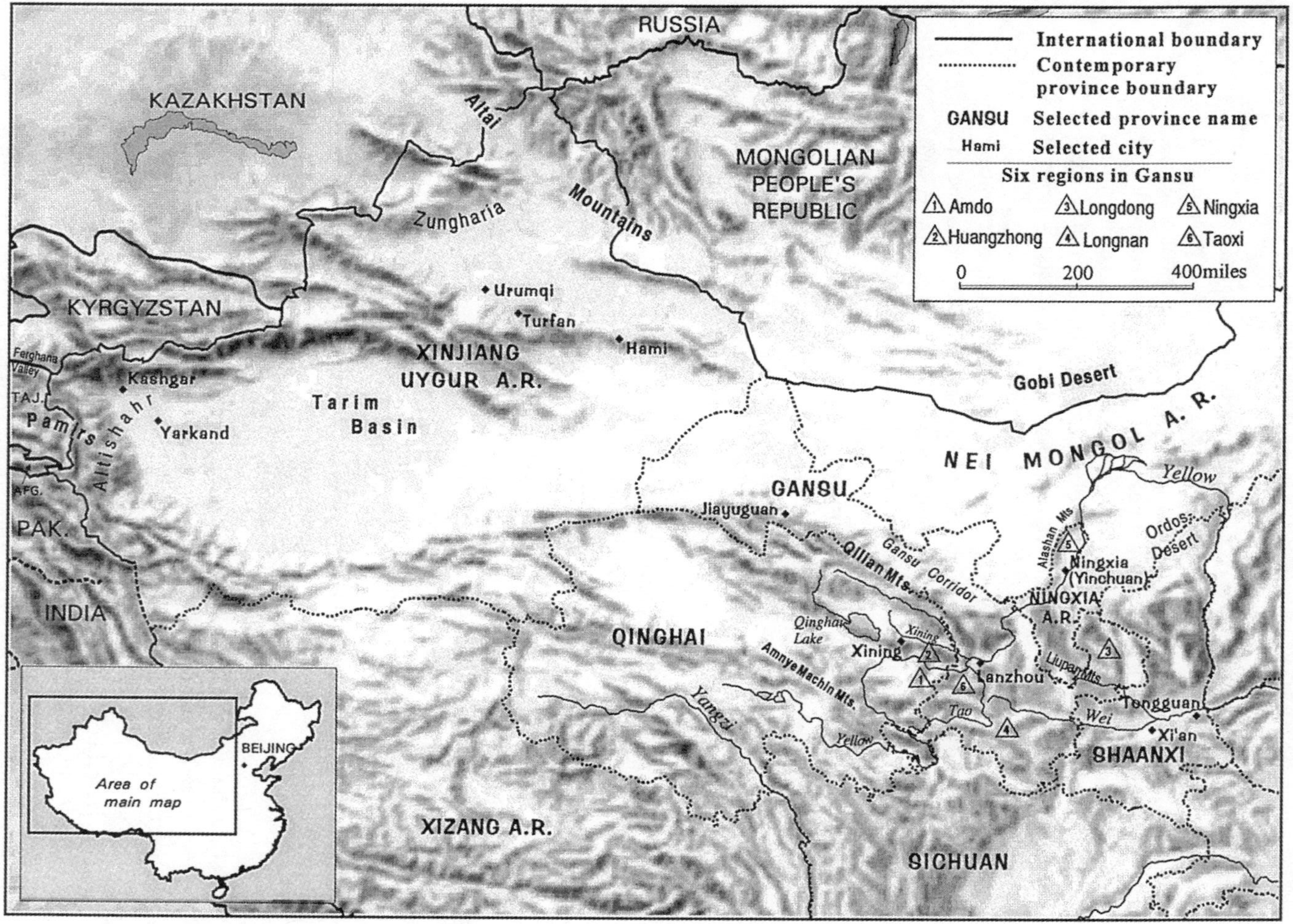

MAP 2. The five provinces and autonomous regions of northwest China. (Map by Philip M. Mobley).

Muslim habitation. Through the city runs the Silk Road, now a paved highway, the main land route from central China to Central Asia, as well as a north-south road connecting Gansu to Sichuan and distant Yunnan. Though nearby hills make extensive farming difficult, the Lanzhou region does produce grain and fruit, especially large (and very sweet) pears. Upriver lie the gorges of northeastern Tibet, and downriver dangerous rapids hinder irrigation of the poor farmland along the banks.

Ningxia. The Yellow River finally straightens out northeast of Lanzhou, running sedately across the loess plain east of Alashan to the city of Ningxia (now Yinchuan), the "Lower Yangtze of the steppe." There, at the edge of the Gobi Desert, an ancient irrigation system supports a rich and mixed agricultural economy, including paddy rice. The irrigated plain east of the river stretches toward the alkaline desert of the western Ordos, a source of wealth from salt extraction but a dangerous obstacle to commerce with north China. Southeast of Ningxia, the ill-favored loess country of Haicheng and Guyuan contains some of Gansu's worst land and poorest people, ending in the rugged Liupan Mountains, where Chinggis Khan is supposed to have died in the thirteenth century.

Longdong.[8] The eastern quarter of the province lies at the upper end of the Wei River valley. The Wei, a tributary of the Yellow River at the great bend (Tongguan) in southeastern Shaanxi, flows through one of the earliest centers of Chinese civilization. Shaanxi Province, also called Guanzhong, the "Area within the Passes," saw the flourishing of the Zhou dynasty, the rise of the Qin, and the stable hegemony of the western Han, all before the beginning of the Christian era. The Sui dynasty's canals brought the produce of the south to this yellow-earth country in the sixth century C.E., and a few decades later the Tang emperors built their supremely cosmopolitan Chang'an on the Wei's southern bank, at present-day Xi'an, where many former capitals had stood.[9] The upper Wei valley in Gansu has sufficient water, a temperate climate, and enough flat land for reasonably well-graded roads, with the dry, barren Liupan mountain range as its source and its northwestern

8. The traditional name for Gansu, Long, is often found in geographical names such as this one, meaning "eastern Long."

9. The Chinese word for loess, *huangtu*, literally means "yellow earth," and its intimate relation to Chinese people's conceptions of their own history and culture held a central place in the recent, controversial television documentary "River Elegy" (He shang), which compared China's ancient, yellow, riverine culture unfavorably to the new, blue, expansive, ocean cultures of Euro-America.

limit. Longdong remains more closely connected to Shaanxi and China proper than does the rest of the province, its large towns almost all lying on the Wei River or on the Xi'an–Lanzhou Road.

Longnan. South of the Wei watershed, east of the Tao River, where Gansu and Sichuan meet, the southern part of the province lies partly inside the Yangzi watershed across a divide in the Qinling Mountains. Well watered but high, with a short growing season, southern Gansu farmland produces barley and oats as well as millet and wheat. Protected by its mountains, this part of the province attracted refugees from wars and disasters to the north and east.

The large Gansu tributaries of the Yellow River—the Xining (Huang), Daxia, and Tao Rivers—all rise in the Tibetan highlands. Flowing among chaotic mountain ranges, they subdivide southwestern Gansu into distinct regions: Huangzhong, Taoxi, and Longnan, all bordering northeastern Tibet (Tib. Amdo).[10] Each of these rivers traverses a transitional landscape from its source in the high mountains to steep foothills surrounding narrow valleys, then to broad valleys marking the entrance from cultural Tibet into cultural China. Divided from one another by the rapidly flowing rivers, which could be crossed with ease only in winter, these regions also contain a variety of ecological zones, from high grasslands suitable for nomads to well-watered arable plains, and thus constitute meeting and mixing grounds for a variety of ethnic groups and cultures.

Huangzhong. Centered on the Xining River watershed between the Yellow River and its major city, Xining, cut by rapid rivers and battered by a harsh climate, the narrow valleys of northeastern Tibet nonetheless can yield good crops to their ethnically diverse cultivators.[11] A local proverb says, "Gansu is dry, but Qinghai is green" (Ch. *Gansu gan, Qinghai qing*), the green including both fields in the valley bottoms (which sometimes lie above 8,000 ft.) and dense forests on some of the

10. Current administrative divisions of the People's Republic of China make Amdo the northeastern part of Qinghai Province and the northwestern part of Sichuan Province, quite distinct from the Xizang Tibetan Autonomous Region. I use the term "Tibet" here in a cultural, linguistic sense, which would demand the inclusion of most of Qinghai, western Sichuan, and western Yunnan (as well as some pieces of other countries) in Tibet. No political claim is intended, for the eastern and northeastern parts of Tibet have not generally been governed from Lhasa but rather have often maintained semi-independence under Manchu, Chinese, or other nominal hegemony.

11. The Xining River is usually called the Huang 湟 River, a homophone of the Yellow (Huang 黄) River. I shall use the less common "Xining" name to avoid confusion.

slopes.[12] Bounded by Qinghai itself (lit., "the blue-green lake," Mong. Kökenör), the Tibetan massif, and the Qilian Mountains in the north, this area has often been of strategic importance as a meeting ground for Tibet, Mongolia, and Turkic-speaking Central Asia, as well as for China's relations with all three. Included in Gansu by the Qing but made part of a separate province (Qinghai) in the late 1920s, Huang-zhong also demands a pastoral or semipastoral life from many of its inhabitants, for the steep, high hill country does not offer large expanses of arable land (see plate 2).

Taoxi. The triangle west and north of the Tao River and east of the mountains, with the Dongxiang mountains at its apex, constitutes a core zone for this book. The Muslim-dominated city of Hezhou (now Linxia) and the Tibetan center at Labrang define an ethnic-cultural progression between China and Tibet. Taoxi marks the southwestern boundary of arable loess and the northeastern boundary of Tibetan pastoralism, and its ethnically mixed population reflects the topography. Though much of Gansu has adequate rainfall in good years, the rain often arrives suddenly in large quantities rather than spreading itself over the growing season. Heavy rainfall can be disastrous in loessial areas such as Taoxi, for that dusty soil must be watered evenly and slowly to produce good crops. Both the Yellow River and the Wei carry heavy loads of loess silt away from Gansu, leaving the northwest more leached and less arable every year. Deforestation and subsequent erosion cut sharp valleys through the loess plains, creating a jumble of tiny plots among the steep slopes.

Amdo. West of the Daxia, south of the Yellow River, northeastern Tibet is largely pastoral and inhabited primarily by Tibetan and Turkic speakers. Unsuited to any but high-country agriculture in which barley is the dominant grain, the mountainous Amdo country rewards pasto-ralists more than farmers. Based in the market towns by the rivers, Muslims have for centuries moved between the pastoral and agricultural zones as middlemen, brokers, and translators. Connected to Lhasa only by long and dangerous roads, Amdo nonetheless constituted a crucial transportation link between Tibet and Mongolia, especially once the latter culture area came to be dominated by Tibetan Buddhism and its lamasery-based political culture. Three great lamaseries—Labrang

---

12. Along the Yellow River the mountains east of Lantaishan still have some of their forest cover, but to the west, past Gaizi and Gandu, they stand bare and eroding, their trees lost to forest fires or, more commonly, to human beings hungry for fuel, housing, and wood for tools.

(south of Hezhou), Choni or Zhuoni (on the upper Tao), and Kumbum (near Xining)—and a host of smaller ones controlled the wealth and military power of the region well into modern times.

Multiple Cores, Multiple Peripheries

In such a hodgepodge of environments, Gansu society could hardly have been a unified, geographically centered system. In G. William Skinner's mapping of China's regions, Gansu is the periphery of the periphery, the outer edge of the northwestern macroregion, which has its core at Xi'an. This book argues that such a single-centered view does not adequately describe Gansu. The Tibetans, Salars, Chinese-speaking Muslims, Mongols, and Mongolian-speaking Muslims all had cores and peripheries arranged very differently. Without understanding their systems, and the interactions of these conceptions of spatial relations and hierarchies, we will misconstrue both the geography and the history of the region, as Gu Jiegang did and many scholars still do.

For example, at this distant edge of their civilization, the Chinese of Gansu did not simply display the language, habits, and values of their core; they also adapted to the harsh environment and to the non-Chinese cultures of their neighbors.[13] Frontiers are always in motion and always have two sides, so Gansu cannot be seen simply as an edge of cultural China. It also constitutes an outer edge of Tibet, Mongolia, and Muslim Central Asia. Beginning with their own unique histories, cultures, and cores, the non-Chinese of the frontiers also evolved and changed through their contact with one another and with China. These mutual adaptations, rather than any one-way transmission, encompass the social and cultural processes of this book, as the severe, diverse Gansu terrain forms its geographical setting.

---

13. However the elites of China may have envisioned (or still envision) their civilizing project along the frontiers, the daily exigencies of frontier life made mutual adaptation necessary. In realms as close to the heart as language itself, the frontier peoples influenced one another—the Hezhou (Linxia) dialect of Chinese utilizes Turco-Mongolic case endings, possibly from the Mongolic language spoken by some Muslims in Taoxi, just as Salar has absorbed large numbers of Chinese and Tibetan loan words while retaining Turkic grammar and Arabic-Persian religious vocabulary (Dwyer, "Altaic Elements"). A Japanese anthropologist specializing in Chinese frontier studies proposed (just after World War II) that especially rich social investigation of mutual adaptation would be possible where Muslims and non-Muslim Chinese lived in close proximity. To that end, he recommended parallel study of Sino-Muslims living in China proper and non-Muslim Chinese living in Xinjiang (Iwamura Shinobu, "Chūgoku Isuramu shakai," 12–15).

The process of incorporation that Gu Jiegang recommended and so deeply desired has indeed changed the nature of China's peripheries as China has changed. The Gansu frontier zones, which had been shifting areas of Chinese/non-Chinese interaction and syncretism, have gradually and sometimes painfully given way in modern times to the new and powerful concept of *political boundary,* a demarcation within which *national sovereignty* rather than imperial virtue holds supreme power and demands local loyalty. As the Chinese state changed, so did the pressures imposed on peripheral peoples, especially on leaders who chose to ally or identify themselves with the political center. The Qing *tusi* system, under which hereditary "native chieftains" (to use the most popular nineteenth-century English translation) were granted imperial titles to rule the frontier, had to be replaced by "national" rule or by local leaders thoroughly imbued with the values of the nation-state. Such leaders would generally be from the group who have come to call themselves Han, the "culturally Chinese," or from the elites of non-Chinese groups who see their advantage, and possibly that of their communities, in representing state power locally.[14] The great diversity of Gansu peoples made local leadership a particularly thorny problem, so the emergence of a new northwestern Muslim elite committed to the political center of China—first Qing, then Republican (1912–49)—beginning late in the nineteenth century forms an important part of this book's story.

Gu Jiegang did not tell his audience in 1938 that China, newly self-conscious and struggling to constitute itself as a nation-state, had imposed on its peripheries with a heavy hand as it underwent its painful modern adaptations. National leaders and nationalist thinkers needed to form a new China both as an idea and as an institution, a modern nation-state utterly different from what they saw in the anachronistic Qing empire, yet covering the same territory and tied to the past with the strong bonds of language and historical consciousness. Gu spoke of expanding the center (Ch. *zhongyuan*) until it includes all of China, leaving the national border as the frontier; that is clearly the goal of national integration and nation building all over the world. But even

---

14. As noted in the Introduction, I have tried to avoid terms such as Han and Hui, which bear the heavy weight of contemporary ethnonymic practice in the People's Republic of China. For the Sino-Muslims, the ethnonym Tongan or Donggan referred exclusively to the Sinophone Muslims of the northwest, but it has fallen into disuse in written texts, though it is still used by Turkic speakers in Xinjiang. I prefer to use "Muslim" and "non-Muslim," plus other appropriate ethnic markers, such as language, rather than the *minzu* terminology that dominates Chinese ethnographic discourse.

now Gansu and Qinghai people refer to their provinces as "frontier" (Ch. *bianjiang*) and the rest of China as the "interior," for they live among cultural Others and see themselves as living on China's cultural edge.

The first part of that nation-building process, the conceptualization of a new world, took place almost entirely without reference to China's peripheries. There were a few new-style schools (Ch. *xuetang*) in Gansu after 1900, and small groups of young Communists had to be eliminated by the Lanzhou authorities in the 1920s.[15] But the modern world arrived in the northwest primarily as military technology, wielded by leaders who fought their most important battles back east. The reformers, revolutionaries, cultural essence (Ch. *guocui*) advocates, and New Culture intellectuals neither knew nor cared much about Muslims, whom they knew to be violent, or about wild and woolly Tibetans, except as potential threats to the unity of the nation.

Another part of the modern process, the creation of a new type of state, forcibly included the periphery in the recasting of an imperial (and imperialized) anachronism into a unified polity capable of survival in the hostile, aggressive twentieth-century world system of nation-states. New China engaged its frontiers with power rather than persuasion, so the ideologies and discussions of the 1920s touched Gansu very lightly.[16] The provincial administrators, bureaucrats, and generals of Republican China used the tools and techniques of the modern world in the northwest only to enhance their control over territory. The Christian general Feng Yuxiang arrived in Gansu not with programs against opium but rather with campaigns against local militarists and factions of unruly Muslims.

The late Qing and Republican periods did see the transformation of the northwest, not by the polemics or ideals of modernization or development but by the process of military incorporation. The "new" local elite rose not primarily from the ranks of students or cadets, not from new political activists participating in boycotts or strikes, not even primarily from the more traditional elites who joined the provincial assembly. Among the non-Muslim Chinese elite, local officials of the defunct

15. Mu Shouqi, *Gan Ning Qing,* 31.28a, describes the secret activism, arrest, and imprisonment of eight young Communist women by the warlord government in 1927. Mu Shouqi's vast compendium of documentary extracts, quotations, and opinions will be referred to hereafter as *GNQSL.*

16. Yu Yao, "Wusi yundong," attempts to demonstrate the significance of the eastern intellectual movement in Gansu but presents no convincing evidence.

Qing dynasty retained their high status and gained Republican legitimacy, while a Gansu Muslim elite evolved from the Qing military, sometimes supported by the Muslim politico-religious groups (*menhuan*) that had enough cash to recruit and equip armies.

With elites such as these, Gansu (in contrast to much of China proper) had a period of warlord domination virtually without a New Culture movement of urban intellectuals. The northwestern periphery was a symbol to be secured, a bastion to be defended, a resource to be tapped, but not a place congenial to the self-conscious designers of New China's identity. Gu Jiegang's intellectual contemporaries tended to call the northwesterners outlandish, violent, and hostile to a civilized new order. Gu Jiegang and his companion Wang Shumin, however, trekking between Lanzhou and Xining, visiting schools and soldiers and officials, saw China's Muslims and the whole northwest with very different eyes, describing them as potential wellsprings of virile energy for the building of a new nation. In that fateful year of 1937, Gu wrote: "In the revival of the Chinese race, the Moslems would have a large responsibility."[17] He knew, if many of his compatriots did not, that the Muslims of northwest China were Chinese.

FRONTIER PEOPLES

The Salars have their own independent language, naturally different in basic vocabulary and grammatical structure from the languages of the surrounding Han and Tibetan peoples. It is close to the languages of the Turkmen and the Uzbeks living in Samarkand. . . . They all belong to the Yugus branch of the western Xiongnu group of the Turkic languages, which are part of the Altaic language family. The Salars' relatively tall and large physique, abundant facial hair, high-bridged noses, and deep-set eyes and other external features clearly mark their differences from the neighboring Han and Tibetan peoples and prove that they have a close racial resemblance to the peoples of Central Asia.[18]

17. Schneider, *Ku Chieh-kang,* 279, 286–93. Gu Jiegang was not alone in this observation. Several years earlier the Japanese observer Sakuma Teijirō ("Shina kaikyōto"), though interested more in Muslim separatism than Chinese unity, concluded that the majority of Sino-Muslims thought of themselves as *Chinese* and could be dissuaded from that position only by a wide-ranging Pan-Islamic movement emanating from Xinjiang or further west.

18. *Salazu jianshi,* 9–10.

Many a traveler has tried to describe anthropologically the Salar type—tall, aquiline noses, etc. Such an undertaking has very little value. As we have already seen, the Salars, at least in the past two hundred years, are a great mish-mash of Turks, Mongols, Tibetans, Chinese, and Huihui [Chinese-speaking Muslims].[19]

People of the Frontiers

In Gansu, agriculture, sedentary pastoralism, and various degrees of nomadism could flourish in close proximity. Frontier peoples, including the Chinese, thus evolved their individual and collective identities in extended contact with many cultural Others. In Gansu live a wide variety of mixed peoples, all on the frontiers of their linguistic cultures: Turkic-speaking Muslims, Mongolic-speaking Muslims, Chinese-speaking Tibetans, Tibetan-speaking Muslims, Monguor-speaking Muslims and non-Muslims, and more. These groups, most of them now carefully but inconsistently classified as "minority nationalities" by the state, have in earlier times been more fluid, flexible entities. Individual fronter folks, by conscious choice or unconscious adaptation, defended and altered their identities among their neighbors.[20]

In Gansu a non-Muslim Chinese male might convert to Islam to improve his chances in business, his female cousin in order to marry a Muslim man who had accumulated substantial wealth. A Muslim merchant might eat pork in order to enhance his working relationship with

19. Trippner, "Die Salaren," 261.
20. As noted in the Introduction, the People's Republic of China divides its Muslim citizens into ten *minzu*. According to this category system, the Muslim *minzu* living in contemporary Gansu, Ningxia, and Qinghai may be described as follows: (1) Hui, living throughout the region, are Muslims who predominantly use Chinese as their native language (though some in Huangzhong speak Tibetan); (2) Dongxiang, concentrated in Hezhou and its eastern district, spoke (and some still speak) a dialect of Mongolian, though many now use Chinese, and call themselves Santa; (3) Salar, living mostly along the two banks of the Yellow River above and below the town of Xunhua, now in Qinghai, speak both Chinese and Salar, a Turkic language, related most closely to Turkmen but now containing a vast number of Chinese and Tibetan loan words; (4) Baoan (or Bonan), a tiny group living in and south of the Salar country, speak a Mongolic dialect similar to that of the Monguor people; and (5) Kazak, a nomadic people dispersed west of Kökenōr and in the Gansu corridor, speak the same Turkic language as the Kazaks of Xinjiang and Kazakstan. The non-Muslim *minzu* of the region are classified as Han (Chinese), Tibetans, Yugu (or Qara Yugur), Mongols, Manchus, and Monguors. For a conventional discussion of the current conditions of these peoples, as the People's Republic officially analyzes them, see Gansu Sheng Minzu Shiwu Weiyuanhui and Gansu Sheng Minzu Yanjiusuo (eds.), *Gansu shaoshu minzu*.

a non-Muslim or to avoid offending an important host. A Tibetan nomad might make a permanent home in a village in order to plant crops and avoid the seasonal disasters of herding. A Turkic-speaker might encourage his children to learn the local dialect of Chinese to better their prospects in an area dominated by the Chinese, or discourage them in order to preserve the purity of his Islamic heritage. A Mongolic-speaking Muslim might be able to earn a living only by migrant labor in non-Muslim areas, so he and his family would travel and learn Chinese by necessity. To take a concrete example, in Tangwang-chuan, on the west bank of the Tao River south of Lanzhou, half of the Wang clan were Muslims while the other half were not, and the same happened within the Tang lineage (see plate 3). While kinship ties united Muslims and non-Muslims, members of each clan also could be enemies of kinsmen and allies of coreligionists, when religion became a divisive valence of identity.[21] In some Tibetan families that did business with Muslims, one son might convert to Islam, sharing the family home with a brother who had become a lama. Such decisions and changes, one by one, have created the complexity of Gansu ethnic identities.

According to an ideological tenet held by many Chinese in premodern times, non-Chinese must either remain in the peripheral darkness of barbarism or they must *laihua,* come and be transformed by the civilizing power of Chinese culture. In this mythic construction, China exerts a stable, immobile magnetism that draws the susceptible (that is, the proximate) into sinification by its moral power. This characterization must be carefully glossed by historical reality.[22] Many people have existed along China's borders for millennia, altered by China's presence but never especially attracted to or absorbed into Chinese culture and society, as the case of the Tibetans most vividly shows. Though some Chinese might argue that this demonstrates their reactionary tendencies or sheer barbaric stupidity, as observers we may conclude that not everyone who knows China wants to be Chinese. Some may want to

---

21. Ma Hetian, *Gan Qing Zang,* 3. The language spoken in this little town and its hinterland represents a vivid syncretism of local cultures. With Islamic religious loan-words from Arabic and Persian, some Turkic as well, and its Chinese-cum-Mongolic grammar, Tangwanghua symbolizes the entire ethnic, cultural, and religious frontier region in which it was created, although it does not appear to contain much Tibetan material (A. Yibulaheimai [Ibrahim], "Gansu zhangnei," 33–47). The geographer Li Xudan, investigating the natural resources of the Taoxi region, also noted that Tangwang-chuan was one of the few religiously and ethnically mixed towns of the region ("Xibei kexue," 25).

22. Crossley, "Thinking about Ethnicity," 1–3.

trade, others to raid, but they certainly desire to remain themselves, however syncretically their frontier culture may have grown.

The Gansu Muslims: Patchwork Society

The Muslims of Gansu did not function as a unified community in any sense of the word but were divided along many lines, including geographic ones.[23] A wide variety of Gansu urban neighborhoods, towns, and villages may be described as "Muslim," but they differed in location, size, relations with non-Muslim peoples, economic activities, religious affiliations, and political allegiances (see plates 4–7).

Close to the Shaanxi border, in a loess valley, lay the entirely Muslim market town of Zhangjiachuan. No non-Muslims lived within miles of the place, except a few artisans who were careful to obey the strictures of Muslim dietary purity in order to continue living there. The tax officers from the county seat could visit and collect, but otherwise non-Muslims came only for the periodic hide and leather market and for the livestock fair of nearby Maluzhen. The town was, in the late nineteenth and twentieth centuries, dominated by a religious leader of the Jahrīya suborder of Naqshabandī Sufis, and his justice was supreme in the valley.[24]

In sharp contrast, Lanzhou, the provincial capital, contained several Muslim neighborhoods, but they constituted no more than 10 percent of the city's population. Though the Muslims did prosper in trade, they had no independent sphere of political action. Their communities built some large mosques, but they never functioned as religious centers for Muslims from other parts of the province. Sometimes besieged by Muslims from Hezhou or Xunhua, the Lanzhou Muslims could not or would not rebel in their own right, living as they did under the eyes of the governor and his garrison.[25]

Muslim political hegemony in Gansu, at least in Qing and Republican times, was associated with the community of Hezhou (Linxia), now the central city of Linxia Hui Autonomous Prefecture, set in the valley

23. An earlier version of this argument may be found in Lipman, "Patchwork Society."
24. Iwamura Shinobu, "Kanshuku Kaimin," 144–47.
25. See the population statistics in Botham, "Islam in Kansu," 377–90. *Chongxiu Gaolan xian zhi* (1892), 13.12a–12b, gives the 1887 figures as 478,294 "Han" and 24,863 Muslims, in contrast to Botham's 50,000 Muslims. Though taken from the *baojia* (mutual security system) records, the gazetteer figures cannot be regarded as any more accurate than the missionary's. The relative percentage, 5–10 percent Muslim, is more trustworthy than any specific numbers.

of the Daxia River southwest of Lanzhou. Muslims and non-Muslims lived there in equal numbers, perhaps forty-five thousand of each in the early twentieth century.[26] The non-Muslims lived in the walled city to the north, the Muslims in the suburbs and rural hinterland (see plate 8). In economic and social power, the Muslims dominated the entire region. Even in the realm of coercive power, they controlled elements of the garrison and had powerful local militias of their own for much of the modern period. The Muslim community also supported many religious institutions, including the tombs of several important Sufi saints. Underscoring the city's centrality in Gansu Muslim life, most of the Muslim generals who dominated the northwest during the Republican period claimed Hezhou as their "official" home district, though many lived elsewhere. As a market for both Chinese goods and the hill country produce of Tibet, Hezhou prospered in peacetime but suffered horribly from communal conflict in wartime. The populous but vulnerable Muslim suburb of Bafang was sacked and burned a number of times as frontier violence escalated after the Qianlong period (1736–96).

Tianshui, now an important town in the upper Wei valley, had a Muslim community of about five thousand, with eight mosques, among a population of fifty thousand. But the entire hinterland of this county seat was non-Muslim, so the town's small Muslim community had to maintain a conciliatory attitude, especially since a garrison was usually stationed there. Though the Muslims there belonged to a supposedly militant revivalist organization, the Jahrīya (Ch. Zheherenye or Zhehelinye), headquartered nearby at Zhangjiachuan, they never rose up against their neighbors.[27]

Near Tianshui and Zhangjiachuan the town of Fujiang (now Gangu), a market town and county seat, had only a small Muslim community. To a European anthropologist working there in the early twentieth century,

---

26. Iwamura, "Kanshuku Kaimin," 145, cites the missionary journal *Friends of Moslems* 8:2, 31, for a 60 : 40 ratio of Muslims to non-Muslims. The Muslim population of Hezhou has been placed as low as 41,000 (Zhang Qiyun, "Taoxi quyu," 3) and as high as 112,000 (Ma Zikuo, "Musilin zai Linxia," 15–18). Both Ma Hetian and Nishi Masao record a 50 : 50 ratio of Muslims to non-Muslims, and this is confirmed without any scientific basis by most of the travel accounts. This figure does not, however, include the rural hinterlands, especially the solidly Muslim eastern subprefecture, whose inhabitants may have numbered as many as one-hundred thousand in the early twentieth century (Ma Hetian, *Gan Qing Zang,* 18; Nishi Masao, "Kanshuku Seikai," 8–21 and 41).

27. "Gansu Tianshui xian gaikuang" gives no indication that the local Muslims were other than peaceful citizens, though it maligns the Hezhou Muslims as *tufei* (bandits) for attacking the city in the late 1920s.

the place strongly resembled entirely Chinese towns much further east and seemed culturally very far removed from the geographically close Muslim centers. Indeed, in a lengthy ethnography Joseph Dols did not mention any Muslims at all.[28] But the Muslims were there and did belong to the Jahrīya. Through their leaders, they participated in the anxiety and planning attendant upon that Sufi order's tribulations and uprisings.[29]

With the usual, substantial warnings about the inaccuracy of the late Qing and Republican population statistics, we may plot the modern distribution of Muslims in Gansu and find it very uneven. They gathered in Hezhou, Xunhua, Zhangjiachuan, Xining, Taozhou, Ningxia, and Guyuan/Haicheng. Large sections of the province—between Lanzhou and Ningxia, in the east, and in the south—held only small Muslim communities. The Gansu sections of the Wei valley were completely dominated by non-Muslims, though Muslims lived at Tianshui, Fujiang, Pingliang, and Zhangjiachuan. As Gu Jiegang found to his pain, Gansu roads were notoriously bad, often closed by natural disaster or bandit menace, placing yet another obstacle in the path of Muslim networks of communication.

In sum, the condition of Muslim communities in Gansu and their relations with non-Muslim neighbors depended to a great extent on local factors. For example, after 1873 Muslims were excluded from living within the city walls of most towns in the province, for fear of a repetition of the violence of 1862–73. In Hezhou, Xining, and Ningxia, all of which had large Muslim communities, they continued to live only in the suburbs into the mid-twentieth century. But in Tianshui and Lanzhou Muslims lived in the city with everyone else, so nonthreatening were their small communities. In some districts Muslims and non-Muslims lived in the same village,[30] whereas around Hezhou the separation between them seemed quite strict:

> On one occasion we made a trip with Muslim muleteers. They were
> friendly and suggested that we stay with them in their village, so for

28. Dols, "La vie chinoise." This lengthy article emphasizes repeatedly the "Chinese" quality of the Fujiang community.

29. The interrogation of a Fujiang Muslim in 1781 revealed that the community had raised four-hundred taels of silver to aid Ma Mingxin in fighting the lawsuits brought against his Jahrīya Sufi suborder and during his imprisonment in Lanzhou (Agui and Li Shiyao [Qianlong 46.5.29, June 20, 1781] memorial, in *Salazu dang'an shiliao*, 85–88).

30. Li Xudan, "Xibei kexue," 25, notes zones of exclusively Muslim and exclusively non-Muslim settlement, with mixed villages and towns between.

that night we stopped in a little Muslim world. The children were called I-ssu-mer (Ismael), Fa-ti-mai (Fatima), Er-pu-tu (Abdul). . . . Before darkness fell, pious bearded men said their evening prayers in public places.

We made another trip over the same general route but on this occasion had Chinese [non-Muslim] muleteers. . . . Somehow the landscape seemed to have a much more typically Chinese complexion than before. Again we stayed for the night in the native village of our muleteers. . . . The smell of incense was in the air. . . . pigs grunted in the courtyards, and in the streets, after dark, accompanied by the beating of gongs and the clashing of cymbals, effigies and masks were carried around in celebration.[31]

We must thus pay close attention to the local in our study of Muslims in northwest China, not relying on categorization schemes devised by national institutions, nor on ideologically informed systems of classification ordinarily used by Chinese and Western scholars. Gansu identities were no more rigid or monovalent than others. Locale, family, religious affiliation, occupation, education, and a host of other loyalties affected the choices that Muslims and non-Muslims made along the frontiers of their cultures.

31. Ekvall, *Cultural Relations,* 19–20. The author explicitly refers to the feelings of "we" and "they" that he heard expressed in both villages and emphasizes the strict segregation between them.

2 / Acculturation and Accommodation
China's Muslims to the Seventeenth Century

SOJOURNERS IN TANG-SONG CHINA (618–1279)

How the Muslims Came to China

Muhammad had the power to create Heaven and Earth. . . . He divided the moon into two and put it together again. . . . This was in 621, 4th year of *Wu-te* [Wude]. The imperial order was thereupon given to Ou-yang Hsun [Ouyang Xun], a *shuai keng-ling* [*shuai gengling*] (keeper of the clepsydra) to engrave in seal characters coins for the Commencement of the (Islamic?) Era, in order to record the extraordinary feat. After this, (T'ai-)tsung dreamt that he met a saint and waking up frightened he then sent several missions to the (saint's) land. The saint then ordered his disciple Saad Waqqas to bring the Qur'an in 30 volumes comprising 114 *sura* and 6,666 verses to offer the emperor. . . . T'ai-tsung edited it and promulgated it throughout the empire, and the faith flourished in China.[1]

The T'ang emperor (T'ai-tsung) dreamt that a turbanned man chasing a phantom appeared to him in the palace. . . . The Interpreter of Dreams said: "The turbanned man is a *Hui-hui* (Muslim) of the west. In Arabia is a Muslim king of great virtue. A great sage is born, with favorable omens." A general Hsu Shih-chi [Xu Shiji] stepped forward and said: "Send an ambassador across the western frontiers to the Muslim king, and request from him a sage to be sent to deal with the threatened evils, so that the country may be kept at rest." The great officer Shih T'ang [Shi Tang] was sent as ambassador. Three religious leaders were sent back to China

---

1. *Zhengjiao si bei ji* (1670) by Ting Peng (*jinshi* 1655), trans. in Leslie, *Islam*, 72. For citations on Ting Peng, see Leslie, *Islamic Literature*, 81–82. The stele is preserved at the Fenghuang mosque in Hangzhou.

with him. . . . Two died on the way, only Ko-hsin [Gexin] arrived. Ko-hsin told the emperor of the heaven-sent Fu-erh-ko-ni [Fuergeni, Ar. *furqān*] (the Qur'an), and reproved him for being an idolator.[2] The emperor finally offered to appoint Ko-hsin as President of the Board of Mathematics.[3]

Tang and Song Foundations

We have no historical evidence that Sa'ad Waqqas, the Prophet's maternal uncle, actually traveled to China, and the Tang Emperor surely neither edited the Koran nor tolerated being reproved as an idolator. But stories such as these, popular and never refuted within Sino-Muslim communities, place Muslims in China very early in Islamic history. It is likely that Muslims *did* come to China as political emissaries and merchants within a few decades of Muhammad's flight from Mecca to Medina in 622.[4] They joined large numbers of non-Muslim Central and West Asians already resident in the Tang empire's trading centers.[5] For six centuries thereafter Arabs and Persians—called Dashi and Bosi respectively—played significant roles in China's economic life, especially along the Silk Road in the northwest and in the port cities of the southeast coast.[6] Only many

2. Leslie translates *furqān* as Koran, but it often has the more general meaning of "sacred scriptures, divine revelations," and would thus include the Old and New Testaments.

3. From the *Huihui yuanlai,* an early eighteenth-century Sino-Muslim text, trans. in Leslie, *Islam,* 74. For various attributions of the text, its editions, and its associated manuscripts, see Leslie, *Islamic Literature,* 55–56.

4. The most thorough English-language scholarship on early contacts between Muslims and China may be found in Leslie, *Islam,* chapters 4–7, with the materials on Arab embassies to the Tang in chapter 4. In chapter 8 he summarizes the legendary accounts current among Sino-Muslims from the Yuan dynasty to the present day.

5. Apart from Leslie, Tazaka Kōdō (*Chūgoku ni okeru*), Zhang Xinglang (*Zhong-Xi*), and Yuan Ch'en (*Western and Central Asians*) have done extensive work on Muslims in pre-Ming China, and many contemporary Sino-Muslim scholars have also pored over the difficult primary texts.

6. The term Bosi presents problems in this context. Though Sino-Muslim scholars unhesitatingly identify "people of Bosi" as Persian *Muslims,* it is likely that many of them were Manichaeans, Mazdaists, or Nestorian Christians well into the Islamic era. This type of terminological confusion continued as late as the Mongol period, when the Nestorian Aixie was identified as a Huihui. Even in Persia Muslims and non-Muslims lived side by side for centuries after the Muslim conquest; it is certainly likely that they did so in distant China, where the pressure to convert to Islam was considerably less. Much of the controversy surrounding the term Huihui stems from the *gradual* conversion of the Uygurs (to whom it first applied) from other religions to Islam, a process that took centuries and confused the terminology of contemporary texts.

centuries later, after the Mongol conquest, did they attain to ranks as exalted as president of the Board of Mathematics.

Much of their trade was carried on in the guise of "tribute" (Ch. *gong*), luxury goods delivered directly to the Chinese court by both legitimate and falsely credentialed representatives of Muslim rulers. The Chinese official histories list dozens of caravans arriving in Chang'an and Kaifeng, where they received free lodging, luxurious entertainment, and benevolent gifts usually reported as exceeding in value the "tribute" they had brought. "Tributary" missions could not remain in China for extended commerce but rather returned home, usually within a few months, bearing their profits and the Chinese emperor's largesse. Modern historians correctly suspect the rhetoric of tribute, surmising that the commercial functions of such missions were known and expected among both Chinese and foreigners.[7]

Some foreign traders, however, came to China to stay awhile. Seafaring Muslims lived as far north as Yangzhou, at the intersection of the Yangzi River and Grand Canal, while Silk Road merchants could be found as far east as Kaifeng, the northern Song (960–1127) capital. Few became participants in Chinese politics or society, in part because the state acted to segregate them. In Chang'an, Guangzhou, and other major cities, all foreigners were required to live in separate wards, to trade in specially established markets, and to restrict their intercourse with Chinese. The Tang government sometimes prohibited or discouraged these male foreigners from marrying Chinese women or wearing Chinese clothing.[8] Muslims remained sojourners, obvious and clearly designated by state and society; they were granted a measure of legal and administrative autonomy within their carefully delineated settlements, but they were not supposed to mix with the local population. These regulations, however, did not prevent some Muslims from studying Chinese, intermarrying, and remaining in China for long periods. Though we can only speculate about their relations with local people, there can be little doubt that some of them settled, found wives (Muslims or converts) among the other immigrant groups or locals, and

7. Yang Huaizhong, "Tangdai de fanke," 53, for example, straightforwardly identifies "tribute" as a commercial transaction. Fletcher, "China and Central Asia," 215–16, concludes that tributary relations served a domestic propaganda purpose but often constituted a cover for interstate trade. Hevia, *Cherishing men,* section 1.3, summarizes the historiographical importance of the tribute system in conceptualizing the Qing empire.

8. Ouyang, *Xin Tang Shu* 182.6b–7a records the order of Lu Jun, governor of Lingnan at Canton, that foreigners and Chinese could not intermarry (Ch. *Fan Hua bu de tong hun*), in order to prevent conflict.

created mixed communities unified by Islam, by their "foreignness," and probably by use of Persian as a *lingua franca.*

Throughout the Tang, Five Dynasties (907–60), and especially in the Song period (960–1279), Muslim import-export firms maintained more-or-less permanent residences or representatives in Chang'an, Quanzhou, Hangzhou, Kaifeng, Yangzhou, and Guangzhou, and possibly in other cities as well. They dealt in a vast variety of commodities, and their numbers were not small.[9] For example, Tian Shengong's soldiers killed thousands of Dashi and Bosi at Yangzhou in a Tang battle against local rebels. When Huang Chao's rebel army took Guangzhou in 879, they are reported by Arabic sources to have massacred tens of thousands of foreign merchants, many of them Muslims.[10]

China's imports of spices and herbs, rhinoceros horn and ivory, and precious stones—all light, expensive, and rare, and therefore appropriate for long-distance trade—lay largely in Muslim hands. The official history of the Song dynasty includes the stories of a number of Arab merchants who traded at Guangzhou as well as lists of Arab products presented to the throne as gifts.[11] Foreign merchants paid taxes and enriched the state; fragrances and spices from the west altered tastes and changed customs; and medicaments from western Asia entered the Chinese market in considerable numbers.[12] Frankincense (Ch. *ruxiang*), a fragrant resinous gum used as incense, achieved particular popularity at court, where the emperor sometimes ordered hundreds of frankincense candles lit. Pu Luoxin, a Muslim merchant who brought large quantities of the precious commodity to China, received an official title for his achievement.[13]

The precious cargoes of Muslim caravans and ships did not go untaxed or unregulated by the Chinese government. The state monopolized some cargoes—iron, agate, coral, and especially frankin-

9. Bai Shouyi, *Zhongguo Yisilan,* 134–69. Another list of the products sold by foreign merchants in the southern Chinese markets may be found in Hirth and Rockhill, *Chau Ju-kua.* Zhao's mid-thirteenth century book, drawing heavily on the *Lingwai daida* of Zhou Qufei (1178) and lightly on the *Pingzhou ketan* of Zhu Yu (early 12th cent.), accurately describes many peoples and places between southeast China and the Mediterranean, precisely the world linked by Muslim Arab and Persian traders.

10. Abu-Zaid of Siraf reported that 120,000 foreign merchants were killed by Huang Chao, while the later Mas'udi claimed 200,000. See Levy, *Biography,* 109–21, for an analysis of the Arabic sources.

11. For example, Tuo, *Song shi* 490.17a. The section on Dashi includes stories of the merchant Pu Ximi and the rich gifts he presented to the throne.

12. Bai Shouyi, *Zhongguo Yisilan,* 158–69.

13. Lai Cunli, *Huizu shangye shi,* 76.

cense—so they could be sold only to government officials, with whom the Muslim merchants could not bargain as they might in an open market. Commodity taxes, assessed in tax warehouses at the port of entry, ranged from one-fifteenth to two-fifths ad valorem and constituted a considerable portion of state revenues, especially after the Song loss of north China to the Jin invaders in 1127. Officials in southern ports and in the northern cities used both specially assigned imperial household funds and their own personal capital to purchase the Muslim merchants' stock at low prices, sometimes for delivery to court, sometimes for resale and private profit. Foreign merchants also had to use a portion of their goods as gifts to both local and metropolitan officials to ensure prompt processing of paperwork and uninterrupted permission to trade.

Despite this regulation of their commercial activities, Muslims resident in China under the Tang and Song nonetheless controlled their own community life under Muslim officials who received imperial patents of office. Their neighborhoods, called "foreigners' quarters" (Ch. *fanfang*), resembled the foreign concessions of the nineteenth century.[14] Muslims had the extraterritorial right to be tried under Muslim law for offenses against other Muslims committed in China, and the community's judge (Ar. *qadi*) was recognized as a legitimate community authority by the state. Few Muslims became ordinary subjects before the late Song; as far as we know, neither they nor the Chinese state desired their acculturation or assimilation.

Tang and Song regulations left Muslim sojourners free to dress, eat, and pray as they pleased. They retained their native languages, though they must have learned Chinese for their work in the markets (or from their Sinophone mothers), and they practiced Islam without engaging in any missionary activity. The few who became literate in the Chinese classical canon received notice in the imperial histories, and only one Muslim obtained an imperial examination degree under the Tang.[15] Until the mid-Song, virtually all Muslims in China considered them-

14. Warned by an unpublished essay by Dilip Basu, I have chosen to translate this usage of *fan* not with the conventional "barbarian" but with the less pejorative "foreigner." A debate has recently begun over the evolved historical meanings of this term, with both "foreigner" and "vassal" receiving support.

15. Li Yansheng, a Dashi, is credited with having obtained the *jinshi* degree in the Tang (Zhang Xinglang, *Zhong-Xi*, vol. 3, sec. 2, 232–3). Zhang cites the *Quan Tang wen* as the source for his story, noting that after residing in China and intermarrying with Chinese, some foreigners may be "scoured and washed" sufficiently by Chinese literary culture to become capable of Chinese scholarship.

selves, and were considered by the Chinese, to be temporary residents rather than permanent settlers.[16]

The Beginnings of Belonging

By the late twelfth century, however, some Muslims had been living in China for generations and occupied a special status. Included among the *tusheng fanke* (native-born foreign sojourners) or *wushi fanke* (fifth-generation foreign sojourners), they were allowed to intermarry and to purchase land for mosques and cemeteries in the port cities.[17] The southern Song (1127–1279) government even made provision for foreign merchants to take official positions; after living in China for three generations, a foreigner could marry an imperial princess if at least one member of his household possessed an official title. Many contemporary Chinese Muslim communities claim Tang origins for their mosques and cemeteries—Sa'ad Waqqas is supposed to have built the Huaisheng Mosque at Guangzhou—but, based on a summary of inscriptions and West Asian sources, Donald Leslie concludes that we cannot reliably date the first mosques in China before the Song. Given the size and duration of their communities, Guangzhou, Yangzhou, and Quanzhou probably had Muslim graveyards and mosques in the Tang, but the sources do not yet allow us to be sure.[18]

Though they had been importers and caravaners on a large scale during the first half of the dynasty, Central Asians seem to have become less influential in north China after the mid-Tang, for the Silk Road trade was interrupted by numerous wars and invasions of northern peoples. Nonetheless, the Song history *Zizhi tongjian* (Comprehensive mirror for aid in government) tells of foreigners, probably Muslims, who lived in Chang'an for forty years, married local women, and did not want to return to their homelands.[19] We know that in times of relative peace travel could be fairly smooth between China and Persia, for as early as the Arab conquest, non-Muslim Persian refugees found their way to the Chang'an region, where they were allowed to settle. In

16. Sauvaget, *'Ahbar as-Sin*, 26.

17. These titles are attested in the *Song huiyao jigao* (Zhiguan sec.), according to Bai Shouyi, *Zhongguo Yisilan*, 134.

18. Leslie, *Islam*, 42–46. The argument for Tang origins is made by Yang Huaizhong, "Tangdai de Fanke," 69.

19. Yang Huaizhong, "Tangdai de Fanke," 60.

the Northern Song Karakhanid "tribute" missions had to be reminded to return home from Kaifeng.[20]

The gradual Islamicization of the Central Asian Turkic peoples affected Eastern Turkestan after the eleventh century, as the Kashgar region became the focus of power struggles among Muslim rulers.[21] Despite these alarms and Khitan, Jurched, and Mongol encroachment, however, some of the trade routes remained open. Xining (in modern Qinghai), for example, became a major entrepot when the Tanguts of the Xixia kingdom interrupted the main Silk Road, and Didao (now Lintao), in modern Gansu, was home to hundreds of foreign merchants. Muslims in Hezhou, later to become the "Little Mecca" of Gansu, probably built their first mosque in the Song period. Even after the fall of the northern Song, Muslims remained in north China under Jurched rule; as early as 1228 a Mongol regulation protected the temples of Fengxiang, in southwestern Shaanxi, including a *dashiman mixiji* (Per. *danishmand,* Ar. *masjid*), a Muslim mosque.[22]

We know that by the end of the Song, Muslims had become a common part of the economic and social world in Chinese cities that were connected to international trade. Many knew Chinese, understood the marketplace, and intended to remain in China. Muslim trade provided a share of the empire's tax revenues and brought valuable goods both to court and to public markets. In addition, Persian and Arab merchants brought technology—cotton processing and glassmaking, for example—to their host culture, while providing the Middle East with Chinese advances in the manufacture of porcelain and paper. A more complex and less understood exchange took place in the realm of medicine, for Arabs and Persians brought new materia medica to China and contributed both to the techniques of healing and to the pharmacopoeia.[23]

Though never subject to specific legal discrimination, Muslims were evaluated negatively both as foreigners and as merchants, a degraded class in Chinese social theory. Neither they nor their religion attracted

20. Yang Huaizhong, "Songdai de Fanke," 96–99.
21. Ma Qicheng, "Jianlun Yisilan jiao," 184–88.
22. The inscription may be found in Cai Meibiao, *Yuandai baihua,* 5. The Chinese transliteration *dashiman* for "Muslim clergy" is analyzed in Poppe, *The Mongolian Monuments,* 83. I am grateful to Thomas Allsen for this reference.
23. The complex vocabulary of both pharmacology and botanical taxonomy has prevented me from analyzing the primary sources. Yang Huaizhong, "Dui *Huihui yaofang,*" 224–28, gives a brief synopsis of texts.

positive attention from the Chinese elite—only one reasonably accurate account of Islam appeared in Chinese in the Tang-Song period, Du Huan's *Jing xing ji*.[24] The words *fan, hu,* Dashi, Bosi, and the like, though they may be translated as "foreigner" without any particular negative connotation, certainly could carry the stigmatic nuance of nasty foreign flavor. At the same time, Chinese eagerly sought to purchase and profit from the spices, jewels, aphrodisiacs, and other exotica transported from afar by the foreign merchants. Muslims, on the other hand, gradually found China to be a good place to do business and to set up households. Since few women made the sea voyage from Dashi or Bosi, most of the merchants married Chinese women, who converted to Islam and laid the foundation for permanent Sino-Muslim communities all over China by teaching their children to speak local dialects of Chinese.

MUSLIMS IN YUAN CHINA (1279–1368)

Ahmad Fanakati, Finance Minister: Four Portraits

A Saracen, named Achmac, a crafty and bold man, whose influence with the Grand Khan [Qubilai] surpassed that of the others. . . . It was discovered . . . that he had by means of spells so fascinated His Majesty as to oblige him to give ear and credit to whatever he represented. . . . He gave away all the governments and public offices. . . . Besides this, there was no handsome female who became an object of his sensuality that he did not contrive to possess. . . . He had sons to the number of twenty-five, who held the highest offices of the state. . . . Achmac had likewise accumulated great wealth, for every person who obtained an appointment found it necessary to make him a considerable present.[25]

24. Du Huan was captured by the Arabs at the great battle of Talas (751) and taken westward to the Middle East. He returned by sea to the southeast coast of China over a decade later. His original text has been lost, but extracts, including his description of Islam, may be found in the *Tong dian,* compiled by his uncle, Du You. Leslie (*Islam,* 21–22) has translated the relevant sections; for a Sino-Muslim evaluation, see Yang Huaizhong, "Songdai de fanke," 128. Zhao Rugua also described Islam, granting it only a brief paragraph in his section on Dashi (Hirth and Rockhill, *Chao Ju-kua,* 116).

25. Marco Polo, *Travels,* 275–76. It is almost certain that Marco Polo was present in Khanbalik when Ahmad served as finance minister and when he was assassinated.

The Emir Ahmad held the vizierate with honor for nearly 25 years. . . . he was extremely cautious and alert.[26]

When Ahmad died, Shizu [Qubilai] still was not entirely aware of his debauchery, and he ordered the Zhongshu not to interrogate his wives and children. Inquiring of Boluo, he then learned of all his crimes and evil. Greatly angered, he said, "Wang Zhu's killing him was truly an act of sincerity!" He ordered [Ahmad's] grave opened, the coffin ripped apart, and the corpse displayed outside the Tongxuan Gate, allowing the dogs to tear his flesh. The officials of all ranks all observed and declared themselves delighted.[27]

Summing up Ahmad's life, he served a definite positive function in government finance in the period of Yuan Shizu's process of unifying the nation and stabilizing the situation. . . . But when it comes to his using official power [for private purposes], hiring his cronies, plotting for his private gain, and taking advantage of the powerless, he must be counted among the evil members of the feudal bureaucracy.[28]

Ruling China: The Semu and Mongol Hegemony

The transcultural power of the thirteenth-century Mongol conquests brought to China an influx of Muslims of many professions and cultures, not just as traders or brokers but also as conquerors and governors, artisans and architects, scientists and tax farmers. Unwilling to allow their newly subdued Chinese subjects to govern themselves, Ögödei, Möngke, Qubilai, and their successors created an intermediary bureaucracy of non-Chinese administrators and merchants collectively

26. Rashīd al-Dīn, a great Middle Eastern chronicler and intellectual, was born in 1247 and thus was contemporary to Ahmad's service to Qubilai (Rashid al-Din, The Successors, 291–92).

27. This final judgment may be found at the end of Ahmad's biography in Song, Yuan shi 205.1b–6b, in the "Depraved Ministers" section. The Yuan shi was, of course, written in the Ming period by servants of the dynasty that had driven the Mongols out of China.

28. Bai Shouyi, Huizu renwu zhi (Yuan dai), 51–63, citation at 63. Rossabi, Khubilai Khan, 178–84, attempts an even-handed assessment, concluding that Ahmad probably was no worse than other officials of his day, regardless of ethnicity or religion, and that Chinese historical sources and Marco Polo's account all carry a distorting grudge, the former because of Ahmad's foreignness, the latter because of his religion.

known as *semu guan* (officials of various categories.)[29] The Venetian Catholic Marco Polo was such an official, but the majority of them were Central and West Asian Muslims.

Charged with keeping the peace and collecting revenues, as well as with distributing goods, these outsiders earned an unsavory reputation among the Chinese but established themselves as permanent residents. Reserving the highest positions for themselves and the *semu,* the early Yuan monarchs prohibited indigenous Chinese from holding the highest offices—*darughaci* (provincial commander), for example. Dozens of Muslims held ministerial-level offices during the early Yuan, among them the exceptionally successful Sayyid Ajall Shams ad-Dīn (Ch. Sai Dianchi), whose tenure as governor of Yunnan, following a series of high appointments in the capital, established a permanent Muslim presence in southwest China.[30]

Muslims monopolized or dominated some academic and economic fields within the Yuan bureaucracy. The offices responsible for astronomy, medicine, manufacture of weapons (especially catapults and other siege engines), and foreign languages all had large contingents of Muslim scholars and technicians. The Persian Jamāl ad-Dīn, for example, brought designs for the latest astronomical instruments from Persia and constructed an observatory at Beijing, thereafter becoming Qubilai's favored calendrical scientist.[31] Middle Eastern, especially Persian, astronomy (called "Muslim" in China) became an integral part of Chinese

29. Because the characters used for *semu* can also mean "colored eyes," many Chinese and non-Chinese writers have mistaken this term for a comment on the appearance of these Central Asians. The Yuan period texts make it abundantly clear that *semu* is an administrative term, not a physical description.

30. Endicott-West, *Mongolian Rule,* is a monograph on the office of *darughaci* and its centrality in the Mongol administration of China. The author concludes that the term, which she leaves untranslated, evolved over the course of the Yuan period and thus has no single English equivalent. It always indicates a local or regional governing official whose duties might comprehend both military and civil functions. As the most unambiguously successful and high-minded Muslim *semu* to achieve office under the Yuan, Sayyid Ajall has been the subject of extensive research by Sino-Muslim scholars, e.g., Yang Huaizhong, "Sai Dianchi"; Bai Shouyi, *Zhongguo Yisilan,* 216–98; and "Sai Dianchi Shan Siding," in Bai Shouyi, *Huizu renwu zhi (Yuan dai),* 12–27. Recent English notices include Rossabi, *Khubilai Khan,* 201–3; Leslie, *Islam,* 80, 83–85; and Armijo-Hussein, "The Sinicization and Confucianization." For two generations Sayyid Ajall's descendants continued to hold positions of trust in the Yuan administration, especially the governorship of Yunnan; many contemporary Yunnanese Muslim families trace their ancestry to Sayyid Ajall's lineage.

31. Jamāl ad-Dīn and a Chinese, Guo Shoujing, prepared a calendar for the Yuan court as well as building an observatory. On Jamāl's life, see Yang Huaizhong, "Zhongguo kexue," 205–23.

court life from the late thirteenth century until it was eclipsed by that brought by the Jesuits nearly three centuries later.[32] During the successful invasion of north China by a mixed Mongol-*semu*-Chinese army, two Muslims constructed the ballistae that enabled the Mongols to take Xiangyang (then in Henan, now in Hubei). At the Yuan capital special academies were established for the teaching of Persian and other Central Asian languages.[33]

Acting not only as scientists and officials of the dynasty but also as commercial entrepreneurs, Muslims became *ortaq*, corporate partners with their Mongol overlords, to concentrate and export Chinese goods and import foreign commodities through the open trade routes of the interconnected Mongol empires.[34] These servants of the Yuan enjoyed political and economic advantage in their intimacy with the Mongol court, including direct investment by Mongol princes, loans from government revenues, and even tax-free status under Qubilai and his immediate successors, so they branched out into every region and province of China. Coming primarily from Central Asia (Chinese sources specifically mention Khwarezm and Samarkand) as well as Dashi and Bosi, and dealing not only in luxury goods but also in foodstuffs, salt, and livestock, they multiplied the Muslim presence in China in numbers and in scope.[35] Since their activities included not only commerce but also tax-farming, even rural Chinese knew them—and all the *semu guan*—as objects of scorn, contempt, and fear.

Like some, but not all, of the foreign sojourners of former dynasties, the Muslim *semu* and *ortaq* of the Yuan intended to remain in China. Within two or three generations they learned Chinese, and some became well-known literati in the Chinese style. Muslim poets, painters, and civil officials of high Confucian learning may be found in the cultural history of mid- to late Yuan China.[36] Though Donald Leslie discounts the degree of acculturation of Muslims to China during the

32. The technical language and texts of Yuan-Ming Islamic astronomy have been masterfully explicated in Tasaka (Tazaka), "An Aspect."

33. Leslie, *Islam*, 94–95.

34. On the origins and functioning of the *ortaq*, see Rossabi, *Khubilai*, 122–23; Schurmann, *Economic Structure*, 4–5, 213–15; and especially Weng Dujian, "Wotuo zakao." Two contemporary scholars have done detailed research on the "partnership" nature of *ortaq* commercial enterprise: Allsen, "Mongolian Princes;" and Endicott-West, "Merchant Associations."

35. Lai Cunli, *Huizu shangye*, 125–31.

36. Ch'en, *Western and Central Asians*, 121, 162–63. Biographies of Yuan Muslim literati may be found in Bai Shouyi, *Huizu renwu zhi (Yuan dai)*.

Yuan, the Muslim *semu* soldiers, merchants, and officials certainly established permanent residence, albeit usually in separate quarters from their Chinese neighbors. In the Gansu corridor, the crucial transportation and communication link with Central Asia, the Mongols settled large numbers of demobilized soldiers as agricultural colonists on the fields of fled or dead Chinese farmers.[37] Even artisans brought from Central Asia established themselves in proximity to Chinese, but in clearly defined and "different" towns or settlements.[38] Whether they studied the Confucian classics or not, many of the Muslims who lived in China had every intention of remaining in the service of "their" Mongol dynasty, and their wide distribution and broad range of occupations laid the groundwork for the following centuries of Sino-Muslim acculturation.

Changing Roles, Changing Images

Before the Yuan, antipathy for Muslims among the Chinese followed conventional formulae of Civilized-Us contrasted to Barbarous-Them. Outlandish and distant, the Muslim merchants who sojourned in the Silk Road towns and the southeast coast ports could not have been familiar to more than a small minority of Chinese. During the Yuan, however, *semu* status gave Muslims a special position in Chinese society that made them both familiar and antagonistic to the indigenous people, especially to the elites who would ordinarily have undertaken political and social leadership themselves. Muslims functioning as officials and as merchants enriched themselves and their families, monopolizing many kinds of power that foreigners had not held under the Tang and Song—power that had been reserved for the upper classes of Chinese society, those responsible for committing China's history and attitudes to writing. We must, therefore, attend with a grain of salt to complaints about Muslim culture or behavior, at the same time noting that the antagonism becomes particularly powerful when non-Chinese people dominate China.

The four portraits cited above of one of Qubilai's highest officials, the Central Asian Finance Minister Ahmad Fanakati, demonstrate this histo-

---

37. Gao Zhanfu, "Yuandai de Gansu."

38. Rashid al-Din (*The Successors,* 276) reported a Samarkandi town called "Sinali" or "Simali," complete with Central Asian gardens, on the road from Daidu (Khanbalik, Beijing) to the Mongol khans' summer palace north of the great wall. The *Yuan shi* (122, in the biography of Hasanna) states that three-thousand "Huihui artisans" were settled there after Chinggis's and Ögödei's Central Asian conquests. For a Sinological explication of this community's location and character, see Pelliot, "Une ville musulmane."

riographical problem. Ahmad (Ch. Ahema) served as an advisor and administrator to Qubilai for twenty years.[39] His performance in office, described as reasonable and honorable by Rashīd al-Dīn, brought him the enmity of many Chinese, and he was excoriated after his death for venality, excessive sexual appetites, nepotism, and corruption of all kinds. Marco Polo, too, records an entirely negative portrait in his *Travels*.[40] Some sources report that when Ahmad was assassinated, the people held a festival, drinking and singing for three days.[41] Following his death, Ahmad's reputation was slandered by his enemies at court, and Qubilai condemned him to posthumous disgrace and his family to punishment. But all of our sources are sufficiently biased that we cannot judge fairly what his achievements and crimes may actually have been.

Modern Sino-Muslim scholars also have a hard time with Ahmad, for their Chinese-language sources tend to judge him harshly, while Sino-Muslim solidarity would call for a more positive moral evaluation. A recent biographical dictionary praises his skill as finance minister in managing the monopolies on salt, tea, wine, vinegar, and metals and in setting up a system of adequate emoluments for officials. The anonymous author also delineates the delicacy and difficulty of being a finance official under a conquering foreign power. On the other hand, Ahmad's corruption, nepotism, and alienation from fellow officials, especially the Chinese, bring him harsh criticism, as seen in the portrait above.

Apart from targeting specific individuals such as Ahmad for opprobrium, Song loyalists and anti-Mongol polemicists wrote texts that have become famous for their vilification of the *semu,* especially the Muslims, calling them the Mongols' trusties and a gang of uncivilized, immoral savages. The authors of these texts neither knew nor cared much about Islam, but they had suffered an unprecedented loss of influence and prestige, and their critiques go far beyond the rhetoric of the literate center and the civilizable savage. Passages from the *Guixin zazhi* of Zhou Mi, the *Xin shi* of Zheng Suonan, and the *Zhuo geng lu* of Tao Zongyi, all Yuan period compilations, describe Muslims as lacking the

---

39. For a detached analysis of sources, see Franke, "Ahmed." Translations of a number of sources on Ahmad's assassination may be found in Moule, *Quinsay,* 79–88, including a reconstruction of the process of posthumous punishment meted out to Ahmad's corpse, family, and estate after Qubilai discovered his "crimes" from Boluo (Pulad Aqa).

40. Polo, *Travels,* 275–78. This chapter was omitted from virtually all manuscripts of Polo's work, surviving only in Ramusio's version. Despite its obvious biases, it seems as accurate an account of Ahmad's assassination as we have, though all versions differ considerably in their details.

41. Nakada, *Kaikai minzoku,* 54.

rudiments of morality, decency, and personal hygiene. According to Zheng, "Even when they bathe, the Huihui still stink." Tao quotes a satirical poem—"Their elephant noses all gone flat, their cat's eyes dulled, all their hopes for a long life gone. . . . Alas! When the tree falls, the monkeys scatter"—to illustrate the fate of the bestial Muslim *semu* at the inevitable defeat of their Mongol guardians.[42] Here we find, for the first time but not the last in China, Muslims described as irremediably Other not in the language of Confucian benevolence toward lesser beings but rather in the stark discourse of racism. We will find, with all due irony, that this form of distinction—they cannot be at all like us, for they are incapable of *wenhua* (literary culture)—increased as Muslims became more acculturated to China.

In historical circumstance, however, the Yuan monarchs did not uniformly favor their Muslim servants but kept them under careful constraints. Angered by the unwillingness of some Muslim guests to eat his "unclean" food, Qubilai himself promulgated an edict forbidding Muslims to slaughter animals in the Muslim fashion, requiring instead that they use the Mongol method.[43] Circumcision and the taxation of religious institutions and teachers—whether Muslim, Buddhist, Jewish, or Christian—also became contentious issues between Mongols and their *semu* subjects during the 1280s.[44] But whatever their internecine conflicts, for the first decades of the dynasty Muslims, Mongols, and other foreigners controlled and milked the Chinese economy, dominating the Chinese while gradually becoming acculturated to local ways.

The Muslims, even more than their formerly nomadic overlords, began to belong in China during the mid-fourteenth century. In those decades of violence and lawlessness, Muslims all over China organized or joined local self-defense corps as well as armies loyal to the dynasty.[45] When the Mongols were driven out in the 1360s by rebels under the

42. Franke, "Eine mittelalterliche chinesische Satire," 202–8, translates Tao's ridicule of the Huihui in its entirety. The original text may be found in the *Congshu jicheng* (Assembled collections), no. 220. See also Leslie, *Islam,* 92–93, for brief translations.

43. Rossabi, *Khubilai,* 200–201, notes the anti-Muslim edict of January 27, 1280, recorded in both the *Yuan dianzhang* and the *Yuan shi.* Rashid al-Din's version of this edict and its revocation some years later may be found in *Successors,* 293–95.

44. Leslie, *Islam,* 88–91.

45. One such Muslim self-defense corps, branded a "rebel" army by official histories, took a prominent role in Fujian until it was wiped out at Xinghua in 1366. Maejima, "The Muslims in Ch'uan-chou," concludes that local enmity against these Muslims, perceived as violent and unreliable, sealed the fate of the southeast coast communities under the Ming.

Ming founder, Zhu Yuanzhang (r. 1368–99), many Muslims chose to stay. Indeed, many chose to fight on the side of the indigenes, and Zhu's commanders may have included a fair number of former *semu*: Chang Yuqun, Lan Yu, Ding Dexing, Mu Ying, and many others are unambiguously claimed as Muslims by Sino-Muslim scholars. Not remarkably, these "meritorious ministers who founded the state" (Ch. *kaiguo gongchen*), whether Huihui or not, hailed mostly from Anhui, Zhu Yuanzhang's own province, not from the more obviously "Muslim" southeast coast towns or Silk Road cities.[46] The presence of Muslims— for there were certainly some, even if their commanders were non-Muslim—in the Chinese armies that drove the Mongols northward presages a gradual, but palpable, change in the condition of Muslims in late Yuan and Ming China. Originally *fanke* foreigners and then *semu*, they became Huihui, familiar strangers who came today and stayed tomorrow, ordinary but different.

BECOMING NORMAL IN MING CHINA (1368–1644)

> Mongols and *semu* who live in China may marry Chinese [women] but may not marry from among their own kind. There are Chinese who do not wish to marry Huihui or Qipchaqs, so these *semu* are not included in this prohibition.[47]

> Huihui are shaggy with big noses, and Qipchaqs have light hair and blue eyes. Their appearance is vile and peculiar, so there are those who do not wish to marry them. Mongols and *semu* may not marry their own kind. . . . but the Qipchaqs and Huihui are the vilest among the *semu*, and a Chinese will not want to marry them. They may marry their own kind. . . . Allowing them to marry each

---

46. Their biographies may be found in Bai Shouyi, *Huizu renwu zhi (Ming dai)*, including the location of their homes in Anhui. There is considerable doubt among non-Muslim scholars as to the "Muslim" identity of most of these generals, but Sino-Muslims assert their "Huiness" unequivocally. Tazaka, *Chūgoku ni okeru Kaikyō*, 861, for example, questions not only Chang Yuqun's identification as a Huihui but that of many others as well. F. Mote, in Goodrich and Fang, *Dictionary*, 1079–83, indicates that we have no evidence that Mu Ying was born a Muslim, and the story of his adoption and upbringing in Zhu Yuanzhang's intimate circle certainly indicates that he was not raised as one. The biography of Lan Yu (788–91) also does not mention that he might have been a Muslim, and Mote's article on Chang Yuqun (115–20) concurs with Tazaka regarding his Muslim identity: "This is not verifiable in any source."

47. *Da Ming lü jijie fuli, lü* 6:11a.

other is in sympathy for their [possible] extinction [should they not be allowed to do so]. There is strictly no prohibition against a Chinese marrying a Huihui or Qipchaq [should s/he wish to do so].[48]

Islam and Muslims

Based on the wide distribution of Muslims in China under the Yuan, the evolution of the Sinophone Muslims during the succeeding Ming dynasty took place in a bewildering variety of contexts. Many claims have been made regarding the relationship of Muslims in China to the Ming state, but few have solid grounding in historical sources; they reflect anachronistic political controversy more than careful research, which must be *local* rather than generalized. From the beginning of the Ming, when armies under Zhu Yuanzhang drove the Mongols out of China proper, concern about relations with peoples and states along the northern and western frontiers marked Ming politics, and Ming attempts to acculturate resident "aliens" demonstrate both fear of Others and confidence in the civilizing power of Chinese culture. Zhu Yuanzhang had Muslim commanders in his army, and may have had at least one Muslim wife, but the dynasty he founded neither entirely acculturated its Muslim subjects nor eliminated anti-Muslim prejudice in China.[49]

Ming emperors employed Muslims in high office, including a large number of scientists in the government agencies responsible for astrology, the calendar, and the interpretation of omens. Following on the service and success of Jamal ad-Din under the Yuan monarchs, the Qintianjian (Bureau of Astronomy) had a special section for the study of Muslim calendrical science, and a Chinese-language *Huihui tianwenshu* (Book of Muslim astronomy) remains extant.[50] In addition to describing

48. *Da Ming lü jijie fuli, fuli* 6:36b.

49. Hājjī Yusuf Chang has long claimed that Zhu Yuanzhang was himself a Muslim, but historians have not generally accepted his argument. On the basis of her surname (Ma), or on claims made by "unofficial histories" (*yeshi*, an often gratuitously salacious genre), one of Zhu Yuanzhang's senior wives is said to have come from a Muslim family (Rossabi, "Muslim and Central Asian revolts," 180–81).

50. Leslie, *Islam,* 106. Ho, "The Astronomical Bureau," notes the parallel establishment of Chinese and Islamic astronomical offices under Zhu Yuanzhang and his successors, but does not credit the Muslim astronomers with any greater skill than their Chinese counterparts. Indeed, he attributes the construction of the Yuan period astronomical instruments entirely to Guo Shoujing, ignoring Jamāl ad-Dīn. For a less ethnocentric view, see Tasaka, "An Aspect," 127–40, in which are translated Ming Taizu's (r. 1368–1398) encomiums to the Muslim astronomers and their texts.

specially designated "Muslim" work-units in the sciences, Sino-Muslim scholars also claim Muslim origins for many Ming civil officials and famous intellectuals, including Hai Rui, Ma Wensheng, Ma Ziqiang, and the iconoclastic literatus Li Zhi, originally from Quanzhou.[51] Such attributions are all suspect if we take "Muslim" to be a *religious* category, for they tend to be based on surname and/or place of origin and thus on a definition of "Huiness" appropriate to the *minzu* paradigm. Many of these men, especially Li Zhi, left not a trace of Islamic origins or religion in their writings or in their biographies, so the attribution of Hui status reveals in the twentieth-century claims both an anachronistic desire to have well-known coreligionists and the consciousness of profound acculturation among upper-class Ming period Sino-Muslims.

But neither courtly connections nor acculturation of China's Muslims could entirely prevent discrimination. Local officials, overwhelmingly non-Muslim, often mistreated Muslims before the bench:

> A Muslim [family] of Hanzhong [Shaanxi] had been reformed [honest subjects] for several generations. At that time [one of them] had a dispute with a Chinese man and brought a suit before the magistrate. The magistrate accused [the Muslim] of crime and, on his own responsibility, sent troops to arrest him. The Muslim was furious and escaped to the mountains. [Despite the intercession of Kang Lang, a local gentryman, the official insisted on attacking the Muslim but failed to take him.] Kang Lang continuously tried to persuade the Muslim to be appeased. [Finally], the Muslim said, "You, sir, know our oppression, so I bind myself [for punishment at your disposal]. If it had been the governor, I would simply have been killed."[52]

Very few Muslims were lucky enough to have had someone like Kang Lang as an ally. Unstable economic conditions in many parts of China, increasingly strict commercial regulation in frontier regions, and localized communal conflict all contributed to the impoverishment of Muslims in the mid- and late Ming. Incidents of "Muslim banditry" and Muslim-related social unrest were reported from Yunnan to Gansu to Shandong.[53] In official communications, including the annals of the

51. Biographies of all of these and more may be found in Bai, *Huizu renwu zhi (Ming dai)*. Examples of arguments on their Muslim origins may be found in Pei Zhi, "Hai Rui," 274–75; and Ye Guoqing, "Li Zhi," 276–84.

52. Tazaka, *Chūgoku ni okeru Kaikyō*, vol. 2, 1195–96.

53. Tazaka Kōdō has collected the important texts on Muslim participation in late Ming violence in "Mindai goki."

central government, Muslims who engaged in illegal activity were clearly distinguished as different from ordinary Chinese, and they were treated with special harshness.[54]

As an illustration of the relationship between the Ming court and its Muslim subjects, let us consider the statute cited above preventing non-Chinese in China from marrying within their own communities, requiring them instead to intermarry with the Chinese. This regulation, entirely opposite to the Tang and Song restrictions on intermarriage, demonstrates the powerful effects of the Mongol conquest and a new attitude toward outsiders: since foreigners, especially former *semu,* might be dangerous, they must be subdued by incorporation, by conscious sinification, through constant exposure to Chinese culture in the intimate family circle and through genetic incorporation into civilized China. Originally designed to promote acculturation of the Mongols and *semu,* the statute has often been cited as proof of Ming harshness toward non-Chinese. Though the exclusion of the Huihui and Qipchaqs by virtue of their "vile and peculiar" appearance does allow for endogamous marriage among them, the wording of the statute hardly bodes well for social relations. Neither consistent persecution of Muslims nor liberal ethnic policy informed Ming relations with the Muslims and other resident outsiders, and a great deal of research will be necessary before we can draw firm conclusions.

During the Ming the Muslims of China proper (including the northwest and southwest) found their connections with the western regions (the Muslim lands of Central and West Asia) to some extent controlled and limited by the Chinese state, a development that must have contributed to their acculturation.[55] Both for revenue enhancement and for frontier security, Ming policy makers found it advantageous to attempt control over all communication on both China's landward side and the

54. Tazaka, *Chūgoku ni okeru Kaikyō,* vol. 2, 1230, n76, cites the *Veritable Records* from the Jiajing reign for use of the term Huizei, "Muslim thieves," and also of terms such as "perverse Muslims." In the same note, he claims that the character for Hui 回 was enriched with a component meaning "dog" 狛 during the Ming period. The causes of Muslim violence in China, usually laid either to "fanatical followers of Islam" or to the oppressive policies of the Manchu Qing, must thus be sought in more complex understanding of specific local and regional contexts.

55. The much more complete acculturation of the Chinese Jews seems to have stemmed, at least in part, from their lack of contact with coreligionists outside China after the fall of the Yuan. Leslie, *The Survival,* presents a narrative of the Jews of Kaifeng, summarizing (p. 52) that the community acculturated completely because of its small size and isolation from other Jews. Pollak, *Mandarins, Jews, and Missionaries,* 337 ff, reaches the same conclusion, with a more complex texture.

South China Sea lanes. The Ming did not restrict Islam per se, but rather worried about Muslims as a potential fifth column for invaders from Central Asia. Chinese Muslims were accused of trying "to evade the commercial regulations of the court or planning raids on unguarded Chinese border settlements," the one from within China, the other from outside, confirming an intimate relationship between Muslims on the two sides of Ming China's Central Asian frontier.[56]

During the early years of the Ming, the Chinese were indeed in grave danger from Central Asia, though they probably did not know either its extent or its immediacy. Tamerlane, familiar to both Zhu Yuanzhang and his son, the Yongle emperor (r. 1402–24), did not find the language of the tribute system quaint or amusing; rather, he saw the embassies from Nanjing, demanding submission to the Ming emperor's all-embracing authority, as galling and provocative. The Ming emperors were neither Muslims nor militarily powerful enough to make such claims. As early as 1395 Tamerlane determined to avenge the insulting implications of the Ming communications, but the conquests of Asia Minor and India came first. Finally, in 1404, he impounded the Yongle emperor's ambassadorial caravan of eight hundred camels, raised a giant army, and prepared to conquer China. Fortunately for the Ming state, Tamerlane died before launching his invasion, but his son, Shahrukh Bahadur, would consent only to an equal exchange of embassies, not to the formal language of submission and tribute demanded by Ming theory. And the Yongle emperor, wary of Central Asian Muslim power and eager for the goods (especially horses) of the overland trade routes, did not press the issue and agreed to address Shahrukh as a political equal.[57]

In the aftermath of Tamerlane's demise, trade and "tribute" missions moved continuously between China and Herat, Samarkand, and particularly Turfan, whose population converted to Islam during this same period.[58] By the 1450s Turfan's caravans to Beijing, which had been

56. Rossabi, "Muslim and Central Asian Revolts," 184.

57. Fletcher, "China and Central Asia," 206–26, esp. the translation of Yongle's letter to Shahrukh, 212–14. Tamerlane's military capacities and organizational skills are described in detail in Manz, *The Rise and Rule*; Manz calls the plan to conquer China "the greatest exploit of his life" (73). We know a great deal about Tamerlane's reception of the Yongle emperor's 1404 embassy because, happily, the Spanish ambassador Clavijo (an indefatigable diarist) arrived at the same time and observed the court with a shrewd diplomat's eye (Le Strange, *Clavijo*, esp. chap. 12). Fear of Tamerlane also played a role in Ming China's treatment of its domestic Muslim communities; see, for example, Dazai, *Shina kaikyōshi*, chap. 5.

58. This summary is based on Rossabi, "Ming China."

dominated in the Yongle period by Buddhist envoys, were undertaken by Muslim merchants. They continued, even as the Muslim rulers of Turfan took and held Hami against Ming counterattacks, until the Ming established an economic blockade in the 1490s to force the Central Asians into proper submission. That plan did cause the Turfan rulers temporarily to deal more cautiously with the Ming court, but they never gave up Hami. This struggle concluded in Turfan's favor in the early sixteenth century, with Hami's final inclusion in Turfan's realm and Ming acquiescence in frequent Muslim trade and "tribute" missions to Beijing, where they made sensational profits. Despite the Ming court's efforts, trade flowed from northwest China to the Ferghana Valley, via Hami and Turfan, and Sino-Muslim merchants certainly took advantage of their position as bilingual middlemen on that route.

The Chinese merchants, among whom were many Sino-Muslims, also gained the final advantage in the frontier tea-for-horses trade, which the Ming rulers instituted to ensure a steady supply of warhorses, a commodity China never managed to produce for itself.[59] The foreign demand for tea gave the Ming state some leverage, and an official monopoly kept the private merchants out for the first half of the dynasty, but frontier wars and corrupt administration gave merchants increasing room to buy and sell. By the end of the sixteenth century the government regulations lay in ruins, and the Qing conquests finally incorporated the markets for tea and the pasturelands of Mongolia and Central Asia into the empire, along with a brand-new set of problems.[60]

On the seacoast, too, where Muslim merchants had played a dominant role since the Tang period, the Ming both used the expertise of Muslims and tried to restrict their trade. The most famous genuine Muslim of the Ming period, the admiral-eunuch Zheng He (born Ma He), certainly came from a Muslim family of Yunnan. Zhu Di, then prince of Yan and later to be the Yongle emperor, called him to service at the age of twenty and used Zheng He against rebels in his home province. "Since Cheng Ho [Zheng He] was pre-eminent among the eu-

59. A recent communication from Ruth Meserve indicates that many factors must be blamed for this remarkable failure in a scientific culture that had produced an advanced agricultural technology. Among them are conservative and often incompetent administration of the imperial stud, inappropriate pasturing and penning arrangements, unwillingness to invest in expensive breeding stock rather than battle-ready geldings, and certainly the nomads' reluctance to supply a potential enemy with so important an advantage as quality horseflesh. The subject deserves serious study.

60. Rossabi, "The Tea and Horse Trade." The same transformation of imperial commerce into private trade may be observed in Ming maritime commerce. See below, n65.

nuchs for both good looks and sagacity, the emperor Ch'eng-tsu [Yongle] appointed him to be principal envoy and commander-in-chief of six great naval expeditions which sailed to the 'Western Ocean' between 1405 and 1421."[61] Yongle's successor ordered Zheng on a seventh voyage in 1430. Zheng's Muslim upbringing may well have influenced the emperor's decision to use him in this office, as was the case in the appointment of the Persian-literate Ma Huan to be his assistant on three of the last four expeditions.

The enormous power projected by Ming China under Zheng He's command into the South China Sea and the Indian Ocean, as far as the Red Sea and Malindi, brought wealth, new tributaries, rare and costly trade goods, and exotic animals to court. Perhaps most important within China, the voyages created a profound sense of the Yongle emperor's legitimacy.[62] Foreign rulers from all along the Arab-Persian trade routes sent representatives to Nanjing, then to Beijing (Yongle moved the capital in 1421), receiving valuable gifts in return for their "tribute." In addition to material wealth and exotica, Zheng He's expeditions brought knowledge back to China, awareness that the people of a huge sweep of the world believed in the Huihui religion. The second-hand impressions of South and West Asia recorded by Tang and Song port officials could now be replaced by first-hand accounts, written in Chinese by men who had actually traveled, traded, negotiated, and made war far from China's shores.[63] From Quanzhou to Aden and beyond, they found Muslims. Members of Zheng's crew went on the pilgrimage to Mecca, and their accounts describe accurately the Ka'aba, Muhammad's tomb, the Zamzam well, and other holy sites of Islam.[64]

61. Mills, *Ma Huan*, 5–8, summarizes Zheng He's life.

62. All of these may well have been intended by the monarch; scholars disagree as to their validity or balance. See the brief summary of arguments and motivations in Mills, *Ma Huan*, 1, n1. For an example of the importance of foreign embassies, and foreign relations in general, to the establishment of dynastic legitimacy, see Toby, *State and Diplomacy*, chap. 3.

63. That knowledge is presented, by category and location, in a compilation of primary texts, Zheng and Zheng, *Zheng He*. Among many scholarly efforts to compile the knowledge gained by Zheng He, Mills's *Ma Huan* is outstanding in English; Xu Yuhu, *Ming Zheng He*, studies Zheng in a conventionally Sinocentric style.

64. Both Leslie, *Islam*, 110–11, and Mills, *Ma Huan*, 173–77, translate Ma Huan's account. Edited and punctuated versions of the Chinese texts on Mecca and Medina may be found in Zheng and Zheng, *Zheng He*, 232–40 (geography), 338–43 (cities and sites), 388–92 (climate and calendar), 562–66 (products and resources), 656–60 (commerce), and 838–44 (government, customs, and language).

Muslims in China and Ming Limits on Foreign Trade

After the 1430s, however, the Ming government no longer saw value in these expensive, expansive voyages, either as political propaganda or as covert trading expeditions.[65] They ceased, and both the exotics and the knowledge faded rapidly from Chinese consciousness. Though briefly revived by the Jesuit presence in the late Ming, Chinese scholarly comprehension of and interest in the "western lands" never achieved so high a level until the nineteenth century's pressures forced the gates, confronting China with a world ill-remembered and utterly transformed.

Despite both popular and official Chinese prejudice, the Ming period actually saw resident Muslims forging stronger and more durable ties with China. Sometimes confined by restrictive travel regulations, and clearly belonging to China by social process, many Sinophone Muslims became even more intimate with their native land by intermarriage or by adoption of Chinese children. Both processes increased their numbers while linking them ever more closely to China. Sino-Muslim communities, with the social cohesion typical of minorities in polyethnic societies and in conformity with the charitable requirements of *sharī'a* law (Islam's comprehensive code), provided mutual aid and solidarity that promoted survival in bad times and continuity under acculturative pressures.[66] Intermarriage almost always involved a Muslim male taking a Chinese wife, who converted formally to Islam and became a member of the Muslim community. Very rarely was a Muslim female allowed to be given in marriage to a non-Muslim, for strong community pressure and Muslim law forbade "losing" a daughter to the outsiders. As noted above, the presence of many Sinophone women, however sincere their Islamic conversion, forwarded the acculturation process (precisely as the Ming statute intended) by making Chinese the language of home for Muslims in

65. The causes for the cessation of the voyages are explored by Haraprasad Ray in *Trade and Diplomacy,* with his conclusions on pp. 135–37. He believes that the voyages, which had begun as expressions of imperial strength and as military efforts, gradually became trading missions over the course of the Yongle period and lost their purpose when private traders filled the commercial roles they had played.

66. Muslim conformity to the duty of charity, enjoined by Muslim law, was attested even by admiring non-Muslims. Yan Congjian's *Shuyu zhouci lu,* published in 1574, 11.4b-20a, contains a lengthy section on "Mecca and Medina," most of which deals with the Sino-Muslims; at 11.6a he praises their community-mindedness and willingness to support one another in need. Leslie, *Islam,* 113, cites Lang Ying's *Qixiu leigao* (16th cent.) to the same effect: "They aid equally those who come from elsewhere." These passages have a very different tone from the Tang-Song exotica or the Yuan period anti-Muslim polemics cited above.

China. A third process, conversion of Chinese adults to Islam, also increased the size and diversity of the Muslim communities, though it was not nearly as common as intermarriage or adoption. To enhance their chances of success in commerce, which in some parts of China was dominated by Muslims, to obtain the benefits of a widespread network of traders and caravaners, Chinese became Sino-Muslims by a religious act and joined the Huihui.

Muslim adaptation to China lay primarily in the realms of material culture and language, as the Ming state enhanced the ordinary acculturative pressure on minority communities by attempting to shut off communication with the "homelands" to the west and south. Tamerlane and his successors in Central Asia, pirates of many peoples off the east and south coasts, and a weakening central state all contributed to a less aggressive, more defensive posture that included restriction of commerce and travel by China's peripatetic Muslims.[67] The Ming controls succeeded primarily in the southeast, where Muslim communities found themselves increasingly isolated, both by Ming policy and by their Chinese neighbors' hostility in the wake of the late Yuan Muslim uprisings. In the Yangzi region, to take an extreme example, late Ming Muslim families wrote Confucian-style clan genealogies to honor their ancestors in the Chinese mode. These documents reveal the Islamic practice of these acculturated Muslims to have been degenerate; their ties with the Muslim world outside China had been completely severed.[68]

RESPONSES AND RESISTANCE TO ACCULTURATION

What people call *xiaojing* was originally a kind of *pinyin* using the Arabic alphabet. . . . Most mosque teachers [in China] were illiterate in Chinese, but they were very skilled in representing sounds with Arabic. So when they were studying, if they needed to make a comment in the margin of their text or record a note, the only reliable means for them to do so was *xiaojing*. . . . And its use

67. Rossabi, "Muslim and Central Asian Revolts," 186, notes a number of Muslim cross-border raids (from Turfan, primarily) and Muslim uprisings during the Wanli era (1572–1620), and reports that Ming officials believed these to stem from poor economic conditions in the northwest. Ming over-regulation of merchants exacerbated the problem and may have led directly to raids on frontier towns.

68. Nakada Yoshinobu, "Chūgoku Musurimu." It comes as no surprise that the most heavily acculturated of the Sino-Muslim communities studied by Dru Gladney (*Muslim Chinese*) lived in Fujian.

was not limited to the scripture hall. . . . People who had received a mosque education, whether they worked as religious professionals or not, could still use this *pinyin* for recording accounts, writing letters, or noting events. To this very day there are still a few people who continue to use it, especially in Gansu, Ningxia, and Qinghai.[69]

Belonging: Gedimu and Jingtang Jiaoyu

Until the seventeenth century virtually all Muslim communities in China focused their communal life around the local mosque. No institutionalized Muslim authority existed above the local community, though outstanding individuals did emerge as supralocal leaders through Islamic scholarship, religious charisma, accumulation of wealth, or success in the examination system.[70] Local mosques linked themselves to other communities informally by bonds of shared Muslim identity and minority position, of commerce, and of language—the Huihuihua patois, which inserted Arabic and Persian locutions into the local vernacular.[71] Largely self-governed, the mosque congregations differed from non-Muslim communities in the centrality of their religious institutions and the potential for intercommunity connections created by religious identity.

Most Muslims lived almost entirely within such congregations and networks, meeting non-Muslims only at market. They were not supposed to eat with non-Muslims or marry their children outside the community, effectively blocking two crucial social communications. Depending on their leaders to mediate between them and the state, they nonetheless spoke to one another in Chinese, used the same vernacular as their non-Muslim neighbors (with Huihuihua additions), dressed similarly, and prepared their food similarly, though it had to be ritually pure (Ar. *halāl*, Ch. *qingzhen*). The Muslims of China thus asked the

69. Feng Zenglie, "Ming Qing shiqi," 244. Prof. Feng (who died in 1996) kindly sent me a copy of his 1982 unpublished essay dealing entirely with *xiaojing*, "Xiaoerjin' chutan."

70. Biographies of leaders of many kinds may be found in Bai, *Huizu renwu zhi (Ming dai)*, but, as noted above, readers should be aware that the "Muslim"identification of some, if not many, of the men included in the collection has been disputed. Sino-Muslim scholars' inclusion of an individual in the Hui *minzu* may indicate nothing more than descent from at least one Muslim, or someone with a Muslim name, and cannot tell us much about that person's involvement or faith, if any, in Islam.

71. Feng Zenglie, "Ming Qing shiqi," 217–51, gives many examples of *jingtangyu* that use both Arabic and Persian vocabulary and, occasionally, grammar.

inevitable question of cultural minorities: How can we cope with the acculturative pressures of the majority, the desire of the Others to have us conform to their ways, while still remaining ourselves and affirming as positive those characteristics which differ? Some of their answers may be found in the strategies of Muslim leaders as they planned for Muslim, community, lineage, and personal success.

Every congregation needed a house of prayer, ranging from a small village's single room in a private home to a wealthy trading center's elaborate set of buildings. These mosques needed religious professionals to perform many crucial functions for the congregation (see plate 9). They led the communal daily and weekly prayers, gave the Friday sermon, represented the community to the state's local officials, taught ritual rectitude and sacred languages, and interpreted and enforced Muslim law. Taken together, these roles transcended those of conventional non-Muslim Chinese religious figures. Even the ritual and mediational functions of the Confucian scholar-gentry did not extend to conducting funerals for villagers or praying for sons at the behest of barren women, as Muslim congregational leaders routinely did. Only in Chinese sectarian organizations do we find such intimacy between congregation and leader, one reason why the imperial court and its officials often looked upon Islam as perilously close to heterodox Buddhism or Daoism.

Before the advent of Sufi orders in northwest China, all mosques chose their own religious professionals, including the *imām* or *ahong,* through a council of elders.[72] Selected by the community for their age, high social or economic status, or relatively high level of Islamic knowledge, the elders maintained the functional unity of the local congregation, exercising secular and administrative power in the management of communal property—especially land donated to the mosque in pious endowment (Ar. *waqf*)—and in the selection of the religious functionaries.[73]

Religious professionals, holding credentials from Chinese or Central Asian seminaries, traveled from post to post through a network of advertising and recruitment. Their contracts, and those of their assis-

---

72. Feng Jinyuan, "Zhongguo Yisilanjiao," 144–46. Most Chinese Muslims refer to Islamic teachers as *ahong,* from the Persian *ākhūnd,* rather than *imām* or *mawlā,* though both of those words are known and used in northwest China; the latter term, *manla* in Chinese transliteration, generally refers to a student in a *madrasa* (religious academy). Famous or especially erudite *ahong* receive higher titles, as do the leaders of Sufi orders.

73. Feng Zenglie, "Ming Qing shiqi," 223–28, discusses the organization and functions of a large Gedimu mosque community in Xi'an as an example of a fully formed set of local functionaries and institutions.

tants, stipulated a period of employment (which was sometimes for life), after which they could seek another job or renegotiate the relationship. Thus, local elders governed and represented their own congregations, which collectively employed the *ahong* and/or *imām*. Respected and obeyed, but not necessarily permanent members of the community, the religious professionals carried the charisma of Arabic and Persian learning and served as ritual leaders and judges. In a small village a single *ahong* might work alone, teaching the small children their Arabic prayers and conducting life-cycle rituals. In a large city or county town a mosque (perhaps one of many) might employ an *imām*, several *ahong*, a *khatīb* (preacher), a muezzin to announce the prayers, and a number of religious teachers. Whatever the size, this type of independent mosque organization, with its two distinct types of leadership—lay elders and religious professionals—came to be called Gedimu, from the Arabic *qadīm*, meaning "old." It contrasted sharply with new Muslim institutions, the Sufi orders, which arrived in northwest China in the seventeenth century.[74]

During the mid- to late Ming some Muslim communities began to feel that their children were not receiving adequate Islamic education— the acculturative pressure to educate children in the majority culture and language had considerable power—and so some professional educators undertook to systematize the Islamic curriculum. Now called *jingtang jiaoyu*, "scripture hall education," this Arabic and Persian schedule of lessons had some Chinese flavoring (see plate 10). Modern Sino-Muslim scholars usually associate *jingtang jiaoyu* with Shaanxi province and with the name of Hu Dengzhou, one of its formalizers.

Hu came from the Wei valley of Shaanxi, where hundreds of thousands of Muslims lived in the market towns and villages of a prosperous region. After going on the pilgrimage to Mecca, he decided that Chinese Muslim life had deteriorated, especially in fundamental Islamic knowledge, and he opened a religious school. We can speculate that by the mid-sixteenth century, when he flourished, many Chinese Muslims could no longer understand Arabic or Persian and had to have the sacred texts explained to them in Chinese. Indeed, by this time purely Arabic inscriptions had disappeared, replaced first by Arabic-Chinese texts and then by steles entirely in Chinese.[75] Inscriptional evidence indicates that many generations of Sino-Muslim teachers trace their

74. Feng Zenglie, "Gedimu' bayi." For a general description of this form of community organization, see Ma Tong, *Zhongguo Yisilan . . . shilue*, 119–27.

75. Feng Zenglie, "Ming Qing shiqi," 222.

intellectual and curricular tradition to Hu and his disciples.[76] He is also credited with regularizing the financing of tuition, room, board, and study materials for his religious students, some of whom lived in his home on a work-study arrangement.

Hu and his followers taught a fairly orthodox Islamic curriculum, innovating only in the relative shallowness of the Arabic and Persian knowledge expected of their students. Rather than using the Koran itself as a text, they selected two dozen or more passages as a primer (Ch. *Haiting*) of Koranic Arabic; only after completing that text would students begin the study of the complete Koran. In addition, they used an elementary Islamic studies textbook called *Zaxue* (Diverse studies), which included prayers, presumably in Arabic, and Persian texts on faith, ablutions, worship, fasting, marriage, funerals, and festivals. One modern scholar speculates that this book dated from the late Yuan period, when Persian was still a Muslim lingua franca in East Asia.[77]

Though we still lack text-based study of this reform movement, the main innovation of *jingtang jiaoyu* seems to have lain in the use of *Chinese* phonetic pronunciation of Arabic. Though students still learned the holy books in the original Arabic orthography, they were taught to recite them with Chinese sounds. Thus the Arabic *salām* (peace) came to be pronounced with three Chinese syllables—*sa liang mu*. No original texts from the Ming period have been published, but colleagues in Shaanxi inform me that students, especially in the more Chinese-literate Xi'an community, actually represented Arabic using Chinese characters.

The written transliteration cannot have been widespread, however, since most northwesterners could not read or write Chinese. Indeed, that inability led to a second Sino-Muslim invention, *xiaojing*—the first *pinyin*, or systematic alphabetic representation of Chinese. In the mid- to late Ming Sino-Muslim males educated in the mosque or *madrasa* could read, but generally not compose or speak, Arabic and Persian. At the same time, all of them could speak Chinese, but only a few could read or write it. To answer the need for a usable written language during this period, innovative mosque teachers created an Arabic *pinyin* for Chinese. Called *xiaojing* or *xiaoerjin*, it enabled Muslims who could not read Chinese to represent its sounds in an orthography they knew from their mosque education. They could thus take notes on texts written in languages they could read but not speak or write. Of course this method

76. See, for example, the *Xiujian Hu Taishizu jiacheng ji*, reprinted in Bai, *Huizu renwu zhi (Ming dai)*, 404–7.

77. Feng Zenglie, "Ming Qing shiqi," 229–30.

suffered from some of the same limitations as any alphabetic representation of Chinese. Dialectal differences among its users would create inconsistencies in representation; neither Arabic nor Persian can represent the tonal structure of spoken Chinese; and the Middle Eastern orthographies cannot distinguish syllabic endings (e.g., *xi'an* vs. *xian*).[78] It did survive its limitations, however, and remains extant among Chinese Muslims, though only a few use it regularly. The northwestern Sino-Muslims thus handled their linguistic adjustment to China in two innovative ways: *jingtang jiaoyu* utilized Chinese phonetics to represent Arabic pronunciation, and *xiaojing* adapted the Arabic script to represent spoken Chinese. These two methods, taken together, might well symbolize for us the gradual acculturation processes of Sino-Muslims during the Ming period, processes that enabled them to live as subjects of the Ming state, as participants in Chinese culture, and as practicing Muslims.

Both Gedimu mosque structure and *jingtang jiaoyu* education show little deviation from conventional Sunni, Hanafi Muslim communities elsewhere in the Muslim world. On the basis of current evidence, we can only surmise that more and more Muslims in China had become entirely Sinophone, even in Shaanxi and Gansu. The descendants of the *semu* Muslims had, after all, been living in China for as long as two centuries by the time of Hu Dengzhou—six to eight generations—and could be expected to acculturate in language as well as in many spheres of daily life. Apart from banditry and evasion of commercial regulations (both common among non-Muslims as well) they do not appear to have engaged in collective antisocial behavior, and they accepted the legitimacy of Ming rule unless it obstructed their business or threatened their survival. Their behavior in the troubled times at the end of the Ming certainly confirms that they considered China to be their home and its politics to be their own.

STRANGERS IN BAD TIMES:
THE MING-QING TRANSITION (1644–50S)

He Bi, supervising secretary in the Office of Scrutiny of the Board of War, presented a long and important memorial to the throne

---

78. Feng Zenglie, "Xiaoerjin chutan," 16–17. Prof. Feng derives the name for this *pinyin* from the homophonic *xiaojing*, "to digest the scripture," a northwestern term indicating the written or oral commentaries on sacred texts with which *madrasa* teachers instruct their students (p. 12). A remarkable example of *xiaojing* is preserved in Forke, "Ein islamisches Tractat."

about ways to exert local control over that particularly troubled region [Gansu]. He began by praising the speed with which Meng Qiaofang had succeeded, in less than half a month, in recovering the major cities of Gansu by crushing the Muslim rebels. "Subduing such despicable wretches" (*xiaochour*) was "like catching foxes and rats in your hands". . . . There was nonetheless the very great possibility that conflict with the Muslims might recur. No one— He quickly added—could disagree with the sage policy of imperial clemency, but it might be pointed out that those who committed such ravages . . . were not all killed. Furthermore, Muslims and Chinese were continuing to live alongside each other in the major cities of the northwest. "Their customs are different and this results eventually in mutual suspicion." He therefore proposed that a policy of ethnic resettlement be adopted. Muslim communities, he suggested, should be located at least fifty *li* from the Han *zhou* [prefecture], *xian* [county], or *wei* [garrison] nearest to them, wherever there were secluded areas suitable for colonization. There they should be taken with their families, and transformed from martial horsemen into peaceful peasants.

> Forbid them to breed horses or to keep weapons.
> Command their religious leaders to take charge,
> regulating their movements back and forth. Let them
> all cultivate the soil, and so gradually allay their
> ferocious natures.[79]

Taking Sides

The mid-seventeenth century fall of the Ming, with its attendant social disorder, provided an opportunity for Muslims to act violently against the state, should they have reason; they also had to protect themselves and their homes in unstable times. Muslim "rebels" often joined other antistate forces, in some case in ethnically mixed units, Muslim and non-Muslim making common cause in the face of adversity, Ming maladministration, and state violence. Ma Shouying, nicknamed "Lao Huihui" (Old Muslim), a Shaanxi Muslim general, materially aided Li Zicheng in his successful campaign against the Ming in northwest China. Ma came from the same region as most of Li's generals, and his battle plans did not differ

79. Wakeman, *The Great Enterprise,* vol. 2, 825–26. The original text may be found in Xie, *Qingchu,* 282.

substantially from theirs; he was fighting a Chinese war, participating in Chinese dynastic upheaval. He obviously did not seek Muslim domination of China or even liberation of parts of China as Muslim territory.[80] Muslim rebels who rose against the Manchu Qing after it defeated Li Zicheng and Zhang Xianzhong (Ma Shouying having died, probably of natural causes, in 1644) also seem to have lacked separatist ambitions.

Early in its reign over China proper the Manchu Qing court ruled that merchants from Turfan and Hami, operating within the rubric of the tribute system, could trade only with selected Chinese merchants and Qing officials, and only at Lanzhou or Beijing. The Manchus also intended to reestablish the tea and horse trade state monopolies of the early and mid-Ming.[81] These political intrusions into Central Asian commerce, resented by the private merchants of the northwest, aggravated an already poor economy and stimulated some Muslims to violence, especially in the Gansu corridor, the vital transportation link between Gansu and Turkestan. The Muslims probably knew that the Manchus were meeting stiff resistance all over China and took advantage of the court's scattered forces.

Beginning at Ganzhou in 1646, Muslims named Milayin and Ding Guodong led substantial armies—government sources claimed one-hundred-thousand soldiers, almost surely an exaggeration—down the Gansu corridor, taking Lanzhou and a number of prefectural towns and laying siege to Gongchang, in eastern Gansu.[82] This could not have been a separatist *jihād*, for the Muslims and their non-Muslim allies acted in the name of Zhu Shichuan, the former Ming prince of Yan-chang.[83] As Ma Shouying (Lao Huihui) had risen against the Ming and

---

80. On Ma Shouying, see Ma Shouqian, "Mingdai houqi," 36–40. Rossabi, "Muslim and Central Asian Revolts," and Tazaka, "Mindai goki," cover many of the same texts. We have no evidence that Ma Shouying imbued his wars with any explicitly Muslim content, no talk of *jihād* or even of *shengzhan*, its imprecise Chinese translation. When Li Zicheng needed a place to recover from defeat and wounds, he sought out Lao Huihui and stayed with him for months. Indeed, Ma Shouying formally joined Li Zicheng's army after many years of anti-Ming struggle and took an official title, "Yingwu General of the Yongfu Battalion." Bai, *Huizu renwu zhi (Ming dai),* 160. The biographical notice (154–64) contains a detailed narrative of Lao Huihui's battles and praise for his success in uniting the peoples of various nationalities to fight the feudal Ming.

81. Wakeman, *Great Enterprise,* vol. 2, 795–98.

82. Wei Yuan, *Shengwu ji, juan* 7, cited in Bai, *Huimin qiyi,* vol. 3, 3.

83. Fletcher, "China's Northwest," 30. Qing commander Meng Qiaofang's report of the Ming loyalist component to this "Muslim" rebellion, and his biography in *Qing shi gao,* are also cited by Rossabi, "Muslim and Central Asian Revolts," 191; and Wakeman, *Great Enterprise,* vol. 2, 800. The original texts may be found in Xie, *Qingchu,* 268–69, 279–83.

aided other Chinese rebels, so Milayin and Ding Guodong made their rebellious decisions within a Chinese context and enlisted the legitimacy of the Ming ruling house to their anti-Qing cause. Zhu was killed early in the fighting, but the cause did not collapse.

We certainly cannot ignore the rebels' "foreign" connections to Hami and, more distantly, Turfan. After some months of rebellion, the sultan (governor) of Hami, Sa'id Baba, sent one of his sons, Turumtay, to serve as prince of (rebellious) Suzhou, demonstrating a close link with Milayin and Ding.[84] But we know little else of that connection and can only surmise that political and religious as well as commercial relationships had been forged across the Ming-Hami frontier and that the two sides decided to unite in the face of the usurping Manchus. Fletcher conjectures, on the basis of contemporaneity, that Naqshabandī Sufism might have played a role in linking Suzhou's rebels to Hami, but he acknowledges a paucity of evidence.[85]

The Qing commander in Gansu, Meng Qiaofang, sent a relief force to Gongchang immediately and broke the siege. The rebels lost ground rapidly, retreating first from Lintao and then from Lanzhou in the face of Meng's experienced troops, who advanced in three columns to converge on the provincial capital. Though his rear guard took months to clear out the rebel remnants south and east of the Yellow River, Meng's main force advanced quickly to besiege Milayin and Ding Guodong's main base at Ganzhou, out in the Gansu corridor. After a sanguinary six-month siege, the rebels negotiated with Meng Qiaofang and surrendered. Milayin obtained an appointment as assistant commander in the Qing garrison at Lanzhou, but both he and Ding Guodong remained in northwestern Gansu.[86]

The rebel alliance had calculated correctly that the Qing army had a great deal to do in early 1649. Within weeks of their victory at Ganzhou, the Qing troops were transferred southward to fight the still-dangerous Southern Ming in Sichuan. Taking immediate advantage, Milayin and Ding's forces again drove southeastward, taking cities as far away as Lintao and killing Qing officials as they went. Meng Qiaofang again responded rapidly, pushing the rebels back to their Gansu corridor bases and killing Milayin at the beginning of a second siege at Ganzhou. Ding Guodong continued the fight from Suzhou, further west toward Hami, with little hope of holding out

84. Rossabi, "Muslim and Central Asian Revolts," 192.
85. Fletcher, "China's Northwest," 20–21.
86. Xie, *Qingchu*, 268.

against Meng's superior army; but anti-Qing forces under Jiang Xiang, far to the east in Shanxi, unintentionally gave the Muslims a few more months of life. Leaving irregulars to hold the siegeworks around Suzhou, Meng spent most of 1649 defeating Jiang, not returning to take Suzhou until December. Upon Meng's victory in that month Ding, Turumtay, and five-thousand followers died at Qing hands, and the Gansu corridor was "pacified."[87]

Pacification (Ch. *shanhou*) had to be carefully planned in order to avoid a recurrence of violence. Conventional nostrums of comforting the common people and rewarding the brave and loyal troops could not solve the problems of commercial overregulation and poverty that caused the uprisings in the first place. Milayin's and Ding Guodong's armies had not been simply Muslim rebels—others, including Chinese and Tibetans, had joined them—but the pacification officials nonetheless singled out the Muslims as naturally violent. As we have seen above, He Bi, a metropolitan official, memorialized that segregation of the Muslims from all cultural Others would have the most salutary effect in the long run, for their natures were savage and had to be tamed by long-term exposure to peaceful husbandry.[88] The court accepted his argument and authorized the resettlement of the Muslims of the Gansu corridor well away from its cities and garrisons. In addition, trade with Hami was cut off for five years, until that city's ruler sent an embassy to apologize for its role in the uprising.

Though marked as Muslims and thus different from other rebels or heroes, Ma Shouying, Milayin, and Ding Guodong must nonetheless be seen as culturally Chinese.[89] Their Sino-Muslim identity had

87. Xie, *Qingchu*, 268, quotes Meng Qiaofang's *Qing shi gao* biography: "Our troops took Suzhou, killed [Ding] Guodong, Turumtay, and their crowd, including Hei Chengyin. Beheaded five-thousand. West of the river, all is at peace." Wakeman, *Great Enterprise*, 823, cites the same passage. This cursorily described slaughter of Suzhou Muslims would be duplicated by Zuo Zongtang over two hundred years later, in 1873.

88. Xie, *Qingchu*, 282.

89. Their Islamic orthopraxy certainly did not conform to the funerary and other ritual markers that James Watson finds at the core of "Chinese" culture. I would argue, however, that "Chinese" is the only word appropriate to describe the culture of Sinophone people whose homes, sense of heritage, spheres of political action, and patterns of everyday life may all be found within cultural China. "Islamic" culture certainly played a part in their lives, but there are no "Islamic" foods, "Islamic" clothes, or "Islamic" vernaculars outside particular cultural contexts, and this particular cultural context is definitely Chinese. (A useful analogy might be the cultural, political, and intellectual lives of many American Jews, which, though they are not entirely devoid of "Jewish" elements, nonetheless may only be identified as "American.") I would not go

evolved in a lengthy process of mutual adaptation between Muslim immigrants and Chinese society, a process that had begun in the Tang-Song, accelerated in the Yuan, and come to fruition in the Ming. Smooth in neither space nor time, that evolution had created Muslims whose homeland lay in China, whose language was Chinese. They were as diverse and contentious as the other Chinese among whom they lived—Ma Shouying did not lead or represent *all* the Sino-Muslims, but only a fraction—and, unlike most of the culturally non-Chinese peoples of China, they did not occupy large territories along a frontier.

Concentrated in the northwest, the southwest, and the eastern cities (for the southwestern coastal communities had declined rapidly with the closing of the Arab-Persian sea trade by the mid-Ming), Sino-Muslims had become a ubiquitous, anomalous part of the Chinese landscape. Normal but different, Sinophone but incomprehensible, local but outsiders, they challenged some fundamental Chinese conceptions of Self and Other and denied the totally transforming power of Chinese civilization, couched always in *moral* terms by the Chinese elite. As we shall see, the Muslims of the northwest had tenaciously maintained their connections with Central and West Asia; the Ming decline and Qing conquest did not find all of them passive or acculturated. Some had friends in Hami and were ready to fight. Ironically, given our usual stereotypes of Muslims, they fought *as Chinese,* in the name of a Ming pretender to the imperial throne in Beijing. However, we have no evidence that they constituted any kind of self-conscious entity (e.g., a *minzu*) beyond their local communities. No Muslims from elsewhere in China flocked to Ma Shouying or Milayin's banners, and their communities remained relatively isolated in their local and regional contexts, connected only by sojourning merchants and religious professionals moving from job to job.

For the next century or so, northwest China's Muslims lived in relative peace with one another, with their neighbors, and with the Qing state. We cannot demonstrate that Qing resettlement policies kept the peace, for most of Gansu (not to mention the rest of China) was not

---

so far as Ma Hetian, Chiang Kai-shek, and others, who have claimed that the Sino-Muslims are "just Hans who believe in Islam." The Sino-Muslims' own sense of shared foreign descent militates against such a definition, however dubious that claim might seem to an academic historian. We must see Sino-Muslim identity as processual and highly localized, even individual, in its combination of elements at a particular moment in time. See Watson, "Rites or Beliefs?"

subject to such orders, but Qing officials and garrisons managed to control any trouble that arose, and the various peoples of the northwest found Qing rule, as it gradually expanded westward to include all of what is now Xinjiang, congenial enough to tolerate.

3 / Connections
Muslims in the Early Qing,
1644–1781

WESTERN INFLUENCE: SUFISM IN CHINA

What is to be done, O Muslims? For I do not recognize myself. I
am neither Christian nor Jew, nor Gabr nor Muslim; I am not of
the East, nor of the West, nor of the land, nor of the sea; I am not
of Nature's mint, nor of the circling heavens.

I am not of India, nor of China, nor of Bulgaria, nor of Saqsin; I
am not of the kingdom of Iraqain, nor of the country of
Khurasan. . . .

My place is the Placeless, my trace is the Traceless; 'Tis neither
body nor soul, for I belong to the soul of the Beloved. I have put
duality away, I have seen that the two worlds are one; One I seek,
One I know, One I see, One I call.[1]

The Sufis have relinquished the form and husk of knowledge, they
have raised the banner of the eye of certainty.

Thought is gone, and they have gained light; they have gained
the throat (essence) and the sea (ultimate source) of gnosis. Death,
of which all others are sore afraid, the perfect Sufis hold in
derision.

None gains the victory over their hearts; the hurt falls on the
oyster shell, not on the pearl.[2]

Hidāyat Allāh and Sufism's Entrance into China

In the early seventeenth century, a Central Asian preacher named Muhammad Yūsuf crossed the Pamirs into Altishahr, where he engaged in

---

1. From the *Divan-i Shams-i Tabriz* of Jalal ad-Din Rumi, Reynold A. Nicholson
trans., cited in Iqbal, *Life and Work*, 136.
2. From the *Mathnawī* of Jalal ad-Din Rumi, vol. 1, 3492–96, trans. in Iqbal, *Life and
Work*, 192.

religious and political disputes with local leaders and with distant kinsmen who belonged to a rival faction.[3] Encouraged by his success among
the Chaghadayid rulers of Altishahr, he traveled eastward, acquiring
disciples in Turfan and Hami, then crossed the Ming frontier into the
Gansu corridor to Suzhou—only a few years later Ding Guodong's
bastion—where he won the allegiance of the local Muslim scholars,
who were Chinese speakers.[4] After a successful sojourn in the country
of the Salars, he returned to Altishahr and there was poisoned by his
rivals and died in 1653.

His son, called Khoja Āfāq (or Āpāq) in Central Asian sources, but
known to the Chinese as "Hidāyat Allāh (Xidayetonglahei), twenty-fifth
generation descendant of the Prophet," moved even more effectively
through northwest China in the 1670s. Taking advantage of the relative
order and freedom of movement provided by Qing hegemony, Khoja
Āfāq visited Lanzhou, Didao, Xining, and probably Hezhou, and had a
profound effect on both Muslim and non-Muslim communities.[5]

Muhammad Yūsuf and Khoja Āfāq were Sufis, leaders within a movement that changed the entire Muslim world between the thirteenth and
eighteenth centuries.[6] Usually called "Islamic mysticism," Sufism gave

3. Altishahr (Tur. "six cities") denotes the western rim of the Tarim Basin, also called
Kashgaria, Tianshan *nanlu* (the route south of Tianshan), and eastern Turkestan. Mod-
ern Chinese sources anachronistically call it "southern Xinjiang" (Xinjiang *nanlu* or
Nanjiang), but I prefer the more local and more politically neutral term.

4. Fletcher, "Naqshbandiyya," 10–13. In several footnotes Fletcher presents evidence
from Turkish and Persian manuscript sources on Muhammad Yūsuf's preaching inside
the Ming frontier, including his conversion of the Salars and the *'ulamā-yi Tunganiyyān*
(Chinese-speaking Muslim scholars) to Sufism. (Tonggan, or Donggan, remained a regularly used Turkic appellation for the Chinese-speaking Muslims into the twentieth century.) Chinese oral and written sources differ in many details from this account; Ma Tong,
Zhongguo Yisilan . . . suyuan, chap. 2, sect. 2 and 3, gives 1622 as the date of Muhammad
Yūsuf's death, does not mention his having preached in Suzhou, and gives his son all the
credit for enlisting the Salars among their followers. Fletcher noted the possibility that
many of the acts attributed to the father or son may have been conflated with the other.

5. This account is based largely on Fletcher, "Naqshbandiyya," and on Fletcher's
"China's Northwest." His sources include Trippner, "Islamische Gruppen," but he notes
that Trippner's account is based on very incomplete evidence and contains many errors.

6. Sufism in general has proven frustratingly difficult to define in theological, intellectual, or sociopolitical terms. Geertz, *Islam Observed,* 48, notes that "this term suggests a
specificity of belief and practice which dissolves when one looks at the range of phenomena
to which it is actually applied. . . . Sufism, as an historical reality, consists of a series of
different and even contradictory experiments, most of them occurring between the ninth
and nineteenth centuries, in bringing orthodox Islam (itself no seamless unity) into effective relationship with the world." The great Islamicist Marshall Hodgson called Sufism
"spiritual athleticism," saying of early Islamic mysticism that it "provide[d] an esoteric form

voice to an aspiration to personal or collective unity with the Divine that had existed among Muslims almost since the rise of Islam itself.[7] Its name, derived from the Arabic word *suf*, meaning "wool," indicates another crucial facet of Sufi belief and practice—ascetic self-denial. The "original" Sufis wore coarse woolen garments and practiced austerities as varied as breath control, fasting, chanting, eremitic withdrawal from the world, and meditation in the hope of achieving a higher state of religious consciousness and communion with God.

Gedimu and *Tarīqa*

Like all religious movements, Sufism did not remain long unified. Its teachers in every period drew diverse methods and theological conclusions from their own mystical experiences and from their sociopolitical contexts. The greatest of them founded Sufi "paths" (Ar. sing. *tarīqa*, pl. *turuq*), which gradually became agents of social transformation as well as more literal "ways" to religious fulfillment. This could happen because

---

of piety among them, which allowed those of them who were so inclined to explore hidden meanings and personal resonances not allowed for by the soberly public Shari'ah [law]" (*The Venture of Islam*, vol. 1, 393–94). Later in his history, however, Hodgson (with many other historians) notes that Sufism came into far closer intimacy with Islamic law in many parts of the Muslim world. The Indian reformer Ahmad Sirhindī, for example, "tried to reconcile the very personal mystical experience, to which Sufism gave a place, with an intensely social activism such as the Islam of the Shari'ah demanded" (vol. 3, 85) I present a rudimentary and far too rigid explanation of Sufism here as an aid to readers who may not be familiar with it. The definition's utility will decrease as my narrative progresses, as we become more specific in a northwest Chinese context.

7. Scholars of comparative religion have found similar impulses within most traditions, including the Jewish and pre-Islamic Arabian religions from which Islam derived. Indeed, Sinophone Muslims, when reaching for a terminology to explain Islam in Chinese, found an easy translation for the "Sufi way." They call *tarīqa*, its mystical impulse, Dao *cheng*, "vehicle of the Dao," a combination of the Daoist "Way" of meditative asceticism with the Buddhist notion of *yana*, a means by which human beings may transform themselves. This use of *cheng* moves away from the original Sanskrit meaning (suspiciously close to Dao itself) toward a concrete, instrumental metaphor of transportation along the Way. The other stages of Islam's three-fold path—*shari'a* law and *haqīqa*, the perfected Unity with the Divine—are called the "vehicle of the teaching" (Ch. *jiaocheng*) and the "vehicle of perfection" (Ch. *zhicheng*). The names of these progressive stages, *shari'a-tarīqa-haqīqa*, both in transliteration and in translation, have become standing terms among northwestern Sufis. The resonance between Daoist and Sufi ideas, obvious even from a superficial reading of Rumi's verses at the head of this chapter, has been studied intensively by scholars of religion. See, for example, Izutsu, *Sufism and Daoism*. I am grateful to Prof. Indira Peterson for her Sanskritist's insights.

Islam does not dictate or provide any central institutional authorities beyond the Caliphate, the direct succession to the Prophet's political leadership. Each community's mosque functions autonomously, its leaders and teachers linked to others by personal relationships, inquiring of great teachers regarding legal and religious questions but not subject to any formal authority.

In contrast, Sufi paths could establish centers of authority for their adherents and command their obedience even from a distance. The *shaikh*, either the founder or his successor, carried a special burden of religious charisma (Ar. *baraka*), which endowed him with both spiritual and secular power. This *baraka*—transferred from generation to generation in a spiritual genealogy (Ar. *isnād* or *silsila*)—inhered in the founder, his successors, and in their tombs. The domed tombs (Ar. *qubba*, Per. *gunbad*, Ch. *gongbei*) of Sufis came to be distinguishing marks of their ever-widening presence in Muslim life from Spain to China. At these places their followers sought inspiration through prayer, or God's favor through the *shaikh*'s intercession. Each Sufi community was led by religious professionals appointed or ordained by the *shaikh*, thus creating a tight network of influence and control. Sufi paths and their associated tombs thus provided foci of organization, worship, and loyalty more effective than the earlier noninstitutionalized ideals of the universal Muslim community and the constrained localism of community-based Gedimu mosques.[8]

The existence of many paths, however, fostered rivalry among Sufis for religious authority, which in many cases led to worldly power and wealth. From their inception, Sufi orders (as the paths are usually called in English) competed not only for the religious adherence of ordinary Muslims but also for the allegiance of powerful families and for the donations and pious endowments that would establish the *shaikh*s as wealthy, secular leaders.[9] Each teacher possessed secret initiation rituals,

8. See Gladney, "Muslim Tombs."
9. Like religious movements elsewhere in the world, the Sufi paths found what we call "religious" and "secular" power to be inextricably intertwined: "Its leaders may use it at different times and places for varying purposes; its adherents use it for other ends. . . . It has a useful social role to play besides its purely spiritual or quietistic mystical functions. An order may become involved in politics; it may provide medical or psychiatric help for its members, or it may become concerned with magic or astrology. For these purposes, it may include within its ranks remarkable magic-makers or miracle-mongers. The order is often directed by a highly charismatic personality . . . whose personal attraction for the common man, or for persons in other parts of society, contributes to the fluctuations of the popularity of the order and to the size of its membership" (Martin, "A Short History," 276). Marxist scholars in China have naturally paid considerable attention to the economic aspects of Sufi organization. For a useful summary, see Yang Huaihong, "Dui xibei," 287–89.

passed down through the *silsila,* with which to transmit the original founder's *baraka* and include new followers within the order. As the orders grew, they relied increasingly on a claim of descent from the Prophet, which made each *shaikh* also a *sayyid* and thus required a hereditary chain of succession.[10] Though the founders of these institutions may have been ascetics, their successors and relatives often became men of great wealth and high political position.[11]

*Shaikh*s and their representatives (called variously *khalīfa* and *ra'īs*) moved along trade routes, staying both in established Muslim communities and among non-Muslims who seemed amenable to conversion. They persuaded new followers with a variety of techniques, including eloquent sermons, magical wonders (Ar. *karāmāt*), lectures on sacred texts, and the collective repetition of mantralike "remembrances" (Ar. *dhikr*) of God. This last-mentioned practice, strongly resembling Amitabha-centered Buddhism in its rhythmical meditative repetitions (either vocal or silent), led to the achievement of trance states and direct, personal connection to the Divine. Sufism thus provided a new expression of religious passion for its adherents; a new set of exclusive, even esoteric, techniques for their enlightenment; and a new institutional framework, the *tarīqa.* Within its network, adherents (Ar. sing. *murīd*) could be connected to other Muslim communities and leaders could achieve new wealth and power.

By seeking and accepting initiation into a Sufi order, a *murīd* also pledged his loyal support to his *shaikh* and his successors. Within Islamic communities this intimate link gave the leader unprecedented power, that of personal veneration and unquestioning obedience.[12] A charismatic Sufi leader could command a disciplined, organized following that extended far beyond a single congregation and did not depend on the goodwill of local community elders. Many *shaikh*s moved often, gathering adherents in various villages and towns, linking them together

10. The status of *sayyid,* denoting prophetic descent, carries a great weight of religious (and often secular) authority in most Muslim communities. Difficult to demonstrate (to an academic's satisfaction) at a remove of tens of generations, this claim nonetheless is often made and sustained with oral genealogical evidence.

11. Fletcher, "Naqshbandiyya," 9, for example, notes a political maneuver by a Sufi order in Altishahr. The grand master of a Naqshabandī order, Ishāq, named the secular ruler of the entire region, Muhammad Khan, as his successor within the order, thereby unifying religious and political leadership in a single man. Muhammad Khan achieved titles of great import in Sufi theology, *qutb* (mystical axis) and *ghawth* (mystical helper of the age), assuring his descendants a central position in the region for many generations.

12. Yang Huaizhong, "Dui xibei," 278–81.

in a solidarity of personal loyalty. This system stood in strong contrast to non-Sufi Gedimu communities, in which elders directed local affairs in consultation with religious professionals employed by the mosque. The Sufi hospice (Ar. *zāwiya*, Pers. *khānqa*, Ch. *daotang*) served as a religious and social center alternative to the community-based mosque: "There they [the *shaikh*s] instructed and housed their disciples, held regular dhikr sessions . . . and offered hospitality to wandering Sufis. . . . These institutions, which had some of the same functions as a European monastery, became basic centers of social integration."[13]

Sufi institutions, ideas, and politics varied widely in differing contexts. Fletcher has demonstrated beyond doubt that Chinese Muslims did maintain connections to "the West"—the world of Islam—and that religious and political currents continued to flow across the permeable frontiers of China and its Islamic neighbor states.[14] Since Sufism first came to China from Central Asia, as a foundation for understanding its historical place in northwest China we must examine briefly the role that the *shaikh* and *tarīqa* played in eastern Turkestan.

Though mysticism seems ideologically to encompass a private, non-communicable religious experience, Sufi orders were never reluctant to take part in politics. The most important *tarīqa* in Central Asia, the Naqshabandīya, "rejected religious quietism and accelerated their missionary efforts in search of political support, particularly among the nomads, whose military strength dominated Central Asia's politics."[15] Conversion of non-Muslims to Islam was as central a concern to Sufis as to non-Sufi Muslims, and Sufi preachers persuaded members of many cultures—Tibetan, Mongol, Turkic, and Chinese—of Islam's rectitude, with some success.

Sufism moved from western Turkestan eastward, both in early centuries and during the Ming and Qing, allied with the sultans and kings of both the oases and the nomads. In the late Ming and early Qing, these were the Uiguristan Moguls, the Kashgarī *khojas* (Persian for a religious and political leader), and the amirs of Ferghana and Kokand. Indeed, in the seventeenth century even non-Muslim rulers such as the Oirat Mongol hegemon Galdan were willing to use Sufis—in his case, the same Khoja Āfāq as came to China—as clients on the throne of Kashgar. The entrance of Sufism into northwest China therefore created a politically charged atmosphere, one in which Central Asian rivalries might be

13. Hodgson, *The Venture of Islam*, vol. 2, 213.
14. Fletcher, "Les 'voies.' "
15. Fletcher, "Naqshbandiyya," 5–6.

played out in a very different sociocultural setting. Instead of a world of Muslim rulers vying for hegemony, the political environment in which Sufis in China lived was overwhelmingly dominated by non-Muslims. Sufi orders' struggles with one another therefore had very different effects in Gansu than in Kashgar because of the former's more distant, potentially hostile relationship to secular political power, a power that was inevitably non-Muslim.

As we have seen in the cases of Ma Shouying and Milayin/Ding Guodong, state domination of the northwest could be challenged only by the very daring, and only at a time of disorder, military weakness, or administrative malaise sufficiently profound that an uprising might succeed in toppling the legitimate authority of the throne (Ma Shouying) or placing an alternative leader in its place (Milayin and Zhu Shichuan). The arrival of Sufi orders provided a means of mobilization, a network of solidarity, that had never been present among Chinese Muslims before. Initially, however, they did not challenge the state, for they had to establish themselves in a sufficient number of communities, with sufficient adherents, to ensure their own survival, stability, and prosperity. Khoja Āfāq set in motion the career of a crucial figure in that process— Abu 'l-Futūh Ma Laichi, the founder of the Khafīya suborder of Naqshabandī Sufis in Gansu.

Ma Laichi and the Rise of the Menhuan

Khoja Āfāq's strain of the Naqshabandīya, called the Āfāqīya in his honor, stressed thaumaturgic wonders, study of the *Mathnawī* of Jalal ad-Din Rumi, a renewal of faith, and adherence to Muslim law.[16] In their meditative practice, followers performed the Sufi remembrance in silence, the "remembrance of the heart" common to most Naqshabandīs, earning themselves the appelation of Khafīya (Ch. Hufeiye or

16. At the opening of this chapter (second extract) I have cited a fragment of this giant mystical poem, written in Persian but available in a Turkish translation; it was enormously popular among Sufis in Central Asia as well as in the Muslim heartlands. With its multilayered complexity of image and intellectual depth, it has been the subject of endless debate and interpretation by Muslim and non-Muslim scholars. Hodgson, *The Venture of Islam*, vol. 2, 244–54, presents a brief but rich description and analysis, while Iqbal, *Life and Work*, chaps. 4–6, discusses the poem in light of its author's religious and philosophical life. One of Joseph Fletcher's manuscript sources has Muhammad Yūsuf (or perhaps Khoja Āfāq) telling a Chinese disciple to preach to his congregation upon the *Mathnawī* every Friday and Monday ("Naqshbandiyya," 13).

Hufuye), "Silent Ones."[17] Khoja Āfāq followed his father to northwest China in search of initiates in order to compete for power with other members of his family in Altishahr, a common phenomenon in the intense politico-religious rivalries of Central Asia, often based on hereditary succession to the leadership of Sufi orders and thus to secular power.[18]

Finding willing converts in Gansu, Khoja Āfāq made three visits to Xining, a polyethnic entrepot that had been an important stop on one route of the Silk Road and is now the capital of Qinghai Province. Muslims from all over the region converged on Xining to hear the famous Sufi's preaching; he worked wonders and taught the *Mathnawī*. Ma Tong claims that his visits resulted in the formation of nine Sufi institutions in Gansu, but Fletcher notes only three significant followers.[19] Both agree that the most politically active new group stemmed from Khoja Āfāq's initiation of Ma Taibaba, a rather retiring Islamic teacher from Milagou. Though Ma Taibaba undertook no innovations or organizing, he did appoint as his successor his most brilliant student, Abu 'l Futūh Ma Laichi.

According to his spiritual descendants' account, Ma Laichi's birth,

17. Disagreement over the recitation of the *dhikr*—whether it should be silent or vocal—is often cited as a major cause of communal violence among northwestern Chinese Muslims. No doubt the distinction possessed considerable symbolic value to both sides in disputes between Sufis, but similar contradictions existed in many other parts of the Muslim world without leading to bloodshed. Algar, "Silent and Vocal *dhikr*," notes that most Sufis practice the vocal remembrance. The Naqshabandīs, who do not, are distinguished by "sobriety, rigor, and restraint." He attributes the unusual practice of vocal *dhikr* by Naqshabandīs to simultaneous affiliation with several orders and to the flexibility necessary if Sufism is to unify rather than divide Muslims. Indeed, Sufis could be initiated into more than one *tarīqa*, as Ma Tong claims Ma Laichi was, and many Middle Eastern Sufis practiced both types of *dhikr* without feeling any contradiction (see Fletcher, "Naqshbandiyya," 24–27.) One of the thorniest problems in Sino-Muslim studies, as we will see below, lies in explaining why liturgical arguments such as that over vocalized or nonvocalized *dhikr* were seized upon as causes (however superficial the justification) for violence among Muslims in northwest China.

18. Fletcher, "Les 'voies,' " 15–16, notes that Sufis all over the Muslim world founded "saintly lineages," especially in the seventeenth century, to unify the *baraka* of the *shaikh* and the temporal, secular power of the *tarīqa* through hereditary succession to its leadership and control of its wealth. Some orders (in China, notably the Qādirīya) forbade hereditary succession to the position of *shaikh*, requiring instead that leadership be passed to the *shaikh*'s most able disciple, but most "saintly lineages" claimed prophetic descent and thus passed *baraka* down within the family.

19. Ma Tong, *Zhongguo Yisilan . . . suyuan*, 49; Fletcher, "Naqshbandiyya," 14.

education, and spiritual initiation were all linked to Hidāyat Allāh.[20] Both Ma Laichi's grandfather (Ma Congshan) and father (Ma Jiajun) concerned themselves with military affairs, the former as a general under the Ming and the latter as a graduate of the military examination under the Qing. Ma Jiajun went into business rather than seeking an official position. Wealthy and childless at forty, he traveled from his home in Hezhou to Xining to request that the famous Khoja Āfāq intercede with God to grant him a son. Having recited the petitionary prayers, the Khoja told Ma Jiajun that he should marry a young woman "awaiting faith" in his home town. This non-Muslim woman, twenty-six years old and still single, had been engaged to a number of men, every one of whom had died before the marriage could be performed. Protected by the Khoja's promise, Ma Jiajun married her, and she bore a son. According to Khafiya legends, when Ma Jiajun's business and property were destroyed by a fire not long after, he gave his son the name Laichi, "Arrived Too Late."

In his new poverty, Ma Jiajun could not afford to continue in Hezhou, so he turned to itinerant tea-peddling along the roads from Hezhou to Xining. Unable to keep his young son with him, he sent the boy to a friend in Milagou, who placed him in Ma Taibaba's Koranic school to receive his education. Ma Laichi proved a prodigy, mastering the Islamic curriculum before his eighteenth year and receiving both his Sufi initiation and ordination as an *ahong* from his teacher, who handed on to him the initiatory *baraka* of Khoja Āfāq.[21] For thirty years Ma Laichi worked as a teacher and preacher in the Hezhou region; then in 1728 (according to Ma Tong) he undertook the rigors of the pilgrimage to Mecca.

Sources differ widely on both the chronology and the locations of Ma Laichi's sojourn in the Muslim heartlands. Some accounts have him study in India, others in Bukhara, still others in Yemen. They agree, however, that he remained in some center of Muslim learning, probably more than one, for many years and returned to China bearing a deep desire to reform Islam in his homeland. He also brought books with him, some of them standard (a Koran, for example), but others new to

20. Ma Tong, *Zhongguo Yisilan . . . shilue,* 223–24, narrates the miraculous story, giving Ma Laichi's childhood Islamic name (Ch. *jing ming*) as Abuduli-Halimu ('Abd al-Karim?).

21. This succession by discipleship, on grounds of learning or other merit, was certainly possible within Sufi orders, though the Āfāqīya in Central Asia tended toward hereditary succession.

northwest China, especially the volume of "scriptural extracts" called *Mingshale* or *Mingsha'er* in Chinese, which he had received from his teacher.[22]

Because so few Muslims from China could go on the pilgrimage or undertake to read and explain the holy texts in their original languages, Ma Laichi possessed tremendous prestige upon his return to Gansu. His charisma and his message won many Muslims, both Chinese- and Turkic-speaking, to his version of Sufi ritual practice; and his thaumaturgic skill awed even non-Muslims into conversion. To this day, communities of Muslim Tibetans, Mongols, and Monguors in Qinghai Province venerate him as their spiritual master, the one who converted their ancestors to Islam.[23] Wherever a saint such as Ma Laichi settled, disci-

22. The description of *Mingshale* as *jing jieju* (scriptural extracts) may be found in the *Daqing lichao shilu* (Qianlong) 290:24b. Fletcher, "Naqshbandiyya," 17–18, analyzes this text's name syllable by syllable and hazards a guess that it was a *sharh* (commentary) on a collection of prophetic writings such as Ibn al-'Arabī's *Fusūs al-hikam*. Lacking the text itself, we can only speculate. Ma Tong, *Zhongguo Yisilan . . . shilue*, 225–26, relates an oral account of Ma Laichi's travels and studies. Beginning in 1728, he went via Canton (where he studied for three months with a famous *ahong*), then embarked with four companions for Yemen, where he visited many mosques and met with the great scholars. In Mecca for the pilgrimage, he took as his teacher the head of the Khafiya *zāwiya*, one Muhammad Jibuni Ahmad Agelai (Fletcher has "Ajilai"). He then traveled to Damascus, Baghdad, and Cairo; he "studied" (was initiated into?) the Naqshbandīya, Qādirīya, and Suhrawardīya Sufi paths. In an unidentified place, he took as his teacher the Mawlānā Makhdūm, whom Fletcher also mentions, surmising that he was probably an Indian, though he might have been teaching anywhere in the Muslim world. Before Ma Laichi's return to China, Mawlānā Makhdūm bestowed upon Ma Laichi the name Abu 'l-Futūh, and Agelai gave him eight gifts: a sword, a seal, the text *Mingshale*, a *mawlūd* (a poem commemorating the birth of Muhammad), eighty volumes of *kitab* (writings), a prayer carpet, a woolen garment, and a "Ka'aba cover." He arrived in China, via Hong Kong, in 1734. Fletcher, "Naqshbandiyya," 16, gives an entirely different itinerary, though naming the same teachers, and has Ma Laichi back in China by 1705, which seems very early and does not accord with events in his life that may be more surely dated.

23. Some Tibetans of Kargang, in the region of Bayanrong north of the Yellow River in modern Qinghai Province, confirm orally what Joseph Trippner found in the work of Ma Zikuo—that Ma Laichi lived among them and converted their ancestors to Islam by a variety of techniques, including debating a local *rimpoche* ("incarnation," often misconstrued as "living Buddha" in both Chinese and English) on theological matters (Trippner, "Islamische Gruppen," 154–55, and also Li Gengyan and Xu Likui, "Yisilan jiao zai Kaligang"). The one Muslim clan among the Monguors (called Turen before 1949 and Tuzu now), the Ye family, lived in the same region (Schram, *The Monguors*, vol. 1, 32). The Tuomao, a Mongolian-speaking group who live north of Kökenör in Qinghai, may also have joined the Khafiya under his influence. Though their oral histories as summarized by Li Gengyan and Xu Likui do not mention Ma Laichi, they hold firmly to the Khafiya as "their" solidarity (Li and Xu, "Qinghai diqu"). Ma Tong claims that the Baoan (Bonan), a

ples would gather, and his participation in any dispute would give weight to the side he supported.[24] In the 1740s a conflict had arisen in the Hezhou and Xunhua regions over the breaking of the Ramadan fast at the end of each day. Should one pray first, then eat (*houkai*), or eat first, then pray (*qiankai*)? Ma Laichi threw his considerable influence behind those who ate first, the *qiankai* faction. The controversy grew increasingly bitter, and a *houkai* leader, Ma Yinghuan, brought suit against Ma Laichi in 1747.[25]

Ma Yinghuan's lawsuit, in a Qing court, illustrates the difficulty of resolving complex conflicts in Chinese Muslim communities. Elsewhere in the Muslim world, where "secular" authority would also be Muslim authority, the state's jurisdiction would be somewhat less problematic. Groups in conflict might request a judgment from a famous scholar rather than resort to the law courts, but even in cases of irreconcilable conflict, the legitimacy of Islamic state authority and of the statutory and moral status of the *sharī'a* would be agreed upon, even if the particular results were not. But in Gansu, neither faction in a dispute would recognize the authorities cited by the other, and the state, being non-Muslim, would not act on the same grounds as would Muslim legal institutions. Therefore, Ma Yinghuan's action, which explicitly recognized the legitimacy of the Qing legal system to resolve disputes *within* northwestern Muslim society, demonstrates the degree to which the Muslims of the northwest belonged to China. The suit between *qiankai* and *houkai* set a precedent in which religious conflicts between Muslims could be submitted for judgment to the secular authorities.

It also established parameters of legal controversy within the Qing code and judicial system. Ma Yinghuan accused Ma Laichi of *xiejiao* (heterodoxy) and *huozhong* (deluding the people), the former a very serious crime.[26] He claimed that Ma Laichi had founded Mingshahui

small Mongolian-speaking group from Tongren County, south of Xunhua, also became Muslims under Ma Laichi's influence (*Zhongguo Yisilan . . . shilue*, 227).

24. According to Fletcher, Ma Laichi had attained the degree of *walī*, usually translated as "saint," under Mawlānā Makhdūm's tutelage ("Les 'voies'," 16).

25. A brief account of the case may be found in the *Xunhua ting zhi* of 1844, 8:16b–17a, which Mu Shouqi copies into *GNQSL* at 18:37b–38a. Trippner, "Die Salaren," 264, claims that a similar case of dispute between *qiankai* (fore-breakers) and *houkai* (after-breakers) had been brought to court as early as 1731, but official sources do not record it. It probably represents an error for the well-documented case of 1747, since at least one of the litigants' names is identical in the two accounts.

26. The statute regarding *xiejiao* may be found in de Groot, *Sectarianism and Religious Persecution*, vol. 1, 137–47, with the main statute at 137–38. Based on the Chinese state's

(Bright Sand Societies), at whose meetings initiates had sand blown into their ears.[27] His intention clearly lay in associating Ma Laichi's Khafiya Sufis with Daoist or Buddhist groups, always suspect in China for their bizarre ritual practices and propensity for sedition. A Qing court might well have found merit in such a line of argument, for Ma Laichi's group must have appeared innovative and divisive when viewed from a legal culture that valued conservatism and harmony, while its Sufi practices, however calmly these Naqshabandīs may have undertaken them, were certainly unlike those of Gedimu communities. But the governor-general, Zhang Guangsi, dismissed the case against Ma Laichi, charging Ma Yinghuan with slander and ordering him punished according to the *fanzuo* rule, which stipulates that a false accuser could receive the sentence his victim might have been given had he been found guilty.[28] The *qiankai* and *houkai* adherents were forbidden to conduct funerals together and ordered to respect their ancestral religion without conflict.

This verdict hardly settled the matter. Ma Laichi's entry into the public world of Gansu Muslim religious politics had generated division and conflict, and neither side would give up the struggle. Most texts cite ritual, liturgical, or magical practices (such as sand-blowing) as the overt reasons for conflict, but the charismatic *hajjī* from Hezhou had clearly stepped on sensitive toes in the social and economic realms as well. His conversion of the Salars, in particular, made Gansu people

experience with Buddhist and Daoist groups perceived as potentially subversive, it concentrates on activities associated specifically with them, some of which also point directly at Muslims as well, especially Sufis. For example, the statute forbids meetings that take place at night, which of course are necessary for Muslims during Ramadan and Sufis as part of their *dhikr* practice. The supplementary statutes forbid writing charms, preparing sacred writings (especially esoteric, encoded texts), and collecting contributions, among many other things. Ironically, these statutes, invoked against Sufis in the eighteenth century, specify banishment to Xinjiang and enslavement to the *begs* (who were Sufis) or to other Muslims as fit punishment for the practice of *xiejiao* (Lipman, "Statute and Stereotype"). Iwamura, "Chūgoku Isuramu," compares the status of the Sino-Muslim communities to that of secret societies, firmly lodged within Chinese society but nonetheless segregated.

27. Nakada, *Kaikai*, 88, where his source is the edict cited above in note 19. This "Bright Sand" business, quite common in Chinese accounts, derives from the characters used in the transliteration of the name of Ma Laichi's text, the *Mingshale*. Some versions of this title use the characters for "bright sand" (*ming sha*), while others use a different *ming* to indicate the sinister "dark sand."

28. According to Nakada, whose source is contemporary to the trial, it was Governor-General Zhang who heard the case. *Xunhua ting zhi*, 8:17a, names Gansu governor Huang as the presiding justice.

nervous, as that Turkic-speaking people, living astride the Lanzhou-Xining and Hezhou-Xining roads, had a reputation for bellicosity. Other Gansu people feared that, should Salars be unified under a single leader in a Sufi order, rather than divided into small, mosque-based *gong* communities under several Qing-appointed *tusi,* they would pose a dire threat to public safety.[29] Indeed, when large-scale hostilities did break out in Gansu in the 1780s and 1890s, the Salars and the Khafīya were intimately involved in their inception. Hidāyat Allāh had apparently had great success among them, and so did Ma Laichi.

Ma Laichi's innovations did not stop with initiation into the Khafīya. Building on the models available within the Āfāqīya, the Central Asian Sufism so intimately linked with the political lineages descended from the Makhdūm-i Aʿzam, Ma Laichi established hereditary succession as the principle for transmission of *baraka* within the Khafīya and the centrality of *gongbei,* the tombs of a Sufi order's deceased leaders, in the ritual lives of adherents (see plate 11).[30] His son, Ma Guobao, followed him as *shaikh,* thus ensuring that the family's accumulated wealth would not dissipate nor its religious power wane. He and several others initiated in the line of Hidāyat Allāh are credited by Chinese sources with founding the first *menhuan,* the Muslim saintly lineages of northwest China.

Menhuan, an entirely local term, probably derives from *menhu,* "great family," or "official family," but it has come to refer exclusively to northwestern Chinese Sufi solidarities whose leadership remains within a single lineage. Though far from unusual elsewhere in the Muslim world, the idea of hereditary succession to religious, social, and political authority fell on particularly fertile ground in China.[31] Sufi orders often transmitted charisma in hereditary lines, but nowhere else did they have the comprehensive model of the Chinese corporate lineage (*jiazu*) to follow. Holding common property, diversifying in trade and other eco-

29. The *tusi* system, which boasts considerable antiquity, allowed indigenous non-Chinese-speaking peoples of the frontier to govern themselves under lineages given patents of office by the Chinese state. For the workings of the *tusi* system among the Salars, see Mi Yizhi, *Salazu,* 55–70, and for the system in general, She Yize, *Zhongguo tusi;* and Zhang Jiefu, "Qingdai tusi."

30. Fletcher, "Ch'ing Inner Asia," 74, briefly reviews the history of the Makhdūm-zādas, stressing their claim to prophetic descent and thus the centrality of genealogy—hereditary succession—within their dynasty and their Sufi traditions. Fletcher correctly notes that this type of transmission of *baraka* may be found in Sufi orders all over the Muslim world, though not in every one.

31. See, for example, Ewing, "The Politics of Sufism."

nomic activities, and participating actively in politics, the *menhuan* used strategies evolved by the Chinese *jiazu* for survival and advancement in the rapidly changing world of late imperial China. As a unique blend of Sufi and Chinese forms, the *menhuan* combined the appeal of prophetic descent with Chinese notions of family structure and socioeconomic competition.[32] Deriving legitimacy from two of the worlds that met on this frontier, the *menhuan* proved to be a powerful new instrument of local elite control.[33]

The lineage basis of the *menhuan* also provided rich ground for conflict. Ma Laichi was not the only founder (Ch. *daozu*) authorized by Hidāyat Allāh. The initiate Ma Shouzhen returned from Xining to Didao, on the Tao River, and his lineage became the core of the Mufti (Ch. Mufuti or Mufouti) *menhuan,* which engaged in feuding with the Khafiya at Xining in the nineteenth century.[34] Ma Zongsheng ('Abd ar-Rahmān), a well-known Hezhou *ahong*, received Hidāyat Allāh's initiation and instruction and became the *daozu* of the Bijiachang *menhuan;* his tomb is located west of the city.[35] And others followed, taking advantage of the effective serendipity that united *jiazu* and *tarīqa* in this context. Unlike earlier Islamic institutions, *menhuan* could grow by gaining adherents in many communities, contiguous or not, so they competed with one another for initiates in all the Muslim regions of Gansu. Both numbers of members and their wealth could contribute to a *menhuan*'s rise, for even poor families could provide young men to serve as students and as guards for the *shaikh.*

32. Ma Tong argues that *menhuan* differed from other Chinese and Muslim groups in their unique combination of Sufi religious impulses, esoteric seeking of the Way under the guidance of a *shaikh,* and the establishment of lineages as the focus of loyalty (*Zhongguo Yisilan . . . suyuan*, 45–47). None of these features, however, distinguishes the *menhuan* entirely from Sufi orders elsewhere in the Muslim world; its unique character derives rather from its adoption of corporate lineage forms from the Chinese sociopolitical environment.

33. Because of the *menhuan*'s centrality in northwest China after the 1740s, contemporary Sino-Muslim scholars have produced a huge literature describing, categorizing, and analyzing both the institution and its historical evolution. Based on late Qing and Republican period local wisdom, Chinese scholars often hold that there were "four great *menhuan*," though their lists often differ. Actually, there were (and are) dozens, great and small. Apart from Ma Tong's two books, both cited above, see Jin, "Sufei pai"; Guan and Wang, "Huasi menhuan"; Rehaimude, "Sufei pai"; and Yang Huaizhong, "Dui xibei." Foreign scholars, too, have found the *menhuan* crucial, e.g., Dru Gladney ("Muslim Tombs") and Nakada Yoshinobu (*Kaikai minzoku,* chap. 4).

34. Ma Tong, *Zhongguo Yisilan . . . suyuan,* chap. 2. The Mufti *menhuan* leadership also took a militant anti-Qing stand in the 1895 uprising; see chap. 4, this volume.

35. Ibid., 214–21.

By the mid-eighteenth century northwest China had received from Central Asia a new religious and social form, the Sufi order, which stimulated a strong drive to political activism, Muslim legalism, community solidarity, and horizontal competition. Combined with the Chinese corporate lineage both socially and ideologically, the Sufi *menhuan* became competitive economic institutions as well. The coming of Sufism from the west inclined Gansu Muslims toward their religion's heartlands in Central and West Asia, but their adaptation took place in a culturally Chinese context. In the Qing period new pressures also arrived from China's great cities in the east, where powerful currents were developing that would tie Sino-Muslims more tightly to the linguistic and intellectual culture of their homeland.

EASTERN INFLUENCE: THE *HAN KITAB*

Islam with Chinese Characteristics

Human affairs are reciprocal and complementary. The influence and permeation of Chinese Islam by Confucian thinking seems to have given late Ming and early Qing Islam, which was tending toward decline, a transfusion of fresh, new blood, a new vitality presented to the Muslim scholars. A group of Sino-Islamicists [Yisilanjiao Hanxuejia] sprang forth. They used Confucian language and Confucian ideas systematically to study, arrange, and summarize Islamic religious doctrine; they constructed a complete Chinese Islamic intellectual system, writing a set of Chinese-language [Hanwen] Islamic works with a uniquely Chinese style. These works are called by the Muslims in China the *Han kitab*—that is, the Chinese canon—and they have had a definite influence in Sino-Muslim society.[36]

Over the course of the Ming period, as the Muslims of China became more exclusively Sinophone, intellectuals among them worried that they might lose their faith, their values, and their uniqueness by losing

36. Truly, there is nothing new under the sun. When I penned the clever heading for this extract, thinking to play on the current Chinese state's claim to have invented "socialism with Chinese characteristics," little did I know that it had already been used by a Chinese scholar (see Cong Enlin, "Zhongguo tese"). The extract is from Feng Jinyuan, "Cong Zhongguo," 280.

the ability to read their sacred texts. In Shaanxi and Gansu, this anxiety led to the strengthening of mosque-based education in Arabic and Persian, which, as we have seen, spread all over China through the posting of northwestern-trained *ahong*. But the anxiety was also keenly felt in the substantial and more acculturated Muslim communities of China's large eastern cities. Relatively few Muslims from Nanjing, Beijing, or even Guangzhou could go on the *hajj* or study abroad, their *ahong* could not interpret the holy books profoundly, and their differences with their non-Muslim neighbors grew less distinct. The intellectually inclined among them studied the Confucian classics and sometimes succeeded in the civil examinations, but Islamic learning could not thrive in their isolated environment. Islamic intellectual decline might have been remedied by a new infusion of enthusiasm, knowledge, texts, or leaders from the Muslim heartlands, but those routes were blocked by a Ming policy that forbade, or at least discouraged, maritime trade and contact.

Though Muslims had lived in China since the Tang, and many had become scholars of Chinese learning, none had written *Islamic* texts in their native language, Chinese. Though this may seem surprising after eight or nine centuries of presence, we know that Arabic and Persian remained inviolate languages of religious transmission within Islam, so undertaking that work in another written idiom would certainly have required a pressing need, individual courage, and an innovative spirit. In the mid- and late Ming, anxiety over the survival of Islam in China among the Sino-Muslim elite created precisely the conditions for that innovation, but only where Chinese learning among Muslims had progressed to the point that literati who knew both Arabic and Chinese could contemplate translating texts and ideas from one idiom into the other—that is, in the eastern cities and in Yunnan.

Linked to and influenced by new movements in Central Asia, Muslims in Gansu, on China's northwestern cultural frontier, became Sufis, joined mystical orders, and created the *menhuan*. Closer to China's heartland, Shaanxi Muslims advocated *jingtang jiaoyu* to ensure that the sacred languages would survive another generation. But in Suzhou (Jiangsu Province),[37] Beijing, and especially Nanjing, Sino-Muslim literati created a new genre of texts, the *Han kitab,* their content accurately reflected by their half-Chinese, half-Arabic name—the Sino-Islamic can-

---

37. This Suzhou is the famous lower Yangzi cultural center, *not* the frontier city in the Gansu corridor that had been one of Ding Guodong and Milayin's bases in 1648.

on.[38] By no means all alike, these books reflected their authors' surroundings, religious convictions, and intellectual preferences.

Wu Sunqie, from Jiangning, may have passed the official examinations to the level of *xiucai*, but he withdrew from the search for public office and turned to studying the Islamic curriculum during the Ming-Qing transition. Achieving an advanced level, he became an Islamic teacher in Suzhou, where he undertook the translation of the *Mirsad al-ibad* into Chinese, an effort that required five years and the intimate involvement of his brother, who was possibly more competent than Wu Sunqie in either Chinese or Arabic prose.

The *Mirsad*, a thirteenth-century text by Abū-Bakr ʿAbd-Allāh, traces the soul's journey from its original home, through the present life to the world to come.[39] Clearly of Sufi origins, in Wu's hands it became a manual for proper Islamic belief and behavior, including sections on creation, worldly obligations, good and evil, and methods of self-cultivation for various classes of society. In northwest China Sufis arrived in person, bearing the *tarīqa* as a vehicle of religious and social organization and their own charismatic leadership for mobilization. In east China Sufism arrived as philosophical texts, not especially distinguished from other Islamic books and quite separate from any social or political forms.

According to one biography, Wu did not wish to impose any changes at all on the *Mirsad*. Rather, he used a rigid method of precise translation, commenting only on philology or grammar. After the book's

---

38. Some of the earliest reliable editions of these texts, tracked through the world's libraries by Donald Leslie and analyzed in his invaluable *Islamic Literature,* have been published in a collection of facsimiles by Ningxia Renmin Chubanshe in Yinchuan. Aside from that excellent compendium, they are generally available only in printings from the late Qing and Republican periods, many of which are not as accurate as the earlier woodblock editions. I have been able to use a few of the earlier editions, but most of the following account is based on quotations from secondary sources. Full-scale study of these texts has been undertaken by Chinese scholars such as Feng Zenglie and Na Guochang, but Western and contemporary Japanese scholars should certainly begin this work as well, for it provides an extraordinary view into the minds of Muslim intellectuals self-consciously explaining their faith in the idiom of classical Chinese, and thus a subtle description of the relationship between the two parts of Sino-Muslim identity as these particular men experienced and explained it. The understanding of these texts among contemporary Sino-Muslims is far from unified; they are even called by two different names. In the northwest, they are called the *Han kitab*. Elsewhere in China, especially among intellectuals, the genre is known by the purely Chinese title *Zhongwen Yisilanjiao yizhu* (Chinese-language Islamic translations and commentaries).

39. Rizvi, *Muslim Revivalist Movements,* 436.

completion, members of his family added a commentary at the beginning of each section, making the text much easier to use. So concerned was Wu about the possible misuse of his text that he forbade its publication, so it survived only in manuscript form until the end of the nineteenth century.[40]

Working at the same time as Wu Sunqie, perhaps even earlier, Zhang Zhong (also called Zhang Shizhong) of Suzhou wrote two important books on Islamic philosophy. He based his most important work, the *Guizhen zongyi*, on the discourses of an Indian Muslim scholar, a Sufi whose name appears as Ashige in Chinese. They met in 1638, and Zhang followed his teacher all over east China. In both Ashige's discourses and his own commentary, Zhang focuses on the difficult notions of faith (Ar. *īmān*) and obedience to God as the core of Islam: "In Islam, the crucial thing is acknowledging God; the key to acknowledging God is *īmān*."[41] In Zhang's book we find the first articulation of what would become a crucial principle among Sino-Muslims: In order to know God, we must know ourselves. Compatible both with orthodox Islam (especially with Sufi introspection and quietism) and with Chinese notions such as *xiushen* (self-cultivation) and *yangqi* (cultivating the vital essence), this psychological, self-disciplined religious ideal appealed to a broad range of Sino-Muslim thinkers and practitioners over the centuries.

After Ashige left China, Zhang Zhong journeyed to Yangzhou, where he met regularly with three Muslim disciples, who questioned him on religion. Together they studied a text rendered in Chinese as *Shuaisuli* or *Lusuli*, but which Leslie lists as *Chahar fasl*.[42] Zhang helped them to translate the text and commented on it. After their teacher returned to Suzhou, the students collected his translation and commentary in the *Sipian yaodao*, divided into four sections: *īmān;* God and Islam; prayer and its rules; and "sacred behavior," including ablutions and specific commandments. Though he had not adhered as rigidly as Wu Sunqie to an ideal of translation, Zhang Zhong nonetheless took Arabic texts and the teachings of Ashige as the core of his writing, adding his own ideas in the form of commentary rather than structuring the entire discourse in self-consciously Chinese ways.

Wang Daiyu (1570s–1650s?), a Muslim of Nanjing, published the *Zhengjiao zhenquan* (A true interpretation of the orthodox teaching) in 1642, making it the earliest extant work of its kind, though he probably

40. Bai, *Huizu renwu zhi (Qingdai)*, 42–43.
41. Ibid., 37–41.
42. Leslie, *Islamic Literature*, 23.

was not the first to undertake the explanation and justification of Islam in Chinese or the translation of Arabic and Persian texts.[43] Wang's preface provides us with the earliest statement of why Sino-Muslims needed this type of book. His self-justification describes his motivation and defines his audiences:

> My ancestors came from Arabia as presenters of tribute to Ming Taizu. They could determine the profundities of astronomy and could correct the errors in the calendar. In surveying the Nine Heavens above and penetrating the Nine Depths below, they surpassed all previous ages without the slightest error. They gladdened the emperor's heart, and he felt that if they had not had a true learning, they could not have accomplished this. He appointed them to the Astronomical Bureau, granted them the right to reside here [in Nanjing] and exemption from the corvée, and allied them with China forever. In the last three hundred years, though we have had time enough to become accustomed to the place, still we have not dared forget our origins.
>
> In my youth, I did not study the learning of the Confucians, so as I grew up, though I had rudimentary literacy, I could not be more than a sometime clerk. As I matured, I grew ashamed of my mediocre attainments, so I began to explore nature and principle and the annalistic accounts and on the side turned to the various philosophers. As I came to some understanding of the general meaning, I felt that their argumentation was perverse and their Way erroneous and mutually contradictory in places. Compared to Islam [Qingzhen], they seemed as night and day. Though not wanting to speculate, I absurdly wished to leave worthy writings for posterity, to clarify [this matter] and arrive at correct [understanding]. So I met with the various thinkers and initiated much debate; though they persevered, they could not compete [with me], and I left them always in the wrong. Of those superior men who willingly submitted, every one regretted that there existed no complete guidebook to the Correct Teaching [Islam]. So whenever I had been among them, I went home and noted down what had been said. Furthermore, in leisure hours, I unsystematically organized my notes and collected them into several [categorized] sections. There was too much to keep, so I had to cut it back, and the result was forty chapters. The principles and Way [discussed] therein are all

43. Ibid., 21, lists three Islamic works in Chinese with prefaces dated before the *Zhengjiao zhenquan*, but none is extant; all are known only through Liu Zhi's preservation of their prefaces or postscripts.

based entirely on reverence for Scripture, with reference to the commentaries, and I have not dared to interpolate my own personal feelings, to add or subtract, or divide the various scholars.[44]

Wang maintained the fundamental truths and superiority of Islam, and certainly did not intend to toady or to flatter the Confucians, but he nevertheless wrote his treatise in a self-consciously Confucian vocabulary. The concepts and arguments of Song and Ming *lixue*, the orthodox Neo-Confucianism associated with the Cheng brothers and Zhu Xi and legitimized by the state, constituted the only acceptable philosophical discourse available to him outside the Arabic and Persian texts that took Islam's verities for granted. He could not write about Islam using the vocabularies associated with Buddhism or Daoism—God forbid!—for that would accomplish neither of his purposes. As he notes in his preface, he wished to communicate the truths of Islam to Muslims literate only in Chinese ("still we have not dared to forget our origins"). He had also to demonstrate the moral qualities of Islam to non-Muslims for whom the Neo-Confucian conceptual framework represented the sole path to ethical or even logical rectitude ("everyone regretted that there was no complete guidebook to the Correct Teaching").

Wang's *Zhengjiao zhenquan* contains twenty brief essays on philosophy and religion, and twenty on ritual and laws. Rather than translating a text or compilation of texts from Arabic or Persian, Wang organized his thinking both in conventional Muslim categories and by Chinese themes that his non-Muslim interlocutors suggested. His initial chapters, on the unity of God and on creation, include quotations not only from the Koran but also from Chinese texts, including the *Laozi*, to prove that Islamic monotheism can be defended within—indeed can improve and complete—the Chinese tradition. In syntax reminiscent of the *Four Books*,[45] he writes: "If one does not comprehend the true Unity [of God], then the root will not be deep; if the root is not deep, the Way will not be fixed; if the Way is not fixed, then faith will not be profound—lacking unity, depth, and profundity, how can their Way long endure?"[46]

---

44. Wang Daiyu, *Zhengjiao zhenquan*, 16. This translation owes much to the skill of Daniel Gardner, to whom many thanks.

45. *The Great Learning* (Da xue), *The Doctrine of the Mean* (Zhong yong), *The Analects* (Lun yu), and *Mencius* (Mengzi). Wang's syntax is especially reminiscent of the powerful parallel sentences that lie at the core of the *Da xue* text.

46. Ibid., *shang*, "Zhenyi," 19.

In his sections on ritual and practice, Wang justifies, often in a prickly and aggressive fashion, Islamic religious life as against the claims not only of Confucian philosophy but also of Chinese popular religion. His arguments sound as if they really were transcribed from conversations in which he held his own against non-Muslim debaters. For example, in his section on geomancy, he answers the criticism that Islam ignores human feelings by burying the dead without a coffin:

> They say, "Orthodox Islamic law is far too sharp and harsh. In embalming and burial, this teaching does not allow the use of a coffin or outer coffin, and that does not accord with human feelings." I reply, "Not using coffins attains to two [high] principles: one is nature, and one is purity. By nature, I mean that the origin of humankind is earth, so going back to the root, returning to the origin, that means returning to the earth, and we call that nature. As for purity, when we bury human flesh and blood in the great earth, it can be transformed and become earth. . . . How can this not be pure? . . . The dead are without [worldly] knowledge, so even a gold inner coffin and a jade outer coffin cannot benefit them."[47]

In the *Zhengjiao zhenquan* Wang Daiyu presents his own strongly held opinions, calling on both Chinese and Islamic canonical texts to support him, arguing forcefully for Islamic orthodoxy and orthopraxy in a language shaped by the Chinese elite's moral concerns, which often differ sharply from those of Muslim theologians, logicians, and legalists. In a closely argued section, he equates the Five Pillars of Faith of Islam with the Five Virtues of Confucianism, calling them both Wuchang, the Five Constants. Subtly including a Confucian virtue in the description of each Islamic obligation, he makes good Chinese sense of the fundamental Muslim duties: creed (*ren,* benevolence), charity (*yi,* righteousness), prayer (*li,* propriety), fast (*zhi,* knowledge), and pilgrimage (*xin,* faith in humankind).[48]

Wang's books were reprinted in many editions and have remained popular among Sino-Muslims, but they did not have the desired impact on non-Muslim thinkers. Islam's outlandish origins, its denial of some basic and obvious truths of Chinese religion, and, perhaps most important, its assertion of Tianfang (Arabia) as a radiating center of civilization prevented its being taken seriously by most Chinese intellectuals.

47. Ibid., *xia,* "Fengshui," 132.
48. Ibid., *xia,* "Wuchang," 82–87.

Wang never claimed Arabia as the sole source of revelation or enlighten-ment; like other Sino-Muslim authors, he cited the classical prediction that a sage would arise in the east (Confucius) and another in the West (the Prophet Muhammad). But so strong was the commitment of China's non-Muslim literati to the exclusive centrality of China to Civili-zation that even parallel or coequal cultural truths expressed in literary Chinese could not be accepted. Within the intellectual world of the Sino-Muslims, however, Wang occupies a crucial place as the innovator who made possible several genres of Islamic writing.

Though the works of Wu Sunqie, Zhang Zhong, and Wang Daiyu all have come to be included within the *Han kitab,* the Chinese Islamic canon, clearly they had very different purposes and methods in presenta-tion of Islamic content to a Chinese-literate audience. Wu wanted to present a Middle Eastern text, a Sufi philosophical treatise, in a Chinese version as close as he could to the original, with little commentary. Zhang based himself on his teacher's discourses and created a general book of Muslim knowledge as the basis for writing his own comments on Islamic ideas and practice. Wang Daiyu, the most innovative, uti-lized the entire Neo-Confucian philosophical discourse in order to criti-cize some of its fundamental concepts and to justify Islam in his own prose. All three acted within a Muslim world in which Arabic and Persian no longer sufficed for Islamic education, and in a Chinese world that demanded of Muslims that they be participants in a universal moral discourse, not immoral foreigners. Their successors continued to re-spond to those dual pressures and created a substantial Sino-Muslim literature.

The Flowers of Sino-Muslim Scholarship: Ma Zhu and Liu Zhi

Born in 1640 in Baoshan County, Yunnan, Ma Zhu studied primarily the Confucian curriculum as a child. His father, who died when the boy was only seven, had been a classical scholar, and his mother encouraged him to follow in the examination pathway. Passing his *xiucai* exam at sixteen, he obtained a position under the last claimant to the Ming throne, the Yongli emperor (r. 1644–62), whose court had been pushed southwestward into Yunnan by the Qing invaders.[49] Unlike his royal employers, Ma Zhu successfully weathered the Qing conquest, and by 1659 he had published his first book and obtained a teaching position.

---

49. Lynn Struve has translated a vivid account of life in that pathetic and roving court by one of its eunuchs (*Voices,* chap. 15).

His essays were well known all over the province by 1665.[50] But as Wu Sangui, a Chinese general in the Qing army, began the political maneuvers that would bring him into direct conflict with the Manchu court, Ma Zhu decided to move to Beijing in 1669.

In the reviving Muslim community of the early Qing capital, Ma turned toward Islamic studies and spent over a decade immersing himself in the languages and texts of his religion. As he probed deeper into Islam, he realized how useful it would be if the new Qing imperium recognized the faith officially. Trading upon his putative descent from Sayyid Ajall Shams ad-Dīn (in the fifteenth generation) and therefore from the Prophet Muhammad (in the forty-fifth), he used official connections to request that his status as *sayyid* be sanctioned by the Kangxi emperor (r. 1661–1722). Though he failed to obtain imperial recognition, he did communicate to fellow Muslims how important it was for the Qing state to place an imprimatur on Islam's presence in China.

To forward that ambition, he spent much of his time in Beijing compiling his research results into a comprehensive guide to Islamic thought and practice, the *Qingzhen zhinan* (Compass of Islam), one of the most popular and massive of the *Han kitab* texts. Then, in 1684, with manuscript in hand and family (his wife and two sons) in tow, Ma Zhu set off on a journey that would take him to most of the important Muslim communities in China, except Gansu. In four years on the road, he visited Nanjing and the other Muslim centers of central China, the major cities of the Yangzi valley, Shaanxi, and finally Sichuan on the long road home to Yunnan. Wherever he stopped, he met with famous *ahong* and local scholars to show them his book, asking them for instruction and gathering prefaces, essays of greeting, and postfaces by the dozen. When he got home, he set about revising the text to include all their suggestions, criticisms, and addenda, a process that took another fifteen years and more.

Ma's book circulated in a variety of manuscript editions, which he distributed along his route, long before it was ever published. The final version of the *Qingzhen zhinan* was complete by 1710. The main portion of the book, in eight *juan* (volumes), includes sections on orthodoxy and orthopraxy, some addressing the issues and problems of Chinese Muslim society more practically and concretely than did Wang Daiyu's *Zhengjiao zhenquan*.[51] The two new *juan* written in

---

50. Bai, *Huizu renwu zhi (Qing dai)*, 44–45.

51. Ibid., 48, where the anonymous author notes particularly the section of *juan* 8 titled *Jiaotiao bakuan*. Ford, "Some Chinese Muslims," 148, discounts Ma's originality and dismisses his work as a repetition of Wang Daiyu's.

Yunnan consisted of a set of queries and responses, like Wang Daiyu's, and a record of Ma Zhu's successful campaign against some of the Sufi teachings and "heterodox" practices that were being taught in Yunnan at that time, having been introduced from India. The final *juan*, *Zuodao tongxiao* (A public denunciation of the perverse way[s]), narrates Ma's opposition to the Qalandarīya (Ch. Gelandai), unconventional Sufis who had converted many Yunnanese Muslims to their own versions of mystical practice. Ma Zhu found their doctrines and behavior abominable, violating both *sharīʿa* law and the core morality of Confucianism, and he recommended (and obtained) official persecution of them.

Ma Zhu, possessing a classical Chinese education, skill at Islamic philosophy, and motivation to obtain state validation, undertook to connect China's Muslim communities to one another by actually traveling among them. Much of his career, including his lengthy sojourn in Beijing and possibly the composition of the *Qingzhen zhinan*, stemmed from his ambition to become the empirewide leader of the Qing's Muslims by having himself proclaimed an official, state-sanctioned *sayyid*, thus making himself the Muslim analogue to the descendants of Confucius. He failed in that mission, but that should not discount his success in composing a lengthy and popular work or in carrying news and scholarly currents among the scattered Sino-Muslims.

The most famous of all the Sino-Muslim writers, Liu Zhi (also called Liu Jielian and Liu Yizhai), remained all of his life in the narrow corridor between the lower Yangzi valley and Beijing.[52] A native of Nanjing like Wang Daiyu, Liu came from a family schooled in both Islam and the Chinese classics. His father had met with Ma Zhu and added a dedicatory poem to the *Qingzhen zhinan* but had never attained his desire to make his own contribution to the Chinese discussions of Islamic philosophy. His son, however, received an education that enabled him to surpass his father by far. Beginning with eight years of Confucian schooling, he then concentrated on the Arabic and Persian curricula for six years. After that, he spent another four years reading widely in Buddhist, Daoist, and "Western" (Ch. Xiyang) writings, which at that time meant the Roman Catholic and scientific treatises of Matteo Ricci and his successors, probably available in a private library in Nanjing. He is said to have studied geography, astronomy, psychology, and other subjects that had been important to Muslims in China

52. As far as we know, the only pilgrimage Liu Zhi ever undertook was to Qufu, in Shandong, to visit Confucius' grave.

over the centuries.[53] Competent in all the necessary languages and canons, Liu Zhi set out to stabilize and confirm Islam's intellectual position in China by writing its history, clarifying its doctrines, and equating its truths and profundities with those of the Confucianism that dominated the philosophical discourses of his day (see plate 12).

The author of many books, of which at least ten are extant, Liu Zhi achieved considerable fame and moved in exalted circles for part of his life. He had some of his books presented to the throne and included in them prefaces by non-Muslim officials ranked as high as vice-minister. These encomiums did not simply increase sales or circulation. By distinguishing Islam clearly from Buddhism and Daoism and by placing upon Liu's books the firm imprimatur of the state, they ensured that the works, and Islam itself, would be regarded as compatible with Qing intellectual orthodoxy by the strict and wary censors, always on the lookout for subversive religious doctrines:

> After discussing the Muslim religion with Liu [Zhi], [the vice minister of the Board of War] found that it upheld the Confucian principles of loyalty to the sovereign, respect by sons for their fathers, brotherly love, and so forth; the Muslims' religion, he added, was not to be spoken of in the same breath as heretical and vicious sects.[54]

The vice-minister's words, written in 1710, might have helped to protect Muslims as a group and Islam itself from persecution seventy years later, when some Muslims—Sufis in the northwest—did in fact turn violently against the Qing state.

Liu's well-known works include a biography of the Prophet, its basic text translated from the Persian and supplemented by a wide variety of important inscriptions, legends, and scholarly studies relevant to the study of Islam in China. This book preserves many otherwise unavail-

53. Several authors have located collections of Arabic and Persian works that Liu Zhi used, to a total of sixty-seven titles, most of them religious in character. Ford, "Some Chinese Muslims," 151, notes that the relative rarity of Muslim books in China forced Liu to use a Shi'i version of the *Hadith* (Traditions of the Prophet) as well as a number of Sufi texts, though Liu himself was certainly not a Shi'ite nor did he belong to a Sufi order. In "Islam littéraire chinois" Françoise Aubin argues that all the writers of the *Han kitab* were Sufi adepts, steeped in mystical doctrine, especially that of the three stages toward ultimate apprehension of God, *sharī'a-tarīqa-haqīqa*. More research in the texts, and more discussions of definitions, will be needed to determine whether these writers may be accurately described as Sufis.

54. Several citations from Liu's works may be found in Ford, "Some Chinese Muslims," 149–52.

able primary texts in a sort of Sino-Muslim encyclopedia. Aiming at Sino-Muslim schools as well, he wrote a primer for children, an Arabic language handbook, and a treatise on the Five Pillars of Faith.[55] He also composed two descriptive texts on Islam: the *Tianfang xingli* creates a complete philosophical and religious system combining Islamic and Confucian ideas in a systematic whole, while the *Tianfang dianli* presents Muslim ritual and other religious and secular behavior as entirely compatible with the highest standards of Chinese society.[56]

The *Tianfang dianli* became Liu Zhi's most famous work because it was the only Muslim book to be included in the *Siku quanshu*, the giant effort initiated by the Qianlong emperor to locate, compile, judge, and censor all extant literature. Though the compilers' comments on the book were negative—"The style of this work . . . is extremely elegant, but if the base is wrong to start with, fine words avail nothing"—its very inclusion guaranteed its unique status among the *Han kitab* and Liu's elevation to the highest ranks of Sino-Muslim intellectuals.[57]

The *Tianfang dianli* does contribute to our understanding of Islam's course in China by providing a wonderfully symmetrical analysis of the relationship between Islam and Confucianism. Liu begins by claiming that "the Ways of the Hui [Islam] and Ru [Confucianism] have the same original source, and from the start their principles [*li*] were identical."[58] Knowing well the Confucian stress on ethical behavior and his Islamic texts' more intense focus on theology and humankind's relationship with God, Liu divides the Dao in two, claiming that the Tiandao (Way of Heaven) is most effectively expressed through Islam, while the Rendao (Way of Humankind) may be found in the Confucian canon and the practices of its followers. Like Wang Daiyu, Liu places Islam's Five Pillars of Faith parallel to a Chinese group of five, but he chooses not the Five Constants but the Five Relationships (Wugang), which form the basis of Confucian interpersonal ethics. By creating this ethical parallelism, Liu Zhi placed Islam and Confucianism on an equal footing: "The sacred book . . . is the sacred book of Islam, but principle (*li*) is the same principle which exists everywhere under Heaven."[59]

55. For citations and textual variations, see Leslie, *Islamic Literature*, 46–53. Liu's family apparently thought him eccentric because he sought neither success in the examination system nor a position as *ahong*, but only studied and wrote. Later in life he lost his friends, and was quite alone when he completed his life of the Prophet.

56. This account relies heavily on Feng Zenglie, "Liu Zhi."

57. Quote from Ford's translation, "Some Chinese Muslims," 151.

58. Feng Jinyuan, "Cong Zhongguo," 257–300.

59. Ford's translation, "Some Chinese Muslims," 150.

In its substantive chapters the *Tianfang dianli* progresses from the abstract and cosmological to the practical, from sections on original teaching and true dominion to the Five Pillars, the Five Relationships, collective prayer, and life-cycle rituals. Often criticized by both Muslim and non-Muslim scholars as too Confucian, too conciliatory to China's hegemonic philosophical discourse, Liu actually walks a line between Wang Daiyu's feisty defense of Islamic uniqueness and the writings of entirely acculturated scholars from ex-Muslim families, which are indistinguishable from non-Muslim texts.

Of course, many *ahong* continued to maintain that only Arabic and Persian could be appropriate vehicles for Islamic scholarship, but Liu Zhi and his predecessors had struck a powerful chord among the Sino-Muslim elite. Their works provided both a revivalist impulse, kindling a new interest in Islam among Muslims more oriented toward the Confucian classical curriculum and the examination system, and a propaganda tool for enlightening non-Muslims as to Islam's high moral standing. "Use Confucianism to transmit Islam" could become an effective Muslim technique only when a sufficient number of Muslims in China had become illiterate in the sacred languages but literate enough in Chinese to handle complex philosophical and ritual texts. Despite the scorn of Muslim traditionalists, who called them antiscriptural and perverters of customs, the writers of the *Han kitab* brought to the fore elements of their faith that resonated most harmoniously with the dominant political and moral philosophy of Qing China.[60]

As Qing rule grew more stable and more repressive in the eighteenth century, Muslims in eastern China could ill afford to alienate the officials. Rather, they provided an intellectual justification by which Muslims could live comfortably in China, remain Muslims, and still participate in the larger culture within which they constituted a minority. This strategy, so obviously different from that of the Sufis, grew out of the context of the eastern cities (even the Yunnanese Ma Zhu did his research and writing in Beijing), where the non-Muslims constituted an unassailably vast majority.

This contrasts sharply with the northwest. There the *ahong* had more power, and intellectual life (in any language) was less easily available, as were books. Very few men could follow the examination system path,

---

60. As Aubin states, many of the *Han kitab* texts emphasize the Three Vehicles of increasingly esoteric Sufi knowledge. I would argue that their authors chose these particular concepts in part because they work so well in a culture devoted to self-cultivation as humankind's highest activity. See Li Xinghua, "Zhongwen Yisilanjiao," 282.

and far fewer Muslims could read Chinese. In Gansu the presence of large, successful Muslim communities, antagonistic perceptions of cultural Others, and a rowdier, more militarized atmosphere stimulated Sufi orders to create solidarities of Muslims based on loyalty to a *shaikh* and a desire for widespread self-defense. The spark that touched off long-lasting violence was the arrival of another Sufi order, the Jahrīya, in the person of another pilgrim returned from Yemen, Ma Mingxin.

NAQSHABANDĪ REVIVALISM IN CHINA

On July 25, 1946, the Rev. F. W. M. Taylor wrote to his fellow missionary, Claude L. Pickens, Jr., to clarify a "chain of succession" for the Jahrīya Sufis of Ningxia, who, he reported, called themselves "dervish," a common Turkic appellation for Sufis. Taylor had worked among the northwestern Muslims for many years, unsuccessfully arguing the virtues of Christianity against their stubborn adherence to their ancestral religion. He had sent an earlier version of the *silsila* to Samuel Zwemer, Pickens's father-in-law and the dean of Muslim studies among the American Protestant missionaries, but it had included errors. Unlike virtually every other such document from China, this *silsila* included the generations *before* the order's arrival in China; it thus constituted the starting point for Joseph Fletcher's detective work to uncover the origins of Naqshabandī revivalism in China.[61] The Arabian generations (in Taylor's imperfect romanization) were:

1. Uways-al-Qarani
2. Jami
3. Sheikh Muharyindi
4. Abu Uesaidun (Yezid)
5. Junayd
6. Tajr
7. Dahawandini, i.e., Naqshband, who died in A.H. 791–A.D. 1389
8. Zayn
9. Abu Duha Halik

After years of effort, in the late 1970s Fletcher finally discovered the identity of the last two men on this list, thus demonstrating conclusively what was already recorded within the Jahrīya suborder but unknown

61. Fletcher, "The Taylor-Pickens Letters," 24.

outside it—that the Jahrīya Sufis of Gansu were Naqshabandīs, that their Sino-Muslim founder had studied in Yemen, and that they were intimately connected to Sufi revivalism all over the Muslim world. Research done in China has since deepened that connection, and an Arabic document from within the Jahrīya has largely confirmed it.[62]

Ma Mingxin and the Jahrīya: The Arabian Connection

All over the Muslim world, the great wave of Sufism changed its character during the seventeenth and eighteenth centuries. Renewal (*tajdīd*) movements grew from West Africa to China, advocating purification of Islam from local cultural accretions and from the abuses (social and economic, as well as theological) possible within Sufi orders. In many parts of Asia, the Naqshabandī order stood at the forefront of this new movement, epitomized by the career of Ahmad Sirhindī, the Mujaddid i-Alf i-Sānī (Renewer of the Second Muslim Millennium), in India in the early seventeenth century.[63] This Sufi revivalism reached northwest China most dramatically in the person of ʿAzīz Ma Mingxin (1719?–81), a Gansu Naqshabandī who, like Ma Laichi, had studied for many years in Mecca and Yemen.[64] His teachers there came from the school of Ibrāhīm ibn Hasan al-Kūrānī, one of the best-known Sufi revivalists of the Arabian peninsula. Among several generations of disciples, al-

---

62. Ma Xuezhi, *Zhehelinye daotong shi*, a translation of about one-third of the Arabic original, existed only in an "informal" version in 1984. I was thus able to read it, but not to copy or retain it. The text includes stories of the Chinese *shaikh*s of the Jahrīya, the miracles they worked, and their victories over their Muslim and non-Muslim enemies. The section on Ma Mingxin makes it clear that he studied in Yemen; Ma Tong, *Zhongguo Yisilan . . . shilue*, 364–65, concurs, identifying Ma Mingxin's teacher as Muhammad "Bulu Seni," probably a mistransliteration of Muhammad ʿAbd al-Bāqī b. az-Zayn, the father of the az-Zayn discussed below. Ma Tong's *silsila* also includes ʿAbd al-Khāliq, though in a different position in the list, an inconsistency possibly due to his oral sources, as compared to Fletcher's written Arabic documents. Ma Xuezhi's abridged Chinese version has now been supplanted by a complete translation of the text, called *Rashuh* after its first Arabic word. Done by two Jahriya *ahong*s and the famous Sino-Muslim novelist Zhang Chengzhi, the published translation is an important addition to our primary sources on Sufism in China. The reference to Ma Mingxin's sojourn in Yemen may be found in Guanli Ye, *Reshihaer*, 10.

63. For a review of Sirhindī's career, politics, theology, and disciples, see Khan, *The Naqshbandis*, esp. 40–98; and Friedman, *Shaykh Ahmad Sirhindī*.

64. Ma Mingxin had several names, both Arabic and Chinese, and scholars disagree as to which one(s) might be most authentic. According to Ma Tong, he came to be called ʿAzīz only after his return from Arabia; his Islamic given name was Ibrāhīm. He also had a Sufi name (Ch. *daohao*), Wiqāyat Allāh (*Zhongguo Yisilan . . . shilue*, 363).

Kūrānī's intellectual and spiritual descendants included the leaders of socioreligious movements in Sumatra, Java, north India, Arabia, China, and west Africa, evidence of the remarkably open communication among international Sufi elites during this century.

Joseph Fletcher has demonstrated how two Naqshabandī Sufis from China, Ma Laichi and Ma Mingxin, obtained quite different versions of their order's tradition, though they both may have studied within the same schools in the Middle East.[65] As we have seen, Ma Laichi had returned to China as a practitioner of the silent *dhikr* characteristic of the Naqshabandī order. Ma Mingxin, a decade or two later, studied with the next generation of Yemeni teachers, who taught that the *dhikr* of God could be chanted aloud as well. His teacher, ʿAbd al-Khāliq b. az-Zayn al-Mizjājī, participated in a scholarly world much more receptive to new forms of remembrance, and he himself is reported to have taught both the silent and the vocal *dhikr* to his disciples.[66]

The *dhikr* was certainly not the only contentious issue among the Naqshabandīs of Yemen in the early eighteenth century; *tajdīd*—commitment to political, social, and religious renewal of Islam—divided them even more profoundly. Among the students of al-Kūrānī, especially in the second generation, were fundamentalists who shook the Islamic world with their negative evaluations of contemporary practice. Muhammad Hayāt as-Sindī, for example, who was one of ʿAbd al-Khāliq's teachers, also included among his disciples Muhammad b. ʿAbd al-Wahhāb. The latter became the most famous anti-Sufi, anti-accretion polemicist of his generation in Arabia and founded a movement that still reigns supreme in the Arabian peninsula. Indeed, "Wahhabi" became synonymous for European scholars with the most intolerant, most reactionary revivalism of the modern period. Activist revivalists such as Shāh Walī Allāh of Delhi, Muhammad as-Samman, and ʿAbd ar-Raʾūf as-Sinkilī of Sumatra all partook of the same atmosphere as Ma Mingxin. For them, as for Ahmad Sirhindī, politics and social reform constituted a crucial focus for Naqshabandīs.[67]

65. Fletcher, "Naqshbandiyya," 27–33.

66. Ibid., 30, esp. n48.

67. It may seem contradictory that Muslim leaders educated within Sufi orders would have become anti-Sufi activists, but by this point in Muslim history virtually every major teacher belonged to one or more orders, so that "Sufi" could encompass the entire, vast variety of Muslim intellectual and political life, including anti-Sufism. In China the range was narrower, but "Sufi" could still include both the well-organized, military-minded Gansu *menhuan* and solitary Sino-Muslim intellectuals, such as Liu Zhi, in Nanjing or Suzhou.

Trained with budding revivalists from all over the Muslim world, Ma Mingxin returned to China in 1761 intending to purify Islam, establish Koranic orthopraxy, and purge the faith of accretions from the surrounding culture. Like all mainstream Naqshabandīs, he held the observance of Islamic law, *sharīʿa,* to be central to Muslim orthopraxy. According to Ma Tong's oral sources, Ma Mingxin's reformist program included unimpeachable Sufi and Sunni tenets: opposition to religious leaders' accumulation of wealth through donations; opposition to grandiose mosques and elaborate decoration; emphasis on emotion in mystical practice, including the use of music; and advocacy of Sufi succession by merit rather than heredity.[68] Though a Naqshabandī like Ma Laichi, Ma Mingxin did not practice the silent *dhikr,* the "remembrance of the heart" characteristic of most Naqshabandī groups. Rather, he and his followers chanted the vocal remembrance called *jahr* (Arabic for "aloud"), from which his suborder took its name, Jahrīya. This vocal *dhikr* was often accompanied by rhythmic swaying, hand movements, even ecstatic dancing.[69]

Ma Laichi and his disciples and descendants, resting on the Āfāqī tradition of Central Asia and their own local self-interest, disapproved of Jahrī rituals and deeply resented the presence of a rival for religious hegemony in the northwest. By the late 1760s, with Jahrīya and Khafīya adherents active all over Gansu, deep, long-lasting conflict *within* the northwest's Muslim communities began to complicate the already difficult relationship between Muslims and the Qing state.[70]

68. Ma Tong, *Zhongguo Yisilan . . . suyuan,* 123–25.

69. Algar, "Silent and Vocal," 44–46, attributes the use of vocal *dhikr* by Naqshbandīs to the practice of multiple affiliation, but also to the existence of a secondary line of spiritual descent within the order, one that justifies *jahr* through the Prophet's initiation of Ali b. Abi Talib. Though he does not believe *jahr* proper to Naqshbandīs, Algar nonetheless admits that it can be of benefit to its practitioners, if done with good intention. Ma Tong notes that precisely during the period of Ma Mingxin's pilgrimage, via Central Asia, the Qarataghliq (Black Mountain, Ch. Heishan) Sufis were in ascendance on both sides of the Pamirs. The Heishan, whom Fletcher ("Naqshbandiyya," 10, n3) identifies as the Ishāqīya, also used the vocal *dhikr,* so Yemen would not have been the only place Ma Mingxin could have practiced this particular ritual innovation. Ma Laichi would not have received the same influences, since his suborder was so closely identified with Khoja Āfāq and the Baishan, the Ishāqīya's sworn rivals.

70. Another popular Sufi order, the Qādirīya, arrived in the Hezhou region in the early Qing, its Chinese founders initiated by a peripatetic Arab missionary who styled himself Khoja ʿAbd Allāh (Ch. Huazhe Abudu Donglaxi), a twenty-ninth-generation descendant of the Prophet. (*Khoja* is not an Arabic title, but ʿAbd Allāh is reported to have studied all over the Muslim world, from Medina to Baghdad and India, so he might

When Sufism first arrived in China, many local Muslims had opposed the new wave, finding its meditative forms and pursuit of the esoteric Way incompatible with their conventional Gedimu lives. But the Central Asian and Chinese Sufi missionaries such as Hidāyat Allāh, Ma Laichi, Ma Mingxin, and Khoja ʿAbd Allāh had powerful advantages in the symbolic capital they brought from the Muslim heartlands. Many had been to Mecca, and at least two claimed Prophetic descent, attributes embodying very high status in the Muslim communities of the Qing empire. They knew Arabic and Persian well, which most Gedimu clergy did not, having been educated entirely within the local *jingtang* and *madrasas*. The Sufis' possession of "pure" texts from West Asia, and their ability to interpret them, added to their influence on potential converts to the Sufi ways. Some of them also became adept at thaumaturgic wonders, which swayed people toward conversion to the path both by direct observation and by the powerful voices of embellishment and rumor.

Conflict among Sufis

Charismatic *shaikh*s such as Ma Laichi and Ma Mingxin obtained substance and standing in their communities once sufficient numbers of local Muslims had committed themselves to their respective paths. Ma Laichi used his personal magnetism and the organizational innovation of the intercommunity Sufi order to amass great wealth from the donations and tithes of initiates. Property donated in pious endowment, often land but also flocks, swelled his fortune and made it permanent. This wealth, of course, was no longer available to the conventional mosques or to other Sufi orders. Sufi elites, beginning with the Khafīya but later including the Jahrīya as well, competed with one another and

---

have picked it up elsewhere.) Though very important in the history of Sufism and the *menhuan* system in China, the Qādirīya did not play a prominent part in the violence of the mid-Qing and will therefore not be discussed here (Ma Tong, *Zhongguo Yisilan . . . suyuan*, 82–92). Since the Qādirīya did not practice hereditary succession to the *baraka* of the *shaikh*, the term *menhuan* seems inappropriate, but Chinese sources regularly include the Qādirīya within that category. I am grateful for this information to the current Qādirīya *shaikh* Yang Shijun *ahong*, a 92-year-old celibate who has lived all his life within the order, based at the Dagongbei complex in Hezhou. Yang *laorenjia*, as his followers call him, graciously spent two hours with me in May 1996, telling me stories of Khoja ʿAbd Allāh's visits to Hezhou, the founding of the Qādirīya, and the past century of Gansu Muslim history. Like his predecessors, he will choose his successor from among his disciples, who live with him and study religion as their sole occupation.

with Gedimu institutions for the resources of their communities, for property, money and religious authority, for the status attached to Islamic learning and orthopraxy, and for congregational decision-making power.

The most divisive conflicts, which produced long-term and disastrous consequences for the Muslims of the northwest, occurred not between Sufi orders and Gedimu congregations but between rival Sufi orders. The Khafiya and Jahrīya came to be personified in their leaders, who preached what Gansu Muslims heard to be different messages, practiced what they observed to be different rituals, and advocated different social and political ideals. Khafiya Sufis claimed to find Jahrīya practices superstitious, heterodox, and sometimes—as in the case of rhythmic motion during vocal *dhikr* recitation—downright immoral. Ma Mingxin, on the other hand, criticized the excessive contributions demanded by Ma Laichi's successors for their religious services, the emphasis on veneration of saints and tombs, and the development of hereditary succession within the Khafiya. This last became a central issue as Khafiya *shaikh*s, beginning with Ma Laichi himself, passed the *baraka* of the saint down to their sons, an act with great socioeconomic significance. Hereditary succession led directly to the formation of *menhuan,* of which Ma Laichi's Huasi *menhuan* was the first.

In addition to differences over ritual minutiae, which provided many of the overt issues in conflict between Khafiya and Jahrīya, Ma Mingxin, bearing al-Kūrānī's political and religious commitment to Islamic renewal, gave the Jahrīya a far more militant attitude toward reform of Muslim practice and toward the non-Muslim state. Ma Laichi's Khafiya, in contrast, tended to follow the political traditions of Khoja Āfāq in cooperating with state authority—Khoja Āfāq had, after all, ruled Kashgar under a non-Muslim imprimatur from Galdan.[71] During the years after Ma Mingxin's return to Gansu in 1761, the rivalry between Khafiya and Jahrīya escalated into open and violent feuding, for all of these Muslim communities were armed. Indeed, the martial arts were known to be a Muslim specialty in the northwest. The militarization of Qing society, sometimes perceived as beginning only in the 1790s, began earlier and proceeded more rapidly on the northwestern frontier. Borderland people, both for protection and for hunting, possessed weapons, including firearms, and trained their sons to use them. Each mosque community, especially those in areas of mixed Muslim and non-Muslim settlement, developed at least some paramilitary capacity.

71. Fletcher, "Les 'voies,' " 21.

Single villages or local alliances prepared hilltop forts and stockades against attack, as did their non-Muslim neighbors. Sufi orders, larger and supralocal, organized their own militias on a wider scale, with more effective centralized command coming from the headquarters of the *shaikh*.

From the 1760s on Muslim communal violence and the state's reaction to it dominate the historical record of northwest China. The Khafīya tended to ally with the state and remained the "established" Sufi order, given the positive appelation Old Teaching to honor its pro-Qing stance. Both officials and non-Jahrīya Muslims labeled the Jahrīya with the pejorative epithet New Teaching and consistently described it as threatening and heterodox.[72] With its militant commitment to Islamic renewal, the Jahrīya frightened local officials by "creating" numerous violent incidents between Muslims. Official fear increased when Khafīya adherents attacked the Jahrīya in lawsuits and in the streets. The sanguinary results will be described below.

Sino-Muslim scholars have not yet successfully dealt with the root causes of violence between competing Sufi orders in eighteenth-century Gansu. Why did advocates of silent and vocal *dhikr* confront one another with fatal consequences in northwest China? In Arabia, after all, Sufis could and did practice both types of remembrance without any apparent contradiction or conflict—indeed, an individual could be initiated into two orders that differed in the matter. The answers, therefore, must lie in northwest China, not in Islam itself, in the characteristics of Gansu Muslim society and its history, not in any inherent qualities of Sufism, Naqshabandism, or Islamic doctrine. We are now prepared to examine a wide variety of possible causes: local ecologies, local eth-

72. A great deal has been made of this Old Teaching vs. New Teaching dichotomy within Sino-Muslim studies, including attempts to find a single movement or organization or theology to which the terms might be attached. A close examination reveals a bewildering variety of usages. "Old Teaching" has been used to describe non-Sufi Gedimu communities (early 18th cent.), Gedimu plus the Khafīya (late 18th–mid-19th cent.), or *all* nonfundamentalist groups (Gedimu, Khafīya, Jahrīya, and the other *menhuan*) as opposed to the New Teaching, which has meant the Khafīya, Jahrīya, Ikhwan, Xidaotang, and others. Saguchi, "Chūgoku Isuramu no kyōha," notes that "New Teaching" was even used to describe reformist attempts in eastern China in the eighteenth–twentieth centuries. Whenever one of these words turns up, we must probe carefully into the local context to discover the points of contention and the leaders/organizations in conflict rather than assigning some absolute meaning to either term. The Chinese officials and Muslim leaders who used them were neither ethnographers nor Islamicists but rather politicians, using loaded terminology to make polemical points. The words "liberal" and "conservative" in American political discourse have similar power, variation, and ideological vagueness.

nographies, pressures internal to the northwestern Muslim communities, and influences from both local non-Muslim society and the Qing state.

The immediate proximity of the Gansu corridor to Hami had facilitated Sa'id Baba's aid to Milayin's rebels back in the 1640s. During the century following Meng Qiaofang's massacre at Suzhou, religious leaders continued to move between northwest China and Central Asia, creating far more durable, institutional connections. As we have seen, from the 1650s to the 1780s the Muslims of the northwest received two new ways of conceiving of Islam, of themselves, and of their place within Chinese culture and society. They came more or less simultaneously, one from the west and one from the east, bringing new ways of belonging, both to China and to the Muslim *umma*, but also the possibility of new and much wider conflict.[73] From the Muslim lands, Sufism spread to the Qing empire as it had to most of the Muslim world, through the charisma of powerful saints who both initiated Muslims into their institutions and converted non-Muslims to their version of Islam.

In contrast, Sino-Muslim intellectuals in eastern cities, trained in both the Islamic and the Confucian curricula, produced synthetic analyses of Islam (including Sufi ideas) in the vocabulary of conventional Neo-Confucianism. Both of these visions of Sino-Muslim society—revivalist and militant, emphasizing tension (from the Muslim heartlands), and syncretic and adaptive, emphasizing compatibility (from the major Chinese cities)—continue to enliven Sino-Muslim life to the present day. Their contradictions, internal and with one another, represent symbolically the difficulties of being both Chinese and Muslim. As Sino-Muslims came to understand the possibilities for unity inherent in

73. I have separated "western" and "eastern" Islamic influences on northwest China too radically here. The two currents, Sufism and the Han *kitab,* actually shared many ideas, even some texts, as Françoise Aubin has made clear in "En Islam Chinois" (esp. pp. 493–515). Sufi texts had been available to Muslim scholars in China (in Arabic and Persian of course) long before Wang Daiyu and his colleagues undertook to render Islamic ideas into Chinese. We have seen that Liu Zhi embedded many mystical notions in his descriptions and justifications of Islam. According to Ma Tong, (*Zhongguo Yisilan . . . shilue,* 387), Ma Mingxin had read Liu Zhi's works and admired them enough to say, "Jielian [Liu Zhi] planted the flowers, and I reap the results." (This saying will turn up again, altered to fit the circumstances, in chapter 5.) However, given its obviously Arabian origins, it would be an exaggeration to claim that Ma Mingxin's Jahrīya was somehow an indigenous, synthetic Sino-Islamic movement. Nor have we any evidence that Sufi *orders,* as distinct from Sufi ideas or texts, made their way to eastern China at any time before the early nineteenth century.

1. Eroded, dry eastern Gansu hill country

2. The Bayanrong valley in Huangzhong

3. Tangwangchuan, from a nearby hilltop.
(Holton Photographs, Harvard-Yenching Library, Harvard University)

4. Elderly Muslim

5. Muslim grandmother and child

6. Poor Muslim working man

7. Muslim family of Amdo (note Tibetan-style hats)

8. A view from the Muslim suburb (Bafang) to the Hezhou wall

9. *Ahong* of a mosque at Guyuan, Gansu

10. Muslim schoolboys with books and bone "slates"

11. A *gongbei* (Sufi saint's tomb) at Pingliang, Gansu

12. Liu Zhi's gravestone, inscribed entirely in Chinese
(restored, 1870 and 1908)

13. Salar man, looking neither ferocious nor Chinese

14. Ma Mingxin's memorial marker at his *gongbei* in Banqiao

15. A large hilltop fort (*zhaizi*) near Xunhua

16. Dong Fuxiang

17. An arch (*pailou*) in honor of Ma Anliang

18. Gatehouse of a Sino-Arabic school near Ningxia

19. A Yunnan Muslim on pilgrimage to Gansu

20. A Jahrīya Sufi, with his distinctive pointed cap

21. Eastern Gansu town gate with slogan
"Do not divide Muslims and Han!"

22. Grave of Ma Yuanzhang and his son at Xuanhuagang

23. Young men selling "Muslim" flatbreads and crocheting white caps

24. Students at an Ikhwan school in Xining

these two modes, or decisively selected one over the other, they created many individual and collective solutions to that dilemma.

External factors were also clearly at work. The corruption of the Qing court, especially the Qianlong emperor's favorite Heshen and his cabal, caused a degeneration of local government in late-eighteenth-century northwest China. A major financial scandal among provincial officials in Gansu revealed widespread malfeasance on the frontier. In addition, the *qiankai-houkai* disturbances had called official attention to the danger of internecine quarrels within Muslim communities, and the state was keeping a more-than-usually watchful eye on Hezhou, Xunhua, and Xining. In this atmosphere of suspicion, corruption, and prejudice against Muslims, the Qianlong emperor tried to implement the policies handed down to him by his father.

THE EIGHTEENTH-CENTURY TRANSFORMATIONS

> The Muslims of every province, as well as the brigands of
> Hebei . . . and Anhui . . . all form bands to feud and kill. In such
> cases, if there are some who call themselves "hired guns," employed
> for violent action . . . their sentences of military exile should be
> raised by one degree.[74]

The arrival of Sufi orders in northwest China did not utterly transform local society. The agricultural and pastoral economies continued to evolve in their long-standing patterns, transportation remained slow and uncertain at times, and wool and leather goods were carried from highland to valley, while pots, tea, and grain moved the opposite way. Chinese, Turks, Tibetans, and Mongols of many faiths and in many combinations met on the grasslands, on the roads, and in the markets to haggle and deal, to intermarry, and sometimes to fight. In that local context, Sufi religious solidarities became wealthy saintly lineages, *menhuan,* which competed for power and disrupted local order precisely at a time of rapid change in the Qing empire. With the Khafiya and Jahrīya orders present and growing in Gansu, in the second half of the eighteenth century, let us now examine the larger world of the Qing, to discover the external pressures that impinged on Gansu in this crucial period.

74. *Duli cunyi* 302.11, cited in Kataoka, "Keian shiryō," 23, n25.

CONNECTIONS

The Conquest of Xinjiang

For over a century after their invasion of China proper, the Manchu Qing extended their empire westward and northwestward. This period of conquest, which created the "China" we now recognize, culminated in the complete subjugation of eastern Turkestan and Zungharia. Though the Kangxi emperor had defeated Galdan's Zunghars, it was left to his grandson, the Qianlong emperor, to finish off indigenous resistance and foreign invasions, all led or inspired by Sufi *shaikhs*.[75] With the final defeat of the Āfāqī branch of the Makhdūmzāda *khoja*s, a Naqshabandī lineage descended from Khoja Āfāq and thus related to the Khafīya of Gansu, by 1759 the Manchus controlled the vast sweep of territory from the Altai all the way to the southern side of the Tarim Basin, and west as far as the Pamirs.

The Qing government's strategic purposes in taking and holding this enormous and potentially very expensive territory included preventing an alliance between Mongolian (including Zunghar) rulers and those of Tibet and "controlling" the potentially violent Kazakhs who lived west of Zungharia.[76] Beyond occupation by about twenty-five-thousand troops of many cultures, the Qing governed the "New Dominion" (Ch. Xinjiang) with a light hand, desiring not assimilation of the predominantly Turkic-speaking Muslim population to Chinese or Manchu ways but rather cooperation in maintaining an orderly society and commerce in this buffer zone. North and east of the Tianshan, direct military government and substantial Chinese (Muslim and non-Muslim) in-migration gradually transformed Zungharia into a polyethnic agricultural-pastoral region. In Altishahr, south of the mountains, local hereditary leaders administered a lenient tax system with appropriate corruption, while sojourning Chinese and Central Asian merchants kept the goods flowing despite a (generally ignored) ban on their permanent settlement. All over Xinjiang merchants from Shanxi, Jiangnan, and the northwest, including many Sino-Muslims, found profitable markets for both staples and luxury goods, which they exchanged either for cash or for jade, the territory's main export to China proper.

75. For a summary of Xinjiang's government, economy, and society in the eighteenth and nineteenth centuries, see Fletcher, "Ch'ing Inner Asia."

76. The first century of Qing rule in Xinjiang, especially its economic and social history, is described with clarity and accuracy in Millward, *Beyond the Pass*. James Hevia (*Cherishing Men,* chap. 2) discusses Qing overlordship in Inner Asia primarily with reference to Tibet, but his arguments apply largely to Xinjiang as well. The most comprehensive published work on Xinjiang in this period may be found in two books by Saguchi Tōru: *Jūhachi-jūkyū seiki* and *Shinkyō minzoku*.

We can only speculate as to the effects of these remarkable conquests on the Muslims of northwest China. By ending a century of warfare in Turkestan and including the entire region in their empire, the Qing had opened up a new domestic arena for Sino-Muslim economic enterprise and cultural exchange. Though they regulated the activities and settlement patterns of Chinese in Xinjiang, the Manchus certainly enabled northwestern Muslims to escape from sometimes dire conditions in Gansu, to seek a better life on the newly available Zungharian arable, which they could not have done under the Ming. The Qing also drew on the resources of the northwest, both products and people, to supply and transport the enormous quantities of material needed by the armies that took and then garrisoned the New Dominion. All Gansu Muslims— including muleteers, caravaners, purveyors of food and fodder, livestock breeders, and farmers—could profit from producing, brokering, and hauling military supplies.

But the demise of independent Islamic political power east of the Pamirs had the same effect as the even more expansive rise of Europe had elsewhere in the Muslim world—it caused Muslims to question their own rectitude in the face of non-Muslim political power. Renewal movements, not coordinated or united across the Islamic world, nonetheless reacted to similar phenomena in similar ways, especially when shaped by the hierarchical, intercommunity potentials of the Sufi orders. Thus we may find both the militance of Ma Mingxin's Jahrīya and the compliance of Ma Laichi's Khafīya comprehensible in the face of overwhelming Qing military might and political control. The Khafīya accepted the obvious domination of the dynasty to thrive under its expanded rule, while the Jahrīya demanded reform and renewal of Islam to counter the triumph of Qing—that is, non-Muslim—hegemony.

Qing Maladministration

Just as Qing power was most convincingly displayed in Central Asia, the seeds of disaster were sown within the bureaucracy in Beijing and all over China proper. The corruption and maladministration usually associated with Heshen and his followers touched the northwest early and hard. We cannot easily ascertain the relationship between the greed of officials and conflict in society at large, but the two coincided with dire results in mid-Qianlong period Gansu, as the Grand Council noted:

> [In Gansu] the Fan [Tibetans] and Muslims live intermingled, and
> You favor them with "impartiality and equal benevolence." You do not

set up distinctions and categories or forbid their customs, so all can imbibe Imperial Virtue and be steeped for generations in the court's favor. That the rebellious Muslims could dare such reckless behavior is beyond reason and principle. If we seek the cause, it lies in the Gansu officials, high and low, who fabricate "disasters" and injure the people in their boundless greed. The severity of years of accumulated offenses finally broke down Heaven's harmony, created malign energy, and led to this poisonous calamity and military burden.[77] As we read Your Majesty's edicts to local officials, [we recognize that] Your Majesty long ago understood and revealed this.[78]

The actions of the rebellious Muslims will be described in the next chapter, but we must first examine what the officials were doing that might have stimulated or at least aggravated their anger.

Beginning in the 1770s Gansu Province's revenues began to disappear into officials' private purses in very large quantities.[79] The Qianlong emperor's investigators discovered three main types of corruption: direct embezzlement of grain from the ordinary land tax and ever-normal granaries; embezzlement of a portion of funds requested for the construction of new granaries; and, most spectacularly, conversion into cash and embezzlement of donations, which were legal only in grain, from purchasers of examination degrees. This last method was extended by a system of false reporting in which those districts with high donation rates would also be slated to receive high levels of "famine relief," whether they experienced famine or not. The "relief" was, of course, pocketed by local officials in collusion with the provincial treasurer. In a province as poor as Gansu, one might expect only paltry amounts to be available from these sources, but the provincial treasurer, Wang Danwang, made millions of taels from his various schemes, while his subordinates and

77. "Malign energy": the Chinese word *qi*, usually translated as "vital essence" or, to follow Daniel Gardner, "psychophysical stuff," in this phrase approximates the 1960s locution "bad vibes."

78. *Qinding Lanzhou jilue*, 153, the Grand Council's appendix to an edict of July 9, 1781. This officially sponsored compendium of documents was compiled by the staff of Agui, the imperial commissioner deputed to subdue the rebellious Muslims of Gansu in the 1780s.

79. Many of the sources for this case may be found in the *Qinding Lanzhou jilue*, as its prosecution was both contemporary to and causally linked by analysts in Beijing with the Muslim rebellion of 1781. The best secondary analysis and compendium of sources may be found in Yang Huaizhong, "Shiba shiji."

local officeholders all over the province cleared from a few thousand to a hundred thousand each.

Not only Qing Grand Council members but also contemporary scholars have concluded that the corruption of Qing officialdom had a great deal to do with rapidly increasing violence in society after the mid-Qianlong period. The analytical vocabularies of Confucianism, Marxism, and the liberal social sciences have all been employed to describe the connections, but often without reference to the complexities and eccentricities of specific local systems. Certainly the extraction of millions from the Gansu economy by Qing officials had a deleterious effect on ordinary people's lives, especially when grain prices and supplies were so shamelessly manipulated by the state's functionaries. But that does not necessarily lead to the formation of secret societies, heretical sects, or rebellious bands. After all, similar corruption took place in Zhejiang—Wang Danwang had been transferred there before his arrest and prosecution—without the kind of results that occurred in Gansu. That is, the financial despoliation of the region by Qing officials played a part in alienating the Muslim population from the state, but was not in itself sufficient to cause widespread violence. Qianlong's officials had, despite his ancestors' and his own admonitions, also created conscious policy toward Muslims as a group that encouraged communal violence in the northwest by encouraging officials to discriminate against them.

Muslims in Qing Law

In 1730 Lu Guohua, the chief prosecutor of Shandong, memorialized requesting that Islam be banned from the Qing empire, for its customs were different and deluded the people. The Yongzheng emperor (r. 1722–35) entirely rejected Lu's view, reiterating what his father had often stated: Muslims living under Qing rule fall within the bounds of civilization, among the emperor's own children, and are to be treated with the same benevolence as all his subjects. The differences between *min* (non-Muslim Chinese) and Hui consist only of "native customs handed down by ancestors from generation to generation," not heterodoxy or treason:

> Why should the Muslim people alone be provoked and made the subject of criminal charges? If the Muslim people indeed transgress, laws and statutes exist under which they will certainly be punished. . . . Henceforth, when the Muslims have basically done nothing wrong but officials, whether high or low, seize on the pretext of minor differences

in customs in order to memorialize wildly, I shall certainly administer severe punishment.[80]

This evenhanded stance on the part of the early Qing emperors boded well for Muslims all over the empire, had local officials been willing or able to enforce their sovereign's will. But memorials such as those of Lu Guohua, and many others, indicate that the Qing employed many men strongly prejudiced against Islam—indeed, against all "different" teachings—and that imperial impartiality faded rapidly beyond the emperor's own gaze. The emperor's officials saw themselves as defenders of the entire Qing order—its law, ideology, customs, language, and more—against any barbaric Others. They probably also faced considerable pressure from local non-Muslims, including gentry, to protect local society from the ferocious and criminally inclined Huihui. It is nonetheless significant that no large-scale Muslim violence against the state or its local officials occurred for over a century after Milayin and Ding Guodong's rebellion was crushed in 1648—not until the mid-Qianlong period.

Like his father, the Qianlong emperor often repeated the time-honored nostrums of imperial benevolence, specifically endorsing the view of a Shaanxi official who found Islam harmless and Muslims to be law-abiding subjects.[81] Even during the literary inquisition, when he might have been expected to be particularly sensitive to unusual or potentially heterodox doctrine, he ruled openly and straightforwardly that there was nothing inherently subversive about Islam. By 1782 "Muslim violence" in Gansu had caused great anxiety and expense for the court, and in that same year a Cantonese Muslim seminarian named Hai Furun was arrested in Guangxi. The literary inquisition was in full swing, and the prefect impounded all his Muslim texts for

80. This rescript, found with Lu's memorial in the Yongzheng *Shilu,* 94:4b–5b, is widely cited in works on the Chinese Muslims, including Leslie, *Islam,* 124, and Saguchi Tōru, "Chūgoku Musurimu," 127. This translation is Leslie's.

81. Bi Yuan, the acting governor of Shaanxi, reported on the reaction of the Xi'an Muslim community to violence by Jahrīya Muslims in neighboring Gansu: "The Hui of Shaanxi feared that they might be dragged in and were inevitably plunged into some apprehension." To defuse the situation, Bi proclaimed the emperor's impartiality to the local Muslims: "As for those who just perform their religious rites normally and break no law, new provisions to deal with them are unnecessary and should be avoided so as not to alarm and spread doubt among the people" (Leslie, *Islam,* 127, citing an edict found only in Liu Zhi's encyclopedic biography of the Prophet, not in any official Qing compilation. The translation is Joseph Ford's).

examination and indictment. Hai's books included Arabic and Persian "scriptures," which the officials of course could not read, and a number of *Han kitab* by Liu Zhi. Zhu Chun, the Guangxi chief inspector, memorialized that the Chinese texts were "presumptuous and reckless . . . containing more than a few wild and deviant passages," and he recommended harsh punishment.[82]

In a pair of firm edicts that summer, the Qianlong emperor denied Zhu's charges, analyzing Islam as a harmless religion, albeit a foolish one, and insisting that Muslims deserve the same protection as other subjects of the empire:

> The sacred texts which they regularly recite consist of books handed down from of old containing no really scurrilous or plainly seditious language. Furthermore, the phrases in these books to which Zhu Chun has drawn attention are on the whole crude expressions which cannot be described as violent and rebellious. These are simple, ignorant Muslim people, faithful to their religion. . . .
>
> The sacred books which they revere are household knowledge among the Muslims. There is no difference here with the Buddhists, Daoists, and Lamas. Surely they could not be exterminated and their books burned![83]

Clearly the emperor had no intention of discriminating against Islam itself, or against law-abiding Muslims in his domains, so he chastised Zhu Chun for overzealousness, and Hai Furun was released unharmed. The emperor saved his ire for what he perceived to be the cause of violence by Muslims—the "New Teaching" of Ma Mingxin, that is, the Jahrīya.

But Qianlong could not control the anti-Muslim sentiments or practices of his officials in the field any better than his father had been able to do. Indeed, under Qianlong and his successors, even the statutes of the dynasty began to reflect the perception that Muslims are somehow more violent and ferocious than other subjects. The distinctions between Hui and *min* in criminal law were subtle but real indicators of prejudice on the part of the Board of Punishments and its magistrates. The first statute directed specifically at activities by Muslims dates from

82. Zhu's memorials may be found in the collection *Qingdai wenziyu dang* (1938), cited in Ma Ruheng, "Cong Hai Furun," 8–12.

83. The edicts may be found in the Qianlong *Shilu*, and are cited by both Ma Ruheng and Leslie, *Islam*, 128, from which this translation is taken.

Qianlong 27 (1762), demanding that Muslim *jiaozhang* (religious professionals) report any untoward activity in their communities and specify-
ing punishment for local officials who do not report *Muslim* criminal
acts.

The first case invoking this statute came at the end of that same year,
when a local Shandong official reported that Muslims, rude and brutal,
had formed a secret party to become bandits (Ch. *feitu*). He requested
severe punishment from then on for such "crowd-gathering collective
crimes." The Board of Punishments, with the emperor's permission,
approved banishing *Muslim* thieves found with weapons in groups of
three or more, with no distinction between leaders and followers, to the
southwest frontier regions as guards. Similar crimes by non-Muslims
would be distinguished by whether they had succeeded in stealing anything, and if so, how much, while leaders and followers would be
punished differently.[84] But official (and unofficial) assumptions about
the Muslims' fierce natures argued against making such fine distinctions
in cases involving Huihui, and the Board's discriminatory precedents
and decisions gradually accumulated.

Beginning in the 1770s the Qing annals contain reports of Muslim
street brawling, feuds (Ch. *xiedou*), and other forms of collective violence. Metropolitan officials became quite suspicious of Muslims in
general, so when the Board of Punishments received a Shandong report
of a murder case involving Muslims, they created a new Muslim-specific
statute. *Dou'ou* (brawling) was the category: If more than three armed
Muslims kill a person, the perpetrator should be punished under the
ordinary regulations, and the rest should be banished to the southwest
as guards. If they are not armed, then the sentence should be reduced
one grade, to one hundred blows and three years of servitude. If ten or
more are involved, even if they are not armed, and if someone is
wounded, they should be sentenced under the statutes for collective
armed brawling. These punishments are one to several grades heavier
than those meted out to non-Muslims for the same offenses.[85]

The trend was clear. The Qing state gradually created a body of law
that distinguished Muslims as a special category of persons who, if they
violated the criminal law, should be dealt with more harshly than others.
Strongly reminiscent of the discriminatory behavior we have seen in
Ming period officials, this prejudicial treatment helped to create an
atmosphere within the government ranks that militated against the im-

84. Kataoka, "Keian shiryō," 4, citing the *Da Qing lüli genyuan,* 64.
85. Ibid., 19, citing the *Da Qing lüli genyuan,* 83.

partiality proclaimed by the emperors. These regulations remained well within the Qing system of precedents, but their proclamation certainly demonstrated to Muslims all over the empire that they were to be treated differently by their magistrates. By the Daoguang period (1821–50) the substatute cited at the beginning of this section made perfect sense in its equation of *all* Muslim offenders with the most feared, most violent members of non-Muslim society, the fierce brigands of Anhui and Hebei. Reacting to increasing disorder, the Board of Punishments later added the bandits of Henan to the list.

Militarization and Local Violence

As a final factor in this history of external influences on mid-Qianlong Gansu, we must cite the violence that struck more and more Chinese locales during and after the 1770s. Much more obvious after the Qianlong emperor's abdication and the White Lotus uprisings (post-1795), the degeneration of local order had nonetheless already begun, as had the defensive, militarizing reaction of local elites and their self-defense associations.[86] The Wang Lun uprising of 1774 is usually held to have been the first major outbreak in China proper, though Turke-stani rebellions had taken place following the Qing conquest of Xinjiang in the 1760s, and the Muslim uprising of 1781 followed seven years later.[87]

China's elite has, for millennia, claimed a harmonious and peaceful character for Chinese society, a Confucian vision in contrast to the barbaric Others that surround it. Violence within the empire could be laid to the continuing existence of evil men and evil ideas, both of which could and should be extirpated by a virtuous state. Thus, even when its officials killed Muslims wholesale or created discriminatory statutes, the Qing state continued to claim that it need only do away with the "weed" Muslims and leave the good ones in peace. An alternative construction of outsiders, that of bestial and irremediably savage Others, could be used to justify full-scale interstate warfare (as against Galdan or the Makhdūmzāda *khojas*), but had to be tempered when conquered peoples became children of the emperor, their leaders made subordinate lords. Both of these views of social disorder blinded central and local officials to the multiple causes of local violence, to the complex combinations of antagonism among "different" people at the local level, feuding

86. Kuhn, *Rebellion and Its Enemies.*
87. Naquin, *Shantung Rebellion.*

within Muslim communities, and socioeconomic dysfunction that had begun to plague Gansu in the mid-eighteenth century.

No single innovation, invasion, or domestic development triggered the violence that rocked Gansu in 1781 and 1784. The Qing state's inept military reaction, eventual brutal pacification, and proscription of the Jahrīya (called New Teaching) took place in a context shaped in part by the changes described above. The conquest of Xinjiang, corruption of the Qing administration, legal discrimination against Muslims, and the gradual increase in violence in society at large all played their part in causing the outbreak led by Su Forty-three (Su Sishisan), which opened a sanguinary century and a half of killing by and of Muslims in northwest China.

4 / Strategies of Resistance
Integration by Violence

FIRST BLOOD IN THE 1780S

After the morning prayers, as I passed Ma Laichi's street, oh God! A crowd gathered against me. Taking long poles and short sticks and whips, they beat me, and the women stood in the doors and threw garbage. With God's help, not knowing how I found the courage and strength, I beat them one by one, broke their weapons, and defeated them. Thus the vengefulness grew deeper, for Ma Laichi's fourth son took a crowd to the magistrate and said we had set up a new teaching to deceive the people. The court decided against us, and I was dragged in and beaten forty strokes, while Ma Mingxin received three. As they beat him, the bludgeon split in two! . . . The next day after dawn prayers, I again went by Ma Laichi's street and cursed the people from one end to the other. The revengers said, "How can he be so bold?" and again went to court. The magistrate decided, "All should return to their native places."[1]

Khafīya vs. Jahrīya at Xunhua

After Ma Mingxin's return from "the west" and his successful campaign of conversion, Khafīya and Jahrīya adherents in "Salar country" (Huangzhong)—and elsewhere in Gansu—became rivals. The Muslims themselves and the Qing state called their altercations "religious disputes," and official documents record religious justifications for violence to bear out this judgment—vocalization of the *dhikr,* wearing of shoes at funerals, the length and cut of beards or mustaches, and other ritual minutiae, as well as the more generic but more serious charges of heterodoxy and deception. But these "religious" conflicts clearly had secular

---

1. Ma Xuezhi, *Zhehelinye daotong shi xiaoji,* cited in Yang Huaizhong, "Lun shiba shiji," 320–21.

causes as well. A wide variety of hot and divisive issues beyond the vocal *dhikr* compelled the two orders first to confront one another, then to seek redress from the local authorities: rivalry over the profits of religious institutions, establishment of control over converts to Islam, personal conflicts between lineages and individual leaders, and, as the Jahrīya history recorded, the boldness of young men bearding their "enemies" in their lairs and brawling in the streets.[2]

The confrontation between Ma Mingxin's and Ma Laichi's followers might well have been an ordinary event, just another gang war or feud in the complex shuffle of frontier history, had it not taken place among the Salars. The officials of Gansu feared Salar violence, as did many non-Salars who lived within range of Huangzhong, for their reputation as raiders had spread from the Gansu corridor to Shaanxi. This labeling of the Salars as inherently, genetically violent and ferocious had been done so often, in so many official documents and local discussions, that it came to be *known* as true (see plate 13).

The Salars' ancestors had migrated from Central Asia to China, probably during the fourteenth century.[3] The Chinese accounts of their journey, undoubtedly influenced by centuries of antagonistic hindsight, maintain that the Salars were cast out of their homeland for their violent behavior.[4] Isolated by the rough terrain from state power, the Salars earned a reputation for violence that belied their numbers, fewer than fifty thousand in the early twentieth century.[5] With a comparative eye

2. Elsewhere I have argued (unfortunately without sufficient care regarding words such as "ethnicity") that local feuding and street violence, almost always undertaken by young males, must be understood at least in part as a stimulating, enjoyable activity (Lipman, "Ethnic Conflict," 79–81). Michael Ignatieff, traveling in Croatia, found the combination of young males, guns, ethnicity (including religion), and alcohol particularly potent and dangerous in creating an atmosphere of murderous violence (*Blood and Belonging,* 3–5).

3. For a recent investigation of their origins, see Mi, *Salazu,* esp. chaps. 1 and 2.

4. Trippner, "Die Salaren," 241–76, esp. 241–50. According to a legend quite general in the sources, the Salars migrated eastward guided by a white camel and carrying a bag of Central Asian soil. They settled around Xunhua, where the local earth matched that in the bag, and the white camel transformed itself into a prominent white boulder.

5. Population statistics for the Salars, like those of any group in China, must be evaluated with great care. The *Xunhua ting zhi* of 1844, 4.28a-31b, gives 2,780 households for the eight main Salar communities on the south side of the Yellow River. This would indicate a much smaller population than the thirty thousand Salars counted by the newly established People's Republic in 1953. But there were five other Salar communities on the north side of the river, outside Xunhua Subprefecture, as well as many Salars residing elsewhere or living on the road. We also have no way of knowing how Salar identity, or any other ethnic identification, was determined in the 1953 census, not to mention the censuses conducted by the Qing and Republican governments.

on the Montagnards of Vietnam, the hillbillies of Appalachia, the Karen of Burma, and many others, we may surmise that we have received the flatlanders' view of the Salars, one thoroughly prejudiced against them. The Salars engaged in dangerous, low-status occupations such as long-distance trade by raft and caravan. Many of them settled far from the Xunhua region, and many joined the military. In sedentary, civil China, such professions and mobility sufficed to earn a people the reputation of being congenital bandits. Some Salars did prey on merchants, but their mobile, mercantile professions would have marked them as vagrants, if not bandits, whatever they might have done. We cannot trust the Chinese imagery, which would automatically type the Salars as uncivilized.[6]

As elsewhere among the Chinese Muslims, the local mosque constituted the core of the Salar communities, which were known as *gong*. The eight *gong* on the south side of the Yellow River and the five on the north all supported numerous religious institutions despite relatively small population and poverty. Xunhua County alone counted sixty-two mosques of various sizes in the early twentieth century.[7] Salars intermarried with other groups, including Chinese and Tibetans, and adapted in a variety of ways to their frontier environment. They wore the queue under Manchu rule, for example, but many of them successfully resisted footbinding. Physically they appeared to be a combination of all the northwestern peoples, as Joseph Trippner pointed out in the passage translated on page 18. To maintain their connections with their Islamic roots, and to tap wider commercial markets, the Salars allegedly established and maintained connections with Muslim Central Asia that were stronger than those of their Sinophone Muslim neighbors. Their religious tradition gave them motivation, their Turkic language gave them the necessary means of communication, and their far-ranging trade gave them greater opportunity.[8]

The Xunhua region, which most Salars called home, was a backwater

6. Trippner, "Die Salaren," 261. The late Rev. Claude Pickens, Jr., a missionary with long experience among Chinese Muslims, traveled to the northwest in 1936. In response to an early draft of this book, he wrote that he deplored the overemphasis on Muslim banditry, calling it a Han perversion of the truth. The Muslims had received this characterization, in his opinion, without earning it, victimized by ethnic prejudice and Han control over the written record.

7. Zhou, *Qinghai*, 185.

8. "Sara Kai oyobi Mōko Kaikai," 76. Arienne Dwyer, who has done the most extensive contemporary work on their language, informs me in a personal communication that the Turkic elements in the Salar language most closely resemble the Turkmen language, from west of Samarkand.

from a Chinese point of view, a frontier town with few eminent literati in its gazetteer and little but conflict to mark its history. Lying amid steep hills on the south bank of the Yellow River, the town had a subprefectural yamen (*ting*) and a small garrison. These represented the only state authority for miles around, authority over a mixed hill-country population of Tibetans, Salars and other Muslims, and Monguors, but very few Chinese-speakers.[9] What seemed to any sensible Chinese to be the back of beyond constituted a cultural homeland for the Salars, who had by the mid-Qing lived there longer than Europeans have lived in North America. When conflict arose among its diverse peoples, however, Xunhua became an unstable social, military, and cultural environment.

In harsh natural conditions, with potential enemies on all sides, none of the frontier peoples could have survived without a martial tradition, without both weapons and the skill to use them, and survive the Salars did.[10] We can hardly blame them, but we can also understand the development of stereotypes and fears among non-Salars who lived nearby. An anxious twentieth-century missionary summarized the local stereotype of the Salars, one he shared wholeheartedly:

> The geographic situation of [Salar] territory, adjoining as it does upon Tibet, enables them to engage in constant warfare with that people, and thus to nurture within them the fierce spirit of their forefathers. Word that the Salars are out upon the warpath will throw the largest Chinese trading community into a panic. It is commonly said that the Salars can only be governed by a Salar, and even for him the task is not always easy.[11]

We need not accept this stereotype at face value to understand its evolution or its power. The non-Muslim Chinese and other local peoples formed rigid images of some of their neighbors as brutal, warlike,

9. Monguors, or Tu people (lit. "indigenes, autochthones, people of this earth"), occupy much of the Huangzhong triangle. They live in lineage settlements. Their language, folkways, history, and ethnic interactions have been studied by Louis Schram, who lived among them for many years. Though biased in their favor, his monograph (*Monguors*) contains a wealth of information on the border region as a whole.

10. Arienne Dwyer's as-yet unpublished fieldwork indicates that the ethnocultural distinctiveness of the Salars is rapidly disappearing under the acculturative pressures of the Chinese-dominated state and both Chinese-speaking and Tibetan-speaking neighbors. She believes that their Turkic language, already replete with Chinese and Tibetan grammatical and lexical influences, will not survive another generation.

11. Andrew, *The Crescent*, 17.

uncivilized and predatory—in short, barbarous beyond rescue. The appearance of feuds, apparently based on ideological differences, among the Salars created a volatile atmosphere all over the province, for their very name evoked fearful images, and their armed affrays evoked a violent response from the state.

The Sufi combatants in Xunhua or Hezhou were certainly not planning the "great enterprise" of dynastic replacement or a political secession from Gansu, much less a *jihād* to convert pieces of the Qing empire into the territory of Islamic government. Rather, they sought local revenge on local enemies. Lacking any effective central authority within their own communities—a *qāḍī* to whom one side had recourse would have been rejected as heterodox by the other—both Old and New Teaching, as the Khafīya and Jahrīya were called in the reports of Qing officials and the diaries of local gentry, took their cases to the secular officials. They also took matters into their own hands, with young men beating each other in the streets, which called their conflicts clearly to the attention of the authorities.[12]

From Feud to "Rebellion"

The Khafīya as a religious order had not caused much violent feuding in Gansu until the establishment of the Jahrīya, Ma Mingxin's revivalist followers, who came to be seen as the destroyers of a once-stable social order. As demonstrated above, the Sufi paths were not merely religious collectives devoted to meditation but rather loci of loyalty for many types of social and political activity. Their internal cohesion and devotion to a single leader made it possible for them to mobilize passion and armed force against their enemies, in this case other Sufis. Twenty years of escalation culminated in 1781, when law cases and street violence between the competing orders brought the Qing authorities to Xunhua to investigate.[13] Learning more of the Jahrīya leadership and its apparently subversive activities, they arrested Ma Mingxin, who was not anywhere near Xunhua at the time, as the chief troublemaker, imprisoning him in Lanzhou. Xinzhu, adjutant general at Hezhou, was sent to Xunhua with Yang Shiji, prefect of Lanzhou, to round up Ma's cohort and end their threat to social harmony.

Some of the Salar Jahrīya Muslims, under the military leadership of Su Forty-three, met the two officials and their small company of troops

12. Yang Huaizhong, "Lun shiba shiji," 311–16.
13. Nakada, *Kaikai minzoku*, 88–89.

at Baizhuangzi. Obviously prepared for trouble, the Muslims had concealed their weapons and presented themselves as a welcoming party of Old Teaching adherents. When Xinzhu told them he intended to eliminate the New Teaching, Su and his men overpowered the military escort and killed both officials.[14] With this violent act, the internecine strife among Muslims became secondary, and "rebellion," as defined in Qing law, began. Not only had feuding among Muslims created intolerable social disorder, but even worse, officials—the local representatives of imperial majesty—had been murdered. The state's theory, and its own claim to legitimacy, demanded that Qing troops intervene quickly and violently to punish the miscreants who appeared to challenge central power.

The Muslims responded with violence of their own, and more of them became "rebels." This legal charge, combined with the widespread perception of the Jahrīya as heterodox, placed these particular Muslims in direct confrontation with the legitimacy of the Qing state, though the Salars had not initially intended to question that legitimacy. Their actions up to the attack on the government officials, and much of their strategy thereafter, aimed primarily at other Muslims, at the Khafīya, at their local enemies. In their own perceptions, to the extent that we can deduce them from their actions, by killing Yang Shiji and Xinzhu they were reacting to an outside threat—military intervention in their internal affairs and the threat of massacre against their *tarīqa*. In Qing eyes, however, the Salars under Su took a critical step when they killed officials—from being potentially subversive or heterodox Muslims to being rebels—and the echoes of that act lasted over a century.

To illustrate the power of folk memory in perpetuating fear and violence, and the extent to which the Qing state could engage to keep the peace on its frontiers, let us consider "The Ballad of Su Forty-three," collected by the ethnographer Wang Shumin, who accompanied Gu Jiegang around the northwest in 1937. The ballad evokes local attitudes toward the 1781 violence from a distance of over a century:

> Hush up, hush up, listen to me,
> From Xitou here comes Su Forty-three.
> Su *ahong* has Salars in tow,
> Ready to fight all the way to Lanzhou.
> Su *ahong*, he hasn't much brain,
> So he follows a teacher named Ma Mingxin.

14. *GNQSL* 18.47a–b.

Ma Mingxin, he's a really smart guy,
Has thousands of Salars ready to die.
Thirty-six hundred are ready for war,
But Su can't move without something more.
When cherry-tree leaves roll up like beans,
Su found Hann Number Two, it seems.[15]
Hann Number Two was smart as hell,
Going to help Su beat old Qianlong well.
Hann Two's wife was a very bright dame,
And she wanted her man to give up that game:
> Husband, you hear!
> And Su hear, too!
> You bug the Emperor,
> And he'll get you!
> You bug the man,
> That's a heavy crime!
> The moment he's mad,
> That's the end of your time!
> The emperor's men are as hot as the sun,
> Your Salars are a cloud on the run.
> As soon as the sun shines, the cloud is done.
> How many Salars are left there? None!
> As soon as the sun shines, the cloud is dead.
> Can't you get that into your head?![16]

Hann's wife appears to have been more aware of the consequences of attacking government forces than were her man or Su Forty-three, at least in this ballad.

Despite the threat of Qing retaliation, Su intended to punish the Khafiya for bringing down official wrath on the Jahriya and to rescue Ma Mingxin from unjust imprisonment in Lanzhou. From Xunhua, he led his two thousand Muslim troops rapidly toward Hezhou, where they invested the town, killing a number of Old Teaching adherents, Qing soldiers, and government officials. Not allowing the provincial military

15. The surname Hann, belonging to the leading families of the Salars, romanizes a Chinese character different from but homophonous with the ethnonym Han.

16. The ballad may be found in its entirety in Wang Shumin, "Qianlong sishiliu nian." It has been reprinted in several anthologies, including *ZYSCZX,* vol. 1, 802–19. Gu Jiegang included an assessment of the Muslim problem, in embryonic form, in his diary of his trip to the northwest, *Xibei kaocha riji.* His views on non-Chinese minorities within China may be found in Schneider, *Ku Chieh-kang,* esp. chap. 8.

leaders enough time to organize effective resistance, the Jahrīya Muslims secretly crossed the Tao River on hide rafts (Ch. *pifazi*) to besiege Lanzhou.[17] The authorities inside the city, reacting in haste and fear, brought Ma Mingxin onto the Lanzhou wall to show him to the besiegers. The Jahrīya adherents showed Ma immediate devotion and respect, despite his chains, so the Lanzhou officials recognized in him a subversive, a destroyer of the dynasty's sacred order. They took him down from the wall and beheaded him immediately. In their perception of the danger they faced, this action could be justified despite Ma Mingxin's lack of direct involvement with Su Forty-three's attack on Xinzhu and his men (see plate 14).

The "New Teaching bandits," as Qing officials had begun to call them, attacked the Lanzhou city walls but failed to make any headway. They lacked even rudimentary siege equipment or experience, and all of their military successes had depended on rapid movement rather than careful planning or positional battles. Determined on revenge against the evil officials who had murdered their *shaikh*, they barricaded themselves, perhaps one or two thousand strong, on the mountains south of the city. The Qing court, thoroughly alarmed at this sudden assault on a provincial capital, sent Imperial Commissioner Agui from the capital to "pacify" them. Unable to reduce the hillside stockades with his regular troops and burdened by the military incompetence of his colleague, Heshen, whom he sent back to Beijing, Agui called in the armed militia of the southern Gansu Tibetans, the Alashan Mongols, and the local Chinese garrisons, all nearby and endowed with a reputation for valor. Agui's multicultural army cut off the Muslims' water supply and eliminated them after a three-month siege, killing Su with all his Jahrīya followers in the final battle.[18] This success against the Jahrīya continued a longstanding Qing policy of using frontier people to control other frontier people.

17. These *pifazi*, a mode of transportation uniquely suited to the rapidly flowing rivers, bulky cargoes, and easily available materials of the northwest, have been the subject of much curiosity among foreigners and non-northwestern Chinese, nowadays appearing in many travel brochures and videos as a noteworthy tourist attraction of Gansu. For sources on their history, see Iwamura Shinobu, "Kōga jōryū." Both Moore, "Raft Life," and Köhler, "Die Bedeutung," offer excellent pictures of the rafts.

18. The copious memorials and reports regarding this bloody uprising and its repression may be found in *Qinding Lanzhou jilue*. Agui's participation is particularly noteworthy, and his own literary and official descriptions may be found in Nayancheng, *A Wenchenggung nianpu* (1813), from 22.43a, where the first emergency memorial from Lanzhou is reported, through Agui's final reports, ending at 25.18b. Some Sino-Muslim historians proudly note that none of the "bandits," as the Qing called them, surrendered, choosing instead to die heroically, while other scholars find this self-sacrifice for religion foolish.

This violence in 1781 provided motivation for further armed affrays, stimulating hatred against cultural or religious Others and desire for revenge on all sides. It also vividly illustrated real contradictions within the Gansu Muslim world. This war did not simply pit Muslims against the Qing state, against the Manchus or the non-Muslim Chinese, but also Muslims against other Muslims. Some Khafiya Muslims fought on the side of the government against Su Forty-three. Evidence of similar divisions among Muslims may be found in the annals of every subsequent conflict, an important advantage for the officials enforcing social order and an important caution for us to be very wary of the words Chinese scholars use to describe such wars: "nationality struggle" (*minzu douzheng*), "nationality righteous uprising" (*minzu qiyi*), and so forth. By essentializing peoples as *minzu* categories ("the Salar, Dongxiang, and Hui *minzu* battled the feudal Qing oppressors," etc.), such descriptions distort more than they explain, depriving the events of their contextual richness.

The Jahrīya's Revenge in 1784

After Agui's victory near Lanzhou and the elimination of Su Forty-three, Qing officials exerted themselves in locating and punishing New Teaching Muslims. Mistakes were made, including the transportation of Ma Laichi's third-generation successor, Ma Wuyi, and other Old Teaching adherents to the southwest as "New Teaching rebels." The "pacification" process made more enemies for the Qing, as local officials tried to impress the throne and their superiors with their assiduous prosecution of rebels and their allies. It should be no surprise that some Jahrīya Muslims who escaped the dragnet immediately began to plan revenge for the death of their *shaikh* (brutally murdered in Lanzhou), their comrades slain in battle, and their fellow Jahrīya adherents persecuted in the pacification process.

Under the leadership of Tian Wu, a Jahrīya *ahong* but not a Salar, they stockpiled arms, built forts, prepared banners, and gathered substantial food supplies to resist siege.[19] Tian's preparations centered in the highlands on the north side of the Wei River watershed and at Guyuan, in the barren valleys of northeastern Gansu, both far from Xunhua. Jahrīya

---

19. Saguchi Tōru, "Chūgoku Isuramu," 79–80; and Schram, *Monguors*, vol. 3, 64. For one perception of Tian Wu's vengeful motivation, see the *Ping Hui jilue*, an anonymous account of Muslim violence in the northwest written by a minor Gansu official, in *HMQY*, vol. 3, 12.

Sufism, anti-Qing sentiment (shared by some non-Jahrīya Muslims), and the desire to avenge Ma Mingxin combined to evoke a wide response in these particular Muslim areas, but not in others. Tian Wu's religious vocation and base area indicate that the Jahrīya organization extended well beyond Salar country by 1781. The Sinophone Muslim communities of eastern Gansu, more culturally Chinese than were the Salars, had also been deeply affected by the coming of Sufism and the fear that Qing reprisals against some Muslims would spread to all.

In 1784, three years after Ma Mingxin's death, Tian Wu and Zhang Wenqing, possibly a relative of Ma Mingxin's wife,[20] called for revenge and attacked local garrisons in eastern Gansu, geographically and culturally distant from the Salar country of the earlier uprising.[21] Tian was killed early in the fighting, but this upheaval grew even larger than Su Forty-three's and took the Qing several months and much expense to quell. Despite pious declarations that only the rebellious miscreants themselves would be punished, Li Shiyao nonetheless executed over a thousand women and children among the eastern Gansu Jahrīya adherents, earning yet another measure of long-lasting Muslim enmity.[22] Even the local chroniclers—staunch supporters of the state and the Qing-endorsed superiority of Chinese culture—noted that this massacre of the innocent stimulated the fighting spirit of the remaining rebels.

In the aftermath of this second victory over local Muslims, some Qing commanders realized that this outbreak of violence had been due, at least in part, to the ferocity of anti-Jahrīya violence three years earlier. Fukang'an noted that neither he nor the other Qing generals could actually exterminate the New Teaching, as they had been ordered to do, and that some Old Teaching Muslims, hearing rumors of anti-Muslim massacres, had indeed joined the rebels. To attempt a wide-ranging slaughter of Jahrīya adherents, or forced reconversion to the Old Teaching, would permanently alienate all the Muslims of Gansu, among whom were both good and evil people. He recommended a more lenient pacification than had been practiced in 1781.[23]

20. Local sources in Xinjiang, where Ma Mingxin's wife and daughters were sent in exile, record that her surname was Zhang, and that she came from the same town as Zhang Wenqing in Tongwei County (Wu Wanshan, *Qingdai xibei*, 40, n6).

21. The official compendium of campaign documents, authored primarily by Agui and his colleagues, the same group who succeeded against Su Sishisan, was published as the *Qinding Shifengpu jilue*. A secondary account may be found in Wu Wanshan, *Qingdai xibei*, 39–52.

22. An Weijun, *Gansu xin tongzhi* 17.3.

23. Wu Wanshan, *Qingdai xibei*, 50.

Despite Fukang'an's plea, the government again proscribed the New Teaching, by which it still meant the Jahrīya, and instituted heavy penalties against any Muslim participating in religious disputation. Not limiting pacification to the Jahrīya alone, the official pronouncements forbade all Muslims to build new mosques, convert non-Muslims to Islam, or adopt non-Muslim children. *Ahong* could no longer preach outside their own locales, a prohibition aimed at peripatetic Sufi missionaries.[24] Those crimes and their penalties, of course, applied equally to non-Jahrīya Muslims, but Khafīya adherents nonetheless continued to serve the Qing in many local capacities, and they obtained some of the lands confiscated from the families of the New Teaching "criminals." The Qing tried to suppress not Sufism itself, which officials could not comprehend, but the New Teaching, which had been identified as the instigator of violence.

Contrary to their intentions, Qing officials encouraged the Jahrīya by linking it so directly to subversion. Muslims dissatisfied with Qing rule gravitated to the militant suborder as to an underground movement. Its propagation continued, and its anti-Qing character, though no more inherent in its rituals than in those of the Khafīya, was reinforced by its proscription. The *ahong* who felt themselves responsible for the Jahrīya's cohesion and continued activity began to write covert collections of miracle stories in Arabic and Persian, describing and praising the *karāmāt* of Ma Mingxin and his successors. One such book by a Gansu *ahong* known as Guanli Ye, recently translated into Chinese by two young Jahrīya *ahong* and a well-known Muslim novelist, was used to transmit not only the suborder's traditions but also its *silsila,* which had to be kept entirely secret to avoid Qing persecution.[25] Despite the ban on their organization, Ma Mingxin's initiates found converts from Turkestan to Manchuria, and as far south as Yunnan, where many Gansu adherents were exiled (see plate 15).[26] This contrasts sharply with the other Gansu Sufi orders and suborders, which restricted themselves almost entirely to local activity and, as institutions, remained respectable in Qing eyes. The

24. Fletcher, "Naqshbandiyya," 34.
25. As noted above, Guanli Ye's entire text has now been translated into Chinese. Zhang Chengzhi, "Kakusareta Chūgoku," is a brief description and analysis of the text and its importance. The book's description of the Jahrīya *silsila* agrees with that of Aubin, "En Islam Chinois," though they give different Arabic names to the second *shaikh,* Ma Mingxin's immediate successor.
26. There have been many studies of the Jahrīya and its transmission after Ma Mingxin. All of them cite Shan Huapu, "Shaan-Gan jieyu lu," an oft-reprinted source, as an authority. The most important Euro-American version is Aubin, "En Islam Chinois."

Jahrīya's uniqueness as a transregional Muslim organization provided even greater evidence to Qing authorities of its menace to social order. Not until the founding of "national" Muslim institutions by Beijing, Nanjing, and other eastern Muslim "new intellectuals" in the twentieth century did Sino-Muslims have any noncommercial structures with so wide a range of activity.

These eighteenth-century wars should not be described as "ethnic conflict" or "Muslim rebellions" but rather as local feuds over both religious and secular issues, inflamed and polarized by heavy-handed state violence wielded by local officials terrified of the Salars' reputation, men who worried about their careers and their dossiers in the capital more than the lives of the subjects over whom they ruled. Since they would be blamed for disorder in the territory under their temporary control, the spread of the outlawed New Teaching beyond the Xunhua district caused them considerable anxiety, but neither they nor their non-Muslim subjects could distinguish clearly between "good" Muslims and "bad" ones except by membership in a "teaching." Some Muslims also had a stake in labeling some of their coreligionists as "the wrong kind of Muslims," and they regularly did so in court after Ma Mingxin's return from his pilgrimage in 1761. We can see how the complex of national policy decisions regarding the New Teaching, provincial malad-ministration, local religious and political rivalries, military officials over-zealous in their obedience to unenforcable orders, and currents from the Muslim west combined to begin a sanguinary history in Gansu, one that was to last more than a century and a half.

The Qianlong emperor himself was baffled by the northwestern rebellions. In a poignant letter to Fukang'an, he wrote:

> In this instance of the Muslim rebels under Tian Wu—how could they manage, without cause or reason, to collect a crowd, set a date, and rebel? Why would Muslims from far and near join up and follow them like sheep? I have pondered this over and over, and I examine myself to find the answer: In the decades since I ascended the throne, I have acted with great caution, not daring to allow myself the slightest arrogance or pretense. I have constantly attended to the people's sufferings. . . . As for Gansu, I have given exceptional relief—for the past many years I have not heard of floods or drought, famine or shortages, and never of the poor losing their homes, nor of bandits stirring up trouble, nor of local officials extorting or harshly accusing, thereby causing thieves to run amok and disturb the peace. Or did news of Li

Shiyao's investigations of Muslims leak out, so rebels could start rumors flying of [a government campaign to] "exterminate the Muslims" as an excuse to incite riots? I have thought of all these things, but
none seems to be the true reason. In the end, why did they rebel? We
must get to the bottom of this![27]

EVERY SIXTY YEARS A BIG REBELLION

These differences of religious faith led to constant conflicts between
Chinese and Moslems. (Chu Wen-djang)

The Muslim revolt in Shensi and Kansu was, however, not just a
religious movement. Like the revolt in Yunnan, the Tungan
Rebellion was a large-scale community conflict—the coalescence of
the persecuted mosque-centered communities for the purpose of
survival. (K. C. Liu and Richard J. Smith)

The Shaanxi Muslim uprisings were the inevitable results of the
Qing's reactionary oppression, religious prejudice, and harsh
economic exactions, all policies of feudal oppression; they were the
explosion of Shaanxi's social contradictions. (Chen Chongkai)

The Shaanxi-Gansu Sino-Muslim uprising was a struggle of the
people of the Hui *minzu* to resist Qing reactionary control, which
included opposition to the systems of feudal control and class
oppression and exploitation; most important, it was a struggle to
resist the Qing rulers' *minzu* prejudice and *minzu* oppression. (Wu
Wanshan)

This new Islam [the *xinjiao*], which started by disseminating Islamic
puritanism among Muslims, partly through the use of *jihād,* turned
into an extremist Mahdi movement which attempted to use *jihād*
(mainly against non-Muslims) to bring the millennium, and ended
up as a multifarious range of sects and sub-sects which, in effect, set

---

27. Wu Wanshan, *Qingdai xibei,* 48. The emperor disingenuously neglected to mention the financial scandal in Gansu that had only recently been cleaned up. He can hardly
have forgotten such a major law case, which resulted in the execution or severe punishment of dozens of provincial and local officials for some of the crimes he mentions here.

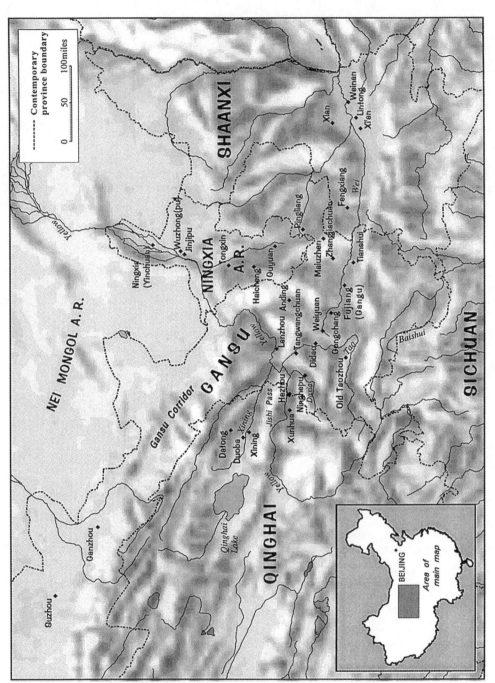

MAP 3. Area of the mid-nineteenth-century Muslim rebellions. (Map by Philip M. Mobley)

116

themselves apart from Islam and turned to ritual introspection.
(Raphael Israeli)[28]

Historiography of the Great Rebellion

The contemporary Chinese historical literature on the Muslims of the
northwest pays close attention to the violence of the 1860s and 1870s,
using two evocative and revealing vocabularies, one in the People's Republic, another in Taiwan. Self-consciously reversing the Qing officials'
language, *The Righteous Uprising of the Shaanxi Hui People, 1862–1875,*
recently published in Xi'an, employs the unassailably virtuous term *qiyi*
(righteous uprising) to define the moral quality of the Muslims' military
action.[29] In its analysis of conflict between local Muslims and non-
Muslims, the latter bear the heavy, judgmental appelation *dizhu tuanlian,*
"landlords' militia." The anti-Qing armies of the mid-nineteenth century
all receive approbation as antifeudal forces, but the Muslim rebels of the
northwest (and the southwest as well) carry the additional positive cachet
of being *minzu* heroes, fighting for the independence and unity of *all* of
the diverse *minzu* of China against Manchu hegemony. In this way
of thinking, the Manchus are defined as evil not because they are
Manchus—in the dominant *minzu* paradigm, that minority status
should carry a positive nuance—but because they are feudal, oppressive,
or incompetent.

In Taiwan, however, scholars employ a vocabulary entirely lacking
class and *minzu* terminology, as in the title of a recent monograph by
the late Gao Wenyuan, *The Anti-Qing Movement of the Northwestern Hui
People in the Late Qing.*[30] His list of "immediate causes" of the violence
includes a wide variety of political, economic, and social shortcomings
of Qing government, all covered by the PRC literature as well, but not
antifeudal class struggle or the depredations of "landlord" militias inspired by *minzu* hatred. In Gao's view Sino-Muslims acted against the
Qing as good Chinese, for morally sound reasons—the state's lack of

28. These epigraphs are taken from Chu Wen-djang, *Moslem Rebellion,* 4; Liu and
Smith, "The Military Challenge," 217; Chen Chongkai, "Cong Shaanxi Huimin," 52; Wu
Wanshan, *Qingdai xibei,* 144; and Raphael Israeli, *Muslims in China,* 204.

29. Shao Hongmo and Han Min, *Shaanxi Huimin.* This vocabulary, of course, does
not originate in the 1980s but descends from the revisionist work on structures of power
in traditional society, especially peasant rebellions, done by many twentieth-century Chinese scholars. It finds obvious expression in works such as Bai Shouyi's *Huimin qiyi,* the
compendium of primary sources compiled in the early 1950s.

30. Gao Wenyuan, *Qingmo xibei.*

virtue is clearly established—and the local anti-Muslim forces receive a negative judgment in terms reminiscent of Confucian historiography.

None of this is new, of course, in Chinese historical studies, for we have become accustomed (perhaps deadened) over the course of more than four decades to this contradictory cacophony of dueling paradigms presented in the secondary literature. In this particular case, however, neither set of historians highlights what might seem to Euro-Americans to be a crucial fact: the rebels were *Muslims,* and Islam may have played a role in motivating them. After all, we have been taught by years of Orientalist discourse to expect violence from Muslims, and all of the Chinese judgments of Islam and Muslims recounted in the previous chapters have included a proclivity for antisocial behavior. Raphael Israeli's book on the subject is subtitled "A Study in Cultural Confrontation," and in it he claims almost exclusively religious rather than contextual causation for Ma Hualong's uprising.[31] What role did religion actually play in this context? Are the historians of the People's Republic correct in seeing Islam as nothing more than one factor unifying the Hui *minzu* with its brother Muslim *minzu* against the feudal Qing? Are the Taiwan scholars justified in presenting nineteenth-century Muslim opposition to the Qing as a problem of imperial political virtue? Is Israeli correct to see Islam and the Confucian ideology of the Chinese order as inevitably and permanently incompatible and Islam itself as the primary cause of violence? We will pursue these issues here as we examine the most widespread violence in Sino-Muslim history—twelve years of bloodletting that devastated several provinces, left millions dead and homeless, and advanced the process of frontier incorporation that Gu Jiegang lamented as still unfinished in 1939.

Multifocal Rebellions: Shaanxi

The decades after the 1780s had seen no major Muslim actions against the Qing in Gansu, but during this time the widespread networks of Muslim traders and wandering religious professionals brought news of increased violence and agitation all over China, as well as specific intelligence regarding the Qing military's incapacities.[32] As we have seen, this period also saw subtle but marked discriminatory precedents emerge in

31. Israeli, *Muslims in China.*
32. C. K. Yang has studied the "mass actions" reported in the *Veritable Records* of the Qing for the years 1796–1911 and reports more than six thousand of them ("Some Preliminary Statistical Patterns").

the Qing criminal statutes. Dealing primarily with cases in Shandong, Anhui, Henan, and other central provinces, the Board of Punishments affirmed the general perception that Muslims are inherently more violent people than non-Muslims and thus should be punished more severely for the same acts. We have no evidence of Sino-Muslim reactions to these changes, but Muslims certainly knew that their "Huiness" would be a negative, perhaps even dangerous, attribute if they came before the Qing officials' bench.

After 1850, with the outbreak of the Taiping wars in the south and then hostilities between Muslims and the Qing in Yunnan, the atmosphere in the northwest grew very tense. Violence on a small scale—market brawls or intervillage feuds—became more and more frequent.[33] Qing civil administration, which had been shaky since before the 1781–84 uprisings, had not recovered. Corruption and official malfeasance, overwhelming taxation, neglect of the military, and confiscation of food supplies by local troops continued to plague both Muslim and non-Muslim residents of Shaanxi and Gansu.

Muslims suffered from social discrimination as well, enforced not only by the state but also by local security organizations, often organized by local gentry specifically to confront them. The militarization of society had proceeded apace all over the Qing empire, but in the northwest the non-Muslim *tuanlian* (militias) had an obvious target in the large local Muslim communities, who responded by forming their own armed bands. This process advanced most rapidly in the Wei valley of southern Shaanxi Province, where agriculture and trade supported a dense population that may have included as many as a million Muslims by the mid-nineteenth century. Most Shaanxi Muslims had not been persuaded to join Sufi orders, so their villages and urban neighborhoods remained Gedimu, mosque-based local solidarities connected to one another by the emotional ties of shared Islamic identity but not by any institutional bonds. Faced with hostile, armed non-Muslims, however, these Muslims did form multivillage associations for self-defense, and they constructed several series of stockades and fortified strong points on the hillsides north of the Wei River. The forts of the Fengxiang Muslims, for example, stretched "over a hundred *li*" in south-

---

33. Schram, *Monguors*, vol. 3, 66, notes a number of local disturbances, some of them sizable, in Huangzhong between 1859 and 1862. Communal relations had clearly deteriorated all over the region, and the vast violence taking place further east, with its consequent channeling of Qing coercive resources away from the northwest, had predictably stimulating effects on simmering local conflicts.

western Shaanxi. To no one's surprise, these forts and their armed young men came into regular, violent confrontation with non-Muslim *tuanlian* in the vicinity, but the Muslims never created any provincial or even regional leadership. Elites and their militias, like most people's concerns, remained almost entirely local, rarely extending beyond a few counties.

The most vicious battles took place in the southeastern part of the province in the early 1860s. Attested in local sources, these feuds alarmed local society in a number of counties and involved thousands of armed men. In addition, the years 1861 and 1862 brought outside forces to play a role in stimulating local conflict. Taiping armies moved north from Sichuan under Shi Dakai and from Henan under Chen Decai, and the western Nian threatened from the east, so friction increased in Shaanxi. Knowing the Qing's military ineptitude and inadequacy, Muslims and non-Muslims reinforced their stockades, and some Muslims made contact with the invaders as potential allies against the local non-Muslim *tuanlian*.[34]

Shaanxi was not the only locus of confrontation. All over Gansu as well, local leaders provided weapons to their followers and organized militias. Mosques affiliated with *menhuan* had especially effective networks of intelligence and supply, since their members could easily move between communities and their religious leaders owed allegiance to a single *shaikh*. The Sufi suborders could also concentrate economic resources effectively, for their members regularly contributed to the *menhuan*'s treasury. Without any central coordination, the

---

34. Wang Zongwei, "Qingdai Shaanxi"; and Zeng Liren, "Xi Nian jun." The role of the Taiping, Nian, or other non-Muslim rebellions in causing or stimulating or encouraging the northwestern Muslim rebellions has yet to be elucidated in a nonpolemical fashion. Fletcher, "Naqshbandiyya," 40, argues that the Taiping invasion of Shaanxi in 1862 touched off communal violence. Curwen, *Taiping Rebel*, 264, finds that the Taipings intended to take advantage of already-existing unrest. Jen, *The Taiping Revolutionary Movement*, 470–71, states that the Taiping general Chen Decai linked his army with rebels in Hanzhong, southern Shaanxi. The combined army, led by Lan Dashun, was to be responsible for the death of Dolongga in 1864. Li Xiucheng, however, in his deposition to Zeng Guofan's staff, said that the Taipings had not been in communication with the Shaanxi or Gansu Muslim rebels (Curwen, *Taiping Rebel*, 311). Work on the Taiping invasion of Shaanxi is now being done by provincial and local historians in China. See, for example, Wu Wanshan's explanation in *Qingdai xibei*, 65–66; he finds that the eastern Shaanxi Muslims had already planned to move against the Qing but used the arrival of the Taiping armies as an opportunity rather than part of a self-conscious alliance. His argument that anti-Qing rather than communal elements prevailed among the rebels ignores plenty of evidence of already-existing local conflict.

Gansu Muslims created no fewer than four large military regions, each controlled by charismatic religious and military leaders. Across the Yellow River from Ningxia, at the town of Jinjipu, the Jahrīya leader Ma Hualong made his headquarters. At Hezhou, Ma Zhan'ao of the Khafīya, both an *ahong* and a *tuanlian* commander, became the primary leader. Ma Guiyuan led the Muslim militias at Xining; Suzhou, out in the western Gansu corridor, saw an independent Muslim force take shape under Ma Wenlu. The connections among these centers consisted primarily of information networks, not any coordinating structure, and no historian has been able to document effective decision-making discussions among them, though Jahrīya adherents in all four owed loyalty to Ma Hualong. As we shall see, they met very different fates as local *xiedou* violence escalated into full-fledged military confrontation in the 1860s.

The initial local cause of the 1862–73 violence, according to Wendjang Chu, was a brawl over the sale of some bamboo poles at a Weinan County market. Other historians have discovered other accounts, all describing events that increased communal tensions. One author, for example, claims that a group of Muslims attempted to break into a non-Muslim theatrical performance toward which they had not contributed.[35] Reports from elsewhere in the northwest indicate that localized warfare, including conflicts between competing Muslim groups, occurred in many regions during those same years. News of these conflicts traveled rapidly via the Muslim trading networks as well as Qing official channels, increasing tensions all over Shaanxi and Gansu. The Xining area, for example, suffered from serious *xiedou* clashes that spring between competing Khafīya suborders, who had been feuding for several years.[36] In sum, the "rebellion" was an escalation of existing tensions in a variety of settings rather than a centralized, planned uprising caused by an explosion of new conflicts or contradictions from a single flash point.

All agree that violence of an unusually general nature erupted in the

35. Chu, *The Moslem Rebellion*, 25, mentions the bamboo poles. See also Mei, "Stronghold." As part of an important oral history project in southern Shaanxi, Ma Changshou collected many local tales and versions of "the beginning" of this violence (*Tongzhi nianjian*, esp. chaps. 1–4). The multiple incidents, local conflicts, and lack of Muslim central leadership in these accounts accurately represent the conditions in Gansu as well.

36. Wu Wanshan, *Qingdai xibei*, 114, reports violence among Muslims at Tankar, Bayanrong, and Xining, especially between adherents of the Huasi and Mufti *menhuan*, both suborders of the Khafīya.

Wei valley and spread with great rapidity in the spring of 1862.[37] The fighting did not follow any prearranged plan but rather ran along the roads and rivers that connected the Muslim communities, all of which reacted against the threat of attack by *tuanlian,* withdrawing to their forts or attacking non-Muslim villages. Southeastern Shaanxi has become known as the origin of rebellion both because of the arrival of the Taiping and Nian armies and because the Muslims of that area were able to kill high officials and gentry. Zhang Fei, a Hanlin scholar and formerly a high-ranking censor, came from Xi'an to Lintong to organize *tuanlian* and to persuade both Muslims and non-Muslims that the "national enemy," the Taiping army, was the main threat to social order. After ordering the local non-Muslim *tuanlian* to leave him unguarded and parlaying unsuccessfully with the two sides, Zhang and his party were captured by Muslims, taken to Cangtouzhen, and killed, making the local Muslims "rebels" in Qing perception and law.[38] Elsewhere the local non-Muslim *tuanlian* mobilized and struck first.[39] Generally the

37. Chu, *Moslem Rebellion,* is a study of government minority policy and the military strategy of Zuo Zongtang. With a similar perspective, Lanny Fields has studied Zuo's "statecraft" (*jingshi*) orientation in a useful book on the mid-century wars, *Tso Tsung-t'ang and the Muslims.* The best study of the official documents on the rebellions remains Nakada, "Dōchi nenkan." An English narrative, with some attention to the interaction of Zuo's policies and the Gansu environment, may be found in Liu and Smith, "The Military Challenge," esp. 211–34. All of these are solidly based in the primary sources, but Chu's book in particular contains errors of interpretation due to its national policy perspective, while Liu and Smith claim, without any evidentiary citations, that Ma Hualong's command network covered all of Gansu. Scholars in China cited above—Feng Zenglie, Wu Wanshan, Ma Changshou, Gao Wenyuan—and many others, including the dean of Sino-Muslim scholars, Bai Shouyi, have produced voluminous and detailed histories of these events. Primary sources include the massive official compendium of military documents, Yixin, *Qinding pingding Shaan Gan Xinjiang Huifei fanglue* in 320 *juan,* published during the Guangxu period; local gazetteers; collections of personal writings from Qing commanders and occasional Muslims; Mu Shouqi's *Gan Ning Qing shilue,* 20–24; Ma Changshou's oral history project, cited above; and accounts by local gentrymen in Shaanxi and Gansu. Many of the Qing sources are listed in Chu's bibliography, *Moslem Rebellion,* 207–19.

38. Chu, *Moslem Rebellion,* 25–27. Some of the primary texts may be found in Gao Wenyuan, *Qingmo xibei,* 191–203.

39. The geographical spread of the violence may be traced in the *Qinding pingding Shaan Gan Xinjiang Huifei fanglue* (see n37) and other contemporary sources. Shan Huapu has done a preliminary survey ("Shuo Shaan-Gan"). In areas of endemic conflict, we must assume that villages were organized over a wide area, constituting what Phillip Kuhn has called "multiplex *tuan,*" unless geography made complex structures impossible. Certainly many non-Muslim areas possessed subcounty military units, some with formidable stockades, against what they perceived to be a constant threat of Muslim violence

Muslim violence, not that of the semiofficial *tuanlian,* was held to constitute "rebellion," and local officials certainly perceived it within that
category of crimes.[40]

Faced with epidemic violence and murdered upper gentry, a series of
inept Qing commanders, including Yingqi and Shengbao, wavered as to
general policy: should they take a hard line and treat all Muslims as rebels,
or should they try to separate "good" from "weed" Muslims as their
theory demanded? Military contingency argued for the latter solution;
given the heavy demands on their military resources for fighting the
Taiping and other insurgents, the Qing could put only a few thousand
poorly armed troops into the field against an enemy potentially number-
ing hundreds of thousands. But the local non-Muslims, terrified of the
hideous violence of which they believed the Muslims to be capable,
demanded the former, an option known as "washing away the Muslims"
(Ch. *xi Hui*).[41] One source reports that unofficial "proclamations appeared declaring that all Muslims were 'to be killed without further
inquiry.' "[42] In these Shaanxi non-Muslims' eyes, their government could
protect them only by ending the Muslim threat permanently—by killing
all the Muslims or allowing the *tuanlian* to do so.

Policy options also divided the Muslims. Some commanders, fearing
the worst from the state and knowing the worst of the *tuanlian,* argued
for a full-scale strike against the provincial capital at Xi'an, to neutralize
resistance and force the Qing to pardon them and remove the potentially fatal "rebel" label. Others rejected this radical course and pleaded
for more diplomatic methods. In an atmosphere already rife with rumors of sanguinary deeds (some of them true) and intensified by the
alarms of many armed bands, the bellicose arguments carried the day.
Some dissenting Muslims were killed by their coreligionists, while others committed suicide in despair, and in late June the organized Muslim

---

(Kuhn, *Rebellion and Its Enemies,* 67–69). The possibility of "extended multiplex *tuan*"
seems somewhat more remote, given the lack of high-ranking gentry and the relatively
sparse resources of the northwestern countryside.

40. *Ping Hui zhi,* in *HMQY,* vol. 3, 61, relates that Zhang Fei threatened to accuse non-
Muslim militia of rebellion if they did not disperse, but this seems to have been extremely
rare.

41. We should certainly take note of this sinister name's resemblance to the "ethnic
cleansing" practiced in Eastern Europe and the former Soviet Union after 1989, especially
in former Yugoslavia. The sickening violence perpetrated in the name of local purity there
certainly found its match in northwest China during the 1860s, 1890s, and 1920s.

42. Ma Xiaoshi, *Xibei Huizu geming jianshi,* cited in Liu and Smith, "The Military
Challenge," 217.

tuanlian besieged Xi'an.[43] For over a year Qing troops from Shanxi to the east and Sichuan to the south tried to relieve the city. Fierce fighting between Muslims and Qing armies, with their non-Muslim *tuanlian* allies, took a terrible toll on both fighters and civilians. With the relief of Xi'an in the fall of 1863, and the relatively competent Dolongga leading troops westward toward Fengxiang, Qing victory seemed assured. But government troops remained too thinly spread across the province, and the anti-Qing Muslims counterattacked and remained in control of substantial parts of Shaanxi for five more years. Not until the defeat of the Taipings and the arrival of Zuo Zongtang as supreme commander, bringing his veteran Hunan troops and methodical logistics, could the Qing finally retake all of Shaanxi in late 1868.

In the meantime, the fighting had created a vast number of homeless Muslim refugees, of whom a majority fled westward to Gansu, where their "Eighteen Great Battalions," organized according to their native places and leaders, concentrated in eastern Gansu and sought to rebuild their strength until they could fight their way home. These military units remained the Shaanxi Muslims' institutional form and focus of loyalty for the remainder of the period of violence. In each of the Gansu centers, local Muslim commanders had to decide what to do about the Shaanxi refugees, who were both "us" (Muslims) and "them" (nonlocal, and often members of different religious solidarities). The Gansu leaders were unwilling to integrate the Shaanxi fighters and their many dependents entirely into their communities, so the Shaanxi Muslims came to constitute not only nuclei of resistance to Qing "pacification" in Gansu but also a contentious issue among Muslims. Their horrifying experience in Shaanxi and their vengeful, homeless presence in Gansu contributed to violence in many parts of that province, and their dispersal at the end of hostilities troubled the northwest for years. They never succeeded in forming any effective central command, remaining in eighteen units, whose manpower and then number gradually decreased as disease, warfare, and desperate conditions took their toll.

What began as a brawl, or series of brawls, became a succession of tragic massacres and flights. Literally decimated, the once large and wealthy Shaanxi Muslim communities never regained their position. The 1953 census found only fifty-four thousand Muslims in the entire province, far less than 10 percent of what the population had been a century earlier. The Xi'an community, a few thousand strong, escaped unscathed from the rebellion only by promising again and again, under

43. *Ping Hui zhi*, in *HMQY*, vol. 3, 62.

close military scrutiny, that they would not under any circumstances join the rebels.

Multifocal Rebellions: Gansu

In Gansu, with its more dispersed and much larger Muslim population, the Qing could not hope to inflict so crushing a defeat, nor had the Gansu Muslims any place to which they might flee. The rest of China offered no refuge, nor did Turkic-speaking Xinjiang appear an attractive alternative to most. Qing commanders and policy makers differed on the extent of violence necessary to pacify the Muslims, and in the end they treated each center differently, depending on the resistance offered, the military options available, and their perception of the Muslims' motivation. After "pacifying" Shaanxi in 1868, Zuo Zongtang turned his attention first to Jinjipu, the well-defended headquarters of the Jahrīya under Ma Hualong, spiritual descendant of Ma Mingxin.[44] Ma Hualong had engaged not only in battle but also in negotiation with provincial and national government forces over the years since 1862; he had surrendered on at least one occasion and taken a new name, Ma Chaoqing (One Who Attends upon the Qing). On that occasion, Mutushan, the Qing general at Ningxia, had beaten his more militantly anti-Muslim rival general Duxinga in a policy debate over accommodating the Muslims, and he had accepted Ma's surrender. The court, hoping to avoid the high costs and difficult logistics of a frontier war, believed Mutushan when he claimed that Ma's proposed surrender was sincere. Zuo Zongtang, among others, sided with Duxinga. On the Muslim side, rather than quietly returning his troops to their farms, Ma Hualong had instead continued to strengthen his base, building a wider circle of defensive fortifications around Jinjipu and actively aiding the Shaanxi Muslims in their attempts to return to their homes by force.

When Zuo Zongtang finally solved his financial and logistical problems, through a combination of careful planning and foreign loans, he sent three columns into eastern Gansu in 1869, converging on Ma Hualong's headquarters. Overcoming strong Muslim resistance and two mutinies within Qing ranks, Zuo's generals reached Jinjipu with

---

44. The Qing continued to refer to the Jahrīya as the New Teaching throughout this period, and they saw it as the main disruptive influence in the northwest. Zuo and his superiors debated whether to proscribe it, allow it to exist under strict controls, or treat it like any other Muslim group. A relatively liberal policy prevailed over Zuo's objections, and the Jahrīya was not forbidden.

their Krupp siege guns in September of 1870 and forced Ma Hualong's surrender in January 1871.[45] At Zuo's insistence, the entire leadership of the Ningxia Jahrīya, including Ma Hualong and as many of his family as could be captured, were executed following the siege, and thousands of ordinary Jahrīya adherents were massacred during "pacification." As we will see, Zuo never succeeded in exterminating the New Teaching, but he certainly did try, by strenuous argument in letters and memorials and by one-sided violence after Ma Hualong's surrender.[46]

Neither Muslim defense nor Qing suppression followed this same course at Zuo's next target, the frontier entrepot of Hezhou, a Muslim-dominated trading town lying between China and Tibet.[47] The most important rebel leader at Hezhou, Ma Zhan'ao, was certainly not an anti-Qing holy warrior. Like Ma Hualong both an *ahong* and a general, he was head of the Huasi *menhuan*, associated with Ma Laichi's Khafīya. Ma Zhan'ao managed to preserve his political prerogatives and his territory by astutely handling Zuo Zongtang. After seizing Hezhou in 1862, he had established a stable base for antigovernment activity or, as the Muslims saw it, a haven for protection against the hostile Qing order.[48] Though Zuo prepared his campaign against Hezhou in 1872 with great care and stockpiling of supplies, he could not overcome Ma Zhan'ao's carefully positioned troops in the Taoxi triangle.[49] The Qing armies crossed the Tao to fight the crucial battle around the town of

45. These mutinies are generally believed to have stemmed from the activities of the Gelaohui, a secret mutual-aid society that played a major sociopolitical role in Shaanxi, Gansu, Sichuan, and Henan throughout the nineteenth and early twentieth centuries. Many of Zuo's troops were Gelaohui members, so when he garrisoned the northwest, the secret society extended its influence all the way to Xinjiang through migration and troop movements. See Yang Zengxin, *Buguo zhai wendu,* 2nd (*yi*) collection, 3.1a–5a, which describes the presence of the Gelaohui from the Xinjiang provincial governor's point of view. A secondary account has been published by Kataoka Kazutada ("Shinkyō no karōkai").

46. Zuo's apparently contradictory analyses of the causes of the rebellion—that it was the fault of the non-Muslims and that it was the fault of the New Teaching—can be reconciled if we recognize that he had different audiences and different purposes as he described the rebellion to his staff, to his superiors in Beijing, to members of his family in letters, and to posterity in reports written for the permanent record.

47. Here again I use these terms not in reference to nation-states or other "legitimate" authorities, but rather to describe cultural zones.

48. Yixin, *Qinding pingding Shaan Gan Xinjiang Hufei fanglue,* 83.7b, notes that when Ma Zhan'ao took over Hezhou at the beginning of the disturbances in the early 1860s, he aided local Qing officials in their escape from the town, doing his best to protect life and property.

49. On Zuo's logistical preparations, see Chu, *Moslem Rebellion,* chap. 4.

Taizisi late in that year, and the Muslims drove the government troops back on the river, then out of Taoxi, killing several commanders and retaining complete control of their territory and supply lines. Though the waters of the Tao may not have run red with blood, as one missionary reported, Zuo's legions fled before the Muslim counterattack.[50]

Had Ma Zhan'ao been a separatist fanatic, as the typical Muslim leader is often portrayed, he surely would not have behaved as he did after this battle. While still mopping up the Qing remnants in Taoxi, Ma sent his own son to Zuo's field headquarters at Anding to propose immediate surrender of Hezhou.[51] He declared his loyalty to the Qing and his willingness to aid the imperial armies in further campaigns against any rebels, including Muslims. Ma's effectiveness in dealing with the Qing and protecting his own community may be demonstrated by his influence on Qing policy in the wake of the fighting. As Zuo Zongtang shuffled surrendered Muslims from place to place in Gansu, following He Bi's seventeenth-century recommendation that the Muslims be isolated, he undertook the reduction of conflict near Hezhou by moving the non-Muslims away. This happened nowhere else in northwest China.[52] After the surrender Ma Zhan'ao executed local Muslims foolish enough to disagree publicly with his decision to ally himself with the Qing state.[53] For his loyalty and subsequent success in campaigns against "rebellious Muslims" at Xunhua and Xining, he received the feathered cap of the fifth rank (Ch. *hualing wupin dingdai*), a token of prestige and merit requested for him by Zuo Zongtang.[54]

---

50. Andrew, *Crescent,* relates a complete Muslim victory. Lattimore, *Inner Asian Frontiers,* cites the Russian scholar V. Shakhmatov, who agrees. Other sources that confirm this account include at least one Republican-period local gazetteer from the region, *Chongxin xian zhi* of 1926, 4.50b, and Tian, "Longshang qunhao." For extensive primary source citations, see Gao, *Qingmo xibei,* 293–309.

51. Zuo's first meeting with his victorious enemy's son impressed Zuo sufficiently that he renamed the young man Anliang, an abbreviation of *anfen wei liangmin,* "making peace for the good people." Even decades later, Ma Anliang reminded his own violent and rebellious son of the meaning of that name—their family, beginning with Ma Zhan'ao, had determined to build a safe haven for Muslims in Gansu, with themselves leading the elite under a Qing and then a Republican state aegis (*GNQSL* 29.23b–24b).

52. See Chu, *Moslem Rebellion,* 150; Liu and Smith, "The Military Challenge," 234.

53. *GNQSL* 24.9a–10a.

54. Ma Zhan'ao has not fared so well at the hands of PRC historians. In time-honored fashion, they judge (*pingjie*) him severely for his collaboration with feudal forces. Though approving of his surrender, for it saved tens of thousands of lives, they find him and his descendants to have become willing servants of the oppressors and the founders of the exploitative, semifeudal Ma family warlords. For a succinct statement of this judgment, see Li Songmao, "Qing Xian-Tong."

His army buttressed by the newly recruited Hezhou Muslims, Zuo Zongtang turned his commanders toward Xining. Though his ultimate objective lay in opening the road to Xinjiang through the Gansu corridor—which meant dealing with the Muslim-held fortress at Su-zhou—Zuo calculated that Xining's strategic position south of the road, and the large number of Shaanxi Muslims who sheltered there, argued for taking that major city first. Well protected by its mountains and rivers, Xining held out against Zuo's commander Liu Jintang for three months but fell in the late fall of 1872. The gentryman Ma Guiyuan, who commanded the Muslims, was captured in Salar country, and thousands of armed Muslims were killed. But Zuo did not mete out severe justice to the Xining Muslim community itself. Rather, he arranged for the resettlement of the surviving Shaanxi refugees, as he had done after Jinjipu and Hezhou, on arable lands distant from other Muslim centers, mostly in eastern and southern Gansu.

Finally free to recapture Xinjiang for the Qing, Zuo's forces faced the last Gansu obstacle at Suzhou, a heavily walled fortress astride the main highway through the Gansu corridor, defended by a large number of Muslim commanders from all over the northwest. Ma Wenlu, who held highest local authority, came originally from Xining, and many Shaanxi Muslims had joined his banner. As in his previous campaigns, Zuo moved cautiously, assuring his supply lines and sufficient ammunition for his German siege guns by reinforcing Lanzhou and establishing an arsenal there. By September of 1873 Suzhou was entirely cut off from the east and surrounded by fifteen thousand Qing troops under Zuo's personal command. Ma Wenlu surrendered on October 24, his walls battered by heavy shells and undermined by tunnels and explosives. The next month Zuo ordered and oversaw the execution of *seven thousand* Muslims, most local but 1,500 of them from other Gansu and Shaanxi communities. This number surpassed those executed when Meng Qiaofang took the same city from Ding Guodong in 1649. To guarantee that the Gansu corridor would remain open and unthreatened, Zuo removed the few surviving Muslims from all the cities and towns in the corridor, from Lanzhou to Suzhou, and resettled them in southern Gansu: "Their seed will no longer remain in these three prefectures, and one need not worry about collusion between Muslims inside and outside the Chia-yü Pass [Jiayuguan]."[55]

55. Cited in Liu and Smith, "The Military Challenge," 235. Though Qing policy makers had worried about collusion between Gansu and Xinjiang, the Shaanxi and Gansu anti-state forces and actions were overwhelmingly local throughout the nineteenth cen-

Thus ended the "great rebellion" of the northwestern Muslims, in total defeat. As we have seen, it actually consisted of multiple rebellions, local in both personnel and outcome, and its objectives, as far as we know, had never included toppling the government or setting up an independent Muslim state.[56] The flight of the Shaanxi Muslims, the only connective tissue among the various rebellious centers, did not create or enable any unified leadership. The Shaanxi Eighteen Great Battalions were forced to be outsiders in Gansu, and they never found a home until Zuo Zongtang resettled their remnant survivors by force after his victories.[57] One Shaanxi Muslim commander, Bai Yanhu, held his refugee force together and retreated from one Gansu Muslim refuge to another, fighting all the while, then fled after the Xining debacle to Xinjiang, where he joined with several Turkic-speaking Muslim leaders to continue the anti-Qing fight. He ended his days under Russian rule, west of the Pamirs, and his followers are numbered among the ancestors of the Dungan "minority nationality" of Kyrgyzstan.[58]

tury. Xinjiang's various rebels, most of them Turkic-speaking and well connected to Muslim centers west of the Pamirs, rarely made any connections with their predominantly Chinese-speaking coreligionists east of Hami.

56. That objective, attempted only once in a Chinese-speaking part of China, belonged to Du Wenxiu and his "State that Pacifies the South" (Ch. Pingnan Guo) in Yunnan, an entirely different environment in which Muslims rebelled against the Qing in the 1850s and 1860s. Only a few direct links have been conclusively documented between those two Muslim anti-Qing movements, though a large literature on the Yunnan rebellion has been produced by Chinese, Japanese, and Euro-American scholars. A recent doctoral dissertation from Sweden makes an important contribution to the sociocultural background for a study of the Yunnanese Muslims (Wang Jianping, "Concord and Conflict").

57. Chu, *Moslem Rebellion,* 149–56, describes and tabulates the resettlement program.

58. A large literature on Bai Yanhu and his Shaanxi band's long flight has been produced in both China and the former USSR, and Svetlana Rimsky-Korsakov Dyer has done linguistic and ethnographic work on the Dungan in the Central Asian republics. Bai was not the only anti-Qing Sino-Muslim commander to flee to Russian territory, but he is certainly the best known. In the judgments of contemporary Chinese historians, the Muslim rebel Bai Yanhu and the victorious Qing general Zuo Zongtang share an ironic juxtaposition. Zuo Zongtang's brutal victory over the "righteous uprising" of the northwestern Muslim peoples certainly makes him a supporter of reactionary, exploitative, corrupt Qing power, but his recovery of Xinjiang from the separatist Muslim leader Yakub Beg earns him positive evaluation as a reunifier, a restorer of China's legitimate authority over eastern Turkestan. Bai Yanhu, on the other hand, began in Shaanxi as a righteous rebel, stayed that way throughout his legitimate wars in Gansu, then became a much more problematic and negative presence by supporting the separatists in Xinjiang and then— greatest sin of all—fleeing the homeland into Russian territory. Clearly, the Xinjiang Muslims' separatist movements and the Shaanxi-Gansu Muslim uprisings take very differ-

Muslim Rebellion or "Muslim Rebellions"?

The above narrative, schematic and rapid, can nonetheless inform our discussion of Muslims in China by challenging a number of paradigmatic constructions: the unified *minzu,* the fanatical Muslims, the rational and statecraft-practicing Qing officials, even notions such as "rebellion" itself. For none of these is a natural, inherent quality of persons or events; rather, we must use the evidence to describe what people did—that is, we must construct narratives—and modify our paradigms and vocabulary accordingly. To take one dramatic example from this complex series of events, let us consider the Muslim militias of the Wei River valley. Conscripted by their communities for self-defense, armed and drilled, provided with fortifications both physical and ideological, these young men could have had a wide variety of motivations to attack a nearby non-Muslim village. Were they simply ordered to do so by manipulative, fanatical *ahong?* Did they lust after loot or violence for its own sake? Or had they heard reports (true or not) of massacred Muslim villages down the road, of *tuanlian* on the rampage, of Qing armies raping and pillaging? Were they predatory or protective, rapacious or terrified, or did they change over time? These questions can be answered only through the construction of focused narratives on the basis of local evidence, not by wholesale, essentialized characterization of religious groups, *minzu,* or other collectivities.[59]

These conflicts, like those of 1781 and 1784, pitted Muslim and non-Muslim Qing loyalists against Muslim (and occasionally non-Muslim) insurgents, righteous rebels, or rioters (depending on the historian's vocabulary).[60] "Muslim unity," a concept dear to scholars, missionaries,

---

ent places in this historiography. Ma Tong, the most senior scholar of Sino-Muslim studies in Gansu, visited Bai's descendants in Kyrgyzstan in 1991 to investigate the dual charge that Bai had treacherously betrayed China by joining Yakub Beg's separatist movement in Xinjiang and that he had also intended to help imperial Russia invade China. He found both allegations unfounded and now maintains an entirely positive evaluation of Bai's anti-Qing movement (*Gansu Huizu shi,* 95–97). Bai Yanhu presents no problem at all for Taiwan-based Gao Wenyuan, who unambiguously regards Bai's long-term, uncompromising, peripatetic struggle against the Qing as heroic (*Qingmo xibei,* 407–24).

59. Elizabeth Perry analyzed armed peasant groups in Huaibei, Anhui Province, using precisely this method, and discovered fundamental differences between bands that were protective and others that were predatory (*Rebels and Revolutionaries*).

60. Zhu Chongli, "Tongzhi shiqi," reminds us that though undeniably ethnoreligious conflicts dominated this period, instances did occur in which Muslims and non-Muslims cooperated against the state.

and many northwesterners when describing the Muslims, did not prevent numbers of Gansu Muslims from joining the Qing forces or siding with them. Such people found greater advantage in alliance with the state, and they did not hesitate to kill coreligionists. Wang Dagui of the Haicheng region, for example, fought effectively for the Qing and was awarded a cap button of the sixth rank (Ch. *liupin dingdai*). Local anti-Qing Muslims caught up with him during a counterattack in 1863 and killed him, with his entire family.[61] It would be comfortable to say that Old Teaching Muslims were loyalists and New Teaching Muslims rebels, but the evidence does not support such a contention. Though anti-Qing activism in northern Gansu (now Ningxia) centered in the Jahrīya, some of the most successful resistance to the Qing came from within the Khafīya and from the refugee Shaanxi Muslims, very few (if any) of whom were Sufis at all, not to mention adherents of the New Teaching.

Nor did Ma Hualong, fifth-generation holder of Ma Mingxin's position as head of the Jahrīya, oppose the Qing with the fanatic's lust attributed to him by most accounts.[62] Branded by the Qing as the main leader of this rebellion, Ma was not a secessionist, and he sought to protect his followers and his territory around Jinjipu, suing for peace when possible until forced to last-ditch military resistance. He often requested amnesties for various groups of Muslims and was reported to be treating non-Muslims well in the territory under his control.[63] Even according to official accounts of the campaigns against him, Ma initially had no desire to establish an antidynastic enterprise. He took no royal titles of office within his movement, though one of his Jahrīya subordinates did, under the influence of Taiping and Yunnanese rebellious styles.[64]

61. Wang Dagui is discussed at some length in Chu, *Moslem Rebellion*, 58–59, 65–66, and in the *Haicheng xian zhi* of 1908, 9.1b.

62. Aubin, "En Islam chinois," 524–28, lists the masters (*shaikh*s) of the Jahrīya in a chronological table, with their various appelations, dates, and the locations of their tombs. Ma Tong, *Zhongguo Yisilan . . . shilue,* 491, constructs a less detailed table.

63. Ma Shouqian, a senior historian at the Central Nationalities University (Zhong-yang Minzu Daxue) in Beijing, has evaluated Ma Hualong positively, despite his status as an elite Muslim landlord and *ahong,* because the anti-Qing struggle he led was fundamentally defensive in nature. Had Ma Hualong taken a separatist stand, like that of Yakub Beg in Xinjiang, he would certainly be viewed very differently by contemporary Chinese scholars ("Qing Tongzhi nianjian," esp. the final section).

64. Nakada, "Dōchi nenkan," 91–92, 133–34. Mu Shenghua *ahong,* of northeastern Gansu, chose to call himself the "king who pacifies the south and restores the Ming" (Ch. *pingnan fuming wang*), recalling the multiple Taiping kings, Du Wenxiu's Pingnan Muslim state in Yunnan, and the desire to restore the Ming, which had motivated so many anti-Qing rebels (Ma Chen, "Mu Shenghua").

Jihād, Islamic "holy war," has held pride of place in Euro-American thinking about Islam since the Crusades. A vision of fanatical hordes unafraid of death has dominated our perceptions and prevented a clear understanding of wars fought by Muslims. Literally "effort directed toward perfection," *jihād* became a general term for military action by Muslims to expand Islamic territory or, if need be, to defend it. The idea of a war to convert Qing territory into Islamic territory could almost never be entertained by a Sino-Muslim leader, as compared to Turkic-speaking Muslims in Xinjiang, who often did declare *jihād* against the Qing. Indeed, virtually all of the Shaanxi and Gansu Sino-Muslims, as we have seen, shared a strong sense of *belonging* in China and of the Qing state's legitimacy. *Shengzhan* (lit., "sacred or holy war"), the Chinese translation of *jihād,* came to mean self-sacrifice for Islam, a call to heroism rather than political domination.[65] Muslims in Shaanxi and Gansu engaged in *shengzhan* not to topple the state but to attack local officials, to take revenge on local enemies, or to defend themselves.

The bloodshed and sacrifices of Ma Hualong's stubborn defense of his main base at Jinjipu might well have been avoided had Zuo Zong-tang or his superiors in Beijing been willing to talk peace with the "fanatical Muslim rebel," as Mutushan had done. But Zuo was pressed for victory, imbued with the monolithic Confucian conception of impe-rial authority, and convinced that the New Teaching lay at the root of Gansu's troubles. He foiled Ma's attempt to surrender to Mutushan and threw army after army at Jinjipu, determined to set an example for all rebellious frontier peoples. In light of this evidence, Zuo Zongtang appears as much a fanatical defender of his faith, the Qing imperium and its bureaucratic Confucianism, as Ma Hualong was of his Jahrīya and his territory.[66]

Neither the creation of negative images of Muslims nor the usefulness of such images to the Qing state should surprise Euro-American histori-

65. *Encyclopedia of Islam,* rev. ed., vol. 2, 538–40. The expansion of Islam's territory at the expense of non-Islamic territory is seen by Raphael Israeli as a primary motivation for Muslim rebellion in China ("The Muslim Revival," 121–23), but I find no evidence for this assertion in the Chinese record or in the scattered statements from the rebels. *Jihād* as a formal legal concept has not been demonstrated in any primary sources from China; rather it seems to be part of a complex of images of Islam—partially Middle Eastern, partially Orientalist—transported to China. *Shengzhan,* on the other hand, meant a reli-giously sanctioned war, an "us" vs. "them" communal war, not *jihad* in its legalistic Islamic sense.

66. For Zuo's ideology and politics in the context of Qing period *jingshi* activism, see Fields, *Tso Tsung-t'ang,* passim.

ans. Lacking texts from the Muslim side, we cannot rely on evidence manufactured by self-serving military officials to deduce Muslim fanaticism. Such tactics have long been a mainstay of official Chinese historiography when describing those who failed to achieve their goals in opposing the state—"A winner a king, a loser a bandit." We can read the sources carefully to comprehend the discriminatory, prejudiced filters through which Qing officials and local gentry viewed the Sino-Muslims and also search outside the official correspondence and military compendia for evidence regarding Muslim motivation and behavior.[67]

We must also remember that the flood of Shaanxi refugees into Gansu, driven from their homes amid slaughter and pillage, helped to keep anti-Qing sentiment alive in communities within which they settled. Jinjipu, Xining, and Suzhou sheltered large numbers of Shaanxi Muslims, and those areas became strongholds of anti-Qing Muslim bands. But even as they worked together to resist the Qing, the Shaanxi Muslims and the Gansu Muslims—including Ma Hualong's Jahrīya—viewed the conflict differently. According to one source, Ma Hualong tried to use the Shaanxi Eighteen Great Battalions as a front line of defense, protecting his northern Gansu troops and forts. Many Gansu Muslims mistrusted the outsiders, and Zuo Zongtang's lieutenants later summarized: "Ma Hualong was a New Teaching Muslim, holding to different religious objectives than those of the Shaanxi Old Teaching [in this case, Gedimu] Muslims, and they were mutually incompatible [lit., 'fire and water']."[68] Hezhou's Muslims, led by Ma Zhan'ao, successfully controlled the Shaanxi refugees' local potential for violence and thus placed themselves in an advantageous position to hold their territory after "pacification." Thus, the Shaanxi Muslims and the Jahrīya—not Muslims in general—provided crucial nuclei of resistance, and those two violently anti-Qing groups differed considerably in motivation. The Shaanxi refugees wanted to fight their way back home, while the Jahrīya adherents seem to have been moved deeply by commitment to

67. Ma Changshou, *Tongzhi nianjian*, presents new personal and local data germane to understanding the motivations for violence among both Muslims and non-Muslims in Shaanxi, county by county. Among the yet-to-be-mined sources for this rebellion, the depositions and confessions of captured rebels will certainly give us a much clearer idea of their organization, their motivation (as the rebels themselves presented it, under duress, before execution), and their behavior. Various provincial "literary and historical materials" series have also published reminiscences collected early in this century.

68. Yi Kongzhao, *Pingding Guanlong jilue* 7, in *HMQY* vol. 4, 8. For a general summary of conflict within Muslim communities and its relationship to Muslim uprisings, see Gao Zhanfu, "Guanyu jiaopai."

their *shaikh* and to Islamic revival, by the Qing's policy of proscribing their *tariqa* and exterminating them, and certainly by the desire to protect their homes.

Zuo Zongtang's lenient, even generous acceptance of Ma Zhan'ao's surrender stands in strong contrast to the brutality meted out at Jinjipu and to the massacre at Suzhou. Nakada Yoshinobu explains Zuo's benevolence as the result of several lines of reasoning. A campaign against Hezhou would have taken a long time, and Zuo's superiors looked to him for a rapid, inexpensive victory after the protracted battles in Shaanxi and northern Gansu. It had, after all, been almost a decade since the beginning of the troubles. Appeasement of the Hezhou Muslims, which could be made to look like victory, produced success and fame for Zuo without incurring high costs.

In addition, Ma Zhan'ao had volunteered to serve the throne, allowing Zuo to "use the Muslims to control the Muslims," a conventional and attractive solution to frontier problems. This variation on an ancient Chinese political theme saved lives and expense for the Qing commanders while preventing unified Muslim resistance to Qing power, a unity inaccurately predicted by Qing ethnography to be inevitable and permanent. Zuo exacerbated already-existing divisions among Sino-Muslims by supporting some groups and persecuting others, and by physically separating communities of Muslims from one another by large-scale resettlement. This strategy proved particularly effective in dealing with the Shaanxi refugees, who had become so intractable wherever they lodged. Zuo moved them to isolated Muslim enclaves in eastern Gansu—at Zhangjiachuan and Pingliang, especially—to prevent them from returning to their Wei valley villages. Their homes and fields in Shaanxi had already been taken over by local non-Muslims, and Zuo knew the refugees would demand satisfaction if they returned.[69]

Ma Zhan'ao had been willing to negotiate and had demonstrated no antistate, dynastic, or *jihād*ist ambitions, so his "rebel" status might be negated rather easily and made to appear temporary. Unlike Ma Hualong, who had been associated with the heterodoxy and long-term violence of the Jahrīya, Ma Zhan'ao led one part of what the Qing called the Old Teaching, which at this point included both the Khafīya, with its many subgroups, and the Gedimu congregations of both Shaanxi and Gansu. The Qing had blamed the entire northwestern debacle on

---

69. There seems no doubt that the Shaanxi Muslims' main desire was to *go home,* and that Zuo Zongtang's refusal to allow them to do so kept them fighting as long as they did (Luo and Wu, "Lun Qingdai," 81).

the New Teaching for almost a century. The active participation of an Old Teaching leader in anti-Muslim campaigns served to divide the Muslims further, to isolate the New Teaching more effectively, and to establish more firmly the "legitimacy" of the Old Teaching.[70] First as a rebel leader, and then as a "returned" loyalist, Ma Zhan'ao built an alliance between Muslim local elites and Qing authority in order to control local violence while retaining a measure of local power in the face of Qing officials and armies. Events after 1873 bear out the ironic observation that Ma Zhan'ao, by surrendering Hezhou, had preserved it as a territorial base for himself and his descendants, for the entire Hezhou region remained under the control of his family for another half century.

To Hezhou's northwest, the Xining Muslims had been engaged in local feuding with one another before 1862, and many Shaanxi refugees made their way across Gansu to this multicultural outpost to intensify already-existing tensions. Local Muslims knew that the Qing armies would follow the Shaanxi refugees as soon as they could mount a campaign, and controversy arose over the appropriate response to Qing oppression and violence. Despite feelings of loyalty and solidarity with their coreligionaries from Shaanxi, fear of the army and of local non-Muslim *tuanlian* hindered organization until the attack finally came. Once Liu Jintang's army started killing in the Muslim suburbs, whole communities lay open to massacre, however law-abiding they may have been. Official pronouncements to the contrary notwithstanding, Qing soldiers could not easily distinguish "good" Muslims from "weed" Muslims—troops do not take the time to make such subtle distinctions among civilians assumed to be armed and hostile. From immediate experience, the Muslims knew that they would be treated as enemies by the Qing military. Ma Guiyuan's small army held off the enemy for a few months, but he was defeated and executed by a coalition of government troops and local militia, some of them Muslims. Ma Zhan'ao's troops participated in this campaign on the Qing side, ensuring that the Salars at Xunhua did not join Ma Guiyuan's army. With the execution of Ma Guiyuan, the final massacre at Suzhou, and the flight of the remnant Shaanxi refugees under Bai Yanhu to Xinjiang and then Russia, the long violence in Gansu came to an end. The triumph of Qing arms has been attributed to the abilities of Zuo and his commanders, to the harsh terrain and scattered Muslim communities, and to the logistical and technical superiority of the Qing armies. We may now add one more

70. Nakada, "Dōchi nenkan," 150.

crucial factor: the Muslims did not act from any unified strategy, nor did they unanimously oppose the Qing authorities.

This interpretation of the 1862–73 rebellion helps us toward a new understanding of Islam in China, especially the Old Teaching–New Teaching conflict, and of Muslim relations with non-Muslims in Gansu. We find mutual fear, economic rivalry, and influence from the Taiping and Nian rebellions to have been important stimuli to violence, added to the state's corrupt, incompetent fiscal administration and its endemic suspicion of closed voluntary associations within Chinese society. This last motivation found expression in a continued demonization of the Jahrīya. Zuo Zongtang argued strenuously in government councils for complete proscription:

> The reason why the New Teaching must be prohibited is that it claims to be from God and makes ridiculous prophecies. This group's behavior is very strange and often lures foolish Muslims into willing slavery. The victims often are trapped into conspiracy without knowing how and are even willing to face execution without the slightest regret. . . . This makes the New Teaching a potential danger to the Empire. . . . [Ma Hualong] healed the sick and granted children to those who prayed for the birth of children. . . . When the New Teaching is eliminated . . . then Shaanxi and Gansu can expect to be safe for a hundred years.[71]

Zuo lost that political battle, and the Jahrīya recovered from the terrible devastation of Jinjipu, but not without changing both its behavior and its organization, as we will see in chapter 5. Some modern scholars have concluded that the New Teaching represented a decadent, corrupt form of Islam. In fact, as we have seen, it was part of an Islamic revival, a movement to return to Koranic purity through mystical unity with the divine and a purging of Chinese-influenced customs, but neither its doctrine nor its behavior were inherently anti-Qing.

An essential part of this Sufi faith lay in obedience to the leader of the order, in whose hands lay the power of initiation into the order and whose tomb provided individual and communal inspiration to his descendants and followers. Such leaders may be found all over the Muslim world, including the *darwish* of Turkey, the *pir* in India, the *serigne* of the Wolof, and China's *jiaozhu*. The extraordinary loyalty they inspired in their followers constituted an important element in their potential threat to Qing state interests. With China's long history of peasant

71. Chu, *Moslem Rebellion*, 157–58.

uprisings, rebellious sects, and millenarian movements very much in mind, officials reacted with extreme hostility to the activities of "heterodox" religious groups in times of social unrest. Voluntary association, always problematic in totalitarian states, became identified with subversion in the eyes of the Qing authorities.[72] In the nineteenth century the Jahrīya embodied structural and ideological characteristics that, seen from the Qing point of view, made it subversive even in times of peace and made Ma Hualong an intolerable menace, despite his willingness to negotiate and to protect non-Muslims under his control.[73]

We may thus conclude that religion did indeed play a role in the violence of mid-nineteenth-century northwest China, but it was neither a consistent nor a dominant role. Local economic, social, and political conditions certainly loomed large in the calculations of all protagonists, as did state policy toward the Muslims and Qing decisions on taxation, military preparedness, and local control. Like ethnic identity, religious identity can never be an absolute predictor of behavior, and in these alarms and clashes we see Muslims making a wide variety of decisions—some active, some reactive—in the face of a majority society and state they correctly perceived to be potentially hostile.

Islam did not *determine* the actions of the Shaanxi Muslim battalions, Ma Zhan'ao, or even Ma Hualong, but all of them acted inside frameworks of Muslim community and identity, which were different from those of their non-Muslim neighbors. Sometimes led by *ahong*, engaged in what they called *shengzhan*, answering a *shaikh*'s call to unified resistance, going into battle prepared for *shexide* (the Sino-Muslim transliteration of the Arabic *shahīd*, "martyrdom"), these Muslims do not seem to have been very Chinese. Yet, as we have seen, they *were* Chinese, like other anti-Qing rebels—fighting for the safety of their villages and families, reacting to a state authority to which they granted legal legitimacy as long as it did not attack them, fighting against the Qing or making local peace deals as they judged most expeditious or noble or

72. This subject, very much à la mode in Chinese studies of the 1960s and 1970s, is reviewed in Wakeman, "Rebellion and Revolution," which notes the scholarly conflict regarding the Islamic content of Muslim movements (p. 227).

73. The same may be said for the White Lotus, that complex amalgam of Buddhist and other folk organizations falsely conflated by Qing authority into an inherently rebellious, heterodox unity. For the Qing's reaction to White Lotus activism, see Overmyer, *Folk Buddhist Religion*, esp. chap. 5. A comprehensive analysis of the transformation of "White Lotus" from a religious to a sociopolitical construct may be founnd in Ter Haar, *The White Lotus Teachings*. The difficulty of analyzing such religious movements accurately is discussed in Esherick, *The Origins*.

safe. Therein lies the historical puzzle of Muslim "rebellion" in China, a puzzle we confront again in the 1890s.

EVERY THIRTY YEARS A SMALL REBELLION

[Hann] Nuri was a Xunhua Salar Muslim, leader of the Old Teaching at Gaizigong. He and the New Teaching adherent Hann Si accused each other over an old grudge and started a feud [Ch. *xiedou*].[74] Their contention was most turbulent, and could not be settled rationally. Governor-General Yang Changjun drew up an indictment and commanded the Xining prefectural office to hear the case, for Xunhua was in Xining Prefecture. Woshikeng'e presided, and both litigants followed correct procedure.

Nuri came to the prefect's court and deposed that the Old Teaching esteemed and loved the Koran and saw the New Teaching as a heretical doctrine. He cited many precedents as proof, talking with confidence and composure. . . . [He said that] the former governor-general, Zuo Zongtang, had held that Gansu Muslim rebellions' origins lay in religious disputes [between Muslims]. If religious litigations do not cease, armed conflict will be born. The roots of conflict are surely in the New Teaching.

[At the end of Nuri's deposition] Hann Si sensibly stayed silent, not saying a word. Woshikeng'e held that Muslim religious disputes were commonplace, and sent both litigants back to Xunhua, ordering them to settle their quarrel and feud no more.[75]

The New Old and New New Teachings

Is the above case not history repeating itself, as the Jahrīya and Khafīya go at it again?[76] On the surface, the case of Hann Nuri and Hann Si,

74. These two Hanns were not related to one another, as far as we know, and neither was a Han, that is, a non-Muslim Chinese. A number of families surnamed Hann held the position of *tusi* over the Salars under the Qing.

75. *GNQSL* 24.40a–41a.

76. The title of this section is not intended as a translation of any Chinese terms, though terms such as New-New Teaching (Xinxinjiao) and New-Flourishing Teaching (Xinxingjiao) do appear in Chinese texts. Rather, I intend to indicate that the entities designated as Old and New Teachings in 1895 were not the same as the Old and New Teachings of the 1780s or even the 1860s. That is, the terms have only contextual meaning, no absolute meaning, and must be examined carefully whenever they appear, to discover to what they might refer.

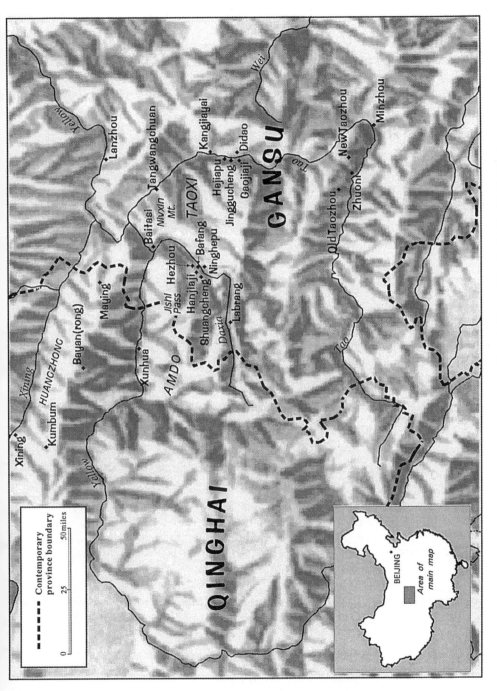

MAP 4. Center of the 1895–96 Muslim rebellions. (Map by Philip M. Mobley)

139

who is conflated with Hann Musa in some sources and called Hann Laosi in others, could have been adjudicated in the 1760s or 1860s. We find the same sorts of people (feuding Muslims) in the same location (Xunhua) suing one another over the same sorts of things (accusations of heterodoxy). But it was not repetition, for this case came before the Xining judge Woshikeng'e in 1894, and northwest China had undergone many dramatic changes since Ma Mingxin's time, as had the rest of the Qing empire.

In the almost two centuries since Sufism had made its first inroads among the Gansu Muslims, the *menhuan* had arisen as a dominant institution in many centers, especially Hezhou, Xining, and Ningxia, but also in smaller towns such as Didao and Xunhua. Saintly lineages that led Sufi suborders, the *menhuan* also constituted crucial loci of secular power, bearing strong structural resemblance to the corporate lineages that controlled local systems all over the Qing empire.[77] The division between "Old" and "New" at Xunhua stemmed from a power struggle within a single *menhuan,* for both litigious Hanns belonged to the Huasi *menhuan* of the Khafiya, which the Qing had called part of the Old Teaching. Nuri and Musa followed different leaders within their solidarity, and their *xiedou* involved not only currents of revivalism from the Muslim world to the west, as Ma Mingxin's and Ma Hualong's had, but also Zuo Zongtang's pacification of Gansu in the 1870s.

When Ma Zhan'ao surrendered after defeating Zuo Zongtang in 1872, his supporters included two brothers, Ma Yonglin and Ma Yongrui, who were *ahong* from the Huasi *menhuan*'s leading family, the descendants of Ma Laichi. Ma Yongrui had played an important military role in the 1860s, while his brother Yonglin had provided wealth to the cause through his commercial success. After "pacification" had been completed through the elimination of Muslim dissenters, Ma Yongrui retired in Hezhou, while Ma Yonglin continued as a leader in local politics and in the *menhuan*. Ma Yongrui's son, Ma Rubiao, followed his father and uncle into religious studies, and the story of the new New Teaching revolves around him.

Either through the influence of an Arab missionary named Selim who came to Gansu, or during his pilgrimage to Mecca, or both, Ma Rubiao became involved in the Shādhilīya, a Sufi order popular throughout the

---

77. Mary Rankin and Joseph Esherick have reviewed the literature and theoretical spectrum on local elites, especially in relationship to state power, in their "Concluding Remarks," in Esherick and Rankin, *Chinese Local Elites,* 305–45.

Muslim world.[78] Though not very different from the Khafīya of his ancestors, this new affiliation gave Ma Rubiao the impulse to reform his own *menhuan*, to purify religious practice and bring it into conformity with what he had come to regard as "pure" Islam. Returning from his pilgrimage, Ma Rubiao followed a familiar pattern; he gathered disciples, drawn by his charisma and that of his texts and reformist ideas, and split the Huasi *menhuan*. While Ma Zhan'ao lived, he was able to mediate between the reformist and conservative elements within the Huasi, but after his death in the late 1880s internal conflict over leadership, ritual practice, and finances spread from Hezhou to other Khafīya centers, especially Xunhua.[79] As the latest innovators, for so they were branded by their opponents, Ma Rubiao's reformist followers bore the condemnatory appelation of New Teaching, while his uncle Ma Yonglin led the Old Teaching resistance to change.

By 1887 *xiedou* had broken out between the rival Huasi factions at Xunhua, and the escalation of fear and violence began again. Given their ferocious reputation, religious feuding among the Xunhua Salars always represented danger to Qing officials, though in this case the initial impetus to conflict did not lie among the Salars but among the Sino-Muslims at Hezhou. As the troubles continued and lawsuits multiplied, the authorities all over the province grew more concerned about widespread violence. In the fall of 1894, as the Xunhua litigants argued in court, their followers fought it out in the streets of Xunhua, and Muslims were killed. The Hezhou commander Tang Yanhe decided to send Ma Yonglin and Ma Yongrui to mediate, since they held high status in the *menhuan* within which the *xiedou* were taking place. Eager to forward his antireformist cause within the Huasi, Ma Yonglin secretly encouraged Hann Nuri to attack the New Teaching, which he did, killing at least two *ahong*. Khafīya adherents also believe that Ma Yonglin knew that the Qing had severely depleted their northwestern defense forces in order to fight the Sino-Japanese War, and that he told Hann Nuri that there were no Qing armies west of Tongguan, in Shaanxi.[80] Following long-standing Khafīya custom, the New Teaching

78. Guan Lianji and Liu Cihan ("Yibajiuwu nian") hold that Selim's influence caused Ma's conversion; Gao Wenyuan (*Qingmo xibei*, 433) claims that Ma became a reformer on the pilgrimage; and Ma Tong (*Zhongguo Yisilan . . . shilue*, 238) writes that Ma took Selim as his teacher in Gansu, then went to Mecca and received initiation in the Shādhilīya.

79. Ma Tong's informants told him that Ma Zhan'ao favored the New, forcing Ma Yonglin to forego any public opposition to the reformists until after Ma Zhan'ao's death (*Zhongguo Yisilan . . . shilue*, 239).

80. Ibid., 240. Unfortunately for the Muslims and Gansu, this claim was false.

group sought relief from the Qing law courts, sending representatives to Lanzhou, where they accused both Hann Nuri and Ma Yonglin before Governor-General Yang Changjun.

Qing Action, Muslim Reaction

Xunhua. In the spring of 1895, Yang Changjun sent Chen Jiaji, a Xining military official, to Xunhua with a small military force and orders to end the troubles. By the time he reached Xunhua, Chen seems to have decided that Ma Yonglin and Hann Nuri's Old Teaching, the antireformist group within the Huasi *menhuan,* was responsible for the *xiedou.* He locked the Xunhua town gates against the Muslims who had gathered to present their cases to him, arrested eleven Old Teaching leaders, and had them executed, displaying their severed heads to awe the Salars into submission.[81] His troops fired on the protesting crowds from the walls, and the Old Teaching Muslims reacted by surrounding Xunhua, several thousand strong, on April 2, 1895. Thus began a year of warfare that devastated southern Gansu from the Tao River to Xining (see plate 15).

Chen Jiaji had acted in what he perceived to be a productive manner, punishing the destroyers of public order and parading the grisly results as a deterrent to further crime. From the Old Teaching Salars' perspective, their leaders had been unjustly slaughtered by an evil Qing official, and, for all they knew, they were next. From this point on, Chinese sources limit themselves to descriptions of troop movements, battles, strategies, and massacres. We must infer the personal and collective motivations of the belligerents (and the bystanders) from the extent of their participation.

Fearing that the violence might spread to other Muslim centers, Governor-General Yang planned a rapid military campaign to relieve Chen Jiaji at Xunhua. Within a few days of Chen's debacle, General Deng Zeng, who had participated in the wars of the 1860s, moved east from his base at Xining, and Tang Yanhe was to cross Jishi Pass from Hezhou to catch the Xunhua besiegers between two Qing armies. Before Tang even reached the mountains, however, he attacked several Muslim villages near Hezhou and announced that he would kill all Muslims, regardless of their *menhuan* affiliation or behavior.[82] Muslims

---

81. *GNQSL* 24.42b.

82. Guan and Liu, "Yibajiuwu nian," 48–49. Mu Shouqi also mentions proclamations, but narrates a different, probably apocryphal beginning to the violence. According

all over the province heard immediately and reacted to Tang's threat of massacre, so the Old vs. New Teaching controversy within the Huasi *menhuan* disappeared rapidly in the fear inspired by this brutal, publicly stated intention. Thereafter, the violence was no longer limited to the Old Teaching or the Salars, though it remained geographically confined.[83] Muslims in areas attacked by Qing troops had little choice but to oppose them. As in the 1860s, soldiers operating in hostile territory could hardly be expected to inquire as to the "good" or "weed" status of Muslims, all of whom they perceived as potential enemies. Yang Changjun tried to quell the fear with proclamations declaring Qing benevolence and demanding an end to the fighting:

> Initially the Muslims of Gansu were without religious conflict. From the early Qianlong period, the "Eat Befores" and "Eat Afters" arose [referring to the *qiankai-houkai* conflict]. With such theories came *menhu* [*menhuan*] and from *menhu* came conflict over power and profit. The religion divided Old from New, who accuse each other and take murderous revenge. . . . What good do all these rebellions do? . . . Immediately turn back and peacefully pursue your occupations![84]

Once Muslim leaders had been declared "rebels" by the state, it would be hard to imagine them believing any promises of Qing benevolence, with the memory of the 1870s still fresh and raw and Tang Yanhe's extermination order being enforced in local fact and general rumor.

Yang's proclamation encapsulated the perceptions of both the state and the local non-Muslims: Muslim violence, which they called rebellion, stemmed from conflict within the Muslim communities. Violence in society may not be tolerated, so Muslim internecine strife must be condemned, along with all institutions that appear to promote it, such as New Teaching and *menhuan*. If conflict occurs, the state *must* intervene, despite the antistate unity created by direct military interference in Muslim affairs. This dogmatic, straightforward analysis, reinforced by

---

to Mu's story, Yang Changjun unintentionally instigated the Hezhou violence by trying to save characters in his announcement. Instead of writing "Sa-la-er Hui," which unambiguously means "the Salar Muslims," he wrote "*sa* Hui," which might refer to the Salars or might mean "disperse and scatter the Muslims." Fearing the latter import, the Hezhou Muslims rebelled (*GNQSL* 24.44a).

83. Rijnhart, *With the Tibetans,* 58.

84. *GNQSL* 24.43a.

centuries of precedent, dominated Qing policy toward the northwestern Muslims, contributing to violence and tragedy.

The local non-Muslims, as frightened of the infamous Muslims as the Muslims were of them, locked themselves in their walled cities and stockades. They called for protection from the state and for extermination of the Salars. Over a century of violent confrontations and their subsequent exaggeration in oral tales had taught Gansu people that Muslims on the rampage, especially Salars, killed non-Muslims wholesale. The governor-general blamed the *menhuan,* solidarities that he perceived as subversive to the all-encompassing legitimacy of the Qing state. Christian missionaries, with their own particular vision of Islam and Muslims derived from the Middle East and Orientalism, theorized a *jihād* in Gansu. Seeing the Near East's holy wars mirrored in this distant corner of what they called the Celestial Empire, they misunderstood the workings of communal hatred and community memory in northwest China, the inertia of local feuding and thirst for revenge, and the ineffectiveness of the Qing government in preventing violence or stemming it once it began.[85]

Hann Nuri, knowing that he faced superior forces once the government mobilized, used the Muslim domination of the Yellow River to cross from Xunhua to the north side in secret. He surprised and defeated Deng Zeng's relief force moving south from the Bayanrong garrison, while Tang Yanhe's column from Hezhou was halted at Jishi Pass. Successful in blunting the first Qing attempts to subdue them in the spring of 1895, the Xunhua Muslims alone had neither the numbers nor the weapons to resist an onslaught by concentrated armies.[86] The diverse Muslims of southwestern Gansu all feared the ethnocentric wrath of the majority and the state, violently expressed by local militia and government troops, so the insurgents worked to convince other Muslims of the immediacy of the danger.

Hezhou. The largest concentration of Muslims lay at Hezhou, where Tang Yanhe commanded the garrison inside the walled city, while Ma

85. The late nineteenth century brought Euro-American missionaries to Gansu, and their direct observations enrich our understanding of the region, despite their clearly stated and consistent religious biases.

86. Despite the Sino-Japanese War, which was just ending back east, the Qing did have plenty of troops available in the northwest, apart from Deng Zeng, Lei Zhengguan, and Tang Yanhe's local garrisons. Yang was able to call upon forces under Dong Fuxiang from Xinjiang; the Muslim cavalry under Ma Anliang; Li Peiying from the corridor; He Jianwei from eastern Gansu; Wei Guangtao from Shaanxi; and Niu Shihan from Ningxia, all within the space of a few months (Wu Wanshan, *Qingdai xibei,* 244–47).

Yonglin and the Khafiya held sway in the Muslim suburbs, with their headquarters in Bafang, south of the city wall. Within Hezhou Prefecture only large settlements, such as the market towns of Hanjiaji and Tangwangchuan, had mixed populations; the rural villages were exclusively Muslim or non-Muslim. In peacetime travelers remarked on the delicious produce, delightful climate, and bustling markets of Hezhou, especially its Muslim suburbs. A wealthy borderland entrepot, the town attracted non-Muslims from all over China as well as Muslims of many languages and cultures.[87] Hezhou's Muslims paid great attention and devotion to their religious institutions. Like Naqshabandīs all over the world, Hezhou Sufis built tombs, some of them elaborate and large, to venerate their *shaikh*s and to seek their intercession. The various solidarities supported at least seven large tomb complexes, each with its prayer halls, as well as a dozen major mosques and many small ones. *Madrasas* in Hezhou sent graduates to Muslim communities all over China, and hundreds of religious professionals led the liturgy and read the sacred books.[88]

The Hezhou city wall was strong and easy to defend, but the suburbs, without walls, often fell victim to manmade disaster. If contemporary reports are to be believed, each victory for Muslim or non-Muslim was accompanied by slaughter among the non-Muslim, Muslim, Tibetan, and other civilians, for communal war never excludes noncombatants from its casualties. Despite commercial symbiosis and the intercommunity cooperation that it entailed, Hezhou had a sinister reputation as a center for heterodox Muslim movements and as a headquarters for Muslim bandits. The Hezhou Muslims served Gansu mothers as a bogeyman for disobedient children: "When I was a baby, whenever I wouldn't stop crying, my mother would say to me sternly, 'Don't cry any more! If the Hezhou Muslims hear you, they'll come and kill you!'"[89] By the late nineteenth century, as we have seen above, those Gansu mothers could draw on a century of violent memories to terrify their children and verify their fear of the Muslims.

The story of Chen Jiaji's murderous attempt at pacification of

---

87. Fan Changjiang, *Zhongguo de xibei jiao,* 90. Ge Chifeng's account of his visit to Taoxi includes oral evidence that many Hezhou people, Muslim and non-Muslim, came from Nanjing and still spoke a Yangzi dialect (*Zangbian caifeng ji,* 2). Studies of the wool and hide trade mention merchants from Shandong, Shanxi, and Mongolia purchasing and shipping goods from Hezhou. Li Wujin, "Gansu Linxia," gives a lengthy list of the Hezhou market's commodities.

88. Liao, "Gansu zhi minzu wenti," 86; and Ma Zikuo, "Musilin," 16.

89. Xu Wanli, "Cong Hezhou shuoqi."

Xunhua quickly reached Hezhou, as Tang Yanhe's local garrison moved out to break the Xunhua siege, so some Hezhou Muslims organized to defend themselves and to seek revenge against the state, especially after receiving news (or rumors) of Tang's intemperate proclamation that he would "wash away the Muslims." The sources tell us little of the recruiting procedures of these groups, but we know that local anti-Qing leaders rose immediately to the occasion. Chief among them was Ma Yonglin, who actively agitated for violence, resorting to terror against Muslims who resisted his appeals. Reluctant Muslims lost their homes to arson or their families to assassins.

Ma Zhan'ao had trained his son, Ma Anliang, who had gone to negotiate the surrender in 1872, to be both an administrator and a soldier, and Ma Anliang had gone to Xinjiang as a cavalry commander in a Gansu unit of the Qing military. In his role as a Qing military official, Ma Anliang earned the enmity of many Muslims. He led only one faction of the Huasi *menhuan,* and the others had good reason to complain of his access to state authority. Familiar with this local history, the anti-Qing Ma Yonglin sought and obtained the support of a leading Muslim named Min Fuying. Min's grandfather and father had opposed Ma Zhan'ao and rebelled against Ma Zhan'ao's local ascendancy in 1874, two years after the surrender. Their campaign had been brutally quelled, all of its leaders executed. Min Fuying, with many followers, joined Ma Yonglin in the hope of taking revenge on the weakened Qing and Ma Anliang for his ancestors' deaths.[90]

From his headquarters in Bafang, Hezhou's largest Muslim suburb, Ma Yonglin could persuade or intimidate the local people more effectively than could the distant Ma Anliang, clearly an officer of the hostile Qing armies. Perceptions of history, both personally experienced and orally transmitted, taught some Hezhou Muslims that violence did not discriminate clearly between friends and enemies, so they joined the rebels in self-defense. Others had learned, from the same history, that violent opposition to the Qing state brought only sword and fire down upon their homes, so they opposed Ma Yonglin. All Gansu Muslims, whether inclined to violence against the state or not, knew that local officials could attack them without warning. In an atmosphere of such insecurity and fear, being a Muslim could not in and of itself determine the choices any anxious resident of Hezhou might make. People decided to fight for one side or the other, not to

90. For the Min family's conflict with Ma Zhan'ao, see *Hezheng xian zhi* of 1930, 206 ff.

fight, or to flee for many reasons—personal relations with followers or leaders, personal histories of family loyalty, guesses as to who might win, and more. Ma Yonglin, for example, was apparently not yet ready to declare open rebellion against the state, so he continued to play the mediator in negotiations with the officials, a stance reminiscent of Ma Hualong's thirty years before. When Qing commander Lei Zheng-guan arrived at Hezhou with his forces from eastern Gansu, Ma Yonglin offered to be intermediary between the apprehensive local Muslims and the new garrison.

Despite superficial resemblance to earlier conflicts, the 1895 violence did not herald a much wider war, as the Wei River valley battles had in the 1860s. No flood of bitter, homeless Shaanxi refugees urged the Gansu Muslims to fight. No Muslim communities were uprooted, nor, with only one exception, did large numbers of Muslims move across the province to join the struggle. The bellicose Muslims of Xunhua, He-zhou, and Xining remained isolated from other Muslim centers. Though communication certainly did exist between Hezhou and Zhangjiachuan, the Haicheng/Guyuan region, and Ningxia, those communities did not share the immediacy of the threat felt in southern Gansu after Chen Jiaji's brutal warning to the Salars and Tang Yanhe's and Yang Chang-jun's proclamations. As we will see below, even the Taozhou Muslim community, southeast of Hezhou within the Tao River bend, had inter-ests sufficiently different from those of the Xunhua-Hezhou-Xining mili-tants that it armed itself in defense against them. In addition, the Jahrīya, the New Teaching of the 1860s, had changed to the point that its formerly militant centers in Ningxia, Zhangjiachuan, and elsewhere in eastern Gansu took no part in the fighting.

Haicheng. Shortly after the outbreak of violence at Xunhua and Hezhou, a jail break and flurry of military activity did occur at Hai-cheng, in eastern Gansu about 250 kilometers northeast of Hezhou.[91] On May 30, 1895, a band of one hundred Muslims attacked the magis-trate's yamen in Haicheng; killed the magistrate, his clerk, at least two women, and a servant; plundered the storehouses; burned the official buildings; and, perhaps most important, opened the jail to free Muslim

---

91. Haicheng lies at the south end of a broken, eroded loess plain stretching from Ningxia on the north to the Liupan mountains in the south. The population of this region (currently called Xi-Hai-Gu for its three counties), predominantly Muslim, was widely scattered across a landscape suitable for herding, with some poor agriculture in the loess valleys. The *Haicheng xian zhi* of 1908 gives the figures 8,489 Han and 39,051 Hui for the county, a total of 47,540.

prisoners.[92] The alarm spread rapidly, for the "rebels" (as they were immediately branded) had not bothered to cut the telegraph lines, so nearby officials heard immediately of this outbreak and declared martial law in several counties.[93]

Local militia under local leadership made quick work of this minor incident.[94] Not staying to hold the town for long, the escapees and their rescuers fled to Hezhou before the attacks of local *tuanlian* and Qing troops. Yang Changjun reported that the incident had lasted two weeks.[95] At least eight Muslims were executed, and many Muslim civilians lost their lives in the ensuing cleanup by Qing troops, undertaken with brutal inefficiency. The Haicheng incident revealed not a widespread Muslim conspiracy but rather the isolation of the Taoxi and Huangzhong fighting from other Muslim centers. There were no threats in other areas, no reactions even in nearby, heavily Muslim districts such as Zhangjiachuan or Guyuan. The response by Qing authorities in eastern Gansu indicates a *fear* of Muslim violence greater than actual Muslim capacity to act violently against the state or against local enemies outside of Taoxi-Huangzhong.

After reinforcing Tang Yanhe's garrison, Lei Zhengguan closed the gates of Hezhou in the face of Ma Yonglin's agitation in the suburbs outside the walls. His guards checked all travelers on the road through the east gate, the only one left open, while strong patrols held the walls opposite Bafang. The tension rose, and Ma Yonglin, Zhou Shixiang (also called Zhou Qishi), and Min Fuying finally led their armed followers to besiege the city on June 8, 1895. They wanted to join their banners to those of the Xunhua Old Teaching, but as a Muslim force approached Jishi Pass from Xunhua, *Muslim* troops, led by Ma Fulu and Ma

92. There are several accounts of the jailbreak and the subsequent Qing campaign against the Muslims: *Haicheng xian zhi*, 9.5b–6a, and the biography of Ma Yanqun at 8.12a; An Weijun, *Gansu xin tongzhi* of 1909, 17.94b; *Guyuan zhou zhi* of 1909, 4.37b; and several Western accounts, especially Rockhill, "The Dungan Rebellion," 414–18. Although the Chinese accounts do not agree on exact details, none claims that the "rebellion" at Haicheng was of more than minor importance. The Europeans inflate its significance. Mu Shouqi, *GNQSL* 24.47b notes that the yamen was guarded by a ferocious hound, which hated Muslims and killed one of the intruders.

93. *Chongxin xian zhi* of 1926, 3.3a; and *Zhenyuan xian zhi* of 1935, 17.37b. Guyuan, an important town near Haicheng, was reported to be in Muslim hands (*North China Herald*, Sept. 27, 1895).

94. The Haicheng gazetteer gives credit for the operation to a local martial arts specialist who had been an antirebel commander under Zuo Zongtang (*Haicheng xian zhi*, 8.12a).

95. Yang's victory memorial may be found in the *Guyuan zhou zhi* of 1909, 8.29b.

Guoliang, stopped them.[96] These commanders, brothers of Ma Fuxiang and Ma Anliang respectively, clansmen and forerunners of the Ma family warlords of the Republican period, clearly felt no sense of solidarity with the antistate activity of Ma Yonglin or the rebellious Xunhua Muslims. Their interests and loyalty lay with the dynasty, a choice their fathers had made that had served their families well.

Didao. Unable to unite with coreligionists to the west, Ma Yonglin and his allies looked eastward, to an alliance with the sizable Muslim community at Didao. Located on the east bank of the Tao, Didao controlled a vital ferry and floating bridge crossing between predominantly Muslim Taoxi and non-Muslim Taodong. The Muslims of Didao constituted about 10–15 percent of the town's people, and several suborders and *menhuan* had their headquarters there. The Hezhou Muslims did not attack Didao themselves, but rather persuaded some of the Didao Muslims to violence. The Mufti, a Didao *menhuan* that traced its leaders back to Hidāyat Allāh, responded by taking the *tuanlian* forts west of the Tao, crossing the river, and besieging the town. For Ma Yonglin, Didao constituted a crucial military objective. Its floating bridge gave eastward access not only to its own substantial hinterland, but also to the entire upper Wei valley. No forts guarded the mountain road from Didao to Weiyuan, so a successful crossing of the Tao would leave the valleys all the way to Tianshui open to Muslim attack.[97]

In addition to the Mufti militants, Ma Yonglin's supporters enlisted the aid of armed bands among the Mongolic-speaking Muslims of Hezhou's hilly eastern prefecture, the people now called the Dongxiang *minzu* by the Chinese government. Those Muslims numbered 150,000 in the 1953 census, far more than the Salars, but their villages lay scattered over a wider territory.[98] That as late as the 1940s many of these Muslims (who call themselves Santa) had not yet learned Chinese confirms their relative cultural isolation. Of their folkways we know little,

96. *GNQSL* 24.49b.

97. Erich Teichman reported the ease with which the crossing from the Tao to the Wei watershed could be made in the early twentieth century (*Travels of a Consular Officer*, 124–25). The entire upper Wei valley to Tianshui, or even beyond, would be open to a Muslim army that took Didao. That had happened in the 1860s, when Longxi and several other upper Wei towns were devastated by the Taoxi Muslims.

98. In 1941 the Chinese Communist Party reported only 20,000–30,000 Muslims in the Dongxiang. The reluctance of minorities to be counted, often due to fear that conscription and/or taxes would surely follow, may be responsible for the very low figure, which derives from oral and traditional written sources rather than a census (Zhongguo Gongchandang Xibei Yanjiushe, *Kangzhanzhong*, 278–79).

except that they treated Muslim guests with extreme politeness and had, according to Chinese sources, a fanatical loyalty to their local leaders.[99] A Japanese traveler noted that, unlike most Mongols, they did not drink any alcohol, indicating strong adherence at least to that prescription of Islamic law.[100]

Both widespread fear of violence from the Muslims of the Dongxiang and their reputation for lawlessness derived, at least in part, from their physical setting, in the poverty-stricken hill country east of Hezhou, west of the Tao. Their markets lay either at Hezhou or across the Tao on the "non-Muslim" east side. So in order to survive, they depended on the river crossings at Tangwangchuan and Didao. If the non-Muslims who occupied the east bank of the Tao closed the ferries and floating bridges, the people of the Dongxiang could not travel eastward for marketing or for seasonal work, on which they depended for income to supplement their meager hillside agriculture.[101] Much of the violence associated with these Muslims revolves around those crossings and the roads leading to them.[102] The extreme poverty of the hill country also played an important part in their "antisocial" inclinations.[103] We do not know to what extent their Mongolian cultural heritage or language divided them from Chinese-speaking or Turkic-speaking Muslims.

The gazetteer account of the battles around Didao contains further evidence that local Muslims fought local battles in 1895 and confirms the importance of the Qing monopoly of substantial walled cities in defeating Muslim attempts to seize the military initiative. Besieging a fortified city is never easy without artillery; the mobile, often mounted Muslim soldiery found it well-nigh impossible.[104] The inhabitants of Didao

99. Ma Zikuo, "Musilin," 15–16.
100. "Sara Kai oyobi Mōko Kaikai," 75–78.
101. Andrew, *The Crescent*, 32, describes the Salars and "Mongol Hwei-Hwei" of the Dongxiang, heading east with their families to work the harvest season on farms in eastern Gansu and Shaanxi.
102. Fu, "Taiping Tianguo," 7, cites stories from official sources of Muslim complaints against non-Muslims who closed the ferries or harassed Muslims trying to cross.
103. Ma Hetian saw the poverty of the people who lived on Niuxinshan (Oxheart Mountain) in the Dongxiang, commenting that these people were thieves primarily because they were incredibly poor (*Gan Qing Zang*, 15).
104. Note that the sieges of Xunhua, Hezhou, Xining, and Didao described in this section all failed to take the walled citadels. Herbert Franke concludes that "the comparative safety of towns, together with the wide area enclosed within the walls, always gave the defender an advantage over the attacker." This certainly held true for late Qing Gansu, where siege artillery was virtually unknown, except for Zuo Zongtang's Krupp cannon, and where strong fortresses were the rule. Indeed, even the Qing armies found it difficult

town could thus resist a Muslim attack, but the bulk of the non-Muslim population lived in smaller, less protected places, so the prefect requested funds from Lanzhou to raise local braves for resistance. The local gazetteer describes the Didao war, which lasted from mid-June into August, 1895:

> The Mufti rebels ... privately made banners and uniforms.[105] They arranged with Tongzhi period ex-rebels who had escaped punishment to entice thieves and bandits from the Dongxiang to attack Siwashan fort. Altogether they killed and wounded over six hundred Han. They united to force the Shikangcha and Songmingyai stockades, then they surrounded and attacked Jinggucheng [all on the west side of the Tao opposite Didao]. Xining and Hezhou were thoroughly alarmed at this time.
>
> On June 29 they crossed the river, gathering at the lumber mill. They surrounded the city for more than a month, not resting day or night and killing many. The prefect, ... the clerk, ... and local gentry ... did their utmost in defense, so the rebels failed. The rebels heard that General He Jianwei was coming to the rescue, so they cut the floating bridge and escaped in the night. When [He] Jianwei arrived, he ordered his army to advance and relieve Jinggu. The rebels besieging the town congregated at Gaojiaji. Then Imperial Commissioner Dong Fuxiang was ordered to advance over the river and attack the rebel horde at Gaojiaji and annihilate them.... [Qing troops] destroyed the *gongbei* and moved the miscreants to Yongdaojiazhuang, ordering that they not be allowed to resist the Han or again establish *menhuan*. The case was closed.[106]

The composition and outcome of the Didao uprising strengthened the Qing and local perception that *menhuan* and *gongbei* caused the Muslim

---

to take fortified Muslim strongpoints such as Duoba, near Xining. If a city were well defended and provided with food, only rapid breaching or mining of the walls, which had deteriorated in some cases, could prevent a prolonged siege that favored the defenders if rescuing armies were on the way ("Siege and Defense," 194).

105. The Mufti *menhuan*, descended via Ma Shouzhen from Hidāyat Allāh within the Khafīya suborder of the Naqshabandīya, did not naturally or invariably oppose the authority of the Qing state or make war on non-Muslims. Only a month before the 1895 violence began in Didao, Mufti adherents captured a non-Muslim bandit and conveyed him to the authorities for punishment (*Hezheng xian zhi* of 1930, 216).

106. *Didao zhou xu zhi* of 1909, 12.3b–4a.

troubles in Gansu. Both local and national Qing officials had numerous precedents for considering sectarian solidarities to be inherently danger- ous, especially when they espoused a religious ideology that could be branded subversive. Though Islam was not in itself anti-Qing, as the Qianlong emperor had declared, some of its forms could be and were construed in that way by hostile local authorities.[107]

Old Taozhou. Blocked to the east and north, the rebellion also could not spread to the south, where the large and wealthy Muslim commu- nity of Old Taozhou reacted to the violence by uniting with local non-Muslims, both Chinese and Tibetan, in defense. Old Taozhou lies inside the big bend of the Tao River, separated from the rest of Taoxi by mountains and a wide expanse of grassland occupied by seminomadic Tibetans. The town's economic life depended on the roads that led northward to Lanzhou, via Labrang and Hezhou, and southward to Sichuan and Yunnan. To the south and east, the Tao was unnavigable by manned craft, though some commodities such as lumber could be floated downstream, and only a tenuous floating bridge connected the north and south banks at Choni. To the west lay the towering Tibetan massif, culminating in Amnye Machin, a range twice calculated (incor- rectly) to be higher than Everest.[108]

Like Hezhou, Xunhua, Xining, and other towns in southwestern Gansu, Old Taozhou marks the Chinese-Tibetan ethnic frontier with a Muslim-dominated market, its Muslim community vulnerable between potentially hostile non-Muslims. Community-minded Taozhou Muslims supported thirteen mosques, thirty-one *ahong,* and five *gongbei* in the

107. The comparison of Chinese Muslims, especially those associated with the New Teaching (whatever that may have meant) in the northwest, to secret societies has been used for centuries by both military and civilian officials to describe what they see when they look at *menhuan* or other Muslim solidarities. See, for example, the Qianlong em- peror's opinion in the *Daqing lichao shilu* 1208.2. The analogy to the White Lotus sect is particularly germane, for the term New Teaching similarly became an epithet applied rather indiscriminately to Muslims who behaved rebelliously. See also Iwamura Shinobu, "Chūgoku Isuramu."

108. The botanist-explorer Joseph Rock, whose hyperbole was matched only by his ill-humor, wrote to the *National Geographic Magazine* (February 1930) that he had found a mountain range over twenty-eight thousand feet in height, surpassing the Himalayas. His measurements, which he later corrected in *The Amnye-Ma-chhen Range,* were inaccurate, as were those of Leonard Clark. An equally egotistical traveller, Clark repeated the error almost twenty years later while fleeing from the Communists with defeated Muslim and Tibetan troops and printed it in *The Marching Wind,* especially chap. 11. The mountain is spectacular; for photographs and an imperfect historical account of its exploration, see Rowell, *Mountains of the Middle Kingdom,* chaps. 11–12.

early twentieth century.[109] The various Taozhou ethnic groups felt Tibetan political influence much more than Hezhou did, for the headquarters of the Choni *tusi,* a Qing-appointed, hereditary Tibetan leader, lay only twenty-five kilometers away, on the bank of the Tao. Direct Qing power, exercised from Minzhou and the "new city" of Taozhou, also played a considerable role, so in Taozhou we find a truly tripartite world, one in which non-Muslim Chinese, Sino-Muslim, and Tibetan political and social forces coexisted or conflicted more or less in parallel, without complete domination by one group or another. Certainly both the Qing state and the Choni *tusi* could exert coercive power, but from a considerable distance, so the Taozhou peoples governed themselves by cooperation among local elites.

In general terms, the Old Taozhou communities performed different socioeconomic functions. The agricultural and pastoral economy lay primarily in Tibetan hands, though Sino-Muslim and non-Muslim Chinese farmers clustered around the market towns.[110] Like coreligionists all over Gansu, the Muslims of Taozhou undertook distribution of goods and marketing, including interregional trade. The local non-Muslim Chinese farmed and produced artisanal goods such as metalware and pottery. The Muslim gentry (Hui *shen*) of Taozhou, like Muslim elites of other Gansu towns, performed both secular and religious functions. *Ahong,* merchants, successful examination candidates, and military men all partook of this status. By the late nineteenth century, *ahong* were often landlords, merchants, or even local *tuanlian* commanders. Their interests thus included both loyalty to Islamic exclusivity and the very real benefits they derived from association with the Qing state and non-Muslim society.[111]

Physically and socially separated from Muslim centers to the north, delicately balanced between Qing authority to the east and the Tibetans

109. Liao, "Gansu zhi minzu wenti," 85.

110. Travelers reported that, despite the poor quality of the loessial soil, Taozhou peasants cultivated their terraced hills all the way to the top. Both Rock and Ekvall, especially the latter, describe the gradations of pastoralism and agriculture of the Tao valley and emphasize the cultural and economic symbiosis they found there (see Ekvall, *Cultural Relations*). During a field research trip to the Taozhou region (now called Gannan, southern Gansu) in May 1996, I gained the same impression of an intensely cultivated arid region. The hillside fields suffer from lack of water during the growing season, though they are eroded by the snowmelt in springtime.

111. Old Taozhou provides excellent examples of these multiple roles within the Muslim elite. The leaders of the Xidaotang solidarity, based in Taozhou, took all of them. See chapter 5. A typology of Muslim gentry in the mid-nineteenth century may be found in Fu, "Taiping Tianguo."

to the west and south, with nomads and mountains on three sides, the Old Taozhou Muslims had a strong vested interest in peace. Located in an ideal commercial middleman's position, they were correspondingly vulnerable in times of trouble. Their numbers were never sufficient to threaten the Tibetans, nor could they escape the Qing presence. Accommodations, not confrontation, marked their reaction to the violence at Xunhua and Hezhou in 1895. Banditry remained in check that summer, a sign of stable control by local gentry:

> In the fifth month of year 21 of the Guangxu reign period [June 1895], the Hezhou and Huangzhong Muslims rebelled. Dissatisfied elements among the Taozhou Muslims had started rumors, stirring up trouble and inciting disorder, taking a challenging position and wildly rampaging around. Wild stories circulated among the Han . . . who panicked and fled. People's spirits were agitated, and the markets were empty. But the Han and Muslim gentry . . . held to the correct way and did not fear.[112]

The multicultural gentry managed to keep control, despite the provocations of local rowdies. When a Hezhou Muslim led his fighters across the grasslands in pursuit of fleeing Qing troops, the gentry-led locals captured and executed him. Set in its defensive posture, Taozhou saw no major outbreaks of violence in 1895.

The Limits of Violence

We have now seen the spark of violence fall on Xunhua, Hezhou, Haicheng, Didao, and Taozhou in 1895. At Haicheng local troops quickly ended any threat from a large-scale jailbreak. At Didao the non-Muslim majority and Qing officials acted expeditiously, with the help of outside troops, to blunt a rebellious thrust by a local Muslim group (Mufti) and its Dongxiang-based allies. At Taozhou Old City nothing happened at all beyond rumors and local agitation, put down by the gentry. Only in Taoxi and Huangzhong, centered on Hezhou, Xunhua, and Xining, could the anti-Qing Muslims undertake concerted violence. Unable to take major cities, they either kept their forces moving or based themselves in smaller fortresses surrounding the Qing garrisons.

After his subordinates failed to relieve Xunhua, Deng Zeng himself led a column from Xining, via Bayanrong, in early June. The Salars

---

112. *Taozhou ting zhi* of 1907, 18.3b.

could not concentrate enough force on the north or west sides of their siegeworks around Xunhua to stop his column, which reached the town on June 12, ending the two-month siege.[113] Hann Wenxiu, who had emerged as a central Salar leader during the siege, fled across the river to the northern *gong*. Had Deng been able to continue his advance, catching the remaining Salar forces between Lei Zhengguan's Hezhou garrison and his own troops, he might have ended the Xunhua threat. But Deng realized that the violence could easily spread to his base at Xining, so he returned to Bayanrong rather than penetrate more deeply into rebel territory.

Back at Hezhou, Ma Yonglin and other anti-Qing commanders ordered continuous assaults on the city wall and on non-Muslim villages in the immediate hinterland. Throughout June and July small forts and stockades south of the city fell to the Muslims, who slaughtered the defenders in thousands and took their land. The Chinese chronicles extol the heroism of the defenders of Ninghepu (now Hezheng County), where seven corps of militia drove off the Muslim attackers, made some successful forays beyond their walls, and neutralized a large besieging force.[114] During July the Xunhua leader Hann Wenxiu brought his fighters to the Xining region and led them, with local Muslims, to take forts in the northern and southern valleys that converge on that city. From Didao to north of Xining, Gansu burned, but the rest of the province lay relatively quiet, except for the movement of Qing troops and supplies toward the disturbances.

Governor-General Yang Changjun planned to relieve Hezhou by using Tang Yanhe's army, still stationed south of the city, in conjunction with a sortie by Lei Zhengguan's garrison inside the walls. Tang, whose Muslim subordinates Ma Fulu and Ma Guoliang had held Jishi Pass against the Salars, moved north via Laoyaguan in early August. According to several accounts, Tang was persuaded by a promise to surrender and a bribe from Muslim leaders to remain at Shuangcheng for the night, where his army suffered an ambush and scattered in the face of the enemy.[115] Lei Zhengguan, shut up in Hezhou, could not move

---

113. *GNQSL* 24.48b.

114. The story of Ninghepu's resistance is in *Hezheng xian zhi* of 1930, 216–20. Mu Shouqi worried a great deal about the wisdom of arming the common people, for greater harm could come to them if they were armed. In addition, the enemy could provide himself with weapons by taking them away from the inexperienced farmers (*GNQSL* 25.9a). But the Ninghepu militia, organized by local gentry and defending their own homes with semiprofessional élan, made all the difference in resisting the Muslims.

115. *GNQSL* 25.6a–7a; Gao Wenyuan, *Qingmo xibei*, 437; Wu, *Qingdai xibei*, 243.

against the besiegers without the other half of the pincers, so the slaughter continued in the countryside.

Ma Yonglin and the other Hezhou Muslim leaders found themselves with two conflicting objectives. They needed to take Hezhou, consolidate their base, and eliminate the Qing armies and *mintuan* stockades that still threatened their local security. But they also needed to break out of Taoxi, either toward Xining or north and east, to find allies in other Muslim communities before larger Qing armies arrived to "pacify" them. In the end they achieved neither objective. Ma Yonglin did traverse the Dongxiang to cross the Tao in early August, but his invasion was easily turned back by Qing cavalry under the redoubtable Ma Anliang, who remained in the field to lead the Qing forces in counterattacking toward Hezhou. However deeply Ma Anliang may have felt solidarity with other Muslims, it certainly did not extend to Ma Yonglin, who had plundered Ma Anliang's home base.[116]

In August 1895 Dong Fuxiang was in Beijing as a Xinjiang representative at the empress dowager's sixtieth birthday party. Concerned about the Gansu violence and impressed by the powerful Manchu minister Ronglu's recommendation of the young soldier, the court sent him into the field once more against the Gansu Muslims. A central figure in northwestern politics and internationally known for his role in the attack on the Beijing legations in 1900, Dong Fuxiang has been confused with Deng Zeng,[117] erroneously called a Muslim,[118] and maligned by Europeans as an arch-criminal (see plate 16). He first gained prominence during the Muslim rebellion of the 1860s, when he and his father formed a group of local partisans to defend their home county, the son

116. Mu Shouqi records Ma Anliang's devotion to his father's pro-Qing stand, a position that caused him often to be accused of treachery by anti-Qing coreligionists (*GNQSL* 28.18a–18b). He was, however, successful as a mediator throughout his career, dealing with Muslim and non-Muslim elites all over the province, and he remained a popular leader among the urban Muslims, especially merchants in Lanzhou and Hezhou, who stood to lose by widespread violence.

117. Bonin, "Les Mahometans du Kan-sou."

118. Broomhall, *Islam in China,* 161, claims that Dong, though a Muslim, "because of some small personal pique, had sided against his co-religionists." This thoroughly incorrect information, coming from the Western world's most-cited authority on Islam in China, must give us pause to consider the quality of our sources! Tian, "Longshang qunhao," 3–14, is only one of several Chinese sources that unambiguously identify Dong as a non-Muslim. Teichman, *Travels,* 109, relates that Chinese informants told him that Dong was not a Muslim, but that he refused to believe them. The European press had so universally associated Dong with Muslim troops during the Boxer uprising that he could not credit a different version of the story.

finishing the war as a colonel in the Qing army commanded by Liu Jintang.[119] Ma Anliang, Ma Fulu, and other important Hezhou Muslim officers enlisted in Dong Fuxiang's army after Ma Zhan'ao's surrender, hoping for advancement within the Qing military and for social order with a measure of local autonomy for the Sino-Muslim elite.[120]

Coming from Beijing to eastern Gansu in 1895, Dong brought something new to the field against the Muslims, the greatly increased firepower of European small arms. Though Dong's troops had not been trained in the European fashion and still resembled the anti-Taiping armies of the mid-nineteenth century, they were armed with Remingtons and Mausers. Dong used these new weapons, vastly superior to the Muslims' muzzle-loaders, halberds, and swords, to great effect.[121] Never before had the Hezhou Muslims been forced to recognize the superiority of Qing arms. Their experience in the 1860s had led them to believe that the Tao River, the mountains of the Dongxiang, and their own mobile, stout-hearted cavalry would serve to block any invasion.

Dong's successes were not only military. He also used localist politics to halt a movement of Muslims from Ningxia to southwestern Gansu. This episode provides a measure of evidence for contact and cooperation among Muslims all over Gansu, but it must be examined carefully. It took place in the fall of 1895, around harvest time.

> When [Dong] Fuxiang arrived at Pingliang, . . . [two local literati] of Jinjipu came to welcome him there. Fuxiang asked them, "How are the fall crops?" They replied, "All harvested, with only the Muslims' fields yet unharvested." Fuxiang was surprised and asked, "Where have they all gone?" "Most of them have gone to Hezhou." Fuxiang said, "I shall send people to urge them to return home."
>
> After the gentry left, he commanded his clerk quickly to prepare a proclamation to be printed in thousands of copies. . . . In brief, it stated: "At the moment, Hezhou has rebelled and Xining reacted. I, the commander, have received the emperor's command to take forty

119. d'Ollone, *Recherches*, 272.

120. Tian, "Longshang qun hao," 4. While in Beijing, Dong Fuxiang had come to the attention of Ronglu, one of the empress dowager's favorite ministers. Their relationship led to the old empress's admiration for the Gansu army and its commander and her order that the northwesterners be brought to the capital region as part of her metropolitan forces during the Boxer crisis. Dong's connection to that powerful court faction would have enhanced both his reputation and his power in Gansu. See Xue Zhengchang, "Dong Fuxiang."

121. *GNQSL* 25.21a.

battalions of horse and foot [soldiers] to attack Hezhou and Xining. You have all listened to and been misled by rumors and run off, leaving your ripened crops to the birds. Hezhou is in the south, Ningxia in the north, as different as horses and cows. The court clearly differentiates good [people] from evil [people]. Could it possibly exterminate you all without exception? Within one month you must return, each to his farm, never again to be frightened out of your wits in this way," etc., etc.

He chose three of the corporals of the guard who were skilled in rhetoric and gave each a platoon. From Pingliang they went to Guyuan, posting copies of the notice as they went. At large villages, they would exhort people. . . . Those among the Muslim braves who returned to their homes were registered by name, age, and residence and the official list sent first to Ningling subprefecture. Then the provincial capital was notified. When Yang Changjun saw the Ningling report, which said that the Muslims from this district who returned from Hezhou numbered over ten thousand, he said to a provincial official, "Dong Xingwu [Fuxiang] has not even advanced on Hezhou yet, and Hezhou's flank army has disappeared."[122]

Far more effective than Yang Changjun's earlier warning, Dong's traveling lecturers actually thwarted the Ningxia reinforcements, returning them to their unharvested fields. They were frightened by Dong's army and reputation, giving up their expression of Muslim solidarity in the face of threatened Qing repression. The Muslims may also have been persuaded by Dong's evocation of localism, for he was a local man himself and would have chosen the most convincing arguments. This incident, evidence for Muslim intercommunity cooperation, nonetheless had no effect on the southern Gansu violence. Some combination of Dong Fuxiang's skill, Muslim fear, self-interest, localism, and perhaps religious rivalry prevented the northern and southern Gansu Muslims from uniting their forces against the Qing. The Ningxia Muslims made no further concerted efforts to aid the anti-Qing Muslims at Hezhou. Dong Fuxiang set up his headquarters at Anding, Zuo Zongtang's old base east of Lanzhou, and prepared to invade Taoxi.

His first objective was to cross the Tao and break Ma Yonglin's siege of Hezhou, relieving Lei Zhengguan's garrison. As Dong moved toward the river, the Hezhou besiegers renewed their efforts to take the city, for they could not concentrate their forces to repel Dong's invasion

122. *GNQSL* 25.12b–13a.

if Lei Zhengguan's Hezhou garrison remained in their rear. They failed. Beginning on November 17, 1895, Dong killed thousands of Muslims at Kangjiayai, crossed the Tao at Didao, relieved the siege of Jinggucheng, and struck across the Dongxiang. Ma Anliang's cavalry crushed Muslim resistance on the slopes of Oxheart Mountain and broke the Hezhou siege in a week of heavy fighting, relieving the town on December 4. Over four hundred Muslim leaders were captured and executed—Ma Weihan, the leader of the Mufti from Didao, died with Ma Zhan'ao's old subordinate Zhou Qishi, and Ma Yonglin's entire family suffered the extreme penalty. The Hezhou uprising, which had cost tens of thousands of lives and the devastation of Bafang, ended in a complete victory for the Qing state. With the Muslim general Ma Anliang in charge, the Qing could be sure of southern Gansu for the remaining fifteen years of its rule.

Xining. Like Lei Zhengguan's defense of Hezhou, the Xining garrison's successful resistance against Muslim besiegers kept another large Qing army intact and active deep in "Muslim" territory. Xining, like Old Taozhou and Hezhou, stands on the frontiers of several ecologies, cultural groups, and political-military powers, astride the main road between Tibet and Mongolia, a road crucial to the political and religious histories of both peoples. It lay at the western end of Qing administrative penetration into Amdo, and its Muslim trading community occupied the cultural middle ground between China and Tibet.[123] Xining's city wall, one of the most imposing in premodern China, towered over a wide plain at the confluence of three rivers. Its garrison could dominate both the local hinterland (Huangzhong) and the essential caravan routes that passed nearby.[124] If the Qing empire could control Xining, it could maintain its domination over the politics of Amdo, the region's

123. Again, I use these as cultural terms, not as the names of sovereign states or territories enclosed by boundaries drawn on maps by negotiators. Marco Polo, who passed through Xining on his way to the Yuan capital in the late thirteenth century, made careful note of the physical characteristics of the Tibetans who controlled the city at that time. He described the yaks and musk deer and reported "no lack of corn." He observed "idolators," by which he meant the Tibetans, as well as Muslims and Nestorian Christians in the town, a combination that was once again found in the late Qing when the China Inland Mission established a station there. The able missionary Charles Ridley made excellent studies and maps of the area, as did German Catholic priests who lived nearby. The studies of the latter are summarized in Eberhard, "Notes on the Folklore," 306–10.

124. The French priest Evariste Huc, with his traveling companion Joseph Gabet, made the journey from Kumbum, a great lamasery near Xining, to Lhasa in 1845–46. Their account, published in English as *High Road to Tartary,* contains vivid descriptions of Amdo.

communication with the Mongols, and the commerce of its highways. But the roads from Lanzhou and the Gansu corridor to Xining, the city's lifelines to the world of China, passed through several steep, narrow passes, places at which a small defending force could easily prevent passage by a much larger one, rendering the city's position tenuous in times of trouble.

Many aspects of Xining's socioeconomic life showed marked blending of Chinese and Tibetan ways. Xining Chinese built Tibetan-style houses, but local wedding customs strongly resembled those of China proper.[125] Despite their local accommodations, many Xining Chinese saw, and continue to see, the Tibetans as a primitive, inferior, uncultured people, separated from civilization by their barbaric character but useful as mercenaries and auxiliaries in frontier warfare. Xining floated on a sometimes restless sea of non-Chinese people, who put up with Qing (or any other external) hegemony to the extent that it profited them or the state could preserve its prerogatives with troops. Around the turn of the twentieth century many groups lived in significant numbers both in the suburbs and in the hinterlands— Chinese, Tibetans, Mongols, Monguors, Sinophone Muslims, and Salar Muslims. No simple mapping, however, could do justice to the intricate intermixing of groups throughout the region, for they often did not live in clearly delineated areas but rather in adjacent villages or neighborhoods.

Xining's high walls faced those of the Muslim suburb, Dongguan, only a few meters distant. The valleys leading to the city bristled with forts held by both Muslim and non-Muslim militias. Datong, Bayanrong, and other county towns could also be easily surrounded by insurgents based in hilltop stockades. In such an atmosphere, the Qing officials both regularly and brutally used military force against the locals. All the communities armed themselves for defense of their lives against their neighbors and/or the state. Through the summer of 1895 local *tuanlian* and government troops reacted to the escalating violence around Hezhou and Xunhua: Muslim residents of Xining were subjected to searches on the road, exclusion from the city walls for fear of spies, and other official and unofficial discrimination. As the Xunhua Muslim leader Hann Wenxiu raided closer and closer to the city, many suburban Muslims

---

125. Rijnhart, *With the Tibetans,* 27–28. See also Frick, "Hochzeitssitten." The Filchner expedition observed both the strength of Chinese culture in the area and its attraction and accommodation to Tibetan culture, especially in the material realm (Filchner, *Wissenschaftliche Ergebnisse,* vol. 2, 124).

joined him, and Muslim forces attacked stockades and fortified villages throughout Huangzhong.

In these "little wars" around Xining, communal or religious identity functioned very much like lineage identity in Chinese society, creating one vector of unity for villages or groups of villages, a boundary against the dangerous Others. In Philip Kuhn's terminology, the simplex *tuan* of many Xining Muslim villages engaged in vendettas (Ch. *xiedou*) with non-Muslim villages and with Tibetans.[126] The funds to buy arms and provisions for such activities (which, in other parts of China often were provided by lineage organizations) in Muslim Gansu came from the communal treasury of the mosque, to which all were expected to contribute, and from the wealth of successful commercial families. They did not, however, attempt to overthrow the Qing state or found any type of autonomous Muslim polity, for their ability to organize rarely exceeded the confines of their villages or multivillage local systems. The spatial arrangement of Muslim and non-Muslim communities, mixed and limited by the harsh terrain, did not encourage regional organizations, nor did the division of Xining Muslim society by the various religious solidarities. Indeed, as we have seen, fighting *between* Muslims could be as vicious and enduring as Muslim vs. non-Muslim battles.

Tension rose very high as Salars assaulted Deng Zeng's own camp near Bayanrong and took commander Li Shijia prisoner at Jingningpu. Deng's army, positioned primarily to fend off Salar violence emanating from Xunhua, could not prevent local Muslim raiding even within sight of Xining's walls. On September 1 armed Muslims mounted the Dongguan walls to begin a bombardment of Xining that lasted several days.[127] Deng Zeng feared the worst—capture of the main citadel—and brought his entire army back to the city, where he met the Muslims head-on. A major battle ensued, with heavy losses on both sides but no clear victory.[128] Though the Xining garrison ventured out to take the Muslims in a pincer movement, they failed, so Deng entered the city but could not break the siege. The Xining Muslims' decision to attack the city thus followed the pattern of Hezhou and Didao. Local Muslims, fearing an assault from apparently bloody-minded local *tuanlian* or

126. For a complete discussion of the growth and structure of *tuanlian,* focusing on south China, see Kuhn, *Rebellion,* esp. 76–78, on the relationship between militia and lineage organizations.

127. *GNQSL* 25.8a–9a, 10a. Lacking modern artillery, the Dongguan Muslims relied on homemade cannons and small arms, hopelessly inadequate to the task of breaching Xining's high walls.

128. *Xining dengchu,* 1.2b.

from the Qing authorities, struck first in the hope of securing a quick victory and control over the walled town. At the roots of this violence lay local emotions and fears, not any grandiose dream of Muslim hegemony based on religious ideology. The weakening of Gansu's Qing garrisons by withdrawals to fight the Sino-Japanese war encouraged some Muslim leaders, and their motivation to fight overrode their knowledge of the local garrisons' strength and the height of the walls.

Battles continued all over Taoxi-Huangzhong in September, with the Qing garrisons and local *tuanlian* consistently holding the advantage through their control of stockades such as Hejiapu, across the river from Didao on the western, "Muslim" side of the Tao; Baitasi, at a crucial Yellow River crossing north of Hezhou; and Ninghepu, south of Hezhou. Deng Zeng and Lei Zhengguan held out in stubborn defense of Xining and Hezhou, as Qing reinforcements began gradually to arrive from Shaanxi, Ningxia, and Xinjiang.[129]

Overwhelming Force at Xining

The Xining Muslims, scattered in dozens of villages and divided by Qing garrisons and *tuanlian,* established a headquarters and bastion at Duoba, west of Xining City. To this fortified market town, with its large Muslim population and many mosques, came fighters and villagers who feared to remain in the open. The Duoba leaders employed their fortress as a staging area for attacks against Xining and other enemy strong points. When Li Peiying tried to join Deng's defense, the Muslims blocked his relief force for over a month at the narrow passes leading to the city, despite Deng Zeng's efforts from within the citadel.[130]

Deng, waiting for reinforcements and trying to contend with chaotic conditions in Xining's hinterland, enlisted the aid of the Qinghai Tibetans as Agui had done at Lanzhou in 1781. Eager for loot and a chance to strike at the Muslims, the Tibetans joined with alacrity. This alignment— Qing troops, local non-Muslim *tuanlian,* and Tibetans all attacking local Muslims—deepened hatred and rivalry between Tibetan and Muslim common folk, despite their ongoing commercial association in the wool trade. The enmity often burst into brutal, sickening violence during the next few decades of disorder. Tibetan participation in these wars demonstrated yet again to local gentry and Qing officials the wisdom and efficacy of using one group of frontier people to fight another.

129. *GNQSL* 25.8b, 10a, 12b.
130. *GNQSL* 25.17a.

Chinese people have generally seen Tibetan culture as inferior to their own, but the Tibetans maintained their language, folkways, religion, and economy remarkably well in the face of their self-confident antagonists.[131] Only Tibetans could live and produce wealth in the highlands, across which no one could fight as effectively; for this skill they were granted a ferocious reputation as killers and robbers. The experience of Chinese, European, and Muslim travellers who ventured into their territory partially justifies this fame.[132] With some exceptions, Amdo Tibetan society, especially its religious institutions, remained relatively independent of outside control even in areas of Qing or Muslim power, or Chinese cultural influence. The lamaseries held much of the local secular and economic power on the grasslands, often greater than that of the Qing state, which bought partial Tibetan compliance by assessing lower taxes than those of nearby non-Tibetans. In addition, some Tibetan leaders—the *tusi* families—received hereditary patents of office from the Qing.[133] This cultural and political combination resulted in many Tibetans' learning some Chinese and adapting in part to Chinese culture, the while remaining clearly Tibetan.[134] In this complex Muslims played the economic middleman, making available the products of agricultural China and the flatland artisans to the Tibetans, who in turn sold them pelts, wool, and other highland products.[135]

Beyond trade and productive activity, the Tibetans played a role in the military affairs of Gansu. When the *tusi* called for troops, every family had to respond. The lamaseries, too, had extensive arsenals, and the monks organized militias and stockpiled arms to defend their temples. The brutality and extent of conflicts along this frontier, from the

131. Ekvall, *Cultural Relations*, 9–12, 83 in summary, and esp. chaps. 3 and 4.

132. Sutton, *In China's Border Provinces*, contains many harrowing stories of the loathing inspired in the European author by his experience with the Tibetan nomads. The *North China Herald* reported their depredations near Xining and the response by Ma Qi, head of the local Muslim military, in 1924 (see esp. August 13).

133. Zhang Qiyun, *Xiahe xian zhi*, 3.3a–3b, notes Tibetan fluency in the Chinese language, as does Wang Zhiwen, *Gansu sheng xinanbu*, 33. Dreyer, *China's Forty Million*, 10–11, discusses briefly the development of the *tusi* system under the Qing. It was primarily intended to govern "semicivilized" non-Chinese peoples by utilizing a hierarchy of titles granted to powerful local lineages, thereby keeping them contented and loyal.

134. A small group of Huangzhong Tibetans around the town of Kargang even converted to Islam under the influence of Khafiya missionaries, but despite some alteration in their clothing styles and food, they remained Amdo Tibetans in language and culture (Li Gengyan and Xu Likui, "Yisilan jiao zai Kaligang").

135. Ekvall, *Cultural Relations*, chap. 4.

Tao valley to Xining and Kökenōr, illustrate painfully the fear and hatred that sometimes characterized communal relations in Gansu.

The lamaseries concentrated wealth and political power. Contributions flowed in to support the monks and *rimpoche,* whose prayers and pilgrimages spiritually maintained the Tibetan world. The most important *rimpoche* at Labrang, for example, sat on a golden throne, surrounded by precious objects and clad in jewel-encrusted robes in stark contrast to the poverty of the pilgrims praying in his courtyards. Scholars went out from the great lamasery at Kumbum, near Xining, to propagate and strengthen religious practice and allegiance all over Tibet. Their missions also maintained the political power and relationships of the *rimpoche* and their agents, who were often their regents.[136] Using their long experience in dealing with the Qing state and many cultural Others, the Tibetan leaders chose friends and enemies with care. In 1895 they correctly allied themselves with the Qing. They called up their cavalry in the Xining area, operating both independently and under Qing command against the Muslim insurgents.

Early in the fall of 1895 Qing victory had seemed imminent. Wei Guangtao was on his way with a large force of the Hunan Army, Zuo Zongtang's old command; Dong Fuxiang had taken Hezhou and was free to strike through Salar country toward Xining; Niu Shihan had finally left Ningxia to assist in the final victory. But the bitter Gansu winter interfered, as did tenacious Muslim resistance. The Muslims knew that submission meant violent death at the hands of the imperial armies (including Muslim commanders such as Ma Anliang) and their own non-Muslim neighbors. After halting Niu Shihan east of the Xining River gorges, the Salars had offered to surrender on terms favorable to the Qing. But the Qing commanders, many of them Gansu men, felt too strongly about Muslim depredations and the necessity for thorough "pacification." They intended to make no mistakes like those of Zuo Zongtang, who had left too much power in Muslim hands.

So Qing forces converged on Xining from the north, east, and southeast. Wei Guangtao's Hunan braves fell heavily on the Muslim villages, and Dong Fuxiang's troops joined in the despoliation, but the Muslims still held out. As late as mid-February, even with Qing troops stationed

136. The commander of the Labrang monastic army during the early Republican period was the elder brother of the monastery's chief *rimpoche.* The obviously political process of ascendancy to the status of a high *rimpoche* has always been clear, even to most Tibetans, but it has not necessarily diminished their respect or devotion to those same *rimpoche.*

in the villages, Deng Zeng and his commanders were not able to prevent non-Muslims from being ambushed and slaughtered by Muslims in broad daylight, within sight of Xining's walls. Nonetheless, as the weather improved, so did conditions for infantry and cavalry assaults, supported by the few Qing artillery pieces. Finally, in March, the Duoba Muslims, their numbers greatly reduced through unsuccessful sorties and depleted food supplies, surrendered unconditionally. Their leaders lost their heads, and the common soldiers dispersed to their ruined, empty villages. Thousands of Muslims tried to follow the tracks of Bai Yanhu west toward a Muslim refuge. Unlike Bai's veterans in the 1870s, they never reached Russian territory but were hunted down by pursuing armies, frozen by the late winter of the north Tibetan marches, and starved by the barren wasteland. Finally captured and relocated near Korla, in Xinjiang, fewer than two thousand survived.

Lessons Learned

The violence between some Muslims and Qing loyalists and allies of various cultures had devastated a fourth of a province, killed tens of thousands, and sustained the worst fears of all. The Qing officials retained their conviction that religious disputes among the Muslims, particularly those caused by the New Teaching (whatever that may have been) and the *menhuan,* led to conflagration and bloodshed.[137] The local non-Muslim Chinese verified their tradition, that their Muslim neighbors were bloodthirsty fanatics. The Muslims confirmed that they were to be discriminated against, excluded, even slaughtered, because they were Muslims, and thus different. The total Qing military victory did not bring lasting peace, for even brutal pacification could not eliminate communal mistrust and hatred. As long as the Muslims and non-Muslims remained neighbors and state authority could not maintain local order, the problems would continue to exist.

The events of 1895 also illustrated again the disunity of the Gansu Muslims, their vulnerability to piecemeal attack. Official and local fears still emphasized the ferocious loyalty Muslims supposedly felt for one another, but the Muslims could not actually unify their communities in

137. Among the Qing officials who held this view was Yang Zengxin, later the imperious autocrat of Xinjiang, who served after 1895 as prefect of Hezhou. He wrote often that divisions among the Muslims should be blamed for the violence of northwestern society. Mu Shouqi, Republican period gentryman and compiler of local history, agreed, as did many other Gansu elites. It did not occur to them that the state might respond differently to conflict within Muslim communities (*GNQSL* 25.37b–39b).

action. Despite efforts by the Xunhua, Hezhou, and Xining Muslim militants to call for a general uprising, many Gansu Muslims remained aloof or actually opposed their coreligionists. Between the pacification of Gansu in 1872 and that of Hezhou in 1895, a number of Muslim leaders faced realistically the Qing capacity to control its peripheries. Adjusting to that capacity, most of them became Qing commanders or allies in order to preserve their local power and, as they thought, the very existence of their communities.

Poised on the frontier of cultural China, resisting or adjusting to the changes occurring in China, Gansu folk also struggled to remain themselves. Violence from their neighbors or their government often threatened their lives and property, so hatred and fear dominated their memories and their decisions in time of trouble. When Chen Jiaji killed eleven Old Teaching Muslims and displayed their heads at Xunhua, many Muslims felt compelled to act in self-defense and vengeful anger. Their poverty had not changed, nor had their harsh environment, but Qing pressure had grown more insistent, more "modern" in its demand for incorporation and in its enforcing power. The Muslim communities, too, had changed, for most of the *menhuan,* originating as revivalist Sufi institutions, had evolved into essentially conservative local solidarities, organized to preserve the community power and wealth of important lineages.

Neither Ma Anliang, the Qing cavalry commander, nor Ma Yonglin, the disrupter of social order, fits into the standard Qing categories of Muslim villainy. Neither was a "New Teaching bandit" or an anti-Qing state-building holy warrior. Ma Yonglin failed because his coalition of anti-Qing and anti-reformist Muslims could not organize widespread, protracted resistance to state power. Ma Anliang succeeded because he served the Qing loyally against some of his Muslim neighbors, bringing new weapons to frontier conflicts. His reward, like his father's, was local authority, albeit closely controlled by Qing officials, an authority that evolved into Gansu's unique system of Muslim warlordism in the twentieth century (see plate 17).[138] The "Ma family warlords" (Ch. *Majia junfa*) represent a new development in the Muslim worlds of northwest China, the modern nation-state's incorporative power expressed locally through cooptation of existing elites. That process is evident in the following narrations of the lives of four individual Gansu Sino-Muslims who followed very different paths, all of which led toward a closer relationship with New China.

138. That evolutionary process is summarized in Lipman, "Ethnicity and Politics."

5 / Strategies of Integration
Muslims in New China

Our Party [the Guomindang] takes the development of the weak
and small and resistance to the strong and violent as our sole and
most urgent task. This is even more true for those groups which
are not of our kind [Ch. *fei wo zulei zhe*].[1] Now the peoples [*minzu*]
of Mongolia and Tibet are closely related to us, and we have great
affection for one another; our common existence and common
honor already have a history of over a thousand years. . . .
Mongolia and Tibet's life and death are China's life and death.
China absolutely cannot cause Mongolia and Tibet to break away
from China's territory, and Mongolia and Tibet cannot reject China
to become independent. At this time, there is not a single nation on
earth except China that will sincerely develop Mongolia and Tibet.[2]

Becoming a Warlord

Like the 1895 anti-Qing leader Ma Yonglin and many other young
Hezhou Muslim men, Ma Qianling, a small merchant and farmer,
fought against the Qing under Ma Zhan'ao. After the surrender in 1872
he received a Qing reward and prospered in trade, returning to the
military life only briefly when he and Ma Zhan'ao had to drive out a
remnant group of diehard Muslim rebels from the Hezhou hills in 1877.
He had four sons with his three wives, one of whom was a convert to
Islam, and he gave the boys auspicious Chinese names—Fucai (Happiness and Wealth), Fulu (Happiness and Emoluments), Fushou (Happi-

---

1. This phrase from the *Zuo zhuan* (4th cent. B.C.E.) appears in many accounts of
Chinese attitudes toward other peoples and cultures. The original reads, "If [they are] not
of our kind, their hearts must be different" (Ch. *Fei wo zulei qi xin bi yi*).
2. Ma Fuxiang, *Meng Zang*, 1–2.

ness and Longevity), and Fuxiang (Happiness and Good Omens). Ma Fuxiang, the youngest, was born in 1876 in a small town near Hanjiaji, in Hezhou prefecture.

Like many elite Sino-Muslims, he received a dual education in the Confucian and Muslim traditions, reading both the Koran and the *Spring and Autumn Annals* (which he preferred to the *Four Books*).[3] As an adult, Ma Fuxiang grew very fond of elegant prose and calligraphy, but in his youth he had ambitions closer to his roots. His older half-brother Ma Fulu excelled in military exercises, so under the influence of Yang Changjun's 1889 visit to Hezhou to review his troops, Ma Fuxiang joined his brother in the martial arts hall. After three years of local training, he and another brother, Ma Fushou, attended military school.

When the 1895 violence broke out, Ma Fuxiang was twenty and full of martial vigor. Allied with the Qing through their father, he and his brothers all opposed the plans of Ma Yonglin and the rebellious Muslims of their home district, so they joined the Qing army commanded by Tang Yanhe. Ma Anliang's brother Ma Guoliang, Ma Fulu, and Ma Fuxiang commanded the Qing troops that held Jishi Pass against an advancing column from Xunhua and earned province-wide fame. When Tang Yanhe's forces were ambushed and defeated at Shuangcheng, the Ma brothers fled south with their general, then back to Lanzhou. Yang Changjun rewarded them for their steadfast loyalty to the dynasty and sent them toward Hezhou with Dong Fuxiang. They earned Dong's praise during the reconquest of their home district, then participated in the massacre of rebel Muslims in Maying, Milagou, and other Hezhou towns, delivering thousands of severed heads and ears to their superiors.[4] According to Ma Tong's oral sources, Hezhou Muslims said of Ma Qianling's sons that their offices were built of Muslim heads, and Ma Anliang's red cap was dyed with Muslim blood.[5]

After victory in 1896 Ma Fuxiang continued his martial education and earned the military *juren* degree in 1897, while Ma Fulu became a military *jinshi*. Nothing prevented these young Muslim soldiers from serving under Qing generals—their father had, and the increasing militarization of the whole Qing empire pressed them toward enlistment with the

3. Much of the chronological material in this section is taken from He Yan, "Ma Fuxiang." Ma Fuxiang's academic proclivities are discussed on p. 33.

4. Ma Fuxiang, *Shuofang dao zhi* of 1926, 28.21a–21b. Ma Fuxiang sponsored the writing of this gazetteer and listed himself as its general editor, so its accounts may be regarded as his own.

5. Ma Tong, *Zhongguo Yisilan . . . shilue*, 245.

most powerful commander, whatever his place of origin or religion may have been. In Gansu that was their own general Dong Fuxiang, so Ma Fulu and Ma Fuxiang, along with many other young men of their lineage, went with him to Beijing as junior officers when his army was transferred to the metropolitan defense force in 1898. They fought against the foreigners during the Boxer uprising, and Ma Fulu died in the battle for the legations, as did four of his cousins.[6] Ma Fuxiang took over his brother's unit, bringing his Gansu braves home as part of the imperial family's escort on their flight to Xi'an. He received substantial rewards, including an appointment as garrison commander in eastern Gansu. Through the emperor and empress dowager's personal favor, powerful appointments followed at Xining, then in Xinjiang. For ten years he increased his military strength and established political connections all over the northwest, trading on his own military reputation, his brother's, and his father's.

In addition to his loyalty to the Qing state, Ma Fuxiang conceived a strong attraction to Confucianism and Chinese culture. His study of the classics, both in Gansu and in Beijing, led him toward a Confucian-Islamic synthesis.[7] Relying on the translations and commentaries of the *Han kitab,* Ma affirmed the compatibility of Confucian morality and Islamic religion. He combined this ideological persuasion with a realistic assessment of the military and political position of Gansu in the Qing state, forging a lifelong commitment to Muslim participation in the political system of the Qing and then Republican China. Political loyalism also dovetailed neatly with Ma's desire to make money from connections between the northwest and central China. He joined a non-Muslim gentryman to set up one of Gansu's first modern industries, a match factory, and took a financial interest in the Tibet-to-Tianjin wool trade.[8] His love of Chinese culture, including the arts of calligraphy and elegant conversation, certainly influenced his political and social choices. In a memoir one of his young secretaries remembered that Ma Fuxiang enjoyed hobnobbing with high Guomindang officials, an advantage in his career. The Muslim general also made a study of Daoist religion and ancient Chinese texts and set up filial stone steles in memory of his deceased ancestors. His last consort, the daughter of a Lanzhou Muslim official, was famous for her Chinese calligraphy, a very unusual accom-

---

6. He, "Ma Fuxiang," 37.
7. Iwamura, "Kanshuku shō"; and Tian, "Longshang qunhao," 12–13.
8. *GNQSL* 24:45b; and Zhao Songyao, "Gansu Ziyiju," 53–59. The wool trade is described in Millward, "The Chinese Border Wool Trade."

plishment for a Gansu Muslim woman and very appropriate for a companion to Ma Fuxiang.[9]

The intimate relationship between Muslim leadership in Gansu and the Qing state found expression in the provincial leadership's reaction to the Wuchang incident, the dramatic beginning of the revolution of 1911. Both Governor-General Changgeng and Shaanxi Governor Shengyun were loyal Manchu servants of the dynasty, so they determined to oppose the rising tide of anti-Qing activism and republicanism.[10] Ma Anliang, more conservative than Ma Fuxiang, shared their support of the imperial order and occupied a crucial role in their military plans. The most immediate threat lay in the revolutionary army of Zhang Fenghui in Shaanxi. The Qing loyalists had to choose between entrenching themselves as a Gansu "western bastion" or striking eastward against Zhang. With Ma Anliang in command, they chose belligerence. Ma proposed raising twenty battalions of loyal Muslim braves, so Changgeng called a special meeting of provincial leaders to discuss the matter. They shilly-shallied, anxious about the arming of Muslims even for such laudable motives. Ma's demonstrated loyalty carried the day, but Gansu gentry and common folk remained leery of Muslims bearing weapons, even under a dynastic banner.[11]

Ma Anliang attacked Shaanxi successfully, and Yuan Shikai took the invasion seriously enough to alert eastern troops to move against him. As Ma approached Xi'an, however, an intermediary convinced him that the emperor's abdication was real, that the Qing state had declined irreversibly, and he withdrew. Declaring his support for the Republic, Ma Anliang virtually ended northwestern resistance to the new government and earned himself the same chance his father, Ma Zhan'ao, had earned in 1872, after the battle of Taizisi. In company with many Qing provincial officials, he consolidated his local power and remained a mediator and broker in communal relations and local government, promoting the careers of numerous Muslims in provincial and local offices.[12] The diehard Manchu Shengyun kept up the good fight; as late as

9. One of Ma Fuxiang's filial steles may be found in the courtyard of the provincial museum in Yinchuan, Ningxia. The text is carved in both standard characters and in the Han dynasty clerical script at which Ma fancied himself expert. On his youngest wife, see Ma Tingxiu, "Ma Fuxiang shishu."

10. Shengyun had become acquainted with Ma Fuxiang when the latter escorted the imperial family to Xi'an in the aftermath of the Boxer debacle.

11. *GNQSL* 26.41b–42a.

12. Yu, "Xinhai geming." See also Ma Peiqing, "Changgeng Shengyun," 190–97. All of that issue of *Gansu wenshi ziliao xuanji* is devoted to the 1911 Revolution in Gansu,

1918 he was reported as still trying to persuade Ma Anliang to stage a Qing restoration.[13]

Sources differ as to Ma Fuxiang's reaction to the invasion of Shaanxi in 1911, but all agree that he did not participate. Defending his local allies from Changgeng and Shengyun's reactionary violence, he joined with non-Muslim gentrymen to declare provincial independence and nominate candidates for local offices.[14] After the emperor's abdication Ma Fuxiang became a member of the Gansu Provincial Assembly.[15] For his cooperation, and because of his strong army, he received a vice-commander's post at Ningxia, on the Gansu-Mongolian border, from the Republican government of Yuan Shikai. Beginning from that base, he expanded his power in northern Gansu until his army dominated not only Ningxia itself but Suiyuan Province (western Inner Mongolia), Alashan, and the rich plains on the east side of the Huang, between the river and the Ordos desert. That frontier assignment provided him with the military and economic foundation to become a senior member of the "Ma family warlords," three Gansu Muslim lineages that dominated the northwest from Ningxia (Ma Fuxiang's family), Xining (Ma Qi's family), Hezhou, and the Gansu corridor (Ma Anliang's family) through much of the Republican period.[16]

In the northwest, with its long-standing militarization, communal strife, and extreme poverty, "banditry"—that is to say, organized violence and robbery by groups of armed men—became an important secondary occupation for many farmers and townsmen. Though many of his troops and officers had probably been "bandits" at one time or another, Ma Fuxiang's desire for standing within the China-centered state caused him to oppose banditry. Serving in the "legitimate" military, uniformed and sanctioned by a political power regional or national, Ma Fuxiang gained a high reputation by battling against "bandits" around Ningxia and to the north. He captured a Mongol who had taken royal titles in 1913 at Baotou and, four years later, he defeated and executed Daerliuji, a Mongol prince who proclaimed himself emperor

---

including articles on the anti-Manchu uprising at Ningxia, the brief independence movement at Qinzhou (Tianshui), and the telegrams sent by Changgeng and Shengyun to the Grand Council during the crisis.

13. Nakada, *Kaikai minzoku,* 103.

14. "Gansu jiefang qian," 33.

15. Zhao Songyao, "Gansu Ziyiju," 56.

16. For an abbreviated genealogical chart of the Ma lineages and a brief account of their rise to power, see Lipman, "Ethnicity and Politics."

and invaded Ningxia. Both Ma Fuxiang's oldest son Ma Hongkui and nephew Ma Hongbin (his late, heroic half-brother Ma Fulu's son) took detachments out to the Gansu corridor and to Suiyuan to capture or neutralize "bandits."[17]

Becoming a National Figure

Ma Fuxiang emerged from this chaos of the early Republic as ruler of Ningxia and leader of a fairly cohesive, well-organized military command centered on his Muslim cavalrymen. In politics as well as military matters, he had followed Ma Anliang, whose father had been his father's superior officer, so after Ma Anliang's death in 1918 the role of mediator between Muslims and non-Muslims fell, at the provincial level, upon Ma Fuxiang. His base at Ningxia gave him a comfortable distance from the dirty politics of the provincial capital, and his cavalry gave him the clout to argue his points against the Muslim and non-Muslim generals who fought over the northwest for the next twelve years.

The most fundamental conflicts among the Gansu militarists, as elsewhere in China, involved control over territory and taxation of its population. Governor Zhang Guangjian, President Yuan Shikai's appointee, had contended with Ma Anliang for Gansu's economic resources, but he had no choice but to allow Ma Fuxiang relative independence in Ningxia. On the other side of the province Zhang seized the administration of Hezhou, the Muslim center of Gansu, for the provincial government at Lanzhou. In opposition, the often-divided Muslim garrison commanders managed a measure of unity, the result of which was a 1920 telegram to the central government (such as it was) in Beijing demanding Zhang's removal.[18] The economy of Zhang Guangjian's parts of Gansu had eroded, so he chose peaceful retirement, leaving Beijing with a choice to make. Ma Fuxiang might well have been the next governor, for he had served loyally, had fought for the Republic, and had a solid base of support among the Muslims. If power, competence, and experience mattered, he should have been appointed.

But the non-Muslim reaction to his consideration, when it was first rumored, was widespread and strong. A Muslim provincial commander (Ch. *dujun*) meant a Muslim-dominated province, with the terrifying Muslim soldiery in control. For people imbued with decades of fear and centuries of memory of Muslim violence, that would have been an

---

17. Chen Shaoxiao, *Xibei junfa ji*, 5.
18. Nakada, *Kaikai minzoku*, 105.

intolerable threat. Telegrams flowed to Lanzhou and Beijing, particularly from eastern Gansu, protesting against Ma's candidacy in the strongest terms, even citing the old slogan "Chinese and Muslims are eternal enemies" (Ch. *Han Hui shi chou*).[19]

Convinced that Ma's appointment would be inappropriate, Beijing selected Lu Hongtao, Zhang Guangjian's assistant, as *dujun*. Lu's inheritance was a disastrous economy; a weak provincial army; an empty treasury; and a social fabric shattered by opium, drought, unstable currency, and military disunity. The *dujun*'s authority reached no farther than his most distant loyal garrison, and Gansu lay under the sway of eight regional military commanders (Ch. *zhenshoushi*), four Muslims and four non-Muslims. As a part of the "nation," the Chinese Republic, Gansu remained passive and profoundly conservative, only very gradually taking up any of the challenges of modernity. Many Lanzhou and county-level elites felt strong pangs of regret when the government defeated, captured, and executed a Qing restorationist who raised an army in 1920 and attacked the provincial capital.[20]

Lu Hongtao had no better fortune than his predecessor in balancing the competing forces in Gansu. When he left the province in 1925 the petty warlords of eastern Gansu, all non-Muslims, were engaged in inconclusive battle with the Lanzhou authorities. President Duan Qirui appointed the famous "Christian general" Feng Yuxiang as military governor of the northwest in 1925. Feng had heard of Ma Fuxiang's success against bandits and appointed Ma as his codirector of northwestern border defenses, a title that again "legitimized" Ma's already-existing power. Ma used Feng's influence to obtain national-level civil and military posts, including that of national aviation commander.[21] All of the Gansu Muslim militarists found the presence of Feng's powerful Guominjun (National People's Army) tolerable as long as Feng and his Gansu general Liu Yufen directed their attacks eastward, toward the non-Muslim eastern Gansu warlords or Shaanxi. But the Muslims' goal of using Feng to maintain order while enjoying discreet independence could not be realized. Feng and Liu needed to bleed Gansu dry of revenue and manpower in order to participate in major campaigns against Zhang Zuolin, dominant warlord of north China. The imperatives of battle did not allow the existence of independent military power

19. *GNQSL* 30.21b.
20. *GNQSL* 30.20b.
21. Shimohayashi, "Seihoku Shina," 202.

in Feng's rear, nor could he allow the province's revenues to fall into potentially hostile hands.

In 1927–31 the cumulative effects of long-term militarist exploitation, drought, earthquake, famine, and ethnic hatred brought on another round of savage local warfare. Taxed beyond the limit by their government(s), pressed into service as soldiers or transporters, robbed, beaten, and brutalized, the ordinary people of Gansu now had to cope with slow death by starvation and clear natural signs of Heaven's displeasure.[22] The Muslim militarists could gain from this horror if they could direct its violent results against Feng Yuxiang or other local rivals. Most actively anti-Feng was Ma Tingrang of the Gansu corridor, Ma Anliang's third son. He made careful arrangements for delivery of a large shipment of Manchurian arms from Zhang Zuolin, Feng Yuxiang's most powerful enemy, and prepared to move against the Guominjun when the weapons arrived in 1927.

Another young Muslim officer also moved against the Guominjun, though with far less thorough preparation. Ma Zhongying was a cousin of Ma Qi, the Muslim commander at Xining. He left that city with a few foolhardy companions in 1928, intending to attack Hezhou and rid Sino-Muslim country of the outside troops. In those times of extraordinary misery and deprivation, his activist, violent call drew thousands of followers from Huangzhong and Taoxi. Ma Zhongying's Gansu campaigns lasted three years and included three sieges of Hezhou and raids from the upper Wei valley to the Gansu corridor, from the Sichuan border to Ningxia.[23]

Ma Fuxiang, eager to increase his influence, sent one of his sons to try negotiations at Hezhou during Ma Zhongying's sieges.[24] Ma Fuxiang also joined other Muslim gentry, including Ma Yuanchao of the Jahrīya, in writing to Muslims all over the province, exhorting them to keep the peace.[25] But neither the Guominjun nor the "legitimate" local Muslim leaders could maintain order in Gansu, so Ma Fuxiang sought allies outside the province, to stabilize his power and to rid the area of Feng by political alliance rather than military force. By mid-1927 the effectiveness

22. Kang, *Xibei zuijin shinian*, a northwestern "modern" gentryman's account of his region's travails, lists dozens of incidents of sickening violence perpetrated by all sides during the 1920s. A shorter, but equally graphic list may be found in *GNQSL* 31.49a–50a.

23. Fan Manyun, "Liu Yufen"; and Linxia Huizu Zizhizhou Wenshi Ziliao Weiyuanhui, ed., *Ma Zhongying*. The results of Ma Zhongying's raid on Old Taozhou after the failure of his final encirclement of Hezhou are discussed later in this chapter.

24. Iwamura, "Kanshuku Kaimin no niruikei," 149.

25. *GNQSL* 31.51a.

of the Northern Expedition against the southern warlords and the Communists had been demonstrated. Guomindang (Nationalist Party) army commander Jiang Jieshi (Chiang Kai-shek) grew rapidly in power and status, moving toward decisive confrontation with the northern warlords after his victorious march to the Yangzi. Building on three years of gradual approach to the Guomindang, Ma Fuxiang broke openly with Feng Yuxiang, using nationalistic rhetoric to justify a new alliance with Jiang Jieshi. All warlords traded in these sentiments of "for the people" and "unify the nation" to justify their militarism, but this new sloganeering, however superficial, had special significance when it came from a Muslim. For Muslims, even more than non-Muslims, this explicit nationalism contrasted with dynastic loyalty, Islamic isolationism, and Gansu regionalism and meant the end of the imperial era—a new stage in the slow, murky dawning of the polyethnic Chinese nation-state.

Ma Fuxiang was the first Gansu Muslim warlord to join the Guomindang, and he achieved national recognition through national alliances. In the wake of Feng Yuxiang's departure and the creation of Qinghai and Ningxia as independent provinces in 1928, Ma participated in the reorganization of Gansu's provincial government. In his combination of national, regional, and local power and interests, he resembled the Muslim examination graduates of the past, who had left their homes to take official posts elsewhere in the empire, leaving their relatives to safeguard their local interests and to ensure their gentry status for another generation. Ma Fuxiang rose rapidly in the official titles competition of the Guomindang: he served as mayor of Qingdao, governor of Anhui, member of the Guomindang Central Committee, member of the State Council, and chair of the Mongolia-Tibet Commission of the Guomindang government.[26] Playing the militarist politics of the day with considerable skill, he helped to arrange the defeat of Feng Yuxiang and the surrender of several of Feng's subordinates, including Ma's own son Ma Hongkui. Though Ma Fuxiang never held an active civilian post in Gansu after moving east as a Guomindang leader, he nonetheless exercised a lively and direct interest in the northwest, keeping in close touch with his subordinates in Ningxia.

Ma Fuxiang also took the lead in establishing national Muslim organizations sponsored by the Guomindang. Until the 1920s only the Jahrīya—never the Chinese state or any transregional party—had undertaken to unify the Muslims of China institutionally. With a national

26. See Boorman, *Biographical Dictionary*, main entry under Ma Fu-hsiang; and Zhang Wei, "Gu Guomin zhengfu."

(rather than imperial or regional) government finally in power after 1928, Muslims had to be actively incorporated into the citizenry and organized in legitimate special-interest groups with nationally known, easily identifiable leaders, rather than being identified as legally different or potentially subversive. The state supported these groups with money and with recognition of their leaders as symbolically influential political figures. Wealthy and well known, Ma Fuxiang had long taken an interest in Muslim educational institutions and had established a public library in Ningxia. As early as 1917 he had gathered investors and spent his own money to sponsor a Mongolian-Muslim normal school and a number of Muslim elementary schools throughout the territory under his control (see plate 18). Immediately after his removal to the east as a Guomindang official, Ma Fuxiang joined Muslim gentry from several provinces in founding the China Islamic Association (Zhongguo Huijiao Gonghui), and he served for a while as titular director of instruction at the Islamic secondary school in Beijing.

North Chinese Muslim intellectuals and progressive *ahong* had established the Chengda Normal College in Jinan, Shandong, in 1925. This first national institution of higher learning for Muslims in China offered a combined Chinese, "modern" (i.e., Western), and Islamic curriculum. Because of his Confucian and Muslim educations, Ma Fuxiang sympathized with this movement and participated actively, especially when the May Thirtieth troubles brought Ma Songting *ahong* and the Chengda College to Beijing.[27] Never forgetting his early intellectual growth under the influence of the *Han kitab*, Ma Fuxiang invested in new editions of many major texts, including most of the books mentioned in chapter 3. His efforts enabled Wang Daiyu, Ma Zhu, and especially Liu Zhi to find new audiences among twentieth-century Sino-Muslims, and some previously unpublished texts were brought to light.

Ma Fuxiang belonged to the new age of nationalist Confucianism, the "revolutionary conservative" ideology that sought to change China's institutions, national strength, and domestic order while preserving its cultural values and elite traditions. He enjoyed socializing with non-Muslim gentry and Guomindang leaders but was also careful in advancing the careers of promising young Muslims who wanted to emulate his worldly success.[28] Non-Muslim allies praised him for his *guojia yizhi,* his "national consciousness," which they distinguished from the stereotypically "different" Muslim consciousness as well as

27. Ma Songting *ahong,* "Zhongguo Huijiao."
28. Ma Tingxiu, "Ma Fuxiang," 190.

from provincial militarism. In public they admired his Islamic-Confucian synthesis, publicized through his reprint projects of both the *Han kitab* and Chinese classical works. They felt comfortable with his advocacy of national unity, as all of them strengthened their local bases in their home provinces.

In 1932 Ma Fuxiang—a rising star in Guomindang central councils, a crucial power broker in the northwest, the best-known Muslim in China—suddenly took sick and died while traveling from Hankou to Beiping. He left behind a wide variety of projects to forward his ambition of achieving a true Sino-Muslim synthesis, the full integration of the Sinophone Muslims as citizens of the Chinese Republic and participants in Chinese culture. He had planned with Ma Zhenwu, head of one branch of the Jahrīya in Ningxia, to translate the Koran into Chinese. In 1931 he had taken a leading role in proposing formation of the Muslim Educational Progressive Committee (Huimin Jiaoyu Zujin Weiyuanhui), to be sponsored by the central government. When it came into existence in 1933, that organization promoted Chinese education among Muslims. In his military days Ma Fuxiang had led troops to kill coreligionists who opposed what he saw as the Gansu Muslims' best interest, a stable position in a strong Qing state. By the end of his life China had changed radically and the Muslim militarist had become an educator, provincial gentryman, and Guomindang official, protecting his territory and his family's interests while working toward an active role for Gansu and China's Muslims in a strong nation-state. Ma Fuxiang worked all his life to include himself among those who *"are* of our kind," the Chinese. His son and nephew, both staunch supporters of the Guomindang and enemies of the Communists, ruled Ningxia—most local people say very badly—for the remainder of the Republican period.

MA YUANZHANG (1853–1920) AND THE REVIVAL OF THE JAHRĪYA

Ma Guanglie [Yuanzhang] does not look upon other religions with hatred; in fact, he joined [his forces with] the militia to pursue bandits. He may be called a man with national *minzu* consciousness![29]

29. *GNQSL* 28.26a.

Rising from the Ashes

Syncretic assimilation to the new China of the late Qing and Republic could be expected from Ma Fuxiang, the son of Ma Zhan'ao's lieutenant, for a segment of the Gansu Muslim elite identified with the Khafīya had sought accommodation since before the 1780s rebellion. But no one, least of all Gansu non-Muslims, expected the head of the Jahrīya to entertain such notions. Oft-proscribed since Su Forty-three's violence of 1781 and central to the uprising of Ma Hualong, the Jahrīya, under its condemnatory label of "New Teaching," still inspired fear all over the province. Despite the slaughter at Jinjipu, the order revived under the leadership of a new *jiaozhu,* Ma Yuanzhang. He continued his predecessors' devotion to Jahrīya solidarity, but his exposure to Chinese society, his broad education, and the changing times altered his perception of the place of the Muslims, including the Jahrīya, in China, and he did not act as many of his predecessors had acted.

We have seen the influence of Sufism and the *tarīqa* fall on northwest China, with deadly results—conflicts within Muslim communities leading to Qing military intervention, rebellion, and massacre. We must not forget that between, or even during, those warlike events, Sufism as a religious system, as faith and practice and intellectual-emotional experience, played a central role in the lives of its adherents. Though the syncretic texts of the *Han kitab* were produced in eastern China, not in the much larger but less literate world of the northwestern Muslims, Ma Tong's oral histories have revealed that a rich religious and cultural life also animated the Sufis of Gansu. The *ahong* read and interpreted the sacred texts, teachers and ordinary folk told tales of miracle-working Sufis and evil enemies, and everyone "remembered" the glories of their own virtuous ancestors, *shaikh* and *daozu,* embellishing the past to suit their circumstances. The tombs of the *daozu* and his successors provided an especially moving religious environment, as did the periodic collective celebrations (Ch. *ermanli,* Ar. *al-'amal*) of the Prophet or of the *shaikh,* occasions for renewing solidarity and offering gifts.[30] As it did for Sufis elsewhere in the world, the *daotang* provided not only a locus for community organization, which it surely did, but also a hospice, a place of religious refuge. Françoise Aubin has brilliantly reconstructed the Jahrīya religious life in China, focusing on the relationship of saint to follower, the importance of the collective *dhikr* recitation, and the

30. Gladney, "Muslim Tombs."

excitement of understanding the proper approach to the divine.[31] During the life of Ma Yuanzhang, the religious and intellectual power of Jahrīya Sufism in Gansu reemerged from the bloodshed and chaos of the nineteenth century into a new relationship with Chinese culture.

According to his great-grandson, Ma Yuanzhang was a direct descendant of Ma Mingxin.[32] When Agui defeated Su Forty-three and the New Teaching in 1781, he sentenced all of Ma Mingxin's surviving family to exile in Yunnan. There the survivors joined the large and active western Yunnan Muslim community, proselytizing the Jahrīya and serving as the *jiaozhu*'s representatives in the southwest. Ma Yuanzhang's father, Ma Shilin, journeyed from Yunnan to Ningxia twice to visit Ma Hualong, once staying two years in Tongxin, south of Jinjipu, as an *ahong*. When Du Wenxiu set up his Muslim-dominated Pingnan state in Yunnan in the 1850s, Ma Shilin joined him as a garrison commander and civil official. He held his fortress of Donggouzhai for over a year against a Qing siege, then committed suicide in defeat. His sons had been sent to Sichuan for safety, Ma Yuanzhang among them. They disguised themselves as merchants and traveled to Gansu, arriving about a year after the fall of Jinjipu and the death of their *shaikh* (see plate 19).

When Ma Mingxin returned to Gansu from Yemen in the 1760s, he had severely criticized the Khafīya for allowing Ma Laichi's son, Ma Guobao, to succeed to his father's *baraka* as *shaikh,* rather than selecting the most meritorious disciple of the late master. During the decades between Ma Mingxin's execution and Ma Hualong's ascendancy at Jinjipu, that high-principled stand had eroded, as it had elsewhere in the Muslim world, in favor of the hereditary charisma of a saintly lineage. Ma Mingxin's two direct successors to the *shaikh*'s position, the second- and third-generation masters of the Gansu Jahrīya, were indeed chosen by their predecessors or by the high-ranking initiates for their Koranic scholarship, knowledge of Arabic and Persian, and piety.[33] But the fourth master, Ma Yide (late 1770s–1849), was the son of the third, and from that generation onward the Jahrīya moved toward the common pattern of Sufi suborders in northwest China, that of the *menhuan*. Though the transformation was not complete until Ma Yuanzhang's

---

31. Aubin, "En Islam chinois," 493–520.

32. This chronology of Ma Yuanzhang is based on: Ma Chen, "Ma Yuanzhang"; Ma Tong, *Zhongguo Yisilan . . . shilue,* 419–29; and Kawamura, "Ba Genshō." Descent from Ma Mingxin made Ma Yuanzhang's aspiration to the now-hereditary leadership of the Jahrīya legitimate.

33. Aubin, "En Islam chinois," 528.

lifetime, the crucial first step had been taken with Ma Yide's succession in 1817.

With proper devotion to the now-hereditary Jahrīya chain of succession, Ma Yuanzhang tried to find any remnants of Ma Hualong's family who had survived the massacre at Jinjipu. He discovered two of Ma Hualong's grandsons, Ma Jincheng and Ma Jinxi, living under Qing guard in Xi'an. Both boys had been sentenced to castration when they reached twelve years of age, and Yuanzhang arrived too late to effect a rescue of the older son, who suffered the penalty for his grandfather's rebellion. But when the unfortunate boy was sent to Kaifeng as a slave after his punishment, Ma Yuanzhang placed disguised Jahrīya members near him, and they cared for him until he died in 1890. Ma Yuanzhang did manage to have the second grandson rescued uncastrated from confinement and smuggled through a series of Muslim homes to the small but prosperous Muslim community of Hangzhou, in the lower Yangzi valley. Working as a leather merchant, Ma Yuanzhang moved all over eastern China, visiting Jahrīya Muslims in a dozen provinces and gaining fame as a trustworthy *ahong,* returning to the northwest to live only after the 1895 violence had ended.

Ma Yuanzhang established his base in and around the town of Zhangjiachuan, in the eastern part of the province, where Zuo Zongtang had relocated thousands of Shaanxi Muslims after the great rebellion. Far from the feuds and violent histories of Hezhou, Didao, Xining, and Ningxia, Zhangjiachuan became an all-Muslim enclave. No non-Muslims lived within miles of the place, except for a few artisans who were careful to follow the strictures of Muslim dietary law. The Jahrīya controlled the town and the nearby valleys, and there Ma Yuanzhang undertook his work of community building, aiming toward agricultural self-sufficiency, commercial success, religious education and expression, and an end to feuding.[34]

Devoted to the revival of his order, Ma Yuanzhang also directed his

34. Iwamura, "Kanshuku Kaimin no niruikei," 144–47. Zhang Yangming, *Dao xibei lai,* devotes an entire chapter to his stay in Maluzhen, Zhangjiachuan's market. One English account of the place exists, by an incredulous Rodney Gilbert, who combines in his brief article the language of light-hearted travel with that of "Hordes of Semi-barbaric Mohammedan Fanatics." His description, shorn of its more fanciful elements, reveals a tightly organized community, devoted to its leader and to acts of charity, thoroughly Chinese and Muslim. Gilbert found the community's focus on Ma Yuanzhang, with whom he had a cordial conversation, to be shocking and potentially dangerous, at the same time remarking that the aged religious leader was devoted to Chinese republicanism and had sent his son to work in Lanzhou ("Remarkable Development").

efforts toward Muslim solidarity in general. Centering his personal and religious life in the Jahrīya—he married a woman from Ma Hualong's family—Ma Yuanzhang nonetheless cultivated friendships with non-Jahrīya Muslims and with influential non-Muslims as well.[35] He obtained a classical Chinese education, taking three northwestern Hanlin scholars and a member of the Manchu ruling clan as his teachers. Skilled in both Chinese and Arabic calligraphy, he scattered ceremonial scrolls and inscriptions around the northwest. He made three complete copies of the Koran in his own handwriting and composed essays and poems on topics as diverse as the nature of prayer and the obligations of patriotism. His followers venerated their *jiaozhu* and made pilgrimages to his *daotang,* practices common to Sufis all over the world in the nineteenth and twentieth centuries.[36]

Dong Fuxiang, the Gansu general and military superior of Ma Fuxiang's family, could not hold national office after the Boxer debacle. In European minds, he had been the most intractable, most reactionary of the Qing loyalists, and his Gansu Muslim troops had been the most steadfast against the foreign armies during the siege of the legations at Beijing. As one of the besieged wrote:

> Those to the north and west—all Kansuh men under Tung Fu-hsiang—remain[ed] sullen and suspicious. From other directions, and especially on the east, where Jung Lu's troops were posted, it was possible to obtain supplies (small, but welcome) of eggs and vegetables, the sellers being smuggled through the Chinese soldiers' lines in spite of the prohibition of their officers, and it was from this side that the messengers came with all later letters. They declared, in fact, that they could not get through the troops on our western side without being shot.[37]

An international clamor for Dong's execution produced prevarication from the Qing court, which did not want to punish him for having done

35. One of Ma's Hanlin teachers was Liu Erxin, a Lanzhou Confucian scholar ferociously loyal to the Qing. In 1911 Liu founded the Confucian Society, a conservative group that spread rapidly among the gentry. He consciously took Zeng Guofan as his model and proposed firm allegiance to the classical curriculum from his seat in the Provincial Assembly. See Yu, "Wusi yundong," 102; Ma Chen, "Ma Yuanzhang," 292; and Zhao Songyao, "Gansu Ziyiju," 54.

36. Saguchi, "Chūgoku Isuramu," 85–87; and Aubin, "En Islam chinois," 552–53.

37. Tan, *The Boxer Catastrophe,* 114, citing the papers of the British minister, Sir Claude MacDonald.

his job so loyally. Under pressure, the Qing stripped him of his rank, though not his command, and banished him to a remote province— Gansu, where his continued prestige and influence remained a source of anxiety and gall for the European community in China until his death.[38]

Dong Fuxiang remembered Ma Hualong and Jinjipu very well, and he desired to control the economic resources of northern Gansu, so he resented the successful revival of the Jahrīya.[39] Rumors flew that he planned to use his local militia to exterminate the Jahrīya, so Ma Yuanzhang had to respond. Times have changed, he wrote to Dong, this is not the Tongzhi period, and you are not Zuo Zongtang. If you dare to move against the Jahrīya, Muslims all over the country will report your treachery to the foreigners, and you will be finished.[40] Ma Yuanzhang had already used his Manchu contacts to obtain a pardon for Ma Jinxi, so Dong knew that Ma might do as he threatened. Aware of his own unpopularity with the Europeans and the Qing's promise to punish him, Dong backed down, and the region remained at peace. After decades of discrimination and turmoil, the Jahrī Muslims could once again wear their distinctive white caps on the streets of Guyuan or Haicheng and do their business unafraid, thanks to Ma Yuanzhang (see plate 20). His reputation as a *shanren*, a saint, grew apace, and pilgrims flocked to Zhangjiachuan.

Coming to Terms with New China

Anti-Manchu violence broke out at Ningxia in 1911, led by the powerful Gelaohui secret society.[41] The provincial government sent Ma Qi to restore order, and the revolutionaries sent Yu Youren to Zhangjiachuan to see Ma Yuanzhang, to persuade him not to support the Qing. Yu advocated anti-Manchu revolution and left books for Ma to distribute, but Ma did not wish to endanger his relationship with the provincial capital and its distant Qing masters. He sent the eastern Gansu Muslim militia, under one of his sons, to help Ma Qi fight against the Gelaohui,

---

38. Letters regarding Dong's purported rebellious activities in Gansu may be found in the *North China Herald* numbers of July 3, 1901; January 8, 1902; March 12, 1902; April 9, 1902; and many others.

39. Aubin notes the presence at Zhangjiachuan of merchants from Andijan, in the Ferghana Valley west of the Pamirs, as well as pilgrims and merchants from Canton, Nanjing, Guizhou, Yunnan, and all over Gansu ("En Islam chinois," 552).

40. Ma Chen, "Ma Yuanzhang," 298.

41. *GNQSL* 26.42a–44b. A Gelaohui plot at Xining was nipped in the bud at the same time.

including its Muslim members, at Ningxia. After the failure of Sheng-yun, Changgeng, and Ma Anliang's invasion of Shaanxi in 1912, Ma Yuanzhang adapted rapidly to the "Republican" (that is, warlord) administration and the devolution of power to the local level. Ma recognized that Yuan Shikai's government, which could appoint the highest provincial officials, held one key to Gansu's stability.

When the powerful, peripatetic general Bai Lang invaded Gansu with tens of thousands of "bandit" troops in 1914, Governor Zhang Guang-jian had just been appointed by the central government, and real power still lay in local hands, not in Lanzhou. Ma Jinxi, Ma Hualong's pardoned grandson, was arrested and accused by eastern Gansu gentry of collusion with Bai Lang. Ma Yuanzhang went directly to Lanzhou, to Zhang Guangjian, whom he was able to bribe to release Ma Hualong's remaining descendant. In the early Republic, unlike the mid-Qing, the provincial government could use the Jahrīya to cooperate in maintaining social order. From 1911 on ambitious power holders in northern and eastern Gansu sent emissaries to Zhangjiachuan rather than risk disaffection of the Jahrīya. Ma Yuanzhang had achieved legitimacy for himself and his once-proscribed order. His militia could not prevent Bai Lang from taking Zhangjiachuan, but they fought in the unsuccessful defense of Tianshui and gained reknown and non-Muslim gratitude for their leader.[42]

Ma Fuxiang and the other Gansu militarists found governor Zhang Guangjian's domination in Lanzhou both irritating and expensive. By 1916 they were already arguing for a local *dujun*, under the slogan "Gansu people should govern Gansu" (Ch. *Gan ren zhi Gan*). Calling on Ma Yuanzhang as a fellow Muslim and a fellow provincial, Ma Fuxiang, who desired the position of *dujun* himself, asked his support for a message to Yuan Shikai. Instead of cooperating with his coreligionist, Ma Yuanzhang telegraphed Beijing that Zhang remained the best man for the job. He earned Ma Fuxiang's enmity, but he gained stature and influence in Lanzhou and east China by this apparently selfless, "patriotic" act. When Ma Yuanzhang visited Lanzhou in 1918, the people welcomed him warmly and hung out scrolls and banners: "A man of all quarters, a boat for all waters!" (Ch. *Dong nan xi bei ren, jiang he hu hai chuan*) (see plate 21).[43]

On December 16, 1920, a massive and devastating earthquake struck the Haicheng-Guyuan region of eastern Gansu. Because so many of

42. "Gansu dudufu dang'an," 262 ff.
43. Ma Chen, "Ma Yuanzhang," 301.

the residents of that loess country lived (and a few still live) in man-made caves carved horizontally into the steep hillsides, whole villages were buried alive that night. Entire mountainsides slid into valleys, rivers were obstructed and flooded the low-lying areas, and massive cracks in the earth swallowed fields and farms. Estimates of the death toll, always suspect in China, ranged as high as two hundred thousand. A quarter-mile of the Xi'an–Lanzhou highway, along which Zuo Zongtang had planted two continuous rows of willow trees, moved overland to lodge forlorn on a newly created hill.[44]

That earthquake also killed Ma Yuanzhang and one of his sons, both crushed by the collapse of a mosque near Zhangjiachuan.[45] Already in his mid-sixties, he had devoted his life to reviving the Jahrīya, but not in its old form and not with its old purposes. Under his leadership the order no longer functioned as the New Teaching—the fundamentalist, anti-assimilationist, anti-*menhuan* institution created by Ma Mingxin and his disciples in the eighteenth century. Indeed, it had already lost the New Teaching name to a new sub-group within the Khafīya during the 1895 troubles. The Jahrīya under his leadership had become another *menhuan,* split by factional strife, led by wealthy patriarchs and dedicated to conservative goals within Chinese society—Islamic spiritual growth and Muslim economic success. Instead of dying for the Jahrīya and Islam, his followers learned to read Arabic and Chinese and undertook commercial ventures all over north and west China.

This new legitimacy and cooperation were not solely results of the fall of the Qing, though the Republic and its decentralized power structure made Ma Yuanzhang a particularly attractive ally for the Gansu provincial leaders. The new impulses also grew from the new imperatives China brought to its frontiers in the late nineteenth century and from the growing dependence of the northwest on China proper, fostered by the modern growth of the Chinese state and economy. In the mid-Qing a New Teaching leader could be only a *feitu,* an illegitimate antistate

44. Zhao Shiying, "Gansu dizhen jianzhi," 259–67, contains numerous published accounts of the quake's damage and local attempts to aid the suffering and homeless. For an English-language account and some extraordinary photographs, see Close and McCormick, "Where the Mountains Walked."

45. So firm were Euro-American images of Muslims that missionary accounts of Ma's death claimed that he was on the verge of a new "Mohammedan rebellion" when providentially killed by the earthquake. One even reported that killing had already begun in the towns of eastern Gansu. Given the above narrative of Ma Yuanzhang's life to this point, these notices reveal only the fear and prejudices of their writers, not Ma Yuanzhang's activities or condition in 1920.

bandit. By the early Republic, Gansu non-Muslims could call Ma Yuanzhang a *shanren,* and Gansu gentry could praise his "national ethnic consciousness" as they praised Ma Fuxiang's. Ma Yuanzhang responded by publicly proclaiming his loyalty to China, even if that involved political opposition to Muslim countries. When the Ottoman government allied with Germany, technically China's enemy in the first World War, Ma telegraphed Beijing:

> We are the same as the Han except in religion. We are not united in any way politically with Arabia. Our lives, livelihoods, and graves are in China. Why should we harm our country for some foreigners? Though there were Han-Muslim killings in the Qing, since the Republic we have kept the peace and done our duty, not opposing the government or secretly plotting. We have been good citizens among the Five Nationalities![46]

The revival of the Jahrīya did not produce simple, positive results. Ma Jinxi, Ma Hualong's grandson and former castrato-in-waiting, considered himself to be the heir to the *baraka* of the Jahrīya *jiaozhu.* Ma Yuanzhang, on the other hand, had led the suborder's rise from the ashes of Jinjipu and had married a woman from Ma Hualong's lineage in order to tie himself closer to that source of legitimacy. Though he never openly challenged Ma Jinxi's claim to Ma Hualong's mantle, he claimed Ma Mingxin's for himself, thus splitting the seventh generation of Jahrīya masters into two sometimes-rival factions. Ma Yuanzhang's, based around Zhangjiachuan, has come to be called the Shagou lineage, from the site (near Ningxia) of one of his two *gongbei* (see plate 22). Ma Jinxi, who returned to the Ningxia region, set up his headquarters near Jinjipu, and his lineage has come to be known as the Banqiao, after its location. In the eighth generation, which followed, no fewer than six Jahrīya leaders claimed legitimate descent from Ma Yuanzhang, while two of Ma Jinxi's sons competed within the Banqiao family. In short, the Jahrīya became a *menhuan,* with all of the centralizing and fragmenting possibilities of that complex institution and its commitment to stability and continuity within Chinese society.[47]

The career of Ma Yuanzhang, like that of Ma Fuxiang, illustrates an important but ironic theme of modern Chinese history. At its edges, a new nation must assert both political and cultural sovereignty, and

46. Shimohayashi, "Seihoku Shina," 217 f.
47. Aubin, "En Islam chinois," 526–28, 542–51.

convert what had been frontier buffer zones for an empire—those governed by Qing period *tusi,* for example—into integral parts of the homeland, demarcated by national boundaries. This was the substance of Gu Jiegang's message in 1938—that the border and the frontier must be the same line. But that process took a long time, including the Qing conquest of the northwest and then eastern Turkestan; Agui's subjugation of Su Forty-three and Tian Wu; Zuo Zongtang's carefully planned reconquest of the whole northwest; the creation of Xinjiang as a province; and Dong Fuxiang's cooptation of Ma Anliang and his Muslim cavalry to defeat Ma Weihan, Ma Yonglin, and the other rebels of 1895. All of these military acts forwarded the political incorporation of the northwestern frontier into a Chinese-dominated nation-state, centered in the east.

The irony lies in the gradual *disintegration* that characterized political China as a whole during the nineteenth and twentieth centuries. As Qing and then Republican governments struggled to hold at the center, as secessionist movements broke off large chunks of the empire, as the entire political fabric unraveled after 1916, the northwest drew closer to China. Ma Fuxiang, Ma Yuanzhang, and many other northwestern Muslims played roles in that conflicted but nonetheless clearly centripetal movement. By accepting the legitimacy of the Qing and Republican states and actively supporting them, working with or even becoming officials, building their own communities as part of the Chinese nation, these new leaders ensured the inseparable bond between their poor, battered region and the New China a-borning in its cultural centers back east.

MA QIXI (1857–1914) AND HIS SINO-ISLAMIC COLLECTIVIST MOVEMENT IN SOUTHERN GANSU

In 1914, after Ma Anliang murdered Ma Qixi, more than forty young women of the Xidaotang were kidnapped to Hezhou, where they were imprisoned in a cart shop before being bestowed upon men. Two *ahong* from another *menhuan* just happened to be walking by the shop gate and saw what was going on, so they could not help but ask, "You say that your Xidaotang is an orthodox Way, but everyone says you're heretics! What the ear hears may be groundless, but what the eye sees is true, so we'll test you today. Can you answer?" Then the two *ahong* started quizzing them about faith, the six articles of faith, and the five divine commandments, and then moved on to the interpretation of each part of the Koran, *shari'a*, the Three Vehicles [of Sufism], and more. Those young women, using both Arabic and Chinese, cited the scriptures and quoted the texts, answering every question smoothly and fluently. The two *ahong* were deeply moved, and they ran to Ma Anliang and said, "You've made a grave error! Their religious solidarity is a true one." And they demanded that the imprisoned Xidaotang women be released.[48]

On the inside, communist; to the outside, imperialist [Ch. *Nei gongchan, wai diguo*].[49]

Local Leader, National Vision

Ma Yuanzhang rebuilt the Jahrīya, using its already established networks, its interprovincial trade, and its tradition of internal cohesion in the face of social, religious, and political hostility. His expertise in Chinese calligraphy, social relations, and politics earned him the admiration of Qing officials and local gentry, while his Islamic learning, Arabic calligraphy, and ability as a mediator won him the respect and obedience due from *menhuan* adherents to a successful *jiaozhu*. Around Zhangjiachuan, he tried to built a self-sufficient refuge, a place where Muslims could live, not detached from Chinese society but far enough from the real dangers of ethnic strife and prejudice. He also shared with Ma Fuxiang, the cosmopolitan Guomindang warlord based at Ningxia, the need to relocate the Sino-Muslims politically in the rapidly changing world of New China. At home in Gansu, both of them had to deal with Ma Anliang, whose military and political power, based at Hezhou, dominated the region. All players in Gansu public life knew that Ma Anliang would use his cavalry and his close relationship to the Lanzhou authorities against any opposition, a willingness displayed most vividly in his violent attack on the Xidaotang, an apparently innocuous Muslim group based at Old Taozhou.[50]

48. Zhu Gang, "Zhongguo Yisilanjiao," 101–2.

49. This proverbial description of the Xidaotang appears in many articles on the subject, e.g., the comment of Gu Jiegang's companion in his northwestern mission (Wang Shumin, "Xidaotang," 123).

50. Old Taozhou refers to the *jiucheng*, the more ancient and strategically located of two walled towns in the county, both now called Lintan. New Taozhou, for a long time the administrative seat of the county, lies twenty miles to the east, closer to the northward bend of the Tao River and to China.

The Xidaotang grew and thrived in the multicultural atmosphere of a trading town on the frontiers of cultural China and cultural Tibet. There, Muslim merchants of many languages and backgrounds, non-Muslim Chinese from many centers, and Tibetans both sedentary and nomadic met to exchange goods. Wealthy in peacetime, vulnerable in wartime, Old Taozhou had been a meeting ground of cultures since the Six Dynasties period (C.E. 220–589), when it was established to guard the border with the Tuyuhun, who were finally driven out by the Latter Zhou. A millennium later Mu Ying, one of Zhu Yuanzhang's close associates, brought an army to subdue the "eighteen lineages of the Tufan" in 1379. Many of his Muslim soldiers stayed at Taozhou, building the town's first mosque and setting up in trade between the nomads and the sedentary population of the Tao valley, Hezhou, and points north and east.[51]

As discussed above, Taozhou did not share the internecine Muslim battles of suborders and *menhuan* that brought fire and sword down on Xining, Xunhua, Ningxia, and Hezhou after the 1760s. Its Muslim community remained primarily Gedimu, organized in mosque-based local solidarities dedicated to local action through their elites, the Hui gentry—which included *ahong,* merchants, military examination graduates, and landowners. Far from any direct connection with Central Asia, balanced between Tibet and China, Taozhou's Chinese-speaking Muslims were more oriented toward China than toward the Muslim heartlands. They claimed descent from Nanjing natives among Mu Ying's Muslim troops, so their culture remained more "eastern," more associated with China proper than with the frontier.[52] Two suborders of the Khafiya, the Huasi and Beizhuang *menhuan,* sought initiates in the town with some success and were able to establish mosques, but neither serious religious disputes nor violent lineage feuds broke the relative peace of the Taozhou Muslims.

Ma Qixi was born into the family of a Taozhou *ahong* of the Beizhuang *menhuan.* In the early stages of his education, he showed great promise as a scholar, so his father made a fairly unusual choice for a Gansu man of religion. He sent his eleven-year-old son to study with a non-Muslim, a local examination graduate, at his private academy. Amazed by the boy's precocious intellectual skills, the teacher introduced his student to a more prestigious instructor, the locally famous senior licentiate Fan Shengwu, whose school convened at New Tao-

51. *Taozhou ting zhi* of 1908, 106. See also Zhang Tingyu, *Ming shi* 2.15b.
52. Guan, "Xidaotang," 76.

zhou.[53] Following the conventional curriculum for civil service candidates, Ma Qixi placed second in the Taozhou examination, then fourth at the prefectural examination in Gongchang, achieving both the praise of his teacher and the civil rank of *xiucai,* rare for a northwestern Muslim.

Though he had spent much of his time on the standard Neo-Confucian texts, Ma Qixi had also read widely in the *Han kitab* and found there the core of Sino-Muslim knowledge. In his analysis, neither the Confucians nor the Daoists had the highest learning. Rather, Wang Daiyu, Ma Zhu, Liu Zhi, and the others had synthesized the universal Confucian discourse of virtue, morality, nature, and principle with the glorious monotheism of Islam to produce the true way. Acting on his conviction that Sino-Muslims should use Chinese culture as their medium for understanding Islam, Ma Qixi returned to Old Taozhou and opened his own school, the Gold Star Hall (Ch. Jinxing Tang), at a *gongbei* of his own Beizhuang *menhuan.* There he taught Islamic religion, the Chinese curriculum, and the *Han kitab* to a devoted following, which slowly grew to over one hundred students. His students learned the standard vocabulary of *xiushen,* individual cultivation of the inherently virtuous self, but they did so in order to comprehend God's commandments and the model life of the Prophet.

Clearly differing with his ascetically minded, Central Asian influenced Sufi colleagues in the Beizhuang *menhuan,* Ma broke with his original solidarity and became an independent instructor, focusing on Liu Zhi's works. The Sufis of the Khafiya called him heterodox, even a nonbeliever, for his worldly success and his unconventional curriculum; they even went so far as to forbid their followers any meat slaughtered by Ma Qixi or his followers.[54] Since Taozhou's Muslim communities had not been riven by religious conflict before this point, all disturbances could conveniently be blamed on him and his (yet again) New Teaching. By 1902 the strife was sufficiently severe that Beizhuang and Huasi adherents went to court, charging Ma Qixi and his followers with heterodoxy, and the Taozhou subprefect proscribed Ma's teaching and convicted his followers, a number of whom were jailed or beaten.[55] After

53. Zi, "Zhongguo Yisilanjiao Xidaotang shilue," 2.
54. Guan, "Xidaotang," 83.
55. Details of the suit, including the defendants, their sentences, and the verdict's reversal by a higher court, may be found in "Ma Qixi xiansheng," 131–32. This account, very sympathetic to the Xidaotang, was written by an anonymous Muslim associated with the solidarity.

the verdict was reversed a year later, Ma set up a mosque in Taozhou, and the resulting furor threatened to escalate into violence. Taking his cue from Laozi, the legendary Daoist sage who went west beyond the pass, Ma Qixi set out on the pilgrimage to Mecca in 1905 with two disciples.

The three Chinese pilgrims never reached their goal. Trapped by local and regional wars and unsettled political conditions in Russian-dominated Central Asia, Ma spent three years in Samarkand, studying and teaching (his adherents say) among the Baishan suborder of Sufis.[56] After one of his companions died, he returned to Taozhou, more convinced than ever that he should teach Chinese Muslims to understand Islam through Chinese culture, precisely the formula proposed by the authors of the *Han kitab*. Again opening a school, this time he called it the Xidaotang, which could be translated either as Western Hospice or Hall of the Western Dao.[57] Under that name, and in conformity with Ma's unique vision of Sino-Muslim life, the new solidarity flourished. Because of his strong attachment to Chinese culture, Ma Qixi also paid close attention to political developments within China, so when the Qing fell in 1912, the men of the Xidaotang cut their queues and the women unbound their feet.

Establishing the Collective

Appropriate to a young man raised in a mercantile atmosphere, Ma Qixi practiced and taught a very worldly, as well as religious, Islam. He emphasized social practice and economic life, the organization of Muslims for material and spiritual success. To that end, he made the Xidaotang into a collective corporate enterprise in which economic, cultural, and religious life were combined. The capital for this venture came from the possessions of his own family and those of his followers.

56. Baishan (White Mountain), a term common in Sino-Muslim accounts of Central Asian Islam, probably refers to the Āfāqīya, the Naqshabandī suborder associated with Khoja Āfāq and therefore with the Khafīya. That solidarity is called Aqtaghliq, also meaning White Mountain, in Turkic sources. Despite Ma Qixi's difficulties with the Khafīya in his home town, he had been raised within that suborder and probably felt most comfortable with its rituals and texts in the foreign atmosphere of Samarkand (Fletcher, "Naqshbandiyya," 10, n3).

57. The former translation is the more likely, since *daotang* (Sufi hospice) was already an established term among Gansu Muslims and Ma Qixi's mosque lay west of Taozhou's wall. But the ambiguity may well have been intentional, since Ma Qixi's Dao, Islam, came from the west, from Tianfang, from Arabia.

Anyone who entered the Xidaotang as an "inner" (full) member donated all property, personal goods, and wealth to the collective treasury, which the leaders then invested in a wide variety of activities. Beginning with Taozhou's specialty—trade between pastoral Tibet and agricultural-artisanal China—the Xidaotang expanded into agriculture, livestock raising, forestry, and processing. The Xidaotang's trading company, under the corporate name Tian Xing Long, became an important player in the production, concentration, brokering, transport, and sale of goods ranging from grain and vinegar to jade and rare medicaments.

Initial resistance to Tian Xing Long's success came, of course, from its local competitors, chief among them the Huasi *menhuan*'s Yi Xing Gong company, headed by a Taozhou Muslim gentryman. In Huasi perceptions, not only did the Xidaotang teach heterodoxy and lure adherents away from the *menhuan,* it also deprived the established company of revenues and trade. Unfortunately for Ma Qixi and his followers, the Hezhou warlord and Huasi adherent Ma Anliang had invested heavily in the Yi Xing Gong—one source says to the amount of thirty thousand taels of silver.[58] Apart from the obvious economics, Ma Anliang had a variety of reasons to hate, or at least mistrust, Ma Qixi and the Xidaotang. Within the Gansu Muslim institutional world, Ma Anliang supported the Huasi *menhuan,* which had opposed Ma Qixi's "innovations." Allied with the most conservative Manchu ex-governors, Ma Anliang might well have found the Xidaotang's advocacy of Republican loyalty galling. Most telling, the Hezhou warlord certainly wanted to control the commerce of the Taoxi region, a rich source of revenue that was flowing increasingly into the collective coffers of the Xidaotang. Ma Anliang found his solution in the invasion of Gansu by the Bai Lang army in the spring of 1914.

Bai Lang, a talented and charismatic military man from Henan, combined the career and romantic imperial aspirations of a roving brigand with the nationalist politics of the early Republican period. He was denounced as a bandit, touted as a social revolutionary, and widely perceived as the immanent emperor of a new dynasty, an impression he did not hesitate to exploit. He worked for the restoration of the Qing, then accepted the Republican governorship of Henan, and ended by comparing himself to Liu Bang, the founder of the Han dynasty. His campaigns in Henan, Anhui, Hubei, and Shaanxi have been well studied, but the end of his military success, namely his defeat in Gansu, has

58. Guan, "Xidaotang," 85.

not.[59] Unable to reduce Xi'an by siege as Liu Bang had done, Bai Lang's army entered Gansu from Shaanxi at its peak strength, perhaps as many as ten thousand men, heading for Sichuan and a new base. Six weeks later, they emerged from Gansu a straggling mob of disorganized units, fleeing eastward for home. This dramatic change had been wrought by the tenacious resistance of local troops, successful pursuit by central government forces, blockading of the southward passes by Sichuan provincial armies, and by the Gansu terrain. The last stop for Bai Lang had been Old Taozhou.

After taking cities in eastern Gansu in the spring of 1914, Bai Lang lost an important positional battle with Gansu provincial forces along the main Xi'an–Lanzhou highway.[60] He then moved southward only to find the Baishui River uncrossable with the Tibetan snowmelt and the passes blocked by the Sichuanese. With national and Gansu troops behind him, he had to keep moving northwestward to Minzhou, where his frustrated troops looted, raped, and killed inside the walls for a whole night.[61] Unable to follow his original plan, Bai Lang was trapped inside the cul-de-sac of Taoxi—he could not retrace his steps or move south, and Ma Anliang's army blocked the direct route to Lanzhou via Didao, so the Taozhou–Hezhou road offered the only escape route. After defeating the *tusi* Yang Jiqing's Tibetans, Bai's army headed for New, then Old Taozhou, both of which they took, but with very different results. New Taozhou did not resist and was only briefly looted. The gentry and militia of Old Taozhou prepared to defend its stout wall, while the Xidaotang adherents barricaded themselves in their stockade at Xifeng Mountain.[62]

59. Two useful English-language sources on Bai Lang are Hegel, "The White Wolf"; and Perry, "Social Banditry Revisited." Neither deals with the Gansu war, which ended Bai Lang's successful march across North China. Bai Lang was often erroneously called the "White Wolf," for his surname means "white" and his given name is a homophone for "wolf."

60. The surrender of Tongwei County involved the local gentry's welcoming Bai, putting him and his officers up at the local elementary school, and giving them dinner. Bai's social conscience did not allow him to devastate so poor and polite a place, so he donated a substantial sum to the commander to buy books for the schoolchildren (*GNQSL* 28.24b).

61. Mrs. Christie, wife of a missionary, barely escaped with her virtue intact; many local women were not so lucky. Her diary account may be found in the *North China Herald*, June 27, 1914, and a somewhat more cynical version in Farrer, *On the Eaves*, vol. 2, 75–76.

62. A missionary writer claims that the Xidaotang had provided itself with modern weapons, purchased with commercial profits and shipped into Gansu via Hankou and

Descending from the east in the last week of May, Bai confronted the Old Taozhou coalition with overwhelming numbers. Knowing the town's wealth and its Muslim majority, the Henan and Shaanxi troops destroyed the city with a brutality unprecedented in their long march. After a brief battle, the invaders broke the defenders and began a thorough pillage of the walled city, which lay empty even a year later:

> The chief feature was the fact that the four walls enclosed nothing but a mass of ruins, the town having been burnt out by the White Wolf [Bai Lang] rebels the year before; we saw many a ruined city in Kansu in the course of our travels—indeed, in that province ruins are the rule rather than the exception—but nothing so utterly and completely destroyed as Old T'ao Chou.[63]

Reginald Farrer, who was collecting wildflowers in the Tibetan mountains during the battle, heard about it from Mr. Christie and Mr. Purdom, who were in Taozhou only a few days after:

> Tao-jo was taken by storm, and the Wolves immediately set themselves deliberately to destroy every living thing within its walls, not only the men and women, the cattle and horses, but down to the very dogs and cats in the lanes. The gates were stacked up to their arches with carrion, and the streets a chaos of corpses.[64]

The Muslims of the town, many of them Huasi and Beizhuang adherents, held out in one of the large mosques but, facing defeat, either immolated themselves or were burned to death by Bai Lang's men. Between eight thousand and sixteen thousand people died in the sack of Taozhou, a high percentage of them Muslims.[65] Even sources favorable to Bai Lang call the massacre a mistake, and some do not mention it at all.[66]

The social origins of many of Bai Lang's men may hold a clue to the

---

Hanzhong. Certainly the Xidaotang had the money and the connections to accomplish this difficult feat of transport, even under the watchful eyes of Ma Anliang (Andrew, *Crescent*, 58).

63. Teichman, *Travels of a Consular Officer*, 135.

64. Farrer, *On the Eaves*, vol. 2, 101.

65. Pei Jianzhun, "Bai Lang rao Long," 40, reports the higher figure. Most sources lie in between the two.

66. Yu Yao, "Bai Lang qiyi jun," 118.

horrific violence visited on the Taozhou Muslims. They were members of the Gelaohui secret society, which, in the volatile atmosphere of Henan and southern Shaanxi, had become virulently anti-Manchu and anti-Muslim.[67] Contemporary Chinese scholars join Farrer and the correspondent of the *North China Herald* in chorus, accusing Ma Anliang of treachery against his compatriots at Taozhou, of refusal to do battle with Bai Lang. But Ma Anliang's main purpose lay in protecting Hezhou, and beyond it Lanzhou, not the small towns of southern Gansu, and his immobility in the face of an invading army ten thousand strong is certainly understandable, if not forgivable. Passive though it was, his strategy worked. Blocked on the north by Ma's defensive posture at Hezhou, the Bai Lang army had no route except to return eastward via Minzhou. The Tibetans had destroyed the floating bridge over the Tao, and the crossing drowned many of Bai's men. The southern Gansu towns, already pillaged once, held out more effectively than they had before, and the supplies, the loot, and even the food were gone. Bai's career was over, his army a disorganized and hungry rabble splintering and running for home, never to reunite as an effective fighting force. Bai himself was driven to suicide shortly after, but one of his commanders became governor of Shaanxi, and others reintegrated themselves into their home districts.

And the Xidaotang? They held their suburban fortress against an assault by Bai Lang's men and actually left their redoubt to attack the looting invaders, against considerable odds, the day after the city was taken. Retreating further into Tibetan territory with their families, they suffered only minor losses in battle and preserved their strength. And there lay Ma Anliang's opportunity, for he could easily give public credence to the rumors that Ma Qixi had struck a deal with Bai Lang, the murderer of so many Muslims and helpless civilians of all communities. Ma Yuanzhang had resisted Bai Lang in eastern Gansu; Ma Anliang himself had held firm; the Khafiya martyrs of Taozhou had died nobly; but Ma Qixi, he accused, had treacherously sold out.[68] Claiming to be pursuing bandits, in mid-June Ma Anliang sent a battalion to Taozhou, where they entered the Xidaotang compound at Xifeng Mountain and captured twenty-five men, including Ma Qixi, his two

---

67. Reginald Farrer observed the Gelaohui as a menacing presence in Fengxiang a few weeks before the Bai Lang invasion of Gansu (*On the Eaves*, vol. 1, 84).

68. For Ma Yuanzhang's mustering of the Jahrīya militia against Bai Lang, see *GNQSL* 28.25b. For Ma Anliang's use of the rumor of Ma Qixi's connection to Bai Lang, see Guan, "Xidaotang," 85.

younger brothers, his son, and other leaders of the solidarity. Taking them to a nearby riverbank, Ma Anliang's men shot them all.[69]

So personal a vision and leadership as Ma Qixi's might have been irreplaceable, but he had built an institution sufficiently coherent that his successors were able to carry on. For five years after the killings, Xidaotang adherents poured out the collective's wealth in lawsuit after lawsuit, at Lanzhou and then at Beijing, to bring the crime home against Ma Anliang. Each suit was referred back to Zhang Guangjian at Lanzhou, and each time he decided not to interfere. Even after another, smaller massacre of Xidaotang men at Taizi (now Hezheng) during a memorial service, the provincial authorities did not or could not act to censure the powerful Muslim militarist.[70] Finally, following Ma Anliang's death in 1919, the Muslim general Ma Lin brought the Lanzhou authorities and the Xidaotang together to negotiate at Hezhou, and Ma Qixi's solidarity was recognized as a legal Muslim institution rather than a renegade gang.

Fish and Meat: Staying Alive in the 1920s

After its legalization, the Xidaotang had to survive the privations and politics of Gansu in the warlord period. The province had always been poor—had long suffered under the tyranny of a harsh environment, strong military presence, and heavy official exactions—so the 1920s did not bring new kinds of suffering, just more of the old ones. The absence of effective government combined with nature's eccentric depredations to bring the whole region the hardest and poorest of times. Opium cultivation on a vast scale deprived many counties, even multicounty regions, of their grain supplies; multiple currencies made even the simplest market transactions into elaborate calculations; major earthquakes reduced wide areas of eastern Gansu (1920) and the eastern part of the Gansu corridor (1927) to rubble; and drought brought multiprovince famine in the late 1920s.[71]

Even in those awful times, the Xidaotang achieved commercial and

69. The anonymous author of "Ma Qixi xiansheng" (p. 134) writes: "On the nineteenth day of the intercalary fifth month, the warlord Ma Anliang, of the hate-filled movement, used the excuse of clearing out bandits and, without public documents, without legal warrants, shot the master to death. Those who followed him included his brothers, Qijin and Qihua, his son Longde, his nephew Xilong, and [many others]."

70. For a brief account of this incident, see Min, "Hezheng Taizijie," 170.

71. For detailed descriptions of these and other privations, see Lipman, "The Border World," chap. 5.

religious success. The Xidaotang was known as one of the "three great families" of southern Gansu, in company with Yang Jiqing (the Tibetan *tusi* at Choni) and the chief *rimpoche* of the great lamasery at Labrang. At its core lay about four hundred "inner" adherents who lived collectively in a huge compound at Taozhou, administering their commercial empire and common wealth. Each male member received an assignment according to his abilities, so the solidarity made best use of the masculine talent at its disposal. Another one thousand or so adherents lived away from Taozhou, working on the road or at production, processing, and sales enterprises. The Xidaotang bought agricultural land, pastureland, and forest land, all of which they put to profitable use, becoming self-sufficient producers of grain, large-scale traders in livestock, and exporters of wood products. Some Muslims chose not to become fully collectivized members, preferring to remain as private entrepreneurs, working for the Xidaotang but retaining their own possessions; one survey estimated their numbers at around 3,500, for a total of around five thousand members in the entire organization.[72] This large, well-integrated collective structure clearly had very positive benefits, for the solidarity thrived even in the 1920s.

It did not escape unscathed, however, from the warlord battles that plagued the region. After Feng Yuxiang took titular command of the northwest, local commanders of all ethnicities scrambled to accommodate his powerful outside army. Hoping to drive Feng away from Taoxi and Huangzhong, Ma Zhongying, the Little Commander (local Ch. Ga Siling), a Xining Muslim adventurer from Ma Qi's family,[73] raided the entire Hezhou region in the late 1920s, attacking Hezhou three times, and then fled southward toward Taozhou with thousands of young Muslim men, eager to plunder.[74] Ma Zhongying's troops clashed with local Muslims and with the Tibetans in and near Old Taozhou, so the Xidaotang members abandoned their shops, warehouses, and homes,

72. Guan, "Xidaotang," 89, citing "an investigation."
73. The European adventurer Sven Hedin wrote a book about Ma Zhongying's campaigns in Xinjiang, giving him the name Big Horse, but he was always known as the Little Commander in Gansu, for he began his campaign against Feng Yuxiang's Guominjun at the tender age of seventeen (Hedin, *The Flight of "Big Horse"*). After three years of peripatetic campaigning in Gansu, with no apparent effect on the Guominjun but devastating consequences for much of the province, he entered his forces into the factionalist politics of Xinjiang, described (more accurately than Hedin could) in Forbes, *Warlords and Muslims,* chaps. 3–4. Ma Zhongying fled to the Soviet Union in 1934, at twenty-three years of age, and no one knows what became of him (Fan Manyun, "Liu Yufen," 110–27).
74. See Lipman, "Ethnic Conflict," 78–81.

fleeing into Tibetan territory for their lives. The Xidaotang central compound became Ma Zhongying's headquarters.

In three years of complex fighting, the Xidaotang lost a large portion of its wealth, but none of its cohesion or political savvy. Even while its headquarters lived in exile among the Tibetans, branches continued to do business, and a new office opened in Zhangjiakou (Chahar's entrepot, northwest of Beiping).[75] When peace returned after 1932, the solidarity's leaders forged closer ties with the new rulers of the northwest, the Guomindang, and once again thrived. Like Ma Fuxiang, they saw their best advantage in alliance with the Guomindang's national power, which would allow them considerable local autonomy while encouraging peace and order for their commerce. When war with Japan broke out, the Xidaotang was in an ideal physical and economic position to provide the Nationalist government in Chongqing with the Taozhou region's special products, especially leather. Ma Mingren, third *jiaozhu* of the Xidaotang, traveled to Chongqing in 1941 and was introduced to President and Commander-in-Chief Jiang Jieshi by Bai Chongxi, the Muslim general from Guangxi Province.[76]

At its height around 1946 the Xidaotang had retail shops or agents in Chengdu, Songpan (Sichuan), Xi'an, Zhangjiakou, Beiping, Tianjin, Shanghai, and Inner Mongolia. In southern Gansu, it possessed two thousand draft animals, seven thousand *mu* (over one thousand acres) of land, five ranches with three thousand head of livestock, thirteen forestry stations, eighteen water-powered mills, two brick and tile kilns, two oil presses, and shops for making leather, flour, and vinegar. Members traded cloth, metalware, grain, flour, oil, sugar, medicine, and tea to the Tibetans, in exchange for wild animal pelts, rare medicines (especially musk), hides, and wool. They took cattle to Minxian, horses to Shaanxi, coral and jade to Inner Mongolia. In 1927 they had founded a joint company with a Beijing firm to sell borderland goods in Beijing and bring metropolitan products to southern Gansu.[77]

Being a Muslim and a Chinese

So engaged was the Xidaotang in business and politics that we might forget its religious and intellectual character. As one of modern China's most successful collectives, it merits recognition and study as a socioeco-

75. Zhu Gang, "Xidaotang dashi ji," 255–58.
76. Guan, "Xidaotang," 94.
77. Guan, "Xidaotang," 90–91.

nomic institution, but it also stands out as a *Muslim* solidarity. Apart from confirming an ordinary Chinese stereotype, shared by the Muslims themselves, that Sino-Muslims are inherently and uniquely good at trade in the marketplace, the history of the Xidaotang also reveals the flexibility of Chinese culture as a medium for the transmission of Islam (see plate 23).

Ma Qixi and his successors led conventional Muslim religious lives—that is, they (and some of their followers) conducted five daily prayer services, gave sermons on Friday, fasted during Ramadan, and so on. Their religious innovations lay in establishing the centrality of *China* in their interpretation and transmission of Islamic meaning. By relying on Liu Zhi and the other *Han kitab* writers, they enabled their adherents to study and comprehend Islam within China, self-consciously "using Chinese culture to enhance Islamic truths."[78] One of Ma Qixi's surviving texts, a commentary on Liu Zhi's philosophy, succinctly elucidates the Sino-Muslim synthesis, in both language and substance: "The way in which the Five Pillars [of Islam] order a person's life is by controlling the self and expelling the selfish, reviving the true luminous virtue [Ch. *ming de*], so that one might return to the state of perfect impartiality."[79]

Unlike the Khafiya and Jahriya, the Xidaotang did not bring any new texts from Arabia, nor did it create any new rituals that became bones of contention. Rather, the solidarity placed its greatest emphasis on education, conducted both in Chinese and in the Islamic languages, in contrast to the *jingtang jiaoyu* of other groups and times. Xidaotang members, male and female, received a fine Muslim education, as the anecdote at the head of this section on Ma Qixi reveals. Because Ma Qixi and his successors emphasized the *Han kitab,* they also learned to read Chinese at a very high level, and many also studied Tibetan in order to succeed in the solidarity's frontier commerce. The Xidaotang established schools almost immediately upon its founding, and many of their young people went on to high school in Lanzhou, and even to university, not a common achievement among the education-starved Gansu Muslims.[80]

Xidaotang schools thus combined secular education in Chinese texts, Islamic education in Arabic and Persian, and Sino-Islamic education in the *Han kitab,* giving their students an unprecedented advantage in the context of China's expanding involvement on its frontiers. They certainly did not neglect their religion, for Ma Qixi himself claimed that

---

78. Zhu Gang, "Zhongguo Yisilanjiao," 103.
79. Guan, "Xidaotang," 81. Thanks to Dan Gardner for his perfect impartiality.
80. Ma Fuqun, "Xidaotang Ma Qixi," 144–53.

Islam's truth lay at the foundation of all truth, and Xidaotang Muslims paid close attention to their Islamic duties.[81] But Ma Qixi's emphasis on the *Han kitab,* for which the Xidaotang received the sometimes pejorative nickname *Hanxue pai* (the Chinese studies faction), distinguished them from other northwestern Muslims. Drawing on a saying attributed to Ma Mingxin, Ma Qixi recognized both the Sufi and the *Han kitab* influences that shaped him and his movement: "Jielian [Liu Zhi] planted the seeds, Guanchuan [Ma Mingxin] opened the flowers, and I reap the fruit."[82] With the solidarity of a kibbutz, the success of a commercial corporation, a serious Islamic heritage, and strong motivation to be self-consciously Chinese, the Xidaotang members adapted quickly to China's rapidly impinging modernity.

As has been noted above, in this period of its greatest modern disintegration, when central power had virtually ceased to exist, China expanded outward through militarism and modernism, cultural centralization without a political center, to incorporate its frontiers more effectively than the Qing had been able or desired to do. Ma Fuxiang, Ma Yuanzhang, and Ma Qixi all felt that pressure in different ways, and all worked to ensure the success of their communities—defined as lineage, religious solidarity, local community, region, or the Sino-Muslims as a whole—drawing closer to New China. One measure of their devotion to this goal lies in their decisions to pursue Chinese calligraphy as an art, as a cultural expression, as a means of social communication with elite non-Muslims. Ma Fuxiang became known for his prefaces, Ma Yuanzhang for his letters and essays, and Ma Qixi for his ceremonial scrolls (Ch. *duilian*).

Our final Muslim leader, Ma Wanfu of the Dongxiang, took the opposite tack and tried to protect Islam and Muslims in China by an older strategy, by purifying religion and practice through "authentic" texts and rituals brought from Arabia. The fate of his fundamentalist venture will serve as the last chapter in this history, for it, too, could not escape the acculturating power of New China as a nation-state. Though Ma Wanfu himself never became a calligrapher, the second generation in his solidarity included a number of men who did.

81. Zhu Gang, "Zhongguo Yisilanjiao," 104, writes: "Xidaotang adherents prayed all the time. Especially when they were working for the good of the *jiaomen,* or when they met with difficulty in any activity, they would chant the *Kalima* of praise [the profession of faith, 'There is no God but God, and Muhammad is God's Prophet'], rhythmically and in unison. This sound often became an encouragement for people, a mantra to encourage them to brave any hardships."

82. Ma Fuqun, "Liu Jielian xiansheng," 180.

MA WANFU (1853–1934)
AND THE RISE OF THE CHINESE *IKHWAN*

Oh God! Help our government and nation, defeat the invaders, and exterminate our enemies. Protect us from the evil deeds done by the violent Japanese. They have occupied our cities and killed our people. Send upon them a furious wind, cause their airplanes to fall in the wilderness, and their battleships to sink in the sea! Cause their army to scatter, their economy to collapse! Give them their just reward! True God, answer our prayer! Amen.[83]

The Early Life of Ma Wanfu, Hajjī

We have seen Islamic currents from West and Central Asia arrive in Sino-Muslim communities in successive, intermittent waves. The first, the early transmission of Islam, based in sojourning merchant enclaves, lasted from the seventh century to the fourteenth, with a tremendous boost from the transregional, unifying force of the Mongol conquest. The Ming period, one of relative isolation from West Asia, saw the growth of an indigenous Islamic tradition in Chinese, including *jing-tang jiaoyu* and the early *Han kitab*. The second wave, that of Sufism and the *tarīqa*, lasted from the seventeenth century to the nineteenth and culminated in the formation of the *menhuan* in the northwest. Non-Sufi (Gedimu) communities continued to exist, of course, and constituted the mainstream of Sino-Muslim life outside the northwest and parts of Yunnan.

This influx of Sufi ideas and institutions had a complex and subtle relationship to the violent changes going on in Qing China, changes that brought some Sino-Muslims to oppose the ruling dynasty (Ma Mingxin, Ma Hualong, Du Wenxiu), others to defend it (Ma Guobao, Wang Dagui, Ma Anliang). With their non-Muslim neighbors, all of them felt to varying degrees the effects of dynastic decline and the encroachments of Euro-American political and economic expansion. Precisely during a period of intense foreign pressure on the Qing, the 1890s, a third wave of Islamic influence, scripturalist fundamentalism, lapped up onto China's inland frontier. Calling itself names familiar to historians of the Muslim heartlands, this new movement became powerful through allies as unlikely as Muslim militarism and Chinese national-

83. See Ye Zhenggang, "Ningxia Yiheiwani," 319, for a reproduction of the prayer in its poster form.

ism. In the late twentieth century it continues to wield power in many Sino-Muslim communities and constitutes one of China's largest religious associations.

Sufism had come to China through two types of leaders. Some, such as Hidāyat Allāh (Khoja Āfāq) of the Naqshabandīya, were West and Central Asian Muslims who traveled to China as missionaries. Others, such as Ma Laichi and Ma Mingxin, were Chinese Muslims who went west on the *hajj*, to seek texts, inspiration, and teaching in Muslim centers. A major intellectual and religious movement of the Muslim world, scripturalist fundamentalism, arrived late in the nineteenth century by both of these means, with Sino-Muslim pilgrims playing the greater role in its transmission. Chinese Muslim narratives concentrate on one man, Hajjī Guoyuan (1853?–1934), whose Chinese name was Ma Wanfu and whose Muslim name was Nuhai, as the primary carrier of these new ideas.[84]

Ma Wanfu was called Guoyuan after his native town, in the eastern subprefecture (Dongxiang) of Hezhou. Like many Muslims of that region, Ma Wanfu spoke a Mongolic language as his native tongue. People of the Dongxiang also had a reputation as a tightly knit, impenetrable, and intransigent ethnic community. Local non-Muslims feared them, as they did the Salars, as violent and unpredictable, saying that they stuck together and enjoyed a good feud. Ma Wanfu's father and grandfather belonged to the same Beizhuang *menhuan* as Ma Qixi, founder of the Xidaotang. Ma Tong, who conducted field research there during the 1950s, records that Beizhuang adherents claim religious descent from an Afghan Sufi living in Yarkand during the eighteenth century. Several heads of the *menhuan* had gone to Xinjiang to seek inspiration, and the leader during Ma Wanfu's early years had made the pilgrimage to Mecca.[85]

Ma Wanfu's father and grandfather were local religious professionals, so he began his study of Arabic and Persian at an early age and performed brilliantly. At only twenty-two he was initiated into the order ("donned his cloak") and ordained as a religious teacher.[86] During almost two decades of teaching in Gansu, Ma Wanfu became less

---

84. Chronological accounts of Ma Wanfu's life may be found in Ma Kexun, "Zhongguo Yisilanjiao Yiheiwanipai"; Ma Tong, *Zhongguo Yisilan . . . shilue*, 127–54; and Bai Shouyi, "Ma Wanfu."

85. Ma Tong, *Zhongguo Yisilan . . . shilue*, 277–93, 487.

86. The use of the term "donned his cloak" (Ch. *chuanyi*) for initiation into a Sufi order is general throughout the Muslim world.

and less satisfied with the texts and practices of the communities in which he worked. Finally, in 1888, he took to the road with his teacher and a wealthy Muslim provincial graduate (Ch. *juren*) named Ma Huisan, and together they undertook the rigors and dangers of the journey to Mecca. There Ma Wanfu entered a religious academy and pursued advanced studies in Islamic languages, law, and liturgy for four years.

Here we must discuss briefly the political and religious situation on the Arabian peninsula during Ma Wanfu's sojourn there in the 1890s. The coastal plain and the holy cities lay under the rule of Ottoman governors, while the interior was turbulent with the struggles that eventually brought the Ibn-Sa'ud family to power. Since the late eighteenth century an alliance in the arid Najd Desert had united the political ambitions of the Ibn-Sa'ud clan and the religious claims of Muhammad ibn 'Abd al-Wahhāb and his successors. Sometimes powerful enough to conquer the coastal plain, that alliance during the 1890s had been driven back on its desert bases, but it continued to exert strong religious influence while in political eclipse.

Muhammad ibn 'Abd al-Wahhāb belonged to the small, fundamentalist Hanbali school of jurisprudence, which advocated the strictest monotheism, demanded adherence to "original" Koranic principles and opposed later interpretations and individual judgment. In particular, 'Abd al-Wahhāb and his followers found Sufism, with its mystical doctrine of human unity with the Divine, heterodox and abhorrent.[87] The veneration of saints and tombs, especially if taken to the point of worship, repelled them as a polytheistic accretion on the pure monotheism of Islam. Willing to go to war in defense of this fundamentalist purity, 'Abd

---

87. See chapter 3 for 'Abd al-Wahhāb's intellectual and religious relationship to the revivalist impulse of Ma Mingxin and the Chinese Jahrīya: Joseph Fletcher, by brilliant detective work and with conscious irony, linked Muhammad ibn 'Abd al-Wahhāb not only with Sufism but even with Chinese Sufism. Their connection lies in the life and teaching of Ibrāhīm b. Hasan al-Kūrānī (1616–90), a Naqshabandī Sufi as well as an initiate of other orders. Al-Kūrānī and his son, Abu 't-Tāhir Muhammad al-Kurdī, taught Muslims from all over the world, including Shāh Wālī Allāh of Delhi and Muhammad Hayāt as-Sindī, also an Indian, who was Muhammad ibn 'Abd al-Wahhāb's teacher. Among al-Kūrānī's other students we find az-Zayn b. Muhammad 'Abd al-Bāqī al-Mizjājī (d. 1725), a Yemeni Sufi who, probably through his son, 'Abd al-Khāliq (d. 1740), taught Ma Mingxin, the founder of the Chinese Jahrīya. The fact that al-Kūrānī and his son actually came from Kurdistan and taught the vocal *dhikr* to their Sino-Muslim students led Fletcher to name a section of his last paper "The Remembrance of the Kurds and Hui," the only legitimate usage of that dreadful pun, common among English-speaking cognoscenti of the Sino-Muslims, that I have ever found ("Naqshbandiyya," 24–29).

al-Wahhāb and his successors claimed unique truth for their version of Islamic practice, condemning other Muslims as deviants or even as nonbelievers for dissenting. This attitude, often erroneously generalized to include all Muslim fundamentalism, came to be called "Wahhabism" by European scholars and was perceived to lie at the root of Muslim violence all over Asia in the nineteenth century.

In Arabia from 1888 to 1892, Ma Wanfu absorbed a variety of religious teachings, which certainly included fundamentalist ideas such as those of ʿAbd al-Wahhāb. Though influenced by them, Ma did not live under Saʿudi rule in Mecca, nor did he ever publicly renounce the Hanafi school of jurisprudence in which he had been educated. Rather, he came to perceive his mission to be one of sweeping reform, not doctrinaire conversion to Hanbali practice. During those years, he also befriended and guided a number of Chinese Muslims who came on the pilgrimage. Among them were ten *ahong* from the Dongxiang, who returned to China with an abiding admiration for Ma Wanfu and became the core of his scripturalist movement after his return. Persuaded by one of his teachers that his work lay in China, not in further study, Ma Wanfu took ship in Arabia in 1892 and arrived in Guangzhou that same year.[88]

Few Chinese Muslims could undertake the *hajj*, primarily because of their poverty and the distance and danger involved. The holy books and liturgical texts they used, therefore, contained numerous errors, for they were damaged or poorly copied by ill-educated *ahong* and not regularly replaced or replenished by books from the Muslim heartlands. Muslims thus regarded returned pilgrims, especially teachers bearing "authentic" texts and capable of Islamic textual scholarship, with special veneration, as we have seen in the cases of Ma Laichi and Ma Mingxin. So it was with Ma Wanfu:

> [On his way home from Canton] Ma Wanfu was in Laohekou, Hunan, during Ramadan and stayed at the mosque there. The local Muslims expressed a warm welcome for this returned pilgrim, both a *hajjī* and a teacher. The local *imām* allowed him to lead prayers, and during the evening service he bowed four times, then sat and read the hymns of praise aloud. The local people and the *imām* said, "Since Waqqas Baba taught us here, we have always bowed twice and then read the hymns of praise. On what do you base your four bowings?" He

---

88. Ma Tong, *Zhongguo Yisilan . . . suyuan*, 182.

answered, "On the scriptures." . . . He stayed more than a year [to teach] and left a lasting impression on the local Muslims.[89]

Imbued as he was with reformist, even fundamentalist ideas, Ma Wanfu must have been a formidable figure despite his youth, threatening to contemporary practice and therefore to established institutions. In highly acculturated Hunan, there would have been none to dispute him, but Gansu's Muslim elite, with a deeper and stronger tradition of Islamic expertise, would not acquiesce so quickly.

Upon his return to the northwest in 1893, Ma Wanfu accepted an appointment as teacher and *imām* in the home village of Ma Huisan, his pilgrimage companion. Because of his presence, that small mosque became an important center of learning in the Dongxiang region, and teachers from all over Gansu flocked to study with Hajjī Guoyuan. Lacking inspired teachers and eager to study authentic texts from Arabia, these men became his disciples, joining him and his "ten returned pilgrims" in a new movement. Borrowing from the desert-dwelling followers of ibn-Sa'ud, Ma Wanfu called himself and his students Ahl as-Sunna (Ch. Aihailisunnai), the Kinsmen of the Tradition. Later, perhaps after 'Abd al-'Azīz's success in unifying Arabia under his rule and under Wahhabi religious domination, the distant Chinese Muslims borrowed another name for themselves, the triumphant al-Ikhwan al-Muslimun (Ch. Yiheiwani), the Muslim Brotherhood, to signify the unity of all Muslims. That name denoted the fundamentalist, scripturalist impulse, which had such wide-reaching effects all over the Muslim world.[90]

Text and Context: The Diffusion of the Ikhwan in China

Specific cultural contexts determined the reception and use of that fundamentalist impulse within Muslim communities, as they always do

89. Ma Kexun, "Zhongguo Yisilanjiao Yiheiwanipai," 445–46. The Waqqas Baba upon whom the Hunan Muslims call for the legitimacy of their practice was a Companion of the Prophet, perhaps his maternal uncle, Sa'ad Waqqas, who looms large in Sino-Muslim legends of their own origins. Scholarly opinion has rejected all of the tales of his mission to China as fantasy, but they have great power among the Sino-Muslims to this day. For a summary of the texts and stories, see Leslie, *Islam*, chap. 8.

90. Contrary to some Muslim and non-Muslim images, the effects of Islamic fundamentalism are not always and everywhere the same, any more than are those of Christian fundamentalism. See Geertz, *Islam Observed*, chap. 3, for an extended comparison of the results of the scripturalist impulse in Indonesia and Morocco.

with religious, political, or academic innovations. China's "Wahhabis," as their enemies called them, must therefore be studied both as bearers of ideas present elsewhere in the Muslim world and as participants in specifically Chinese, especially northwest Chinese, communities and events. The fate of Ma Wanfu's Ikhwan presents a compelling case for this approach. Within one generation of its fundamentalist, antiacculturationist founder, the movement had become an ally of Chinese nationalism, a tool of an acculturating Muslim elite, and an important bridge between Muslim communities and the burgeoning Chinese nation-state.

Ma Wanfu, opposed to Sufism and to all external influences on Islam, refused to learn to read and write Chinese, forbade his children to learn Chinese, and insisted upon Arabic and Persian education as the foundation of Muslim orthopraxy. He spoke Chinese, but his academy and his movement were based on the purity and distinction of Islam, its sacred languages, and its adherents among the nonbelievers. Like the Hanbali reformers of Arabia, Ma Wanfu also claimed a special truth for the Ikhwan among Muslim teachings. His frequent use of the slogan "Venerate the scriptures, reform the customs" (Ch. *Zunjing gaisu*) led to his movement's being called the "scripturalist faction" (Ch. *zunjing pai*).

Ma Wanfu's program for reform of Islam in China had ten basic tenets, most of them dealing with liturgical practice and directed against Sufism.[91] They were perceived as a full-scale attack on established ways among the northwestern Chinese Muslims, against both Sufi and Gedimu practice. They focus particularly on the *menhuan,* which had accumulated wealth and high status through hereditary succession to the leadership of Sufi suborders. The performance of the veneration rituals at tombs, for example, and the great memorial festivals for saints and *shaikh*s were occasions for massive contributions by members of Sufi orders to their leaders, who would lose that income if Ma Wanfu's program were put into practice. Ma Wanfu also recommended that Muslims read the Koran themselves, which would deprive religious professionals of the income obtained by reading sacred texts on behalf of congregation members at times of religious significance. One of the Ikhwan's favorite slogans, "If you read scripture, don't eat; if you eat, don't read scripture" (Ch. *Nianle buchi, chile bunian*), aimed to end the practice of feeding the *imām* or *ahong* in exchange for the reading of scripture. Indeed, paying religious professionals to undertake tasks originally required of all Muslims struck Ma Wanfu as a forbidden Chinese

91. Ma Tong, *Zhongguo Yisilan . . . shilue,* 131.

accretion. Even the wearing of coarse white mourning clothes (Ch. *daixiao*) by Muslims seemed to him a violation of Islamic distinctiveness and a degradation of Islam.

In Ma's design, the Kinsmen of the Tradition had to be radically separated from non-Muslims, and their common orthopraxy and knowledge of texts had to produce an upsurge of unity. Given the sweeping character of his reform proposals, we should not be surprised that he met with considerable resistance. Though he attacked Gedimu customs as well as Sufism, immediate and powerful opposition came from the *menhuan*. Their leaders saw the Ikhwan as a serious threat to their dominance; as zealous teachers flocked to the Dongxiang to study with Ma Wanfu, his enemies planned to neutralize his influence. In 1895–96 tens of thousands died as internecine Muslim strife brought down the wrath of the Qing state once again on Hezhou, Xunhua, and Xining. Responding, as had Ma Yuanzhang, to the disastrous results of disunity, Ma Wanfu came to a very different conclusion. Declaring that his objective was the unification of all Muslim religious factions in northwest China, he argued that shedding blood for Islam in a war against nonbelievers constituted noble martyrdom (Ar. *shahīd*, Ch. *shexide*).

Since Ma Wanfu directed his movement primarily against the *menhuan*, as well as supporting the anti-Qing struggle, he alienated important Gansu leaders, especially Ma Anliang, who also opposed Ma Qixi's Xidaotang with such deadly purpose. Trained in both the Muslim and Chinese curricula, Ma Anliang had been raised by his father, Ma Zhan'ao, to be a bridge between Islamic culture and Chinese culture, between Qing power and their family's control over the Hezhou region. As Ma Wanfu began to build his movement, Ma Anliang responded with confrontation and repression, using his army to enforce his interests in religious as well as political life. In acute danger, Ma Wanfu fled to Shaanxi—not westward but eastward, away from the Muslim heartlands—where Gedimu communities welcomed him more readily than did the strongly Sufi centers of Gansu. For the next ten years the reformist *hajjī* wandered as an exile, sometimes back in Gansu, sometimes in Shaanxi or even in Xinjiang, but never far ahead of Ma Anliang's pursuit. Despite living and working under cover, Ma Wanfu still managed to maintain his ambition to defeat the *menhuan* and institute a reform of Muslim religion and daily life.

Finally, in 1917, Ma Anliang caught up with Ma Wanfu, then living in Hami. In that chaotic, decentralized period following the fall of the Qing, Ma Anliang and Zhang Guangjian, the non-Muslim governor of Gansu, combined to request the aid of the non-Muslim warlord of

Xinjiang, Yang Zengxin, in doing away with the Ikhwan. Ma Anliang and Yang Zengxin had fought together against Muslim rebels in 1895, while Ma Wanfu had encouraged those same insurgents, so Ma Anliang could call on both comradeship and desire for revenge in seeking a non-Muslim's help in apprehending the renegade Ikhwan leader. Arrested by Yang Zengxin's constabulary and chained in a prisoner's cart, Ma Wanfu and his son were shipped eastward along the ancient Silk Road toward certain death at Lanzhou.[92]

Alliance with Ma Qi

At this point an ironic and dramatic twist of politics intervened in what might otherwise have been a very short history of scripturalist fundamentalism in northwest China. One of Ma Anliang's sometime allies among the Muslim generals of Gansu, Ma Qi, had for some time worked to create an independent territorial base at Xining, at the cultural edges of both China and Tibet, on the vital Tibet–Mongolia road. After the fall of the Qing, Ma Qi obtained dominion over Xining and built up his family's strength and fortune in that isolated but relatively productive region. Despite his prosperity, however, Ma Qi could not match Ma Anliang's military power or his religious and political connections. Searching for means to encroach on his ally-rival's power, Ma Qi discovered Ma Wanfu's predicament and decided to enlist the Ikhwan to his advantage against Ma Anliang's Huasi *menhuan*.

Ma Qi sent a military force through the Biandu Gorge to the main highway. They easily overwhelmed the guards and brought the Ikhwan leader to Xining, where he resided for the rest of his life, depending entirely on the patronage of Ma Qi and his descendants. Ma Qi, for his part, promulgated the Ikhwan's religious tenets as his own. He instituted strict antiopium prohibitions, for example, and reduced the power of *menhuan* within his territory. He did not, however, take Ma Wanfu's entire separatist program to heart. He continued to participate in the China-oriented militarist system, to make allies and enemies among Muslim and non-Muslim generals, and to involve himself in the nationalist struggles of the 1916–30 period of disunion. Ma Qi thus began the process that was to transform the Ikhwan from a radical fundamentalist group to a much less divisive, much more China-centered reformist movement.

After all, the Ikhwan, however appealing it may have been to reli-

92. Ma Kexun, "Zhongguo Yisilanjiao Yiheiwanpai," 456.

gious professionals eager to transcend their imperfect texts, had not succeeded in drawing much loyalty away from established institutions. Even the Gedimu communities of Shaanxi, where Ma Wanfu had worked for many years, had not become hotbeds of scripturalist radicalism. The fundamentalist Ikhwan could not succeed to any great extent in communities that perceived themselves as respectably and correctly Chinese, and most Muslim communities in the northwest either did or wished to appear as if they did. In addition, the solid networks of the *menhuan* and the centuries-old traditions of the Gedimu held great power among Sino-Muslims. The leadership of men such as Ma Anliang and Ma Qi was grounded in their proven ability to protect their communities from the Qing state, from violent coreligionists, and from communal antagonists such as Tibetans and non-Muslim Chinese. Ma Wanfu and his disciples could not replace these established leaders until they joined their banner to Ma Qi's secular power, but in order to serve his purposes, they had to dissociate themselves from a separatist message and embrace a more socially conservative platform acceptable to their patron (see plate 24).

Once that happened, the Ikhwan's advantages as an advocate of Muslim unity became clear. In light of their obvious rivalries with one another, the *menhuan* could not claim to be promoting unity, and Gedimu mosques lacked intercommunity connections. The Ikhwan, therefore, filled an important gap in northwestern Muslim life after 1917, calling for Islam in China to become a coherent and unified force but gradually reducing its potentially separatist demands. So successful was Ma Qi in promoting and using the Ikhwan that Ma Fuxiang's family at Ningxia also decided to identify with its aims and take advantage of the inherent legitimacy of its call for Muslim unity. Though they continued to be members of their family's original *menhuan*, Ma Fuxiang, his son Ma Hongkui, and his nephew Ma Hongbin all encouraged the Ikhwan in their territory, which stretched from the Mongolian desert almost to the Wei River valley.[93]

The Ikhwan and Chinese Nationalism

In its association with Ma Qi, Ma Fuxiang, and their successors, the Ikhwan dropped much of its fundamentalist program, at least parts that impinged on the world of politics. Indeed, following its need to be politically reliable among these rather conservative Muslim warlords, the

93. Mian, *Ningxia*, 118–31.

Ikhwan eliminated any reference to ʿAbd al-Wahhāb from its teachings. Claiming to continue the Sunni, Hanafi teachings universal among Sino-Muslims, the Ikhwan dissociated itself consciously from the Hanbali movement of the Saudi Arabian Ikhwan while retaining its anti-Sufi, exoteric religious perspective.[94] As an example of this transformation, let us consider the career of Hu Songshan (1880–1956), an Ikhwan teacher who became an important figure during the war against Japan.[95] The son of a northern Gansu *ahong* who belonged to a Khafiya *menhuan*, Hu Songshan was raised to continue his father's work and allegiances, but by his eighteenth year he had already surpassed his father and taken a new teacher, Wang Naibi of Haicheng. Advancing rapidly in his studies, Hu became Wang's favorite pupil and joined his teacher in reading the "new" texts made available through Ma Wanfu's Ikhwan.

Deeply moved and convinced of the necessity to reform the *menhuan* system, Hu rushed through the remainder of Wang's curriculum and returned to Ningxia at the age of twenty-one to become the first Ikhwan *ahong* in that heavily Muslim region. He persevered despite attacks from local *menhuan* adherents, including physical violence. Within ten years the Ikhwan had a stable membership in Tongxin County, and a number of teachers promulgated Hu Songshan's version of Ma Wanfu's scripturalist message. He opposed all cash payments to religious professionals for services rendered, striking at the economic base of the *menhuan* system. He opposed expensive and wasteful religious rituals, especially those surrounding funerals, and particularly vilified the obviously Chinese wearing of white mourning garments. Finally, he opposed Sufism in its entirety, the veneration of saints, meditation at tombs, and the mystical doctrine of unity with God. In order to demonstrate his devotion to the Ikhwan's stand against *menhuan*, Hu Songshan took dramatic action and destroyed his own father's *gongbei*, built at Tongxin after 1899.

The course of Hu Songshan's life might have resembled Ma Wanfu's more closely had he gone to Mecca earlier in the century. But Hu delayed that obligation until 1925, when he was forty-five years old. His experience changed his perspective on Islam, on China, and on the role of the Ikhwan. Unlike Ma Wanfu, Hu Songshan suffered prejudice through his long round-trip pilgrimage not because he was a Muslim but because he came from China. He concluded from this painful lesson

94. Ma Tong, "Alabo de Wahabiyapai." I am grateful to Prof. Ma for allowing me to cite this paper.

95. For Hu's life, see Ye Zhenggang, "Ningxia Yihewani," 308–25; Mian, *Ningxia*, 120–24; and Ma Tong, *Zhongguo Yisilan . . . shilue*, 146.

that only a strong China could give the Sino-Muslims the individual and collective freedom to practice their religion and guarantee their status and safety outside China's borders. So he became a fervent Chinese patriot. After returning to Ningxia he continued to preach the Ikhwan's doctrine, but he added to it strong doses of current events and advocacy of Chinese unity in the face of imperialist threats and domestic warlordism.

During the 1930s, as he observed the national and international scene, Hu continued to believe that only Chinese national strength could save the Muslims of China, and that only modern education and science could engender national strength. He thus agreed with the many members of the Gansu Muslim elite—including Ma Fuxiang, Ma Yuanzhang, Ma Qixi, and their successors—that Muslim schools must teach Chinese and modern subjects such as science and foreign languages, as well as the Islamic curriculum. Committed to this idea, Hu Songshan gave up his post as an *ahong* to become the principal of the new Sino-Arabic Middle School (Ch. Zhong-A Zhongxue) established by the Muslim gentry of Wuzhong County, near Ningxia.

After the Japanese invaded China proper in 1937, Hu Songshan espoused the Chinese nationalist cause even more fervently. He decreed that every morning's required prayers would be accompanied by the salute to the flag and an exhortation to national pride and patriotism. When he delivered the Friday sermon in the school's prayer hall, he invoked Koranic authority to urge sacrifice in the anti-Japanese struggle. To spread his message more widely, he penned a prayer in Arabic and Chinese (translated at the head of this section), had it printed bilingually, and posted it in all mosques, schools, and Muslim gathering-places in the area. We see in this prayer an intimacy with China-as-home combined with faith in God that is not often found in the liturgies of dispersed Islam. It resembles closely the vernacular "prayers for our country" said in Diaspora synagogues, after the Enlightenment and the French Revolution brought citizenship and civil rights to some Euro-American Jews. The author of this plea was as clearly Chinese as he was Muslim, and his membership in a putatively fundamentalist movement only underscores the importance of that combination.

Truly, the Ikhwan had come far from Ma Wanfu's original purposes. Instead of resistance even to becoming literate in Chinese, Hu Songshan and other Ningxia Ikhwan teachers translated important Muslim texts into Chinese. Hu Songshan followed the Neo-Confucian Muslim authors of the *Han kitab* by composing a "Muslim Three-Character Classic" as a primer for Sino-Muslim students in their study of Islamic faith, ritual, and daily life. Though Ikhwan mosques, like Gedimu mosques in northwest China, did not have any overarching institutional unity, they did improve upon Gedimu fragmentation by holding major religious ceremonies at larger, central mosques called *haiyisi*. These mosques invited Ikhwan adherents from surrounding smaller communities, generating some supralocal solidarity.[96] The Ikhwan was also held together by the oppositional quality of its religious ideas, by common use of the specific texts Ma Wanfu had brought from Arabia, and by the consciousness of purity and rectitude that belongs to reformers.

Hu Songshan cannot be considered a "typical" Ikhwan teacher, for he stood out by his liberal attitude toward modern ideas and practices. He allowed photographs to be taken of himself and his mosque, he encouraged the students in his school to practice sports, and he attempted to discover a Muslim cosmology compatible with modern science. A tireless promoter of Muslim unity in a strong China, he studied the Chinese classics in order to urge solidarity between Muslim and non-Muslim for nationalist goals. In doing so, he unified the goals of the apparently irredentist Ikhwan with those of the *Han kitab*: to make Islam comprehensible, moral, and effective within a Chinese political, intellectual, and cultural world without compromising its core principles. In apparent contradiction to Ma Wanfu, his anti-Qing, antiassimilationist teacher, Hu Songshan joined his life and work to those of Ma Fuxiang, Ma Yuanzhang, and Ma Qixi, all of whom tried to make a safe place for Islam and Muslims in modern Gansu. Ma Fuxiang chose involvement in national politics and the Guomindang, Ma Yuanzhang the revival of a transformed Jahrīya, and Ma Qixi the creation of an entirely new solidarity, the Xidaotang. All of them became leaders of solidarities coping with the problem of being a Muslim in China. The variety of their solutions, even in a single province in the northwest, reveals the hitherto hidden complexity and richness of the Sino-Muslim world.

---

96. Sources favorable to the Ikhwan credit them with this innovation, but Gao, "Linxia Qingzhen," 197–200, claims that they were created at Hezhou by Ma Zhan'ao and Ma Anliang to maintain control over the Muslims more effectively than did smaller, scattered mosques.

6 / Conclusion
Familiar Strangers

[The Huihui *minzu*] is not one of those native peoples that has always lived on the ancient soil of China (like the Han, Miao, or Qiang), nor one of those purely immigrant groups that came to China from abroad (like the Koreans or Russians), nor one of the peoples of a border region who have long lived in contact (like the Kazaks or the Dai). Rather, it relied upon the tremendous unifying power of Islamic culture, which concentrates Muslims of different countries and different languages into a single entity, causing a *minzu* to form from a blend of foreign elements and partially domestic inhabitants, creating a new species. On the vast, broad land of China it planted roots, sprouted, bloomed, and produced fruit, becoming an important component of the indivisible, great *minzu* family of China.[1]

THE MULTIVALENCE OF SUBALTERITY

Part of the scholarly enterprise of late twentieth-century America lies in missing, then finding and reviving the voices of the silenced, revising our histories to include the women and African-Americans and Indians and Gypsies and others who were there, whose actions surely shaped the past as they do the present, but whose presence and power have been excluded from the dominant narrative. The Sino-Muslims have ever been marginal to China's own history, appearing only as exotics in the Tang-Song, as conquerors and villains in the Yuan, and then disappearing into the category of sinified barbarians until they rise up against the Qing, either as righteous rebels or as murderous and disorderly savages, depending upon the historian's point of view. Only since the founding of overtly Chinese Muslim organizations by both religious and secular Muslim intellectuals in the 1920s have there been national Muslim voices speaking for and about this "minority nationality." This

1. Lin and He, *Huihui lishi*, 1.

chronology would indicate that the notion of *minzu,* of particular peo-plehood within the "indivisible, great *minzu* family of China," had to be invented before those voices could be perceived as legitimate within China.[2] Until then, Chinese conceptions of their own civilization (and all others' strangeness) demanded that Muslims either *laihua,* come and be transformed, or remain beyond the pale as irremediable barbarians.

This grandiose ideological principle could not, of course, work in practice. Muslim voices were heard in China from the Tang onward, and they spoke a variety of languages, including Chinese. Most Mus-lims, however attractive they found living in China, however much particular places in China became home, did not desire to be non-Muslims. As they acculturated in language, first spoken and then writ-ten, and in folkways and customs they found or helped to create in their local ecologies, Muslims were not undergoing some process peculiar to China. All over the Eurasian and African worlds, Muslims made such adaptations, sometimes as a culturally dominant class (as in Java), some-times as a conquering elite ruling a non-Muslim majority (as in India or Spain), sometimes as a mercantile or peripheral acculturating minority (as in the Philippines, east Africa, or China). If this were not so, Mus-lims would be everywhere and always the same, and Clifford Geertz, among many others, has demonstrated conclusively that they are not.[3]

Muslims never achieved a legitimate voice within the awesome history-making apparatus of the Chinese state and its intellectual min-ions both in and out of office. The Hai Furun case and the *Siku quanshu* editor's comment on the *Tianfang dianli* clearly demonstrate that Chi-nese officials could not possibly regard texts in Arabic and Persian, or even Muslim texts written in elegant Chinese, as civilized. Had the Sino-Muslims been completely isolated, cut off from contact with sources of inspiration, knowledge, texts, and experience outside of China, they might well have gone the way of the Jews of Kaifeng, who had utterly lost their sense of differentness from their neighbors, except as a vague memory, by the end of the nineteenth century. That process did take place among the Muslims of southeast China after piracy and

2. Gladney, *Muslim Chinese,* 81–87, cogently argues this position, insisting on its close relationship to the creation of the Han as the dominant *minzu* of China.

3. In 1987 I participated in an ACLS-sponsored conference, in New Delhi, on Muslims as minorities in non-Muslim states. We heard papers on European, South Asian, Southeast Asian, and East Asian Muslim peoples, wonderfully diverse and adapting in fascinating ways to the cultures within which they live. At the end, we found nothing we could isolate as viable themes to tie them together, except the simple fact of their minority status, so closely were their acculturations and resistances linked to their particular environments.

CONCLUSION

Ming defensive policy closed the once-vital sea links between that region and the Muslims to the south and west. Both the formerly Muslim Guo family of northern Taiwan, described by Barbara Pillsbury, and the Ding clan of descendants of Quanzhou Muslims, whose partial re-Islamicization is narrated by Dru Gladney, illustrate what can happen in the absence of reviving external contact.[4]

As they underwent their evolution in official perceptions from *fanke* and foreign merchants (Tang-Song) to *semu* (Yuan) to Huihui (Ming-Qing), Muslims who lived in China became Chinese in a wide variety of places, and they took many professions. The descendants of foreign merchants, artisans, scientists, and soldiers became farmers, officials, *ahong*, migrant laborers, peddlers, doctors, caravaners, raftmen. They married, the men often taking non-Muslim wives in the early centuries; they began to give their children Chinese names as well as *jing ming*; and they lived complex lives inside the local politics of their villages, market systems, and counties—material lives not vastly different from those of their non-Muslim neighbors except for adherence to the strictures of the dietary laws and intercommunity solidarity based on common religion. In structure, however, their communities differed substantially from those of non-Muslims in the centrality of the mosque, its education, rituals, and religious professionals, especially the elders and *ahong* (in Gedimu communities) or the *jiaozhu* and his representatives (in Sufi orders and *menhuan*). We have no evidence of supralocal organization among them before the arrival of the *tarīqa* in the eighteenth century, though Ma Zhu did try to become the Qing empire's official *sayyid*.

If they were aware of the lives of other Muslims in China, it was *as Muslims* that they knew them. If they traveled, as so many did, they could find *halāl* food, a common vocabulary, and a mosque for prayers only in another Muslim community, and there lay one crucial element of the strangeness of Muslims in China. They could be connected to one another by their religion in ways that non-Muslim Chinese could not, except through pilgrimage or sectarianism. Sino-Muslims shared the *jingtang* education, the religious and ritual knowledge of insiders, which distinguished them as individuals from non-Muslims. They could use Huihuihua, the Arabic and Persian lexicon of authenticity, which, despite its local Chinese dialectal base, indicated to other Sino-Muslims

4. Pillsbury, "No Pigs for the Ancestors"; and Gladney, *Muslim Chinese,* chap. 6. The Dings are also one of the clans discussed by Nakada, "Chūgoku Musurimu." It is, as discussed above, no surprise that these entirely acculturated ex-Muslims lived in central and southeast China, not in the north or west.

that they were dealing with coreligionists. Indeed, the Muslim potential for connection with other Muslims transcended in geography and language the bonds of native place and lineage, which gave most Chinese their primary personal relationships in social life. And thus did the Sino-Muslims fulfill Georg Simmel's definition of a stranger—though they stayed, they never quite gave up the freedom of coming and going. To non-Muslim Chinese they looked unified, their solidarity foreign and frightening despite their familiar presence. One can imagine the non-Muslims saying of them, "They always stick together," feeling the uneasy alterity that majorities feel in the face of minority exclusivity.

But they did not stick together. On the contrary, their communities divided along lines of religion, politics, class, gender, and other valences of identity and identification that individuals use to make choices in their lives.[5] As we have seen, everyone in northwest China knew at least one crucial "fact" about the Muslims—they were violent people, and their violence was often directed against one another: "When Old and New Teachings fight, it's a matter for swords and troops before it's over!" On the evidence delineated above, we may conclude that in times of conflict, being a Muslim did not *determine* anyone's behavior, though it probably influenced everyone's. Beyond the context of violence, some Sino-Muslims succeeded in business or the examination system or the army, while others did not; some chose to affirm the legitimacy of the ruling sovereign, while others did not; some chose to educate their children in Chinese, others only in Arabic and Persian, while still others could not educate them at all. Outside of the Jahrīya and Ikhwan, most of the solidarities that unified and divided the northwestern Muslims did not extend beyond Gansu, and even within that region large-scale Muslim action was the exception rather than the rule. In day-to-day life, their local and regional communities did not have much to do with one another, except for connections created by sojourning merchants and *ahong,* so they did not create any wide consciousness of unity before the modern period.

Here lies a difficulty and danger of applying the *minzu* paradigm to the history of the Sino-Muslims (or, I would argue, that of any people). Created only in the late nineteenth and early twentieth centuries, ap-

---

5. These choices, like ours, were not always conscious, instrumental, and rational. An enormous literature provides analyses of the interaction of these valences or elements of identity—which come to the fore when, and how. Prasenjit Duara's recent summary imposes a refreshing simplicity: "The self is constituted neither primordially nor monolithically but within a network of changing and often conflicting representations" (*Rescuing History,* 7).

plied consistently as a political tool by an effective central government only after 1949, the notion of *minzu* asserts that such entities existed as self-consciously unified solidarities long before the technological and social intrusions and capacities of the modern nation-state made that possible. There is no doubt that the Hui *minzu* now exists in China. But did it come into being in the Ming period as Muslims adapted to being Chinese, or did the rise of Chinese nationalism in its particular forms and with its particular concerns create it? As Dru Gladney has also argued, the narrative presented in this book supports the latter assertion with regard to the Sino-Muslims.[6]

The Hui *minzu*, with its wide dispersion and diverse contexts, can exist only as an imagined community, a people with solidarity, as it develops a national leadership, a national consciousness, a sense of China and of itself that transcends the local, particular forms and relationships that governed Sino-Muslim people's lives before the modern era.[7] Thus, I have avoided the term Hui in favor of "Muslim," avoided Han in favor of "(non-Muslim) Chinese." The People's Republic's *minzu* ethnonyms certainly did exist in premodern times, but they did not mean the same things as they do now. Hui or Huihui meant "Muslim," and Han meant "culturally Chinese," as James Watson and others have defined it, but they were not exclusive *minzu* categories. Indeed, a common term for the Sino-Muslims, in addition to the Central Asian Donggan, was Han-Hui, the Han Muslims, while some of the Mongolic-speaking members of today's Dongxiang *minzu* would have been called Meng-Hui, the Mongol Muslims. These combined terms certainly cannot coexist with the *minzu* paradigm, which demands exclusive membership in one *minzu*, but they nonetheless accurately describe the peoples' cultural conditions.[8]

6. Crossley, "Thinking about Ethnicity," and *Orphan Warriors;* Gladney, *Muslim Chinese,* 96–98.

7. This vocabulary for understanding the development of nation-states finds its first expression in Anderson, *Imagined Communities.*

8. An American graduate student who has lived for years in Xinjiang tells me that he is often asked, in local Turkic, "To what *millet* do you belong?" This term clearly does not intend its Ottoman meaning, which indicated religious community, for in the context of the People's Republic, it has come to mean *minzu*. His interlocutors are not satisfied with "America" as an answer, either, for though *millet* has important political implications, it is not the same thing as citizenship. They are asking about *blood—millet, minzu*—and accept "English" as a legitimate response. In this case, I wonder what they would do with the Scotch-Irish-English-French-German reality. We should certainly note the resemblance of this *minzu* paradigm to ideas of race, especially as constructed by nineteenth- and twentieth-century Euro-Americans (Dikötter, *Discourse of Race,* chaps. 3–5).

THE PROBLEM OF VIOLENCE

Here we must confront the question Joseph Fletcher's death left unanswered. Why did divisions among Sufi suborders, usually defined as differences in ritual practice (e.g., vocal vs. silent *dhikr*), result in sanguinary warfare in northwest China, though they did not in other parts of the world? In eighteenth-century Arabia, as we have seen, individuals could even participate in recitation of both kinds of *dhikr* without feeling that they were doing anything odd. We find bloody conflict between Sufis to be sensible in Central Asia—between the Āfāqīya and Ishāqīya, for example—because the stakes lay in political control over territory, the rulership, the state. But in northwest China, such control was beyond the dreams of any sane person, except when the central government was already in a state of collapse, and even then, Milayin and Ding Guodong allied with a Ming pretender, not with a Muslim conqueror. What, then, caused the Gansu Muslims to attack one another so violently?

The narrative presented above argues for multiple causation and for careful examination of the terms of explanation. Certainly we must grant some causal power to pre-existing geographical, social, economic and political conditions, to the pressures inherent in a frontier society with a harsh and unyielding natural environment. The northwest remains China's poorest region, its population overburdening the unproductive arable, its rainfall barely adequate, its infrastructure unprotected against the vagaries of weather and seismic movement. We must also note the presence of many distinctive groups in a restricted space, identifying themselves by culture, religion, language, and local or regional loyalty, competing for scarce resources. In particular, the proximity of agricultural and pastoral peoples and the position of the Muslims as economic middlemen, balanced in a vulnerable position between cultural China and non-China, militate against the region's lying peaceful and serene. Even at Old Taozhou, whose elites resisted splitting along ethnic lines, there was plenty of pressure to do so. Such frontier zones often create communities in arms, ready to resort to the martial arts, men who sleep with their weapons close at hand.

This same frontier quality also created a peculiar tension in Gansu Muslim society, caused by its lack of an intellectual elite apart from the religious professionals. In the Middle East, or other entirely Muslim cultural environments, disagreements over religion certainly did become conflictual, were taken to court, or even resulted in brawling, feuding, and war. But they could also be argued in a context of mutually accepted rules, of religious curiosity and intellectual interaction. On the Islamic frontiers of Gansu, the rigidity of orthodoxies without the possibility of such dialogue created the nexus for religious conflict. Without the confidence of obvious authenticity, as in solidly Muslim contexts, Sino-Muslims required rigid adherence to rules, especially those received from the Muslim heartlands, and could not question or modify them within a shared intellectual tradition. Instead, they resolved conflicts among themselves with violence, sometimes (but not always) encouraged by their religious leaders.

We can also adduce causes external to the Muslim communities. The corruption and incompetence of Qing officials, negative evolutionary change in government regulations and attitudes toward Muslims, and a special vigilance over social order in the northwest following the final conquest of Xinjiang all contributed to rising tension in Gansu in the late eighteenth century. The Sino-Muslims were not, after all, unique in acting violently against the Qing state. Studies of the Taiping, Nian, Miao, Boxer, and other large-scale antistate actions have also indicated the importance of seeing violence as firmly rooted in local contexts, not just as the result of cultural difference, oppositional ideology, or dissatisfied and therefore rebellious leaders.[9]

The initial innovation within Muslim communities in eighteenth-century Gansu came not from the Jahrīya but from the Khafīya, the first Sufi *tarīqa* to win significant numbers of adherents in the region. Hidāyat Allāh's and Ma Laichi's success in building cohesive, multicommunity networks of personal loyalty to themselves and their descendants, especially among the Salars, presented a direct threat to the legitimacy and power of the Gedimu elite, both *ahong* and elders. The Mufti suborder of Didao, also descending in religious succession from Hidāyat Allāh, had similar success, but not among the Salars, who were always perceived as more volatile and dangerous than other frontier peoples. Ma Yinghuan's initial lawsuit, however, couched in terms of *qiankai* and *houkai* factions, did not result in long-term violence. Only with the arrival of the Jahrīya and its conversion of Mongolic- and Chinese-speaking Muslims as well as the Turkic-speaking Salars to a *tarīqa* in direct competition with the Khafīya did street fighting become general at Xunhua,

9. The Miao *minzu*, as currently constructed in the People's Republic, resembles the Hui *minzu* in the wide cultural diversity of its members, who are united primarily by their inclusion in a Chinese category. In the eighteenth and nineteenth centuries some Miao undertook armed struggles against Qing authority, while others did not, another characteristic they share with the Sino-Muslims (Diamond, "Defining the Miao").

and then the local Qing administration had to take more invasive notice, given the precedents and responsibility for social order it bore.

That constituted one of the most important causes of "Muslim rebellion" in northwest China, as it did elsewhere in the empire. Despite imperial pronouncements to the contrary, Muslims were regarded as different and dangerous by Gansu local officials both civil and military. Heavy-handed, brutal, often indiscriminate state violence, or the rumor of its impending onslaught, stimulated Muslims engaged in feuding to confront the armed forces of the state in battle. When Su Forty-three (in disguise) met Xinzhu at Baizhuangzi (1781), when Zhang Fei came to negotiate in southeastern Shaanxi (1862), and when Tang Yanhe despoiled villages west of Hezhou (1895), the Muslims heard, believed, amplified, and spread the word that the Qing intended to "wash away" the Muslims, exterminate them all. People with a martial tradition, organized into local militias (Shaanxi) and by the *tarīqa* (Gansu), following their gentry or *ahong* or *jiaozhu,* might certainly meet such a challenge violently, especially if they knew that the state's local forces were weakened by the Taiping or Sino-Japanese war.

So we have come to another answer to the Qianlong emperor's self-incriminating question, "Why did they rebel?" They gathered their forces against local enemies—Muslim or, in Shaanxi, non-Muslim. Blockaded in their forts, remembering old massacres or hearing of new ones, they reacted against state or militia violence with violence of their own and thus became rebels in the eyes of the state without any plan to seize territory or set up an antistate or proclaim a *jihād.* In short, we must see "rebel" as a state-created category in most of these cases, not as a description of what the Muslims intended to do. Only in 1784, when Tian Wu made banners and planned an uprising, do we see more deliberate intention, and that makes sense as revenge for the bloody pacification and decimation of the Jahrīya in 1781.

To add another multivalent conclusion, not all Muslims agreed with the decision to fight the Qing. We know that some actively opposed it, including Khafīya adherents in 1781, Wang Dagui and many others in the 1860s, Ma Zhan'ao after his surrender to Zuo Zongtang, and the entire contingent of Muslims in the Qing military in the 1890s. We know far less about those who chose not to fight at all, to run or to hide rather than confront either the armed might of the state or the armed wrath of fellow Muslims. They may have hated the Qing for its violence against their people, mistrusted their (or others') leaders for starting the troubles, but we can only surmise that plenty of people took the passive option when they could. We cannot know if they acted on fear or on principle, out of loyalty to the Qing or in quiet solidarity with fellow Muslims, for they have left no traces in our historical record to date, a record dominated by martial action, sweeping generalization, and stereotypical characterization. We can certainly conclude that violence is no more natural to the Muslims of northwest China than it is to other people.

THE PROBLEM OF NAMES

We have already noted the difficulty in understanding the words *minzu* and "rebel" in the context of northwest China. Other terms have figured in this narrative as obfuscators rather than clarifiers of peoples and events, chief among them New Teaching and its putative opposite, Old Teaching. As we have seen, these words have no permanent referents but rather vary over time and space. That is, they are applied in particular contexts to reformist or conservative groups within Sino-Muslim society. If they were neutral terms, they might simply indicate chronological sequence—which teaching arrived first? But in a politicolegal culture that demanded social order, took officials' ranks and lives in chaotic times, and asserted tradition as a crucial arbiter of rectitude, the New and Old labels were far from neutral. Though not invariably proscribed or punished by local judges, especially before 1781, any group targeted as New Teaching had already lost part of the battle for legitimacy in Sino-Muslim society. After the internecine slaughter and state repression of 1781 and 1784, New Teaching, which at that time meant the Jahrīya, had come to be associated with violence, with rending the social fabric, with innovation, heterodoxy, and deceiving the people. The Old Teaching, which meant the Khafiya and Gedimu Muslims, could be viewed as potentially accommodating the legitimate authority of the dynasty, even fighting on the side of Agui and his ethnically diverse troops against Su Forty-three's intractable "rebels."

Other words have often been used to describe the violence narrated above—in Chinese, *minzu douzheng* and *shengzhan*,—"*minzu* conflict" and "holy war." On the evidence presented here, we may conclude that these are far too general to apply conclusively to any of these events. If *minzu* conflict pits one *minzu* against a repressive authority or another *minzu*, how can we use the term when Sino-Muslims fight on both sides, as they did in most of the wars in this book? If Ma Hualong was fighting a holy war, how can we understand his decision to surrender, to take a Qing title, or his unwillingness to unite wholeheartedly with the Shaanxi Muslims? These wars began as local conflicts, between Muslims (in Gansu) or between Muslims and non-Muslims (in Shaanxi), which became polarized by state intervention along lines not purely religious, ethnic, or geographical, though all three identities surely played parts in people's decisions to join one side or another. Some historians are very careful in their application and understanding of these terms, but many are not, and we must beware of the easy characterization, the facile descriptive term.

After all, it was the state that eventually determined what many of the words meant. Categories such as "rebel," "heterodoxy," "New Teaching," and "bandit" are not natural or inherent descriptors but rather legally and politically defined black boxes, into which state authority can place a wide variety of people and behaviors. "A winner a king, a loser a bandit" summarizes useful folk wisdom on the subject. For religious ideologies, one might say, "A winner a teaching, a loser a heterodoxy." By the mid-nineteenth century, some Qing officials had decided that *menhuan* and *gongbei*—that is, Sufi orders with their saintly lineages and saints' tombs—lay at the root of Gansu's sanguinary history, but never did the state try to proscribe them all. Rather, they selected those leaders and solidarities which appeared most dangerous to social order and labeled them as "weeds," evil Muslims who deceive the people, while maintaining that all others were "good" Muslims. This could not work in a local atmosphere laden with fear, bloody memory, and desire for revenge. To many Gansu non-Muslims, and Qing officials as well, the only "good" Muslim was a dead one, or at least one who lived far away from non-Muslims, especially Chinese non-Muslims. From the seventeenth-century official's recommendation of radical separation of Muslims from civilized society until settled agriculture could work its deracinating magic, to the late-nineteenth-century generals' slaughter of Muslim civilians around Xining, this conviction was proposed and sometimes put into practice.

THE PARADOX OF PERIPHERIES

The names of places, like those of groups of people, carry a heavy political load. This book has dealt extensively with "frontier" as a name for Gansu, for the whole northwest. Gu Jiegang was ashamed of the fact that the frontier lay so close to the geographical center of his nation-state. Clearly, Gansu *was* a frontier of China, a zone outside of which Chinese people would find themselves culturally, if not politically, foreign. But Gansu was also a frontier of Tibet, Mongolia, and Central Asia—a meeting ground of cultures—and we might write a very differnt history if we saw Tibetans, Mongols, or Central Asians as the main characters in this narrative.

Not only do frontiers have at least two sides, but they also have residents, for whom the frontier is home. The spatial arrangements we privilege—positionings that define terms such as cores, peripheries, and frontiers—follow closely the relative power and productivity of their inhabitants. China's many centers and edges have been carefully mapped and defined by G. William Skinner and others, but China's Muslim space has been invisible within that mapping, and the two are not congruent. Ningxia, Hezhou, Xunhua, and Xining lie on the periphery of the periphery if one's perspective centers on China, but they are the cores of concern for Sino-Muslims and local non-Chinese. Certainly the Muslims interacted with the systems centering on Lanzhou and Xi'an, with prefectural capitals at places such as Tianshui and Didao, and they participated in an economy with those cities as cores. But they also participated in a Muslim economy, political and religious as well as productive, and that Muslim arrangement influenced their lives as surely as did the "dominant" Chinese patterns. Its symbolic capital flowed among Muslim communities in the persons and ideas of *ahong* and *jiaozhu,* students and pilgrims, while its goods flowed between cultural China and non-China in Muslim hands.

This book's challenge thus lies in identifying parallel structures and positions within which parallel narratives, such as this history of Muslims in China, actually take place. We do not find a simple arrival and transformation here, though Muslims do arrive, and the Muslims of the Qing are certainly very different from those of the Song. But the transformation is mutual, always partial, evolutionary, and unpredictable. Chinese perceptions of themselves and their own culture have been deeply affected by the presence of cultural Others in their local systems and on their frontiers. Northwest China certainly would not be what it has become without the constant mediating presence of its Muslim communities, but they have not all behaved consistently or alike.

Through pilgrimages, missionaries, and trade, Muslims in the northwest also maintained close connections with the Muslim heartlands and were deeply affected by institutions and ideas flowing into China from the west. Even in east China, where Muslims were more acculturated in language and material life than were their Gansu coreligionists, many nonetheless continue to practice their religion, especially its dietary laws and endogamy, to the present day.[10] So we cannot conclude that the Sino-Muslims were somehow not sufficiently Islamic to be a distinctive population. Nonetheless, Lao Huihui aided Li Zicheng (1630s–44), Milayin

10. Gladney, *Muslim Chinese,* chaps. 4 and 5.

and Ding Guodong backed a Ming pretender (1648), and the Khafiya leaders saw their solidarity's best interest in alliance with the Qing (1781). Indeed, this history demonstrates that the most effective Islamic revivals in the past century of Chinese history have directly engaged their own Chineseness: the Ikhwan, which failed as Wahhabi-influenced fundamentalism and succeeded when it allied itself with Chinese nationalism; and Hanxue, centering on the *Han kitab* and expressing Islamic meanings in current Chinese, a movement that began and flourished in Nanjing, Beijing, Suzhou, and Jinan before it reached Gansu.

That recent history leads to a final conclusion regarding space: China incorporated its northwestern frontier most effectively during a period of extraordinary central weakness. During the height of Qing power the *tusi* system allowed considerable local autonomy for frontier elites, and powerful religious figures such as the high *rimpoches* of Tibetan monasteries and Sufi *shaikhs* (e.g., Ma Laichi and Ma Hualong) could establish legitimate local authority parallel to the distant dynasty in Beijing and its local representatives. Even the Qing conquest of Xinjiang between the 1690s and 1750s did not result in decisive central control over Gansu. Only Zuo Zongtang's reconquest, followed by the cooptation of local elites such as the Ma families of Qing generals, later to be warlords, finally guaranteed dominance from the east. Without the active support of Ma Anliang, Ma Qi, and Ma Fuxiang, neither the late Qing nor the Republic could have controlled Gansu as they did.

The methods of nation-building learned or created in the hostile international world of European imperialism served both the old and the new regimes well in the northwest, so Gansu history reflects accurately the processes of transformation from empire to nation-state, frontier to border, imperial virtue to national sovereignty. Sino-Muslim history, however, must also take into account the waves and currents of Central Asia and the Middle East, especially the growth and flourishing of Sufi orders as revivalist movements and the fundamentalist upheavals associated with eighteenth- and nineteenth-century scripturalism. They, too, stimulated change in northwest China, in parallel and sometimes in conflict with the evolution of the late Qing and the rise of New China.

THE PARADOXES OF IDENTITY

Echoing the Chinese logician Gongsun Long, this book has asked, "When is a Chinese not a Chinese?" Answer: When the Chinese is a Sino-Muslim. What does it mean to belong to two cultures at once, when both demand at least a measure of exclusive dominance in individual and collective life? Historians, psychologists, sociologists and anthropologists have analyzed a wide variety of elements that make up human identity. In this study of the Sino-Muslims, I have focused particularly on language, religion, and place, coming to the conclusion that none can be isolated as somehow *more* fundamental than the others, and that all operate all the time. If I have erred on the side of choice, of individual and collective decisions as expressions of identity, I must plead the complex and contradictory nature of the sources, which do not allow simple generalizations to stand.

In a moving essay, the cosmopolitan intellectual Slavenka Drakulic writes of discovering her national identity amidst the slaughter of a disintegrating Yugoslavia:

> Along with millions of other Croats, I was pinned to the wall of nationhood—not only by outside pressure from Serbia and the Federal Army but by national homogenization within Croatia itself. That is what the war is doing to us, reducing us to one dimension: the Nation. The trouble with this nationhood, however, is that whereas before, I was defined by my education, my job, my ideas, my character—and, yes, my nationality too—now I feel stripped of all that. I am nobody because I am not a person any more. I am one of 4.5 million Croats.[11]

This feels like what happened to some northwestern Muslims, though few if any of them articulated their dilemma in prose. In specific times and places, they could be reduced by outside force to their Muslimness, to that one crucial facet of their identities. When Meng Qiaofang, Xinzhu, Zhang Fei, Yang Changjun, Tang Yanhe, Dong Fuxiang, or even Ma Fuxiang or Ma Anliang started killing (or threatening to kill) Muslims, the rumors flew: They are going to *xi Hui*, kill Muslims just for being themselves, and for being at home. In northwest China, with its rich memory of massacre and the protagonists' bellicose reputations, the rumors of extermination edicts would be believed, and some Muslims would react to them, killing local others in self-defense or in revenge.

But they did not act simply as "Muslims." Especially after the arrival of Sufi orders in Gansu, and the militarization of local society in both Gansu and Shaanxi, they also acted as members of local solidarities, as rivals of other Muslims as well as non-Muslims, as residents of particular communities and members of lineages, as Chinese- or Mongolic- or

---

11. Slavenka Drakulic, *The Balkan Express*, 51.

Turkic- or Tibetan-speakers. And they did not all act in the same way. Drakulic's disintegrating Yugoslavia was divided among rival political factions, all of which strove to mobilize ethnicity as a weapon against the others, to control "homeland" and claim authenticity and homogenizing centrality. Some Gansu Muslim leaders used the same tactics, but without the possibility of territorial autonomy. Rather, they utilized the *tarīqa,* the charismatic power of the *ahong* and the *jiaozhu,* the fear of indiscriminate violence, and the slogans of Muslim unity to motivate their followers to violence, in defense of their homes or for revenge against evil others.

Under such circumstances, did individual Muslims in northwest China really have choices? In Shaanxi in 1862, perhaps they did not. Perhaps they had to fight, run, or die, homogenized into a monolithic enemy by their neighbors in the non-Muslim militias and by the Qing army. But in Gansu, Muslims fought on both sides, and some communities, like Taozhou's, chose not to participate if they could avoid it. Overarching all these choices lies the theme of *home,* of one's own place. The mid-nineteenth-century Shaanxi Muslims retained their defensive rage, fled and regrouped and attacked again, in order to go home. The Ningxia, Hezhou, Taozhou, Xunhua, and Xining Muslims all evinced a deep attachment to their own territory, using its familiarity both for strategic purposes and to motivate soldiers and civilians to fight. On the other side, many non-Muslims defended their villages and stockades with ferocity, suffering massacres at Muslim hands or holding out against lengthy siege.

Could not the Muslims have left, settled to the west, among coreligionists? Some certainly did. Bai Yanhu fled to Xinjiang and then Russia (1870s); some of the survivors of Duoba did, too (1890s); and Ma Zhongying followed them almost forty years later. But very few made that choice. However hostile, however conflict ridden, Gansu and Shaanxi were home to these Sino-Muslims, the only places they wanted to live, with familiar livelihoods, mosques, holy tombs, and graves. The four leaders whose stories close this history all spent their lives trying to establish a viable home for the Muslims of northwest China—Ma Fuxiang by connecting Gansu and Ningxia to the nation-state; Ma Qixi and Ma Yuanzhang by creating Muslim solidarities of protection and religious, social, economic, and political stability; and Ma Wanfu by leading the Sino-Muslims to a purer, more authentic religion. Before coming under Ma Qi's aegis, Ma Wanfu failed to provide enough safety for adherents to his vision of Islamic truth, so it was left to the second generation of Ikhwan leaders to follow the path already taken by the Ma family warlords, the Jahrīya, and the Xidaotang. They came to terms with New China and imbedded their religious communities in the rising nation-state.

In the early eighteenth century Liu Zhi wrote his *Han kitab* in Nanjing. A few decades later Hidāyat Allāh, Ma Mingxin, and ʿAbd Allāh of the Qādirīya arrived in the northwest and began the creation of new social institutions, the Sufi orders. These two currents, originally only chronologically linked, have collided and developed and changed one another over the course of over two centuries, producing a rich harvest of conflict and insight. Once the northwest was brought irreversibly into the Qing empire, after Zuo Zongtang's reconquest, the leaders of the Sino-Muslims turned decisively eastward. Never ignoring the Muslim heartlands, many of them still open to new inspiration, texts, and experiences from the west, they nonetheless cast their lot with China and took the *Han kitab* as their guide. Liu Zhi's Confucian vision of Islam has not yet gained final victory, for he wished to construct an identity that would not separate the Muslims from China but unify them with it, an impossible task as long as they remain, to any extent, strangers. But those who read Chinese can find in his books a familiar vocabulary of belief and devotion, a discourse dedicated to making China a home for believing Muslims.[12]

For the writers of the *Han kitab*—and their readers—were and are serious Muslims, not assimilated half-breeds or betrayers of the faith in comparison to Ma Wanfu or Ma Hualong. In the face of ordinary acculturative pressures faced by any strangers—to learn the language, eat the food, wear the clothes, become normal and familiar—they complied and resisted as their mixed culture demanded. For example, many Sino-Muslims retain pork avoidance long after they abandon other Islamic practices, but they all speak Chinese as their native tongue. In the face of the incorporative political and cultural power of the modern nation-state, all the Sino-Muslims have become citizens of China, no longer subjects of the empire. Their story after the 1930s must await another study, but we can say with confidence that they have remained

12. Wang Jianping informs me in a personal communication that Muslim scholars in Yunnan, teaching among Muslims who read Arabic and Persian but not Chinese, have translated some of the *Han kitab* texts into Arabic for instruction in the *madrasa*. I cannot say whether they realize the extraordinary irony inherent in this act.

different from their non-Muslim neighbors, some only in possessing memories of Otherness, others more completely, while working to make a place for themselves in China, the only home they have ever known.

We conclude with a final warning against established categories, against stereotyped characterizations and facile generalizations. Muslims, like many other kinds of people, have been subjected to a variety of analytical oversimplifications, their behavior measured always by some narrow textual standard or predicted by some putatively universal religious ideology. The narrative told in this book cannot be simplified accurately; to the extent that it succeeds, it reflects the messiness of what actually happened in northwest China over the past millennium. Our histories should not be reducible to dichotomies ("Are they more Muslim or more Chinese?") or to black boxes ("the indivisible, great *minzu* family of China"), for they must take into account what Harold Isaacs has called "the essential disorderliness of the truth."[13] In a more human, less cogent history, categories give way to decisions made by individuals and effective solidarities in particular contexts. Only by learning and constructing a myriad of such stories can we piece together what it actually meant, and actually means, to be a Muslim in China.

13. Isaacs, *Idols of the Tribe*, 29.

Chinese Character Glossary

All definitions of nouns are given in the singular form.

Agui 阿桂

Ahema (Ahmad Fanakati) 阿合馬

ahong 阿訇 (洪) (Per. *ākhūnd*), Islamic teacher

Aihailisunnai 哎亥里遜乃 (Ar. Ahl as-Sunna), Kinsmen of the Tradition; the Ikhwan

Ashige 阿世格

Bai Chongxi 白崇禧

Bai Lang 白朗

Bai Yanhu 白彥虎

Baishan 白山 (Tur. Aqtaghliq), White Mountain, Naqshabandī order in eastern Turkestan

Beizhuang 北庄, *menhuan* name

bianjiang 邊疆, frontier

Bijiachang 畢家場, *menhuan* name

Bosi 波斯, Persia

Chang Yuqun 常遇春

Changgeng 長庚

Chantou Hui 纏頭回, Muslim who wraps the turban, eastern Turkestani

Chen Decai 陳得才

Chen Jiaji 陳嘉績

Chengda Shifan Xueyuan 成達師范學院, Chengda Normal College

Daerliuji 達兒六吉

daixiao 戴孝, wearing of coarse white mourning clothes

Dao 道, the Way

Daoguang 道光, Qing reign period, 1821–50

daotang 道堂, Sufi hospice

daozu 道祖, founder of a Sufi order or suborder

Dashi 大食, Arabia

dashiman mixiji 達失蠻密昔吉 (Per. *dānishmand*; Ar. *masjid*), Yuan dynasty term for a Muslim mosque

De Wang 德王

Deng Zeng 鄧增

Ding Dexing 丁德興

Ding Guodong 丁國棟

dizhu tuanlian 地主團練, landlords' militia

Dolongga 多隆阿

Dong Fuxiang (Dong Xingwu) 董福祥 (董星五)

Dong nan xi bei ren, jiang he hu hai chuan 東南西北人, 江河湖海船, "A man for all quarters, a boat for all waters" (said of Ma Yuanzhang)

Donggan 東干, Tungan, Chinese-speaking Muslim

Dongxiang 東鄉, *minzu* name;

the eastern subprefecture of Hezhou Prefecture

dou'ou 鬥毆, armed affray

Du Wenxiu 杜文秀

Duan Qirui 段祺瑞

duilian 對聯, celebratory paired scrolls and their inscriptions

dujun 督軍, provincial military commander (Republican period)

Duxinga 都興阿

ermanli 爾曼里 (Ar. *al-'amal*), celebration in honor of the Prophet or a saint

fan 番 (蕃), foreigner; barbarian; a generic term for outsiders, or specifically for Tibetans

Fan Hua bu de tong hun 蕃華不得同婚, "Foreigners and Chinese may not intermarry"

Fan Shengwu 范繩武

fanfang 蕃坊, foreigners' quarter (Tang-Song period)

fanzuo 反坐, antilitigation regulation stipulating punishment for false accusers

fei wo zulei zhe 非我族類者, "those [people] not of our kind"

feitu 匪徒, bandit

Feng Yuxiang 馮玉祥

Fukang'an 福康安

Gan ren zhi Gan 甘人治甘, "Gansu people should rule Gansu"

Gansu gan Qinghai qing 甘肅乾青海青, "Gansu is dry, Qinghai is green"

Gedimu 格迪目 (Ar. *qadīm*), community-based mosque organization, "traditional" in China

Gelandai 格蘭岱, Qalandarīya, Sufis in Yunnan

Gelaohui 哥老會, the Elder Brothers, a secret society

gong 工, Salar community

gong 貢, tribute

gongbei (*gongbai*) 拱北 (拱拜) (Ar. *qubba*), tomb of a Sufi saint

Gu Jiegang 顧頡剛

Guanli Ye 關里爺

guocui 國粹, national essence

guojia 國家, nation-state (modern term borrowed from Japanese)

guojia yishi 國家意識, national consciousness

Hai Furun 海富潤

Hai Rui 海瑞

Haiting 亥聽 (Ar. *khatm*), primer of Koranic Arabic

haiyisi 海乙寺 (Ar. *hayy*), a large, centrally located mosque

Han 漢, non-Muslim Chinese, the "majority ethnic group of China"

Han Hui 漢回, Sino-Muslim

Han Hui shi chou 漢回世仇, "Chinese and Muslims are eternal enemies"

Han kitab (*Han ketabu*) 漢克塔布, the Sino-Islamic canon

Hann Er 韓二

Hann Nuri 韓奴日

Hann Si (Hann Laosi) 韓四 (老四)

Hann Wenxiu 韓文秀

Hanxuepai 漢學派, Chinese Studies faction; Xidaotang

He Bi 郝璧

He Jianwei 何建威

Heshen 和珅

houkai 後開, breaking the Ramadan fast after prayer

Hu Dengzhou 胡登洲

Hu Songshan 虎嵩山

Hualing Wupin Dingdai 華翎五品頂戴, Feathered Cap of the Fifth Rank

Huang Chao 黃巢

Huasi 花 (華) 寺, *menhuan* name

Hufeiye (Hufuye) 虎非耶 (虎夫耶), Khafiya, a Sufi suborder

Hui (Huihui) 回 (回), Muslim (a term that gradually came to mean Sino-Muslim)

Hui *shen* 回紳 Muslim gentry

Huihe 回紇, Uygur; (non-Muslim) eastern Turkestani during the Tang through Ming dynasties

Huihui tianwenshu 回回天文書, *Book of Muslim Astronomy*

Huihuihua 回回話, local Sino-Muslim patois with Arab-Persian lexical additions

Huijiao 回教, Islam (term no longer used in the People's Republic of China)

Huijiaotu 回教徒, a Muslim (term no longer used in the People's Republic of China)

Huimin Jiaoyu Zujin Weiyuan-hui 回民教育促進委員會, Muslim Educational Progressive Committee

Huizei 回賊, Muslim thief

huozhong 惑眾, deceiving the people

hushang 胡商, foreign merchant (Tang-Song period)

Jiang Jieshi (Chiang Kai-shek) 蔣介石

Jiang Xiang 姜瓖

jianshi 簡史, "simple history" of an individual *minzu*

jiaomen 教門, religious teaching or solidarity associated with a teaching

jiaopai 教派, religious faction

jiaozhang 教長, community religious leader, non-Sufi

jiaozhu 教主, *shaikh*; Sufi leader

jiazu 家族, Chinese corporate lineage

jing ming 經名, Islamic name, given to a Muslim child at birth

jingtang jiaoyu 經堂教育, scripture hall education; religious instruction in Arabic and Persian

jingtangyu 經堂語, same as Huihuihua

jinshi 進士, highest civil-service examination graduate

Jinxing Tang 金星堂, Ma Qixi's first school, the Gold Star Hall

juren 舉人, provincial-level examination graduate

kaiguo gongchen 開國功臣, meritorious ministers who founded the state, Zhu Yuanzhang's ministers

Kang Lang 康朗

Kangxi 康熙, Qing reign period, 1661–1722

laihua 來化, come and be transformed

Lan Yu 藍玉

Laojiao 老教, Old Teaching

Lei Zhengguan 雷正琯

li 理, principle

li 禮, ritual, propriety

Li Peiying 李培簔

Li Shiyao 李侍堯

Li Zhi 李贄

Li Zicheng 李自成
Liu Jintang 劉錦棠
Liu Yufen 劉郁芬
Liu Zhi (Jielian, Yizhai) 劉智 (介廉, 一齊)
Liupin Dingdai 六品頂戴, Cap Button of the Sixth Rank
Lixue 理學, Neo-Confucianism
Long 隴, traditional name for Gansu
Lu Guohua 魯國華
Lu Hongtao 陸洪濤

Ma Anliang 馬安良
Ma Congshan 馬從善
Ma Fucai 馬福財
Ma Fulu 馬福祿
Ma Fushou 馬福壽
Ma Fuxiang 馬福祥
Ma Guiyuan 馬桂源
Ma Guobao 馬國寶
Ma Guoliang 馬國良
Ma Hongbin 馬鴻賓
Ma Hongkui 馬鴻逵
Ma Hualong (Ma Chaoqing) 馬化龍 (馬朝清)
Ma Huan 馬歡
Ma Huisan 馬會三
Ma Jiajun 馬家俊
Ma Jincheng 馬進城
Ma Jinxi 馬進西
Ma Laichi 馬來遲
Ma Lin 馬麟
Ma Mingren 馬明仁
Ma Mingxin 馬明新 (馬明心)
Ma Qi 馬麒
Ma Qianling 馬千齡
Ma Qixi 馬啓西
Ma Rubiao 馬如彪
Ma Shilin 馬世麟
Ma Shouying (Lao Huihui) 馬守應 (老回回)
Ma Shouzhen 馬守貞

Ma Songting 馬松亭
Ma Taibaba 馬太爸爸
Ma Tingrang 馬廷勷
Ma Wanfu (Hājjī Guoyuan) 馬萬福 (果園哈只)
Ma Weihan 馬維翰
Ma Wenlu 馬文祿
Ma Wensheng 馬文升
Ma Wuyi 馬五一
Ma Yide 馬以德
Ma Yinghuan 馬應煥
Ma Yonglin 馬永琳
Ma Yongrui 馬永瑞
Ma Yuanchao 馬元超
Ma Yuanzhang (Guanglie) 馬元章 (光烈)
Ma Zhan'ao 馬占鰲
Ma Zhenwu 馬震武
Ma Zhongying 馬仲英
Ma Zhu 馬注
Ma Ziqiang 馬自強
Ma Zongsheng 馬宗生
Majia junfa 馬家軍閥, Ma family warlords (Republican period)
Meng Qiaofang 孟喬芳
Meng-Hui 蒙回, Mongol Muslim
menhu 門戶, great family
menhuan 門宦, saintly lineage; hereditary leader of a Sufi sub-order
Milayin 米喇印
min 民, common people
Min Fuying 閔福英
Mingshahui 明沙會, Bright Sand Societies, a pejorative for Ma Laichi's Khafīya
Mingshale (Mingshaer) 明沙勒 (明沙爾), a text of scriptural extracts used within the Khafīya
minzu 民族, ethnic group (modern term borrowed from Japanese)

minzu douzheng 民族鬥爭, *minzu* conflict

minzu qiyi 民族起義, *minzu* righteous uprising

Mu Ying 沐英

Mufuti 穆夫提, *menhuan* name

Musilin 穆斯林, Muslim

Mutushan 穆圖善

Naigeshibandingye 乃格什板丁耶, Naqshabandīya, a Sufi order

Nei gongchan, wai diguo 內共產外帝國, "On the inside, communist; to the outside, imperialist" (said of the Xidaotang)

neidi 內地, the interior, China proper viewed from Gansu

Nianle buchi, chile bunian 念了不吃吃了不念, "If you read scripture, don't eat; if you eat, don't read scripture" (Ikhwan slogan)

Niu Shihan 牛師韓

pailou 牌樓, memorial or celebratory archway

pifazi 皮筏子, hide rafts of the upper Yellow River

Pingnan Guo 平南國, Du Wenxiu's secessionist state in Yunnan

pinyin 拼音, transliteration system

Pu Luoxin 蒲羅辛

qiankai 前開, breaking the Ramadan fast before prayer

Qianlong 乾隆, Qing reign period, 1736–96

qingzhen 清眞, pure and true; Islamic; ritually pure (halāl)

Qintianjian 欽天監, Bureau of Astronomy (Ming period)

ren 仁, benevolence

Rendao 人道, Way of Humankind

Ronglu 榮祿

Ru 儒, Confucian

ruxiang 乳香, frankincense

Sai Dianchi 賽典赤, Sayyid Ajall Shams ad-Din

Sala(er) 撒拉 (爾), Turkic-speaking Muslim of northeastern Tibet

semu 色目, foreigner resident in China (Yuan period)

semu guan 色目官, official of the various categories; foreign official in China (Yuan period)

shanhou 善後, state-imposed pacification after violence, especially rebellion

shanren 善人, saint

shaoshu minzu 少數民族, minority nationality; minority *minzu*

Shazilinye 沙孜林耶, Shādhilīya, a Sufi order

Shengbao 勝保

Shengyun 升允

shengzhan 聖戰, holy war

shexide 舍犧德 (Ar. *shahīd*), martyrdom

Shi Dakai 石達開

Su Sishisan (Su Forty-three) 蘇四十三

Sufei *pai* 蘇菲派, Sufi order; Sufism

Tang Yanhe 湯彥和

Tao Zongyi 陶宗儀

Tian Shengong 田神功

Tian Wu 田五

Tian Xing Long 天興隆, the Xidaotang's trading company

Tiandao 天道, Way of Heaven

Tianfang 天方, Arabia

Turen 土人, Monguor, a Mongolic-speaking people of Gansu

tusheng fanke 土生蕃客, domestically born foreigner (Song period)

tusi 土司, hereditary "native chieftain" in frontier zones (Yuan-Qing periods)

Wang Dagui 王大桂

Wang Daiyu 王岱輿

Wang Danwang 王亶望

Wang Lun 王倫

Wang Naibi 王乃必

Wang Shumin 王樹民

Wei Guangdao 魏光燾

wenhua 文化, literary culture; "civilization" in an elite Chinese context

Woshikeng'e 倭什鏗額

wotuo 斡脫 (Mong. *ortaq*), foreign merchant partner of Mongol royalty (Yuan period)

Wu Sangui 吳三桂

Wu Zunqie 伍遵契

Wuchang 五常, Five Constants

Wugang 五綱, Five Relationships

wushi fanke 五世蕃客, fifth generation domestically born foreigner (Song period)

xi Hui 洗回, "wash away the Muslims"

xiaojing (xiaoerjin) 消經 (小兒錦), use of Arabic letters to transliterate Chinese

Xidaotang 西道堂, religious solidarity based in Old Taozhou

Xidayetonglaxi 西達葉通拉希, Hidāyat Allāh, Khoja Āfāq

xiedou 械鬥, feud

xiejiao 邪教, heterodoxy

xin 信, faith in humankind, sincerity

Xinjiao 新教, New Teaching

Xinzhu 新柱

xiucai 秀才, prefectural examination graduate

xiushen 修身, cultivating one's inherently virtuous inner nature

xiyang 西洋, Western (in early Qing refers to the Catholic writings of Ricci et al.)

Yang Changjun 楊昌濬

Yang Jiqing 楊積慶

Yang Shiji 楊士璣

Yang Zengxin 楊增新

yangqi 養氣, cultivating the vital essence

yi 義, righteousness

Yi Xing Gong 義興恭, Huasi *menhuan*'s trading company

Yihewani 伊赫瓦尼 (Ar. al-Ikhwan al-Muslimūn), Ikhwan

Yingqi 瑛棨

Yisilanjiao 伊斯蘭教, Islam

Yisilanjiao Hanxuejia 伊斯蘭教漢學家, Sino-Islamicist, modern term for a *Han kitāb* writer

Yongle 永樂, Ming reign period, 1403–24

Yongli 永歷, Ming remnant reign period, 1644–62

Yongzheng 雍正, Qing reign period, 1722–35

Yu Youren 于右任

Yuan Shikai 袁世凱

Zaxue 雜學, *Diverse Studies*, an Islamic primer

zhaizi 寨子, stockade; fort for paramilitary militia

Zhamalading (Jamāl ad-Dīn) 扎馬剌丁

Zhang Fei 張苻

Zhang Fenghui 張鳳翽

Zhang Guangjian 張廣建

Zhang Guangsi 張廣泗

Zhang Wenqing 張文慶

Zhang Xianzhong 張獻中

Zhang Zhong (Zhang Shizhong) 張中 (張時中)

Zhang Zuolin 張作霖

Zhehelinye (Zheherenye) 哲赫林 (忍) 耶, Jahrīya, a Sufi suborder

Zheng He 鄭和

Zheng Suonan 鄭所南

zhi 智, knowledge

Zhong-A Zhongxue 中阿中學, Sino-Arabic Middle School

Zhongguo Huijiao Gonghui 中國回教公會, China Islamic Association

zbongyuan 中原, central plain; China proper

zhongzu 種族, race (modern term borrowed from Japanese)

Zhou Mi 周密

Zhou Shixiang (Qishi) 周世祥 (七十)

Zhu Chun 朱椿

Zhu Di 朱棣

Zhu Shichuan 朱識鋐

Zhu Yuanzhang 朱元章

zongjiao 宗教, religion (modern term borrowed from Japanese)

zunjing gaisu 尊經改俗, "venerate the scriptures, reform the customs"

zunjing pai 尊經派, scripturalist faction; the Ikhwan

Zuo Zongtang 左宗棠

Bibliography

ABBREVIATIONS

GNQSL   Mu Shouqi. *Gan Ning Qing shilue* (Outline history of Gansu, Ningxia, and Qinghai). 10 vols. Reprint, Taipei: Guangwen Shuju, 1970.

HMQY   Bai Shouyi, ed. *Huimin qiyi* (Righteous uprisings of the Hui people). 4 vols. Shanghai: Shenzhou Guoguang Chubanshe, 1953.

HSG   Yang Huaizhong. *Huizu shi lungao* (Essays in Hui history). Yinchuan: Ningxia Renmin Chubanshe, 1991.

HSJ   Zhongguo Shehui Kexue Yuan Minzu Yanjiusuo (Nationalities Research Institute, Chinese Academy of Social Sciences) and Zhongyang Minzu Xueyuan Minzu Yanjiusuo (Nationalities Research Institute, Central Nationalities University), eds. *Huizu shi lunji (1949–1979 nian)* (Essays on Hui history, 1949–1979). Yinchuan: Ningxia Renmin Chubanshe, 1983.

QTNSH   Feng Zenglie, Li Dengdi, and Zhang Zhijie. *Qingdai Tongzhi nianjian Shaanxi Huimin qiyi yanjiu* (The righteous uprising of the Hui people of Shaanxi, 1862–1875). Xi'an: Sanqin Shuju, 1990.

QZYL   Ningxia Zhexue Shehui Kexue Yanjiusuo (Ningxia Philosophy and Social Sciences Institute), ed. *Qingdai Zhongguo Yisilan jiao lunji* (Essays on Islam in Qing China). Yinchuan: Ningxia Renmin Chubanshe, 1981.

XSJ   Qinghai Minzu Xueyuan Minzu Yanjiusuo (Nationalities Research Institute, Qinghai Nationalities College) and Xibei Minzu Xueyuan Xibei Minzu Yanjiusuo (Northwest Nationalities Institute, Northwest Nationalities College), eds. *Xidaotang shiliao ji* (Historical materials on the Xidaotang). N.p., 1987.

XYY   Gansu Sheng Minzu Yanjiusuo (Gansu Provincial Nationalities Institute), ed. *Xibei Yisilanjiao yanjiu* (Islam in northwest China). Lanzhou: Gansu Renmin Chubanshe, 1985.

YZZ   Gansu Sheng Minzu Yanjiusuo (Gansu Provincial Nationalities Institute), ed. *Yisilanjiao zai Zhongguo* (Islam in China). Yinchuan: Ningxia Renmin Chubanshe, 1982.

ZYSC   Bai Shouyi. *Zhongguo Yisilan shi cungao* (Essays on Chinese Islamic history). Yinchuan: Ningxia Renmin Chubanshe, 1983.

ZYSCZX Li Xinghua and Feng Jinyuan, eds. *Zhongguo Yisilanjiao shi cankao ziliao xuanbian* (Selected reference materials on the history of Islam in China). 2 vols. Yinchuan: Ningxia Renmin Chubanshe, 1985.

al-Din, Rashid. *The Successors of Genghis Khan.* Trans. John A. Boyle. New York: Columbia University Press, 1971.

Algar, Hamid. "Silent and Vocal *Dhikr* in the Naqshbandi Order." In *Akten des VII. Kongresses für Arabistik und Islamwissenschaft* (Proceedings of the Seventh Conference on Arabist and Islamic Studies), pp. 39–46. Göttingen: Vandenhoeck & Ruprecht, 1976.

Allsen, Thomas. "Mongolian Princes and Their Merchant Partners, 1200–1260." *Asia Major,* 3rd ser., 2, part 2 (1989): 83–126.

An Weijun, comp. *Gansu xin tongzhi* (New provincial gazetteer of Gansu). N.p., 1909.

Anderson, Benedict. *Imagined Communities: Reflections on the Origin and Spread of Nationalism,* Rev. ed. London and New York: Verso, 1991.

Andrew, George F. *The Crescent in Northwest China.* London: China Inland Mission, 1921.

Armijo-Hussein, Jacqueline. "The Sinicization and Confucianization of a Muslim from Bukhara Serving under the Mongols in China." Paper presented at the conference "The Legacy of Islam in China," Harvard University, Cambridge, Mass. 1989.

Aubin, Françoise. "En Islam chinois: Quel Naqshbandis?" (In Chinese Islam: Which Naqshbandis?). In *Naqshbandis: Cheminements et situation actuelle d'un ordre mystique musulman* (Naqshbandis: Historical development and contemporary situation of a mystical Islamic order), pp. 491–572. Ed. M. Gaborieau, A. Popovic, and T. Zarcone. Istanbul and Paris: Editions Isis, 1990.

———. "Islam littéraire chinois (XVIIe siècle-debut XXe siècle): Soufisme et anti-soufisme" (Chinese literati Islam from the seventeenth to the early twentieth century: Sufism and anti-Sufism). Paper presented at the conference "Sufism and Its Enemies," Utrecht University, Utrecht, The Netherlands, 1995.

Bai Shouyi. "Ma Wanfu." *Zhongguo Musilin* no. 39 (1984): 2–6.

———. "Sai Dianchi Shan Siding kao" (On Sai Dianchi Shams ad-Din). In *ZYSC,* 216–98.

———. *Zhongguo Yisilan shi cungao* (Essays on Chinese Islamic history). Yinchuan: Ningxia Renmin Chubanshe, 1983. (*ZYSC*)

———, ed. *Huimin qiyi* (Righteous uprisings of the Hui people). 4 vols. Shanghai: Shenzhou Guoguang Chubanshe, 1953. (*HMQY*)

——— et al., eds. *Huizu renwu zhi (Ming dai)* (Biographical dictionary of the

Hui people: The Ming period). Yinchuan: Ningxia Renmin Chubanshe, 1988.

————. *Huizu renwu zhi (Qing dai)* (Biographical dictionary of the Hui people: The Qing period). Yinchuan: Ningxia Renmin Chubanshe, 1992.

————. *Huizu renwu zhi (Yuan dai)* (Biographical dictionary of the Hui people: The Yuan period). Yinchuan: Ningxia Renmin Chubanshe, 1985.

Bonin, Charles-Eudes. "Les Mahometans du Kan-sou et leur derniere revolte" (The Muslims of Gansu and their most recent rebellion). *Revue du monde musulman* 10, no. 2 (1910): 210–33.

Boorman, Howard, ed. *Biographical Dictionary of Republican China*. 4 vols. New York: Columbia University Press, 1967.

Botham, Mark. "Islam in Kansu." *Moslem world* 10, no. 4 (1920): 377–90.

Broomhall, Marshall. *Islam in China: A Neglected Problem*. London: Morgan and Scott, 1910.

Cai Meibiao. *Yuandai baihua bei jilu* (Yuan period vernacular inscriptions). Beijing: Kexue Chubanshe, 1955.

Chen Chongkai, "Cong Shaanxi Huimin qiyi de fuza yuanyin kan qi xingzhi yu tedian" (The nature and uniqueness of the Shaanxi Hui rebellion in light of its complex causes). In *QTNSH,* 36–53.

Chen Shaoxiao. *Xibei junfa ji* (The northwestern warlords). Hong Kong: Zhicheng Shuju, 1974.

Ch'en, Yuan. *Western and Central Asians in China under the Mongols*. Trans. Ch'ien Hsing-hai and L. Carrington Goodrich. Los Angeles: Monumenta Serica, 1966.

Chongxin xian zhi (Chongxin county gazetteer). 1926. Reprint, Taipei: Xuesheng Shuju, 1957.

Chongxiu Gaolan xian zhi (Revised Gaolan county gazetteer). N.p., 1892.

Chu, Wen-djang. *The Moslem Rebellion in Northwest China: A Study of Government Minority Policy*. The Hague: Mouton, 1966.

Clark, Leonard. *The Marching Wind*. New York: Funk and Wagnall, 1954.

Close, Upton, and E. McCormick. "Where the Mountains Walked." *National Geographic Magazine* 41, no. 5 (May 1922): 445–64.

Cong Enlin. "Zhongguo tese de Yisilanjiao—Zhongguo chuantong wenhua yu Yisilan wenhua de zhuangji" (Islam with Chinese characteristics: Traditional Chinese culture and Islamic culture). *Ningxia shehui kexue* no. 55 (1992): 48–55.

Crossley, Pamela. *Orphan Warriors: Three Manchu Generations and the End of the Qing World*. Princeton: Princeton University Press, 1990.

————. "Thinking about Ethnicity in Early Modern China." *Late Imperial China* 11, no. 1 (1990): 1–34.

Curwen, Charles. *Taiping Rebel: The Deposition of Li Hsiu-ch'eng*. Cambridge: Cambridge University Press, 1977.

Da Ming lü jijie fuli (The Ming code: Statutes and commentaries). 5 vols. Reprint, Taipei: Taiwan Xuesheng Shuju, 1970.

Da Qing lichao shilu (The veritable records of the Great Qing). Beijing: Zhonghua Shuju, 1985.

Dazai Matsusaburō. *Shina kaikyōshi no kenkyū* (Studies on the history of Islam in China). Dairen: Mantetsu, 1924.

de Groot, J. J. M. *Sectarianism and Religious Persecution in China.* 2 vols. Amsterdam: J. Miller, 1903–4.

Dennerline, Jerry. *Qian Mu and the World of Seven Mansions.* New Haven: Yale University Press, 1988.

Diamond, Norma. "Defining the Miao: Ming, Qing, and Contemporary Views." In *Cultural Encounters on China's Ethnic Frontiers,* pp. 92–116. Ed. Stevan Harrell. Seattle: University of Washington Press, 1995.

Didao zhou xu zhi (Didao prefectural gazetteer, supplement). N.p., 1909.

Dikötter, Frank. *The Discourse of Race in Modern China.* Stanford: Stanford University Press, 1992.

d'Ollone, H. M. G. *Recherches sur les musulmans chinois* (Studies on the Chinese Muslims). Paris: Leroux, 1911.

Dols, Joseph. "La vie chinoise dans la province de Kan-sou" (Chinese life in Gansu province). Parts 1–5. *Anthropos* 10:11–12:13 (1915–18).

Drakulic, Slavenka. *The Balkan Express: Fragments from the Other Side of War.* New York: Harper Collins, 1993.

Dreyer, June T. *China's Forty Million.* Cambridge: Harvard University Press, 1976.

Duara, Prasenjit. *Rescuing History from the Nation: Questioning Narratives of Modern China.* Chicago: University of Chicago Press, 1995.

Dwyer, Arienne. "Altaic Elements in the Linxia Dialect." *Journal of Chinese Linguistics* 20, no. 1 (1992): 160–79.

Eberhard, Wolfram. "Notes on the Folklore of Ch'inghai." In *China und seine westlichen Nachbarn* (China and its western neighbors). Darmstadt: Wissenschaftliche Buchgesellschaft, 1978, 306–10.

Ekvall, Robert. *Cultural Relations on the Kansu-Tibetan Border.* Chicago: University of Chicago Press, 1939.

Encyclopedia of Islam. Rev. ed. Leiden: Brill, 1960.

Endicott-West, Elizabeth. "Merchant Associations in Yuan China: The *Ortoq.*" *Asia Major,* 3rd ser., 2, part 2 (1989): 127–54.

———. *Mongolian Rule in China: Local Administration in the Yuan Dynasty.* Cambridge: Harvard University Press, 1989.

Esherick, Joseph. *The Origins of the Boxer Uprising.* Berkeley: University of California Press, 1987.

———, and Mary Rankin. Introduction to *Chinese Local Elites and Patterns of Dominance,* pp. 1–24. Ed. Joseph Esherick and Mary Rankin. Berkeley: University of California Press, 1990.

Ewing, Katherine. "The Politics of Sufism: Redefining the Saints of Pakistan." *Journal of Asian Studies* 42, no. 2 (1983): 251–68.

Fan Changjiang. *Zhongguo de xibei jiao* (China's northwest corner). Tianjin: Dagong Bao, 1936.

Fan Manyun. "Liu Yufen yu Hezhou shibian" (Liu Yufen and the Hezhou incident). *Gansu wenshi ziliao xuanji*, no. 9 (1981): 110–27.

Farrer, Reginald. *On the Eaves of the World*. 2 vols. London: Arnold, 1917.

Feng Jinyuan. "Cong Zhongguo Yisilanjiao Hanwen yizhu kan Rujia sixiang dui Zhongguo Yisilanjiao de yingxiang he shentou" (The influence and permeation of Confucian thought in Chinese Islam as seen in the Chinese Muslim translations and commentaries). In *YZZ*, 257–81.

———. "Zhongguo Yisilanjiao jiaofang zhidu chutan" (The independent mosque system in Chinese Islam). In *XYY*, 142–59.

Feng Zenglie. "Gedimu bayi" (Eight points on the Gedimu). In *XYY*, 130–41.

———. "Liu Zhi yu *Tianfang dianli*" (Liu Zhi and the *Tianfang dianli*). In *YZZ*, 301–18.

———. "Ming Qing shiqi Shaanxi Yisilanjiao de jingtang jiaoyu" (Islamic mosque education in Shaanxi during the Ming and Qing). In *QZYL*, 217–51.

———. "Xiaoerjin chutan" (On the *xiaoerjin* script). N. p., 1982.

———, Li Dengdi, and Zhang Zhijie. *Qingdai Tongzhi nianjian Shaanxi Huimin qiyi yanjiu* (The righteous uprising of the Shaanxi Hui people, 1862–75). Xi'an: Sanqin Shuju, 1990. (*QTNSH*)

Fields, Lanny. *Tso Tsung-t'ang and the Muslims: Statecraft in Northwest China, 1865–1880*. Kingston, Ontario: Limestone Press, 1978.

Filchner, Wilhelm. *Wissenschaftliche Ergebnisse der Expedition Filchner nach China und Tibet, 1903–1905* (Scientific findings of the Filchner expedition to China and Tibet, 1903–1905). 10 vols. Berlin: Mittler u. Sohn, 1908–12.

Fletcher, Joseph. "A Brief History of the Chinese Northwestern Frontier." In *China's Inner Asian Frontier: Photographs of the Wulsin Expedition to Northwest China in 1923*, pp. 21–52. Ed. Mary Ellen Alonso. Cambridge: Peabody Museum, 1980.

———. "China and Central Asia, 1368–1884." In *The Chinese World Order: Traditional China's Foreign Relations*, pp. 206–24. Ed. John K. Fairbank. Cambridge: Harvard University Press, 1968.

———. "China's Northwest at the Time of the Ming-Ch'ing Transition." Harvard University, 1974. Photocopy.

———. "Ch'ing Inner Asia c. 1800." In *The Cambridge History of China*. Vol. 10, part 1, pp. 59–90. Ed. John K. Fairbank. Cambridge: Cambridge University Press, 1978.

———. "Les 'voies' (*turuq*) soufies en Chine" (The Sufi orders [*turuq*] in China). In *Les ordres mystiques dan l'Islam* (The mystical orders in Islam), pp. 13–26. Ed. A. Popovic and G. Veinstein. Paris: Edition de l'Ecole des Hautes Etudes en Sciences Sociales, 1986.

———. "The Naqshbandiyya in Northwest China." In *Studies on Chinese and Islamic Inner Asia*. Ed. Beatrice Manz. London: Variorum, 1995.

———. "The Taylor-Pickens Letters on the Jahri Branch of the Naqshbandiyya in China." *Central and Inner Asian Studies* 3 (1989): 1–35.

Forbes, Andrew. *Warlords and Muslims in Chinese Central Asia: A Political History of Republican Sinkiang, 1911–1949.* Cambridge: Cambridge University Press, 1986.

Ford, Joseph. "Some Chinese Muslims of the Seventeenth and Eighteenth Centuries." *Asian Affairs,* n.s., no. 2 (1974): 144–56.

Forke, A. "Ein islamisches Tractat aus Turkistan" (An Islamic tract from Turkestan). *T'oung Pao,* ser. 2, 3, no. 1 (1907): 1–76.

Franke, Herbert. "Ahmed: Ein Beitrag zur Wirtschaftsgeschichte Chinas unter Qubilai" (Ahmed: A chapter in China's economic history under Qubilai). *Oriens* 1, no. 2 (1948): 222–36.

―――. "Eine mittelalterliche chinesische Satire auf die Mohammedaner" (A medieval Chinese satire of the Muslims). In *Der Orient in der Forschung: Festschrift für Otto Spies zum 5. April 1966* (The Orient under research: Festschrift, April 5, 1966 for Otto Spies), pp. 202–8. Ed. W. Hoenerbach. Wiesbaden: Harrassowitz, 1967.

―――. "Siege and Defense of Towns in Medieval China." In *Chinese Ways in Warfare,* pp. 151–201. Ed. F. Kiernan and John K. Fairbank. Cambridge: Harvard University Press, 1974.

Frick, J. "Hochzeitssitten von Hei-tsuei-tzu in der Provinz Ch'ing-hai" (Wedding customs at Heizuizi in Qinghai province). *Folklore Studies,* Sup. 1: 1–102.

Friedman, Yohanan. *Shaykh Ahmad Sirhindī.* Montreal and London: McGill-Queens University Press, 1971.

Frolic, B. Michael. *Mao's People: Sixteen Portraits of Life in Revolutionary China.* Cambridge: Harvard University Press, 1980.

Fu Yiling. "Taiping Tianguo shidai Huiluan lingdao renwu chushen kao" (The social origins of important leaders of Hui rebellions in Taiping times). *Fujian wenhua* 2, no. 3 (1945): 1–12.

"Gansu dudufu dang'an" (Gansu provincial military governor's office archives). In *Bai Lang qiyi* (The righteous uprising of Bai Lang), pp. 246–76. Ed. Du Qunhe. Beijing: Zhongguo Shehui Kexue, 1980.

Gansu jiefang qian wushi nian dashi ji (Important events in Gansu, 1900–49). Hong Kong?: N.p., 1981.

Gansu Sheng Minzu Shiwu Weiyuanhui (Gansu Provincial Nationalities Commission) and Gansu Sheng Minzu Yanjiusuo (Gansu Provincial Nationalities Institute), eds. *Gansu shaoshu minzu* (Minority nationalities of Gansu). Lanzhou: Gansu Renmin Chubanshe, 1989.

Gansu Sheng Minzu Yanjiusuo (Gansu Provincial Nationalities Institute), ed. *Xibei Yisilanjiao yanjiu* (Islam in northwest China). Lanzhou: Gansu Renmin Chubanshe, 1985. (*XYY*)

―――. *Yisilan jiao zai Zhongguo* (Islam in China). Yinchuan: Ningxia Renmin Chubanshe, 1982. (*YZZ*)

"Gansu Tianshui xian gaikuang" (Conditions in Tianshui county, Gansu). *Kaifa xibei* 1, no. 2 (1934): 61–72.

Gao Wanxuan. "Linxia Qingzhen 'haiyi' zhi de jianli ji qi bianqian" (The establishment and evolution of central mosques in Linxia). *Gansu wenshi ziliao xuanji*, no. 2 (1980): 197–200.

Gao Wenyuan. *Qingmo xibei Huimin zhi fan Qing yundong* (The anti-Qing movement of the northwestern Hui people in the late Qing). Taipei: Xuehai Shuju, 1988.

Gao Zhanfu. "Guanyu jiaopai zhi zheng zai Qingdai xibei Huimin qiyizhong xiaoji zuoyong de tantao" (The negative functions of factional struggles during the righteous uprisings of the Hui people under the Qing). In *XYY*, 245–62.

———. "Yuandai de Gansu Huihui ren" (The "Huihui" in Gansu during the Yuan). *Ningxia shehui kexue*, no. 52 (1992): 58–62.

Ge Chifeng. *Zangbian caifeng ji* (Colors and customs on the Tibetan frontier). Chongqing: Shangwu, 1942.

Geertz, Clifford. *Islam Observed*. New Haven: Yale University Press, 1968.

Gilbert, Rodney. "Remarkable Development in Mohammedanism in Western China." *Far Eastern Review* 15, no. 11 (1919): 703–6.

Gladney, Dru. *Muslim Chinese: Ethnic Nationalism in the People's Republic*. Cambridge: Harvard University Press, 1991.

———. "Muslim Tombs and Ethnic Folklore: Charters for Hui Identity." *Journal of Asian Studies* 47, no. 3 (1987): 495–532.

Goodrich, L. Carrington, and Fang Chaoying, eds. *Dictionary of Ming Biography, 1368–1644*. 2 vols. New York: Columbia University Press, 1976.

Gu Jiegang. "Kaocha xibei hou de ganxiang" (My feelings after investigating the northwest). *Xibei shidi*, no. 2 (1984): 12–16.

———. *Xibei kaocha riji* (Diary of a northwestern investigation). N.p.: Hejia Tushuguan, 1949.

Guan Lianji. "Xidaotang lishi gaishu" (A brief history of the Xidaotang). In *XSJ*, pp. 75–96.

——— and Liu Cihan. "Yibajiuwu nian He-Huang shibian chutan" (The Hezhou-Huangzong incident of 1895). *Xibei shidi*, no. 4 (1983): 46–54.

——— and Wang Jin. "Huasi menhuan de xingshuai" (The rise and fall of the Huasi *menhuan*). *Xibei shidi*, no. 1 (1982): 56–62.

Guanli Ye. *Reshihaer* (Rashuh). Trans. by Yang Wanbao, Ma Xuekai, and Zhang Chengzhi. Beijing: Sanlian Shudian, 1993.

Guyuan zhou zhi (Guyuan prefectural gazetteer). N.p., 1909.

Haicheng xian zhi (Haicheng county gazetteer). N.p., 1908.

Harrell, Stevan. "Civilizing Projects and the Reaction to Them." In *Cultural Encounters on China's Ethnic Frontiers*, pp. 3–36. Ed. Stevan Harrell. Seattle: University of Washington Press, 1995.

———. Introduction to *Violence in Chinese Society: Studies in Culture and Counterculture*, pp. 1–25. Ed. Jonathan Lipman and Stevan Harrell. Albany: SUNY Press, 1990.

———, ed. *Cultural Encounters on China's Ethnic Frontiers*. Seattle: University of Washington Press, 1995.

He Yan. "Ma Fuxiang nianpu gailue" (A chronological life of Ma Fuxiang). *Gansu wenshi ziliao,* no. 11, 32–54.

Hedin, Sven. *The Flight of "Big Horse": The Trail of War in Central Asia.* New York: E. P. Dutton, 1936.

Hegel, Charlotte. "The White Wolf: The Career of a Chinese Bandit, 1912–1914." Master's thesis, Columbia University, 1969.

Hevia, James. *Cherishing Men from Afar: Qing Guest Ritual and the Macartney Embassy of 1793.* Durham: Duke University Press, 1995.

Hezheng xian zhi (Hezheng county gazetteer). Reprint, Taipei: Chengwen, 1970.

Hirth, F., and W. W. Rockhill. *Chau Ju-kua: His Work on the Chinese and Arab Trade in the Twelfth and Thirteenth Centuries, entitled* Chu-fan-chi. St. Petersburg: N.p., 1911.

Ho, Peng-yoke. "The Astronomical Bureau in Ming China." *Journal of Asian history* 3, no. 2 (1969): 137–57.

Hodgson, Marshall. *The Venture of Islam: Conscience and History in a World Civilization.* 3 vols. Chicago: University of Chicago Press, 1974.

Huc, Abbe. *High Road to Tartary.* New York: Charles Scribner's Sons, 1948.

Huizu jianshi (A brief history of the Hui *minzu*). Yinchuan: Ningxia Renmin Chubanshe, 1978.

Ignatieff, Michael. *Blood and Belonging: Journeys into the New Nationalism.* New York: Farrar, Straus and Giroux, 1993.

Iqbal, Afzal. *The Life and Work of Jalal-ud-din Rumi.* London: Octagon, 1956.

Isaacs, Harold. *Idols of the Tribe: Group Identity and Political Change.* Cambridge: Harvard University Press, 1975.

Israeli, Raphael. "The Muslim Revival in Nineteenth Century China." *Studia Islamica* 43 (1976): 119–38.

———. *Muslims in China: A Study in Cultural Confrontation.* London: Curzon, 1978.

Iwamura Shinobu, "Chūgoku Isuramu shakai kenkyūjō no shomondai" (Some problems in the study of Chinese Islamic society). *Minzokugaku kenkyū* 12, no. 3 (1947): 1–22.

———. "Kanshuku Kaimin no niruikei" (Two types of Gansu Muslims). *Minzokugaku kenkyū kiyō,* no. 1 (1944): 119–65.

———. "Kanshuku shō no kaimin" (The Muslims of Gansu). *Mōko* 10, no. 2 (1942–43): 39–51.

———. "Kōga jōryū no hibatsu" (The hide rafts of the upper Yellow River). *Minzokugaku kenkyū,* n.s. 2, no. 1 (1944): 21–36.

Izutsu, Toshihiko. *Sufism and Daoism.* Berkeley: University of California Press, 1983.

Jen, Yu-wen. *The Taiping Revolutionary Movement.* New Haven: Yale University Press, 1973.

Jin Yijiu. "Sufei pai yu Zhongguo menhuan" (Sufism and China's *menhuan*). In *XYY,* 187–202.

Kang Jianguo. *Xibei zuijin shinian lai shiliao* (Historical materials on the past ten years in the northwest). N.p., 1931.

Kataoka Kazutada, "Keian shiryō yori mitaru Shinchō no Kaimin seisaku" (Qing policy toward Muslims, as seen in legal case records). *Shigaku kenkyū*, no. 136 (June 1977): 1–24.

———. "Shinkyō no karōkai" (The Gelaohui in Xinjiang). In *Rekishi ni okeru minshū to bunka* (Ethnicity and culture in history), pp. 845–58. Tokyo: Kokushu Kankyokai, 1982.

Kawamura Kyōdō. "Ba Genshō" (Ma Yuanzhang). *Kaikyō* 1, no. 2 (1927): 28–33.

Khan, Almaz. "Chinggis Khan: From Imperial Ancestor to Ethnic Hero." In *Cultural Encounters on China's Ethnic Frontiers*, pp. 248–77. Ed. Stevan Harrell. Seattle: University of Washington Press, 1995.

Khan, Sardar Ali Ahmad. *The Naqshbandis*. Sharaqpur: Darul-Muballeghin Hazrat Mian Sahib Sharaqpur Sharif, 1982.

Köhler, Günther. "Die Bedeutung des Huang Ho innerhalb des nordwest-chinesischen Verkehrsnetzes" (The significance of the Yellow River within the northwestern Chinese transport network). *Petermanns Geographische Mitteilungen*, no. 96 (1952): 85–89.

Kuhn, Phillip. *Rebellion and Its Enemies in Late Imperial China: Militarization and Social Structure, 1796–1864*. Cambridge: Harvard University Press, 1970.

Lai Cunli. *Huizu shangye shi* (Commercial history of the Hui *minzu*). Beijing: Zhongguo Shangwu, 1988.

Lattimore, Owen. *Inner Asian Frontiers of China*. Reprint, Boston: Beacon, 1962.

Le Strange, Guy, trans. *Clavijo: Embassy to Tamerlane, 1403–1406*. London: Routledge, 1928.

Leslie, Donald D. *Islam in Traditional China: A Short History*. Canberra: Canberra College of Advanced Education, 1986.

———. *Islamic Literature in Chinese, Late Ming and Early Qing: Books, Authors, and Associates*. Canberra: Canberra College of Advanced Education, 1981.

———. *The Survival of the Chinese Jews: The Jewish Community of Kaifeng*. Leiden: Brill, 1972.

Levy, Howard S. *Biography of Huang Ch'ao*. Berkeley: University of California Press, 1961.

Li Gengyan and Xu Likui. "Qinghai diqu de Tuomaoren ji qi yu Yisilan jiao de guanxi" (The Tuomao people of the Kökenōr region and their relationship to Islam). In *XYY*, pp. 357–67.

———. "Yisilan jiao zai Kaligang: Guanyu Kaligang diqu bufen qunzhong xi Zang jin Hui de diaocha" (Islam in Kargang: An investigation of the members of the Hui *minzu* in Kargang who were formerly of the Zang *minzu*). In *YZZ*, pp. 417–26.

Li Songmao. "Qing Xian-Tong nianjian Huimin qiyi pinglun" (A critical evaluation of the mid-nineteenth-century righteous uprisings of the Hui people). In *QTNSH*, 23–35.

243

Li Wujin. "Gansu Linxia dili zhi" (The geography of Linxia, Gansu). Parts 1–2. *Xibei lunheng* 7, no. 11–13 (1939).

Li Xinghua. "Zhongwen Yisilanjiao yizhu pingshu" (Evaluating the Chinese Muslim translations and commentaries). In *YZZ*, 281–300.

——— and Feng Jinyuan. *Zhongguo Yisilanjiao shi cankao ziliao xuanbian (1911– 1949)* (Selected reference materials on the history of Islam in China, 1911– 1949). 2 vols. Yinchuan: Ningxia Renmin Chubanshe, 1985. (*ZYSCZX*)

Li Xudan. "Xibei kexue kaocha jilue" (A scientific investigation in the northwest). *Dili xuebao*, no. 9 (1942).

Liao Kaitao. "Gansu zhi minzu wenti" (The *minzu* problem in Gansu). In *Xibei wenti luncong* (Collected essays on problems of the northwest), vol. 1 (1941), pp. 81–96. Ed. Zhongguo Guomindang Zhongyang Shunlian Weiyuanhui, Xibei Ganbu Shunlian Tuan, Xibei Wenti Yanjiusuo (Chinese Nationalist Party Central Training Commission, Northwestern Cadre Training Group, Northwestern Issues Institute).

Lin Song and He Yan. *Huihui lishi yu Yisilan wenhua* (History of the Hui people and Islamic culture). Beijing: Jinri Zhongguo, 1992.

Linxia Huizu Zizhizhou Wenshi Ziliao Weiyuanhui (Linxia Hui Autonomous Prefecture Historical Materials Commission), ed. *Ma Zhongying shibian shimuo* (The Ma Zhongying incident). Linxia, 1963. Mimeographed.

Lipman, Jonathan. "The Border World of Gansu, 1895–1935." Ph.D. diss., Stanford University, 1981.

———. "Ethnic Conflict in Modern China: Hans and Huis in Gansu, 1781– 1929." In *Violence in China: Studies in Culture and Counterculture*, pp. 65–86. Ed. Jonathan Lipman and Stevan Harrell. Albany: SUNY Press, 1991.

———. "Ethnicity and Politics in Republican China: The Ma Family Warlords of Gansu." *Modern China* 10, no. 3 (July 1984): 285–316.

———. "Hyphenated Chinese: Sino-Muslim Identity in Modern China." In *Remapping Modern China: Fissures in Historical Terrain*. Ed. Gail Hershatter et al. Stanford: Stanford University Press, 1996.

———. "Patchwork Society, Network Society: A Study of Sino-Muslim Communities." In *Islam in Asia*, vol. 2, 246–74. Ed. Raphael Israeli and Anthony Johns. Jerusalem: Magnes, 1984.

———. "Statute and Stereotype: Qing Legal Discourse on Islam and Muslims." Paper presented at the conference "Ethnic Identity and the China Frontier," Dartmouth College, Hanover, N.H., 1996.

Litzinger, Ralph A. "Making Histories: Contending Conceptions of the Yao Past." In *Cultural Encounters on China's Ethnic Frontiers*. Ed. Stevan Harrell. Seattle: University of Washington Press, 1995.

Liu, K. C., and Robert Smith. "The Military Challenge: The Northwest and the Coast." In *The Cambridge History of China*, vol. 11, part 2, 202–73. Ed. John K. Fairbank. Cambridge: Cambridge University Press, 1980.

Luo Wanshou and Wu Wanshan. "Lun Qingdai Tongzhi nianjian xibei Huizu de bianqian" (The Tongzhi period rebellion of the Hui *minzu* in the north-west). *Xibei shidi*, no. 3 (1990).

Ma Changshou, ed. *Tongzhi nianjian Shaanxi Huimin qiyi lishi diaocha jilu* (An investigation into the history of the Tongzhi period Shaanxi Hui people's righteous uprising). Xi'an: Shaanxi Renmin Chubanshe, 1993.

Ma Chen. "Mu Shenghua ahong kangqing shilue" (*Ahong* Mu Shenghua's anti-Qing resistance). In *YZZ*, 245–56.

———. "Ma Yuanzhang yu Zhehelinye jiaopai de fuxing" (Ma Yuanzhang and the revival of the Jahrīya). In *QZYL*, pp. 290–307.

Ma Fuqun. "Liu Jielian xiansheng de zongjiao yizhu dui yihou Yisilanjiao de yingxiang" (The influence of Liu Zhi's religious writings on Islam). In *XSJ*, pp. 171–86.

———. "Xidaotang Ma Qixi xingban jiaoyu ji" (Educational activities under Ma Qixi of the Xidaotang). In *XSJ*, pp. 144–53.

Ma Fuxiang. *Meng Zang zhuangkuang* (The situation in Mongolia and Tibet). Ningxia: Meng Zang Weiyuanhui, 1931.

———, comp. *Shuofang dao zhi* (Shuofang [Ningxia] gazetteer). N.p., 1926.

Ma Hetian. *Gan Qing Zang bianqu kaocha ji* (An investigation of the Gansu-Qinghai-Tibetan frontier region). Shanghai: Shangwu, 1947.

Ma Kexun. "Zhongguo Yisilanjiao Yiheiwanipai de changdaozhe—Ma Wanfu (Guoyuan)" (Ma Wanfu [Guoyuan]—The founder of the Ikhwan in Chinese Islam). In *YZZ*, pp. 439–58.

Ma Peiqing. "Changgeng Shengyun jingong Shaanxi minjun shimuo" (Changgeng and Shengyun's attack on the Shaanxi People's Army). *Gansu wenshi ziliao xuanji*, no. 11 (1981): 190–97.

Ma Qicheng. "Jianlun Yisilan jiao zai Zhongguo de zaoqi chuanbo" (Early transmission of Islam to China). In *Minzu yanjiu lunwen ji* (Essays in ethnology) vol. 1, 184–88. Beijing: Zhongyang Minzu Xueyuan, 1981.

"Ma Qixi xiansheng chuangjiao xunnan shi" (The obstacles faced by Ma Qixi in establishing his teaching). In *XSJ*, pp. 130–34.

Ma Ruheng. "Cong Hai Furun anjian kan Qianlong dui Huizu de tongzhi zhengce" (The Qianlong emperor's policies for control over the Hui *minzu* as seen in the Hai Furun case). *Huizu yanjiu*, no. 1 (1992): 8–12.

Ma Shouqian. "Mingdai houqi de Huimin qiyi yu Huizu nongmin yingxiong Ma Shouying" (The late Ming righteous uprisings of the Hui people and the Hui *minzu*'s peasant hero Ma Shouying). *Minzu yanjiu*, no. 1 (1980): 36–40.

———. "Qing Tongzhi nianjian de Ningxia Huimin qiyi—jianlun dui Ma Hualong de pingjie" (The Tongzhi period righteous uprising of the Hui people of Ningxia, with a critical evaluation of Ma Hualong). In *QZYL*, pp. 108–23.

Ma Songting *ahong*. "Zhongguo Huijiao yu Chengda Shifan Xuexiao" (Islam in China and the Chengda Normal School). *Yugong* 5, no. 11: 4–7.

Ma Tingxiu. "Ma Fuxiang shishu" (On Ma Fuxiang). *Gansu wenshi ziliao xuanji,* no. 21 (1984): 173–91.

Ma Tong. "Alabo de Wahabiyapai yu Zhongguo de Yihewani" (The Arabian Wahhabiya and China's Ikhwan). Lanzhou, n.d. Mimeographed.

———. *Gansu Huizu shi* (The history of the Hui *minzu* in Gansu). Lanzhou: Gansu Renmin Chubanshe, 1994.

———. *Zhongguo Yisilan jiaopai menhuan suyuan* (The origins of China's Muslim solidarities and *menhuan*). Yinchuan: Ningxia Renmin Chubanshe, 1986.

———. *Zhongguo Yisilan jiaopai yu menhuan zhidu shilue* (The history of China's Muslim solidarity and *menhuan* system). Yinchuan: Ningxia Renmin Chubanshe, 1983.

Ma Xuezhi. *Zhehelinye daotong shi xiaoji* (A history of the Jahrīya orthodox path). Yinchuan: Xibei Wusheng[qu] Yisilanjiao Xueshu Taolun Hui, 1980.

Ma Zikuo. "Musilin zai Linxia" (Muslims in Linxia). *Xibei tongxun* 3, no. 1 (1948): 15–18.

Maejima, Shinji. "The Muslims in Ch'uan-chou at the end of the Yuan Dynasty (II)." *Memoirs of the Research Department of the Toyo Bunko,* no. 32 (1974): 47–71.

Manz, Beatrice F. *The Rise and Rule of Tamerlane.* Cambridge: Cambridge University Press, 1989.

Martin, B. G. "A Short History of the Khalwati Order of Dervishes." In *Scholars, Saints, and Sufis: Muslim Religious Institutions Since 1500,* pp. 275–305. Ed. Nikki Keddie. Berkeley: University of California Press, 1972.

Mei, Y. P. "Stronghold of Moslem China." *Moslem World* 31, no. 2 (1941): 178–84.

Mi Yizhi. *Salazu zhengzhi shehui shi* (A political and social history of the Salar *minzu*). Hong Kong: Huanghe Wenhua, 1990.

Mian Weilin. *Ningxia Yisilan jiaopai gaiyao* (The Muslim solidarities of Ningxia). Yinchuan: Ningxia Renmin Chubanshe, 1981.

Mills, J. V. G., trans. and ed. *Ma Huan* Ying-yai sheng-lan, *"The Overall Survey of the Ocean's Shores."* Cambridge: Cambridge University Press, 1970.

Millward, James. *Beyond the Pass: Economy, Ethnicity and Empire in Qing Xinjiang, 1759–1864.* Stanford: Stanford University Press, forthcoming 1998.

———. "The Chinese Border Wool Trade of 1880–1937." Stanford University, 1987.

Min Shengzhi, comp. "Hezheng Taizijie Qingzhen Xidasi lishi gaikuang" (A history of the Xidasi mosque, Taizi Street, Hezheng County [Gansu]). In *XSJ,* pp. 166–70.

Moore, Robert W. "Raft Life on the Huang Ho." *National Geographic Magazine* 61, no. 6 (1932): 743–52.

Moule, A. C. *Quinsay, with Other Notes on Marco Polo.* Cambridge: Cambridge University Press, 1957.

Mu Shouqi. *Gan Ning Qing shilue* (A history of Gansu, Ningxia, and Qinghai). 10 vols. Reprint, Taipei: Guangwen Shuju, 1970. (*GNQSL*)

Nakada Yoshinobu. "Chūgoku Musurimu to shūzoku soshiki: Zokufu o chūshin to shite mitaru" (China's Muslims and the lineage system: A view centered on clan genealogies). *Tōyō gakuhō* 38, no. 1 (1955): 89–114.

———. "Dōchi nenkan no San-Kan no Kairan ni tsuite" (The Tongzhi period Muslim uprisings in Shaanxi and Gansu). In *Chūgoku kenkyū*, no. 3, pp. 71–159. Tokyo: Tokyo University Press, 1959.

———. *Kaikai minzoku no shomondai* (Questions regarding the Huihui *minzu*). Tokyo: Ajia Keizai Kenkyūjo, 1971.

Naquin, Susan. *Shantung Rebellion: The Wang Lun Uprising of 1774.* New Haven: Yale University Press, 1981.

Nayancheng. *A Wenchenggung nianpu* (Chronological biography of Agui). N.p., 1813.

Ningxia Zhexue Shehui Kexue Yanjiusuo (Ningxia Philosophy and Social Sciences Institute), ed. *Qingdai Zhongguo Yisilan jiao lunji* (Essays on Islam in Qing China). Yinchuan: Ningxia Renmin Chubanshe, 1981. (*QZYL*)

Nishi Masao. "Kanshuku Seikai shōjō ni okeru Kaikyōto no seikatsu" (The lives of Muslims in Gansu and Qinghai). *Kaikyōken* 5, no. 12 (1941): 8–21, 41.

North China Herald, September 27, 1895; July 3, 1901; January 8, 1902; March 12, 1902; April 9, 1902; June 27, 1914; August 13, 1924.

Ouyang Xiu, comp. *Xin Tang Shu* (New official history of the Tang). Reprint, Taipei: Ershiwu Shi Biankan Guan, 1956.

Overmyer, Daniel. *Folk Buddhist Religion: Dissenting Sects in Late Traditional China.* Cambridge: Harvard University Press, 1976.

Pei Jianzhun. "Bai Lang rao Long" (Bai Lang disturbs Gansu). *Gansu wenshi ziliao xuanji*, no. 1 (1978): 40–43.

Pei Zhi. "Hai Rui shi fou Huizu?" (Was Hai Rui a Hui?). In *HSJ*, pp. 274–75.

Pelliot, Paul. "Une ville musulmane dans la Chine du nord" (A Muslim village in north China). *Journal asiatique*, no. 211 (1927): 261–79.

Perry, Elizabeth. *Rebels and Revolutionaries in North China, 1845–1945.* Stanford: Stanford University Press, 1980.

———. "Social Banditry Revisited: The Case of Bai Lang, a Chinese Brigand." *Modern China* 9, no. 3 (1983): 355–79.

Pillsbury, Barbara. "No Pigs for the Ancestors: Pigs, Mothers, and Filial Piety among the 'Taiwanese Muslims.'" Paper presented at the Symposium on Chinese Folk Religions, University of California at Riverside, 1974.

Ping Hui jilue (Pacifying the Muslims). In *HMQY*, vol. 3, 7–14.

Pollak, Michael. *Mandarins, Jews, and Missionaries: The Jewish Experience in the Chinese Empire.* Philadelphia: Jewish Publication Society, 1980.

Polo, Marco. *The Most Noble and Famous Travels of Marco Polo Together with the Travels of Nicolo de' Conti.* Ed. John Frampton, with introduction, notes, and appendixes by N. M. Penzer. London: Argonaut Press, 1929.

Poppe, Nicholas. *The Mongolian Monuments in hP'ags-pa Script.* Wiesbaden: Harrassowitz, 1957.

Qinding Lanzhou jilue (Imperially commissioned military documents on [the campaigns around] Lanzhou). Annotated and punctuated by Yang Huai-zhong. Yinchuan: Ningxia Renmin Chubanshe, 1988.

Qinding Shifengpu jilue (Imperially commissioned military documents on [the campaigns around] Shifengpu). Annotated and punctuated by Yang Huai-zhong. Yinchuan: Ningxia Renmin Chubanshe, 1987.

Qinghai Minzu Xueyuan Minzu Yanjiusuo (Nationalities Research Institute, Qinghai Nationalities College) and Xibei Minzu Xueyuan Xibei Minzu Yanjiusuo (Northwest Nationalities Institute, Northwest Nationalities College), eds. *Xidaotang shiliao ji* (Historical materials on the Xidaotang). N.p., 1987.

Ray, Haraprasad. *Trade and Diplomacy in India-China Relations: A Study of Bengal During the Fifteenth Century.* New Delhi: Radiant Publishers, 1993.

Rehaimude. "Sufei pai ji qi yu Gaderenye menhuan de guanxi" (Sufism and its relationship to the Qādirīya *menhuan*). *Xibei shidi,* no. 3 (1982): 65–71.

Rijnhart, Susan. *With the Tibetans in Tent and Temple.* Cincinnati: Foreign Christian Missionary Society, 1901.

Rizvi, S. A. A. *Muslim Revivalist Movements in Northern India.* Agra: Agra University Press, 1965.

Rock, Joseph. *The Amnye-Ma-chhen Range and Adjacent Regions.* Rome: Istituto Italiano per Il Medio ed Estremo Oriente, 1956.

Rockhill, William W. "The Dungan Rebellion and the Muhammedans in China." *Asiatic Quarterly Review,* 3rd ser., 3: 414–18.

Rossabi, Morris. *Khubilai Khan: His Life and Times.* Berkeley: University of California Press, 1988.

———. "Ming China and Turfan, 1406–1517." *Central Asiatic Journal* 16, no. 3 (1972): 206–25.

———. "Muslim and Central Asian Revolts." In *From Ming to Ch'ing,* pp. 167–99. Ed. Jonathan Spence and J. E. Wills. New Haven: Yale University Press, 1979.

———. "The Tea and Horse Trade with Inner Asia During the Ming." *Journal of Asian History* 4, no. 2 (1970): 136–68.

Rowell, Galen. *Mountains of the Middle Kingdom: Exploring the High Peaks of China and Tibet.* San Francisco: Sierra Club Books, 1983.

Rubenstein, Richard. *The Cunning of History: The Holocaust and the American Future.* New York: Harper and Row, 1978.

Saguchi Tōru. "Chūgoku Isuramu no kyōha" (Islamic religious factions in China). *Kanazawa Daigaku hōbun gakubu ronshū shigaku hen,* no. 17 (1969): 1–16.

———. "Chūgoku Isuramu no shinpishugi" (Mysticism in Chinese Islam). *Tōhōgaku* 9 (1954): 75–92.

———. "Chūgoku Musurimu shakai no issokumen" (One facet of Chinese Muslim society). *Nairiku Ajia no kenkyū* (1955): 123–65.

———. *Jūhachi-jūkyū seiki Higashi Torukisutan shakaishi kenkyū* (Social history of eastern Turkestan in the eighteenth-nineteenth centuries). Tokyo: Yoshikawa Kobunkan, 1963.

————. *Shinkyō minzoku shi kenkyū* (History of the *minzu* of Xinjiang). Tokyo: Yoshikawa Kobunkan, 1986.

Sakuma Teijirō. "Shina kaikyōto no dōkō ni kansuru ikkōsatsu" (An investigation regarding the movements of the Chinese Muslims). *Tōa* 5, no. 12 (1932): 68–79.

Salazu dang'an shiliao (Historical archives on the Salar *minzu*). Xining: Qinghai Minzu Xueyuan, 1981.

Salazu jianshi (A brief history of the Salar *minzu*). Xining: Qinghai Renmin Chubanshe, 1982.

"Sara Kai oyobi Mōko Kaikai" (The Salar Hui and the Mongol Huihui). *Kaikyō jijō* 1, no. 3 (n.d.).

Sauvaget, Jean. *'Ahbar as-Sin wa 'l-Hind: Relation de la Chine et de l'Inde.* Paris: Belles Lettres, 1948.

Schneider, Laurence. *Ku Chieh-kang and China's New History: Nationalism and the Quest for Alternative Traditions.* Berkeley: University of California Press, 1971.

Schram, Louis. *The Monguors of the Kansu-Tibetan Frontier.* 3 fasc. Philadelphia: American Philosophical Society, 1954.

Schurmann, Franz. *Economic Structure of the Yuan Dynasty: Translation of Chapters 93 and 94 of the* Yuan shih. Cambridge: Harvard University Press, 1956.

Shan Huapu. "Shaan-Gan jieyu lu" (The tragedy of Shaanxi and Gansu). *Yugong* 5, no. 11 (n.d.): 95–102.

————. "Shuo Shaan-Gan 'Huiluan' chuqi shi zhi dili guanxi" (On geographical relationships in the initial phase of the "Muslim uprising" in Shaanxi and Gansu). *Yugong* 5, no. 11 (n.d.): 91–94.

Shao Hongmo and Han Min. *Shaanxi Huimin qiyi shi* (History of the righteous uprising of the Shaanxi Muslims). Xi'an: Shaanxi Renmin Chubanshe, 1992.

She Yize. *Zhongguo tusi zhidu* (China's *tusi* system). Shanghai, 1947.

Shimohayashi Hiroyuki. "Seihoku Shina Kaikyōto ni kansuru chōsa hōkoku" (Report of an investigation on the Muslims of northwest China). *Shina kenkyū*, no. 10 (1926): 177–241.

Song Lian, comp. *Yuan shi* (Official history of the Yuan). Reprint, Taipei: Ershiwu Shi Biankan Guan, 1956.

Struve, Lynn. *Voices from the Ming-Qing Cataclysm: China in Tigers' Jaws.* New Haven: Yale University Press, 1993.

Sutton, S. B. *In China's Border Provinces: The Turbulent Career of Joseph Rock.* New York: Hastings House, 1974.

Tan, Chester. *The Boxer Catastrophe.* New York: Columbia University Press, 1955.

Taozhou ting zhi (Taozhou subprefectural gazetteer). 1908. Reprint, Taipei: Chengwen, 1970.

Tasaka (Tazaka), Kodo. "An Aspect of Islam Culture Introduced into China." *Memoirs of the Research Department of the Toyo Bunko,* no. 16 (1957): 75–160.

Tazaka Kōdō. *Chūgoku ni okeru Kaikyō no denrai to sono guzū* (The transmission and diffusion of Islam in China). 2 vols. Tokyo: Toyo Bunko, 1964.

———. "Mindai goki no Kaikyōto ryūzoku" (The roving Muslim bandits of the late Ming). *Tōyō gakuhō* 37, no. 1 (June 1954): 46–68.

Teichman, Eric. *Travels of a Consular Officer in Northwest China.* Cambridge: Cambridge University Press, 1921.

Ter Haar, B. J. *The White Lotus Teachings in Chinese Religious History.* Leiden: Brill, 1992.

Tian Tongjin. "Longshang qunhao ji Majiajun yuanliu gaishu" (The myriad rowdies of Gansu and the origins of the Ma family armies). *Gansu wenxian* 2 (1973): 3–14.

Toby, Ronald. *State and Diplomacy in Early Modern Japan: Asia in the Development of the Tokugawa Bakufu.* Stanford: Stanford University Press, 1984.

Trippner, Joseph. "Die Salaren, ihre ersten Glaubensstreitigkeiten und ihr Aufstand 1781" (The Salars: Their initial ideological conflicts and their rebellion of 1781). *Central Asiatic Survey* 9, no. 4 (1964): 241–76.

———. "Islamische Gruppen und Gräberkult in Nordwest-China" (Islamic groups and tomb cults in northwest China). *Die Welt des Islams* 7(1961): 142–71.

Tuo Tuo, comp. *Song shi* (Official history of the Song). Reprint, Taipei: Ershiwu Shi Biankan Guan, 1956.

Wakeman, Frederic. *The Great Enterprise: The Manchu Reconstruction of Imperial Order in 17th Century China.* 2 vols. Berkeley: University of California Press, 1985.

———. "Rebellion and Revolution: The Study of Popular Movements in Chinese History." *Journal of Asian Studies* 36, no. 2 (1977): 201–37.

Wang Daiyu. *Zhengjiao zhenquan* (A true interpretation of the orthodox teaching). Punctuated and collated by Yu Zhengui. Yinchuan: Ningxia Renmin Chubanshe, 1988.

Wang, Jianping. "Concord and Conflict: The Hui Communities of Yunnan Society in Historical Perspective." Ph.D. diss., Lund University, 1996.

Wang Shumin. "Qianlong sishiliu nian Hezhou shibian ge" (A song on the Hezhou incident of 1781). *Xibei tongxun* 3, no. 2 (1948).

———. "Xidaotang—xin shehui de muoxing" (The Xidaotang: Model for a new society). In *XSJ,* 122–24.

Wang Zhiwen. *Gansu sheng xinanbu bianqu kaocha ji* (An investigation of the southwestern Gansu frontier). Lanzhou: Gansu Sheng Yinhang, 1932.

Wang Zongwei. "Qingdai Shaanxi Huimin qiyi tong Taiping jun, Nian jun, Li Lan yijun de guanxi" (The relationship of the Qing period Shaanxi Hui righteous uprising with the Taiping, Nian, and Li Lan armies). In *QTNSH,* pp. 158–73.

Watson, James L. "Rites or Beliefs? The Construction of a Unified Culture in Late Imperial China." In *China's Quest for National Identity,* pp. 80–103. Ed. Lowell Dittmer and Samuel Kim. Ithaca: Cornell University Press, 1993.

Weng Dujian. "Wotuo zakao" (Various studies on the *ortaq*). *Yanjing xuebao* 29 (1941): 201–18.

White, Richard. *The Middle Ground: Indians, Empires, and Republics in the Great Lakes Region, 1650–1815.* Cambridge and New York: Cambridge University Press, 1991.

Wu Wanshan. *Qingdai xibei Huimin qiyi yanjiu* (The northwestern Hui people's righteous uprisings in the Qing period). Lanzhou: Lanzhou Daxue, 1991.

Xie Guozhen. *Qingchu nongmin qiyi ziliao jilu* (Historical materials on peasant uprisings in the early Qing). Shanghai: Xin Zhishi, 1956.

Xining dengchu junwu jilue (Military activities around Xining). Xining: N.p., 1896.

Xu Wanli. "Cong Hezhou shuoqi" (Speaking of Hezhou). *Gansu wenxian,* no. 3 (1974): 45–47.

Xu Yuhu. *Ming Zheng He zhi yanjiu* (On Zheng He of the Ming). Gaoxiong: Dexin, 1980.

Xue Wenbo. "Mingdai yu Huimin zhi guanxi" (Relations between the Ming court and the Hui people). In *ZYSCZX,* vol. I, 207–25.

Xue Zhengchang. "Dong Fuxiang yu Ronglu xilun" (Dong Fuxiang and Ronglu). *Xibei Daxue xuebao (zhexue shehui kexue ban)* 23, no. 4 (1993): 111–16.

Xunhua ting zhi (Xunhua subprefectural gazetteer). 1844. Reprint, Taipei: Chengwen, n.d.

Yan Congjian. *Shuyu zhouci lu* (A complete inquiry regarding strange lands). N.p., 1574.

Yang, C. K. "Some Preliminary Statistical Patterns of Mass Actions in Nineteenth-Century China." In *Conflict and Control in Late Imperial China,* pp. 174–210. Ed. Frederic Wakeman and Carolyn Grant. Berkeley: University of California Press, 1975.

Yang Huaizhong. "Dui *Huihui yaofang* de liangdian xiangfa" (Two points of view regarding the *Muslim pharmacopoeia*). In *HSG,* pp. 224–28.

———. "Dui xibei diqu Yisilanjiao Sufeipai de jidian renshi" (Some identifications of Islamic Sufi orders in the northwest). In *HSG,* pp. 278–94.

———. *Huizu shi lungao* (Essays on the history of the Hui *minzu*). Yinchuan: Ningxia Renmin Chubanshe, 1991. (*HSG*)

———. "Lun shiba shiji Zhehelinye Musilin de qiyi" (The eighteenth-century righteous uprising of the Jahrīya Muslims). In *HSG,* pp. 310–70.

———. "Sai Dianchi Shan Siding he tade jiazu" (Sayyid Adjall Shams ad-Din and his lineage). In *HSG,* pp. 177–204.

———. "Shiba shiji de Gansu maozhen an" (The eighteenth-century relief fraud scandal in Gansu). In *HSG,* pp. 371–439.

———. "Songdai de fanke" (Foreign merchants in the Song). In *HSG,* pp. 82–128.

———. "Tangdai de fanke" (Foreign merchants in the Tang). In *HSG,* pp. 50–81.

———. "Zhongguo kexue shishang de Zhamalading" (Jamal ad-Din in the history of Chinese science). In *HSG,* pp. 205–23.

Yang Zengxin. *Buguo Zhai wendu* (Writings from the Buguo Studio). Preface dated 1921. Reprint, Taipei: Wenhai, 1965.

Ye Guoqing. "Li Zhi xian shi kao" (On Li Zhi's origins). In *HSJ*, pp. 276–84.

Ye Zhenggang. "Ningxia Yiheiwani zhuming jingxuejia Hu Songshan" (Hu Songshan, the reknowned scripturalist of the Ningxia Ikhwan). In *QZYL*, pp. 308–25.

Yi Kongzhao et al., eds. *Pingding Guanlong jilue* (Records of pacifying Shaanxi and Gansu). In *HMCY*, vol. 3, 241–vol. 4, 209.

Yibulaheimai (Ibrahim), A. "Gansu zhangnei Tangwanghua jilue" (Tangwanghua [language] of Gansu). *Minzu yuwen*, no. 6 (1985): 33–47.

Yixin et al., comp. *Qinding pingding Shaan Gan Xinjiang Huifei fanglue* (Imperially commissioned compendium of documents on the campaign to pacify the Muslim rebels of Shaanxi, Gansu, and Xinjiang). Beijing, 1896.

Yu Yao. "Bai Lang qiyi jun zai Longnan de huodong" (The activities of Bai Lang's righteous army in southern Gansu). *Gansu shida xuebao*, no. 4 (1981): 116–20.

———. "Wusi yundong dui Gansu de yingxiang" (The influence of the May Fourth Movement in Gansu). *Gansu shida xuebao*, no. 2 (1979): 102–5.

———. "Xinhai Geming zai Gansu" (The 1911 Revolution in Gansu). *Gansu shida xuebao*, no. 3 (1979): 96–99.

Zeng Liren. "Xi Nian jun he xibei Huimin jun lianhe de yixie wenti" (Some problems in the connections between the western Nian army and the northwestern Muslim army). In *HSJ*, pp. 491–510.

Zhang Chengzhi. "Kakusareta Chūgoku Isuramukyō no himitsu shiryō— *Rashufu*" (The *Rashuh*, a lost secret historical text of Chinese Islam). *Tōyō gakuhō* 73, no. 1–2 (1992): 77–82.

Zhang Jiefu. "Qingdai tusi zhidu" (The Qing tusi system). *Qingshi luncong*, no. 3 (1982): 188–202.

Zhang Qiyun. "Taoxi quyu diaocha jianbao" (Brief report on the Taoxi region). *Dili xuebao* 2, no. 1 (1935).

———. *Xiahe xian zhi* (Xiahe county gazetteer). Reprint, Taipei: Chengwen, 1970.

Zhang Tingyu et al., comp. *Ming shi* (The official history of the Ming). Shanghai: Shangwu Yinshuguan, 1958.

Zhang Wei. "Gu Guomin zhengfu Meng Zang Weiyuanhui weiyuanzhang Ma Yunting jinian bei" (An inscription in memory of Ma Yunting [Ma Fuxiang], former head of the Mongolia-Tibet Commission of the national government). *Guoshiguan guankan* 1, no. 4 (1948): 110–12.

Zhang Xinglang. *Zhong-Xi jiaotong shiliao huipian* (Collected historical materials on East-West relations). Beijing: N.p., 1930.

Zhang Yangming. *Dao xibei lai* (Coming to the northwest). Shanghai: Shangwu, 1937.

Zhao Shiying. "Gansu dizhen jianzhi" (A chronology of Gansu earthquakes). *Gansu wenshi ziliao xuanji*, no. 20 (1984): 183–296.

Zhao Songyao. "Gansu Ziyiju ji qi yanbian" (The evolution of the Gansu provincial assembly). *Gansu shida xuebao,* no. 4 (1981): 53–59.

Zheng Hesheng and Zheng Yijun. *Zheng He xia xiyang ziliao huibian (zhong)* (Collected materials on Zheng He's voyages, vol. 2). Jinan: Jilu, 1983.

Zhenyuan xian zhi (Zhenyuan county gazetteer). N.p., 1935.

Zhongguo Gongchandang Xibei Yanjiushe (Northwest Study Group, Chinese Communist Party), ed. *Kangzhanzhong de Gan-Ning-Qing* (Gansu, Ningxia, and Qinghai in the war against Japan). N.p., 1941.

Zhongguo Shehui Kexue Yuan Minzu Yanjiusuo (Nationalities Research Institute, Chinese Academy of Social Sciences) and Zhongyang Minzu Xueyuan Minzu Yanjiusuo (Nationalities Research Institute, Central Nationalities University), ed. *Huizu shi lunji (1949–1979 nian)* (Essays on Hui history, 1949–1979). Yinchuan: Ningxia Renmin Chubanshe, 1983. (*HSJ*)

Zhou Zhenhe, ed. *Qinghai.* Reprint, Taipei: Commercial Press, 1970.

Zhu Chongli. "Tongzhi shiqi Shaanxi Huimin qiyi zhong Hui-Han renmin de lianhe douzheng" (The combined struggle of Hui and Han people during the Tongzhi period Shaanxi Hui righteous uprising). In *QTNSH,* pp. 187–95.

Zhu Gang. "Zhongguo Yisilanjiao Xidaotang xinyang shuping" (Evaluation of the beliefs of the Chinese Islamic Xidaotang). In *XSJ,* pp. 97–116.

Zi Heng. "Zhongguo Yisilanjiao Xidaotang shilue" (A history of the Chinese Islamic Xidaotang). In *XSJ,* pp. 1–74.

Index

'Abd al-'Azīz, 204
'Abd al-Wahhāb, Muhammad b., 87, 202–3, 209
Abū 'l-Futūh. *See* Ma Laichi
acculturation: as local, 213; as ordinary, 226; process of, xix. *See also minzu* paradigm
   of Sino-Muslims, xviii; anxiety regarding, 73; and external contact, 213–14; limits of, 213; in Ming, 39, 40, 45–46, 55–56; in Tang-Song, 28–31; in Yangzi region, 46; in Yuan, 34–38
adoption, 45, 113
Āfāqīya (Sufi order), 64, 70, 88, 94, 190*n56*, 217
Agui, 110, 111, 162, 179, 186, 220
Ahl as-Sunna (Kinsmen of the Tradition), 204
Ahmad Fanakati (Ahema), 31–32, 35–36
ahong (*imām,* religious teacher): as distinctive leader, 214; in Gansu, 178; inadequacies of, 73; limitation on movement of, 113; opposition to *Han kitab* by, 84; as profession, 48–49. *See also* Islam; *madrasa;* mosques; religion
Alashan, 171
Altishahr, 58, 65, 94. *See also* Xinjiang
Amdo (northeastern Tibet), 12; geography and economy of, 13; as independent, 163; as middle ground, 159. *See also* Qinghai Province; Tibet
Anhui, 38
Arabia (Tianfang): scripturalist fundamentalism in, 202–3; as site of conflict, 217; as source of truth, 78–79; Sufi revivalism in, 86–87

Arabic calligraphy, 181, 187
Arabic (language) education, 49–51, 215
Arabic *pinyin* for Chinese, 50–51
Arabs, 25
Aryanism, xx
Ashige, 75
Aubin, Françoise, 178

Bafang, 21, 146, 159
Bai Chongxi, 197
Bai Lang, Gansu campaign of, 183, 191–94
Bai Yanhu, 129, 135, 165, 225
Baishan (Sufi order), 190
Baizhuangzi, 108
banditry, endemic in Gansu, 171
baraka (religious charisma), 61, 66, 185
Bayanrong, 144, 155, 160
beg (hereditary lord), xxix
Beizhuang (*menhuan*), 188, 201
Bi Yuan, 98*n81*
Bijiachang (*menhuan*), 71
Board of Punishments, xix*n4*, 99–101, 119
Boluo (Pulad Aqa), 32
Bosi. *See* Persians
Boxer uprising, 169, 181
brawling (*dou'ou*), 100
Buddhism: in China, xviii; as heterodoxy, 48, 77; resemblance to Sufism, 60*n7*, 62; studied by Liu Zhi, 81; Tibetan, 13–14; in Yuan, 37

category system: as danger, 227; as discourse of power, xxv, 221; *minzu* paradigm as, xxii, 216. *See also* ethnicity; *minzu* paradigm
Central Asia: Amdo as frontier of, 13; com-

INDEX

Tian Wu, 111–12, 114, 186, 219
Tian Xing Long, 191
Tianfang. *See* Arabia
Tianfang dianli (text), 83–84, 213
Tianfang xingli (text), 83
Tianshui, 21, 183
Tibet: cultural continuum of China and,
    13; Gansu as frontier of, xxxiii–xxxiv;
    Qing policy toward, 94; Taozhou
    and, 188
Tibetan language, 198
Tibetan *minzu*, xxiii*n12*, 8
Tibetan culture: in Chinese eyes, 163;
    at Taozhou, 153; at Xining, 160
Tibetans: allied with Qing, 110; in anti-
    Muslim coalition, 162; as converts to
    Islam, 67*n23;* divisions among, 7; as
    frontier people, 19, 221; in Gansu,
    162; in Gansu military, 163; in Taoxi,
    152–54; Xidaotang and, 197
Tonggan. *See* Tungan
tribute system, 26, 42, 43
tuanlian (militias): as anti-Muslim forces,
    117, 119; at Haicheng, 148; as reaction
    to threat, 91, 219; in Shaanxi, 120, 122,
    130; in siege of Xi'an, 124; at Xining,
    135, 160–61. *See also* Shaanxi Province;
    violence
Tungan: in Russia, 129; as term for Sino-
    Muslims, xix*n4,* 59*n4,* 216
Turfan, 42, 43, 53, 54, 59
Turkic-speakers, 8, 19, 70, 105, 132, 150
Turumtay, 54
tusheng fanke (native-born foreign sojourn-
    ers), 29
tusi (local hereditary chieftains): of Choni,
    153; defined, xxix; as local authority,
    223; replacement by nation-state, 186;
    among Salars, 70, 138*n74;* system, 15;
    among Tibetans, 163. *See also beg;*
    Salars; Tibetans

umma (community of Muslim believers),
    xxvi, 92
Uygur *minzu,* xxiii
Uygurs, conversion to Islam of, 25*n6*

violence: 19th cent. increase in, 101, 118,
    119; causes of, 5, 114, 136, 217–20; as

characteristic of Muslims, xxx–xxxi,
    148; in Chinese society, 101; in de-
    fense of home, 225; on frontiers, 5; in
    Gansu after 1761, 91; as gendered activ-
    ity, 104*n2;* internecine Muslim, 111; as
    local, 114, 162, 218, 220; motivation to,
    225; among Muslims, xxx, 100, 111,
    143, 161, 215; between Muslims and Ti-
    betans, 162; as rebellion, 123; relation
    to state, 5, 219; role of religion in, 137;
    in Shaanxi, 120; social roots of, 101;
    between Sufi orders, 103. *See also*
    rebellion

Wang Dagui, 131, 200, 219
Wang Daiyu, 83: in 20th cent., 176; as au-
    thor of *Han kitab,* 75–79; in thought
    of Ma Qixi, 189
Wang Danwang, 96–97
Wang Lun, 101
Wang Naibi, 209
Wang Shumin, 17, 108
Wang Zhu, 32
"wash away the Muslims" (*xi Hui*), 123,
    142–43, 146, 219
Wei Guangtao, 164
Wei River valley, 11, 119, 122, 130
wenhua (literary culture), 37
Western (*xiyang*) writings, 81
White Lotus, 101, 137*n73,* 152*n107*
Woshikeng'e, 138, 140
Wu Sangui, 80
Wu Sunqie, 74–75, 79
Wuchang incident, 170
wushi fanke (fifth-generation foreign
    sojourners), 29

Xi'an, 11, 123–24, 170, 180
xiaojing (Arabic *pinyin*), 46, 50–51
Xidaotang: adaptation to modern China,
    226; alliance with Guomindang, 197;
    called "Chinese studies faction," 199;
    commerce of, 197; as economic collec-
    tive, 190–91; education in, 198; as Is-
    lamic solidarity, 198–99; origins and
    evolution of, 186–99; resistance to
    Bai Lang, 194. *See also* Ma Anliang;
    Ma Qixi; Taozhou
xiejiao (heterodoxy), 68–69, 103